W9-BZK-870

THEY DIDN'T WIN THE OSCARS

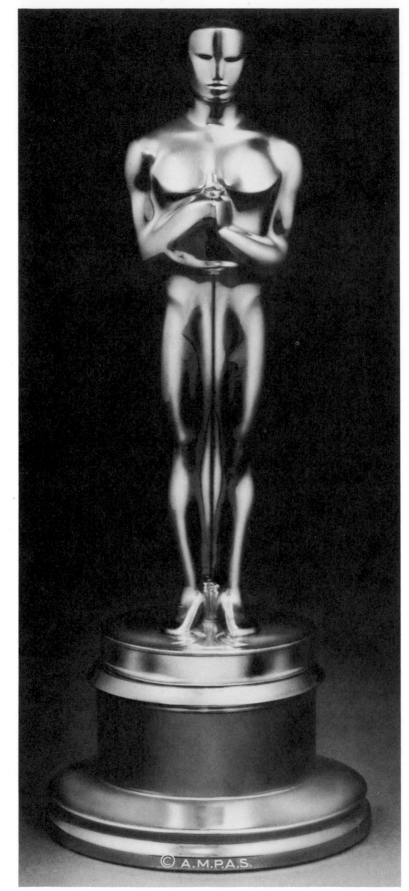

© A.M.P.A.S.

THEY DIDN'T WIN THE OSCARS

by

Bill Libby

ARLINGTON HOUSE PUBLISHERS
Westport, Connecticut

ACKNOWLEDGMENTS

THIS BOOK has been a labor of
love, something the author, long a movie buff, always wanted to do. For the
opportunity to do it and for her work on it, he is grateful to Kathleen Williams and
also to her associate Pat Waill of Arlington House.

For their help and advice, the author is grateful to Charles Champlin of the
Los Angeles Times, Ernie Schwork, and all the critics and fans who participated in
our polls covering the most-memorable film performances.

This was a job of research as well as memory. The author is indebted to many
authors and the most important of the books used as background are listed in the
bibliography at the end of this book.

For the photographs, the author is grateful to:

ERNEST SCHWORK
ESE PUBLISHERS
509 NORTH HARBOR BOULEVARD
LA HABRA, CALIFORNIA 90631

And also to:

Bob Colman's Hollywood Poster Exchange
LaCienega Boulevard
Los Angeles, California

And

Larry Edmunds' Movie Book Shop
6658 Hollywood Boulevard
Hollywood, California

Copyright © 1980 by Bill Libby
All rights reserved. No portion of this book may be reproduced without written permission from the
publisher except by a reviewer who may quote brief passages in connection with a review.

Arlington House Publishers, 333 Post Road West, Westport, CT 06880

Library of Congress Cataloging in Publication Data

Libby, Bill.
 They didn't win the Oscars.
 Bibliography: p.   Includes index.
 1. Moving-pictures. I. Title. PN1994.L482   791.43'0973   80-22925
ISBN 0-87000-455-7

Designed by Sam Gantt · Manufactured in the United States of America

CONTENTS

1. THEY DIDN'T WIN THE OSCARS *3*
2. THE LISTS *19*
3. THE ACTORS *52*
4. THE ACTORS, PART II *73*
5. THE ACTRESSES *102*
6. THE ACTRESSES, PART II *114*
7. THE DIRECTORS *130*
8. THE CLASSIC LOSERS *145*
9. THE CLASSIC LOSERS, PART II *159*
10. WESTERN & ADVENTURE FILMS *173*
11. CRIME & SUSPENSE FILMS *183*
12. COMEDY FILMS *188*
13. MUSICAL & FANTASY FILMS *198*
14. ROMANCE FILMS *211*
15. REALISTIC FILMS *221*
BIBLIOGRAPHY *228*
INDEX *229*

James Cagney gives a surprised Mae Clarke the grapefruit treatment in Public Enemy.

DEDICATION

Orson Welles called movie film "a ribbon of dreams."
This book is dedicated to
my all-time favorite companion at the movies,
my kindest critic,
my wife,
the girl who made my dreams come true,
Sharon.

ONE

They Didn't Win
the Oscars

CITIZEN KANE, considered by many to be the classic film of all time, did not win an Academy Award. Nor did such highly regarded films as *The Grapes of Wrath*, *The Informer*, *Mr. Smith Goes to Washington*, *Wuthering Heights*, *The Treasure of the Sierra Madre*, *The Magnificent Ambersons*, *Sunset Boulevard*, *Singin' in the Rain*, *The Wizard of Oz*, *Who's Afraid of Virginia Woolf?*, *The Maltese Falcon*, *Stagecoach*, *High Noon*, *Shane*, *The African Queen*, *American Graffiti*, *The Last Picture Show*, *2001: A Space Odyssey*, *Star Wars*, *The Turning Point*, and *Coming Home*.

Many of the most memorable performances of all time did not win Oscars. These include Charles Laughton's Captain Bligh, Clark Gable's Rhett Butler, Marlon Brando's Stanley Kowalski, Jose Ferrer's Toulouse-Lautrec, Orson Welles' Citizen Kane, Laurence Olivier's Heathcliff, Henry Fonda's Tom Joad, James Dean's Cal Trask, Montgomery Clift's Pvt. Prewitt, James Stewart's Mr. Smith, Humphrey Bogart's Rick, Greta Garbo's Camille, Olivia De Havilland's Virginia, Rosalind Russell's Sister Kenny, and Bette Davis' Mildred, Judith, and Margo.

Respectively, these portrayals came in *Mutiny on the Bounty*, *Gone With the Wind*, *A Streetcar Named Desire*, *Moulin Rouge*, *Citizen Kane*, *Wuthering Heights*, *The Grapes of Wrath*, *East of Eden*, *From Here to Eternity*, *Mr. Smith Goes to Washington*, *Casablanca*, *Camille*, *The Snake Pit*, *Sister Kenny*, *Of Human Bondage*, *Dark Victory*, and *All About Eve*.

These are the performances that entertainers today mimic when they do routines on movies. These are the performances that are the heart of Hollywood history.

Bette Davis was nominated ten times for Academy Awards and took home two—for Joyce Heath in *Dangerous* in 1935 and Julie Marsen in *Jezebel* in 1938. Yet these are not the performances for which she is remembered—the floozy Mildred in *Of Human Bondage* in 1934, the doomed Judith Traherne in *Dark Victory* in 1939, and the star Margo Channing in *All About Eve* in 1950. Supposedly, she was sentimentally selected for her inferior role in *Dangerous* because of public outrage over the fact that she was not nominated for her superior performance in *Of Human Bondage* the year before.

Many of the actors and actresses I have listed did win Oscars, but not for their most famous performances. It is hard to argue against an Academy Award for Laurence Olivier's *Hamlet*, but it is perhaps even harder to understand how this great modern actor could have been nominated ten times and won just once. It is difficult to figure out how Henry Fonda could have been nominated only once—for his Tom Joad in *The Grapes of Wrath* in 1939 (and he lost)—in more than forty years of fine film performances.

Among actors never even nominated for an Award are John Barrymore, Edward G. Robinson, Joseph Cotten, Lloyd Nolan, Paul Henreid, Robert Preston, Tyrone Power, Pat O'Brien, Peter Lorre, Glenn Ford, and Eli Wallach. Among those nominated but never

Sweat-stained T-shirt and all, Marlon Brando was unforgettable as Stanley Kowalski in A Streetcar Named Desire.

Clark Gable didn't win Oscar as Rhett Butler in Gone With the Wind.

Charles Laughton was denied Oscar as Captain Bligh in Mutiny on the Bounty.

Henry Fonda won his only nomination for his role as Tom Joad. Here he's with "Ma," Jane Darwell, in The Grapes of Wrath.

Montgomery Clift, perfect as Prewitt, comforts injured Frank Sinatra in From Here to Eternity.

Bette Davis won Oscar twice, but not for her memorable role as Margo Channing. Here she's talking to Anne Baxter, as future husband Gary Merrill, center, and George Sanders watch in All About Eve.

Humphrey Bogart was Rick with Ingrid Bergman in Casablanca.

Laurence Olivier, here in Sleuth, *won one Oscar, for the English* Hamlet, *in eleven nominations.*

A winner in life, if not in Oscar races, here's Edward G. Robinson in his later years, with part of his great art collection.

Paul Newman never won Oscar, but might have for Cool Hand Luke. *Here he's helped by George Kennedy.*

winning are Cary Grant, Burgess Meredith, Charles Bickford, James Mason, John Garfield, Raymond Massey, Walter Pidgeon, Orson Welles, Lee J. Cobb, and Kirk Douglas. More recently, there are Al Pacino, Robert Redford, James Caan, and Warren Beatty who have not won.

Richard Burton has been nominated seven times, Peter O'Toole five times, and Paul Newman four times. Not one of them ever has been handed an Oscar. Charles Boyer, Claude Rains, Arthur Kennedy, and Montgomery Clift were nominated four times without winning. It is difficult to imagine actors such as Robinson, Rains, Burton, Cobb, and Massey not qualifying somewhere along the line.

Who has had greater impact on the art of acting in the last twenty-five years than Garfield, Clift, Newman, or Dean? But they were never chosen.

Deborah Kerr has been nominated six times for a starring performance by an actress, but she never has won. Thelma Ritter was nominated six times for a supporting performance, but she never won. Irene Dunne and Geraldine Page have been nominated five times, and Ethel Barrymore, Agnes Moorehead, Rosalind Russell, Barbara Stanwyck, and Shirley MacLaine were nominated four times without winning. Greta Garbo never won. Nor Gloria Swanson, Ida Lupino, Myrna Loy, Betty Field, Jean Arthur, or Margaret Sullavan. Nor, recently, Gena Rowlands, Jane Alexander, Jill Clayburgh, or Marsha Mason.

The first words spoken from the screen were, "You ain't heard nuthin' yet." They were spoken by Al Jolson before he sang in *The Jazz Singer*. That milestone movie, the first talkie, or at least part-talkie, came out in 1927. The first Academy Awards were given for movies from 1927 and 1928, but *The Jazz Singer* was not even nominated. King Vidor's *The Crowd* emerged in 1928 and has come to be considered a classic, but it was not nominated either. Buster Keaton's *The General* was released in 1927 and Charles Chaplin's *City Lights* in 1931; both are now considered classics, but neither was nominated. Nor was Keaton himself. Chaplin was, but did not win.

There was still time to salute the geniuses of the silent films for worthy movies, but the chance was not taken. Many years later, Chaplin and Keaton, for *The Jazz Singer* and *The Crowd*, were given honorary Oscars, but I cannot count these, deserved though they were. Nor can I count those honorary Oscars given to Cary Grant, Roz Russell, Greta Garbo, Judy Garland, Groucho Marx, Stan Laurel, Fred Astaire, and Gene Kelly. They were not the real thing.

Barbara Stanwyck and Fred MacMurray, neither an Academy Award winner, romantically contemplate murder in Double Indemnity.

An honorary Oscar is not the real thing, but Cary Grant seems happy to have gotten this one from Frank Sinatra.

Ironically, there seldom has been a place in Academy Award voting to honor those things that have made movies what they are. For example, slapstick, sophisticated comedy, musical extravaganza, and dancing.

Since Chaplin and Keaton received their honorary Oscars, great comics, such as W.C. Fields, Laurel and Hardy, and The Marx Brothers, and more recently Mel Brooks and Woody Allen, have been neglected. However, Woody Allen did win for his somewhat more serious than usual *Annie Hall*, as Best Picture, and Diane Keaton won for her part in it. Cary Grant and Rosalind Russell, William Powell and Myrna Loy, however, and other masters of sophisticated comedy never won. What would movies have been like without the laughter these fine actors and actresses provided?

Is there anyone who made more memorable movies than Fred Astaire? Yet, he never was nominated for his thirty-five years of sophisticated comedy or for his incredible dancing. Late in his career he was nominated

Denied the real thing, an ailing Rosalind Russell shows off her honorary Oscar shortly before her death.

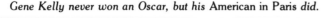

Gene Kelly never won an Oscar, but his American in Paris did.

Disney's Snow White and the Seven Dwarfs.

but lost, for a dramatic part. Some of his films were nominated, such as *The Gay Divorcee* and *Top Hat*, but they did not win. *American in Paris* won but Gene Kelly did not. He was nominated once, but did not win. It was his only nomination in more than twenty-five years of spectacular performances.

Judy Garland was nominated, but never won, except for an honorary Oscar later in her career. Her classic *The Wizard of Oz* was nominated, but did not win. Nor did Walt Disney's milestone movies *Snow White and the Seven Dwarfs* and *Fantasia* win, although Disney did take home more statuettes of one kind or another than anyone else, ever—thirty-five.

Mickey Rooney and Shirley Temple were king and queen of the box office in their day, but never king and queen of the Academy Awards. Rooney did win nominations for Oscars, but not Shirley. An honorary Oscar was awarded to her later, but it was not the real thing.

Who has made more compelling pictures than Alfred Hitchcock? Yet he never won an Oscar, only an honorary one. *Rebecca*, which he directed, won but he did not. His *Psycho* was not even nominated, yet remains one of the most frightening movies ever made. Other Hitchcock classics such as *Suspicion*, *Spellbound*, *Dial M for Murder*, *Rear Window*, *Vertigo*, *North by Northwest*, and *The Birds* were either ignored or denied.

Judy Garland as Dorothy with Tin Man Jack Haley and Straw Man Ray Bolger in The Wizard of Oz.

Paul Newman and Robert Redford, neither an Oscar-winner, come out shooting in Butch Cassidy and the Sundance Kid.

Only five films of crime or suspense have won Oscars. Trailblazers such as Paul Muni's *Scarface* and *I Am a Fugitive from a Chain Gang*, Edward G. Robinson's *Little Caesar*, and James Cagney's *Public Enemy* were not among them. Robinson was never nominated. Cagney won for his portrayal of song-and-dance-man George M. Cohan in *Yankee Doodle Dandy*, not for his landmark public enemy performances. Paul Muni won for high drama, not underworld depictions. Humphrey Bogart won for his role as a rogue in *The African Queen*, not for such milestone performances as Duke Mantee in *The Petrified Forest* or Sam Spade in *The Maltese Falcon*. Recent crime classics such as *Bonnie and Clyde*, *Chinatown*, and *The Conversation* have been neglected.

Horror films have been a staple in Hollywood throughout its history, but *Frankenstein* and *Dracula*, which in 1931 blazed a trail over which so many have followed, were not even nominated for Oscars. Nor were their stars, Boris Karloff and Bela Lugosi, whose performances have been copied or imitated more than any others nominated. *King Kong* was not nominated. *The Lost Horizon* was, but lost. Considered a classic already, *2001: A Space Odyssey* was not nominated when it was released in 1968. Nor was the compelling *Close Encounters of the Third Kind* in 1978. Nominated, but losers, were *Star Wars*, *Jaws*, and *The Exorcist*. Nonsense films? Unreal and of no great social significance? Perhaps. But, classics of their kind, all, and with a great and enduring impact on the movie-going public.

Could there not have been found categories for fantasy, comedy, and musicals so that some of these films and performers could have been honored with

Gloria Swanson regales William Holden with stories of her starry past in Sunset Boulevard. *The pictures are of Gloria in her past.*

cussed in this book. Not all, of course, could be. It is interesting to me that the results of many top-picture polls, as well as my top-performance polls, confirmed my feeling that more deserving pictures and performances have been neglected than honored by Oscars.

A few years ago the American Film Institute membership picked the finest films of all time. Seven of its top ten did not win Academy Awards. These were *The African Queen, Citizen Kane, The Grapes of Wrath, Singin' in the Rain, Star Wars, 2001: A Space Odyssey,* and *The Wizard of Oz.* Oscar winners named in their list were *Casablanca, One Flew over the Cuckoo's Nest,* and *Gone With the Wind.* In all, forty-three films were named and twenty-seven were not Oscar winners. These included *Wuthering Heights, Sunset Boulevard, A Streetcar Named Desire, Snow White, Fantasia, High Noon, The Treasure of the Sierra Madre, A Streetcar Named Desire, Butch Cassidy and the Sundance Kid, Cabaret, Dr. Strangelove, Nashville, The Graduate,* and *Chinatown.*

The University of Southern California Performing Arts Council polled film producers and critics to pick the fifty most significant films ever—milestone movies

which advanced the art. Forty of fifty-four named did not win Academy Awards. *Citizen Kane,* which tied with *Gone With the Wind* for the top spot, did not. Others chosen, but not previously mentioned here, were *Stagecoach, The Jazz Singer, The Informer, King Kong, Who's Afraid of Virginia Woolf?, Little Caesar, Public Enemy, 42nd Street, City Lights, The General, The Maltese Falcon, I Am a Fugitive from a Chain Gang, The Lost Weekend, Shane, Easy Rider,* and *Bonnie and Clyde.*

In 1978, the *Los Angeles Times* poll of fans produced one hundred favorite films. Following *Gone With the Wind* and *Casablanca,* the next three were ones neglected by Oscar—*Citizen Kane, The Wizard of Oz,* and *The African Queen.* Two others in the top ten also were neglected—*The Grapes of Wrath* and *Star Wars,* as well as *2001, Singin' in the Rain, The Graduate, Fantasia, Treasure of the Sierra Madre, Wuthering Heights, To Kill a Mockingbird,* and *Butch Cassidy and the Sundance Kid* in the top twenty-five. Seventy-four of the one hundred did not win Oscars.

The only two American movies in a British Film Institute poll of critics selecting the ten greatest films of all time were Orson Welles' *Citizen Kane* and *The Magnificent Ambersons*. Neither of these films nor Welles ever won an Academy Award. Many films that did win such as *The Broadway Melody*, *Cavalcade*, *The Greatest Show on Earth*, and *In The Heat of the Night* appear on no lists that I've seen.

Six actors' performances in my most memorable performance poll, presented in Chapter Two, made the top ten of both the fans' and critics' lists. Thus, there were fourteen in the top ten on one list or the other. Ten failed to win Academy Awards. These included the first choice of the critics and second choice of the fans— Clark Gable in *Gone With the Wind*—and the first choice of the fans—Marlon Brando in *A Streetcar Named Desire*. Others that made both lists but that were not Oscar winners were Henry Fonda in *The Grapes of Wrath*, James Dean in *East of Eden*, Dustin Hoffman in *Midnight Cowboy*, and Montgomery Clift

in *From Here to Eternity*. Others that made one list or the other but that did not win Oscars were Orson Welles in *Citizen Kane*, Humphrey Bogart in *Casablanca*, Paul Newman in *Butch Cassidy and the Sundance Kid*, and Jack Lemmon in *The Apartment*.

Other non-winners prominent in one poll or the other were Rod Steiger in *The Pawnbroker*, Charles Laughton in *Mutiny on the Bounty*, Richard Burton in *Who's Afraid of Virginia Woolf?*, Al Pacino in *The Godfather Part II*, Cary Grant in *Suspicion*, Humphrey Bogart in *Treasure of the Sierra Madre*, James Dean in *Rebel Without a Cause*, Paul Muni in *I Am a Fugitive from a Chain Gang*, Buster Keaton in *The General*, and Charlie Chaplin in *City Lights*.

Among actresses, there also were six in our poll that made the first ten of both critics and fans, so with a tie for tenth, there were fifteen that made one list or the other. Eight of the fifteen did not win Academy

Cary Grant never won Oscar but Joan Fontaine did, here in Suspicion.

James Dean and Natalie Wood in a poignant moment from Rebel Without a Cause. *All three were denied Oscars.*

The Little Tramp, *Charlie Chaplin.*

Camille *teamed Greta Garbo with Robert Taylor. It appears Taylor later had a nose job.*

Awards. These included the first two choices of the critics—Katharine Hepburn in *The African Queen* and Bette Davis in *All About Eve*. This Davis performance also was the second choice of the fans. The fans' favorite, Vivien Leigh in *Gone With the Wind*, did win Oscar. Others of the top tens that did not win include Judy Garland in *The Wizard of Oz*, Ingrid Bergman in *Casablanca*, Katharine Hepburn in *The Philadelphia Story*, Gloria Swanson in *Sunset Boulevard*, Jane Fonda in *They Shoot Horses, Don't They?*, and Deborah Kerr in *From Here to Eternity*.

Other non-winners prominent in one poll or the other include Olivia De Havilland in *The Heiress* and *The Snake Pit*. Rosalind Russell in *Auntie Mame*, Judy Garland in *A Star Is Born*, Greta Garbo in *Camille*, Deborah Kerr in *The Sundowners*, and Anne Bancroft and Shirley MacLaine in *The Turning Point*.

I was surprised at how well younger fans and critics remember the older pictures and performances, but this is the way it is with those who love movies. Many found a way to see films made before they were born. They

Deborah Kerr, one of the most notable of those overlooked by Oscar, is here with Robert Mitchum, also neglected, in The Sundowners.

cherish them despite differences in time and style. There can be no doubt, in any event, that the most memorable movies and film performances deserve to be honored and recalled, even if they were overlooked by Oscar.

In the following chapter, I include not only a listing of all the Oscar nominated movies and directors, starring and supporting actors and actresses in the history of the Academy Awards, but several of the more important polls of all-time favorite films, as well as the results of my most memorable performance poll. I put them up front in the book rather than in the back, where they would usually go, because I feel that you will find them fascinating and fun to study, and because they single out neglected losers as well as honored winners, thus setting the stage for all that follows.

The neglected Judy Garland with Jack Haley and Ray Bolger in The Wizard of Oz.

T W O

The Lists

IN THE YEARS between 1927 and 1979 there have been fifty-one Academy Awards ceremonies. The results of the votings have never been revealed, only the winners announced. There have been only two ties for major Awards—between Wallace Beery in *The Champ* and Fredric March in *Dr. Jekyll and Mr. Hyde* for Best Actor in the 1931–32 voting year, and between Katharine Hepburn in *The Lion in Winter* and Barbra Streisand in *Funny Girl* for Best Actress in 1968. There were three nominations in the first case, five in the second, but over the years there have been as many as ten.

From the first voting year, 1927–28, through the sixth, 1932–33, each voting spanned two years, but actually covered one year from one election to the next, from August 1 to July 31. From 1934 on, the voting covered each calendar year and the results were announced at ceremonies early the following year. Nominations come in many categories. *All About Eve* drew the most nominations ever, fourteen, in 1950, and won six Awards, including Best Picture. *Who's Afraid of Virginia Woolf?* in 1966 drew the second most, thirteen, and won five, but did not win Best Picture.

Ben-Hur won the most Awards ever, eleven, in 1959. It was nominated for twelve, including Best Picture, and lost only one, for Best Screenplay. *West Side Story* won ten in 1961 and *Gigi* nine in 1958. Such spectacles as *An American in Paris* in 1951, *The Greatest Show on Earth* in 1952, and *Around the World in 80 Days* in 1956 won Best Picture Awards without a single starring or supporting actor or actress

nomination. Their directors were nominated, but lost. It is amazing how many times a picture is deemed best without the director being deemed best.

William Wyler has been the most nominated director, with twelve, winning three. John Ford has won the most with four Oscars out of only five nominations. He also directed the most Oscar-winning starring or supporting performances, fourteen. Elia Kazan ranks next with nine. The directors with the most nominations who have not won are King Vidor and Alfred Hitchcock, with five each.

Katharine Hepburn has drawn the most nominations of any actor or actress, eleven, and is tied for the most Awards, three, all as a starring actress. Ingrid Bergman drew seven nominations and won three, but one win came as Best Supporting Actress. Walter Brennan won three, all as a supporting actor. Bette Davis and Laurence Olivier are tied for the second most nominations, ten, while Spencer Tracy had nine. Two-time winners have been Davis, Tracy, Gary Cooper, Olivia De Havilland, Fredric March, Elizabeth Taylor, Marlon Brando, Jane Fonda, Jack Lemmon, Helen Hayes, Melvyn Douglas, and Anthony Quinn. Aside from Bergman, Lemmon and Hayes also won in both starring and supporting roles. Both of Quinn's and Douglas' wins were in supporting roles.

Davis won two Oscars in ten nominations, Olivier one in ten, Tracy two of nine. On the other end of the scale is Hayes with two victories in two nominations, and Brennan with three out of four. Richard Burton tops the non-winners list with seven nominations, followed by starring actress Deborah Kerr and supporting actress Thelma Ritter, with six.

The oldest winner was George Burns when he gained an Oscar in 1975 at the age of eighty with his supporting performance in *The Sunshine Boys*. Among actors, he supplanted Edmund Gwenn and John Houseman, who each were seventy-one when they won Best Supporting Actor Awards in 1947 and 1973, respectively. The oldest actress to win was Ruth Gordon for a supporting performance in 1968 at the age of seventy-two. The youngest to win was Tatum O'Neal when she won for Best Supporting Actress in *Paper Moon* in 1973 at the age of ten. The youngest supporting actor winner was Harold Russell in 1946 at twenty-three. The youngest nominee for starring actor or actress was Jackie Cooper, who was nominated for Best Actor for *Skippy*, in 1930–31 at age ten, but he did not win. The youngest nominee for supporting actor or actress was Justin Henry for *Kramer vs. Kramer* in 1979, but he did not win. The youngest winner for starring actor or actress was Jennifer Jones, selected for *The Song of Bernadette* in 1943, when she was twenty-four. The youngest starring actor to win was Marlon Brando for *On the Waterfront* in 1954, at thirty—really not so young!

Gable is the only actor or actress to have starred in three Oscar-winning pictures—*It Happened One Night* in 1934, *Mutiny on the Bounty* in 1935, and *Gone With the Wind* in 1939, though he won only for the first. Those who consider him more a personality than an actor might think about this.

Donald Crisp, Jack Hawkins, and Hugh Griffith gave prominent supporting performances in three winners—Crisp in *Mutiny* in 1935, *The Life of Emile Zola* in 1937, and *How Green Was My Valley* in 1941; Hawkins in *Bridge on the River Kwai* in 1957, *Ben-Hur* in 1959, and *Lawrence of Arabia* in 1962; and Griffith in *Ben-Hur* in 1959, *Tom Jones* in 1963, and *Oliver* in 1968. Hawkins, Lawrence Harvey, Peter Sellers, and Dirk Bogarde are notable Britons who did not win the Academy Award, but this book is primarily concerned with Americans.

Briton Peter Finch was the first to win posthumously when he was voted Oscar in 1976 for *Network* shortly after his death. Previously, James Dean in 1956 and Spencer Tracy in 1967 were nominated after their deaths, but they did not win.

Burt Lancaster is the only actor to have costarred with four actresses or actors when they won Oscars— with Shirley Booth in *Come Back, Little Sheba* in 1952, with Anna Magnani in *The Rose Tattoo* in 1955, with David Niven in *Separate Tables* in 1958, and with Maximilian Schell in *Judgment at Nuremberg* in 1961. He also starred with Frank Sinatra and Donna Reed in *From Here to Eternity* in 1953, Wendy Hiller in *Separate Tables* in 1958, and Shirley Jones in *Elmer Gantry* in 1960 when they won supporting actor or actress Oscars. For the latter, Lancaster won his only Oscar. Obviously, he gave a great deal to his fellow performers.

Who is the leading American actor or actress in film history? According to the polls taken for this book, the number one actor is either Clark Gable or Marlon Brando, the number one actress Katharine Hepburn. More than a hundred critics and almost 2,000 fans responded to my request for the ten most memorable male and female film performances in the history of this country's movies, and the totals seem to me sufficient to be significant. They are, at the least, interesting.

In the critics' category, Marlon Brando received the most votes, followed by Humphrey Bogart, Spencer Tracy, Montgomery Clift, Laurence Olivier (though not American, he was in many American films), Dustin Hoffman, Jack Nicholson, Paul Muni, George C. Scott, Clark Gable, Henry Fonda, and James Stewart. Tracy, however, was nominated for the most different films, six, followed by Olivier, Muni, and Clift with five each.

Among fans, Gable was the top choice, followed by Tracy, Bogart, Brando, Nicholson, Clift, Hoffman, James Dean, Paul Newman, John Wayne, Cary Grant, and Jack Lemmon. But Grant was nominated for the most films, twelve—in some cases only one or two votes for a particular performance—followed by Tracy, eleven, Wayne, nine, and Olivier and Brando, eight each.

As for the ladies, the critics cast the most votes for performances by Katharine Hepburn, followed by Bette Davis, Vivien Leigh, Jane Fonda, Ingrid Bergman, Judy Garland, Deborah Kerr, Elizabeth Taylor, Anne Bancroft, Olivia De Havilland, Judy Holliday, and Shirley MacLaine. Hepburn was nominated for the most performances, eight, followed by Davis, seven, and Garland and Fonda, six each.

The fans and critics saw the ladies much alike. As far as most votes go, the first three on both lists were the same—Hepburn, Davis, and Leigh. These were followed in the fans' vote by Taylor, Fonda, Bergman, Garland, De Havilland, Greta Garbo, Audrey Hepburn, Marilyn Monroe, and Judy Holliday. Hepburn was nominated for the most performances, eighteen, followed by Davis, eleven, Bergman, nine, and Taylor, eight.

Hepburn and Davis were one-two among the performers receiving the most votes, male or female, in both the critics' and fans' polls. Brando, Leigh, Bogart, Tracy, Clift, Olivier, Hoffman, and Nicholson followed in the critics' voting. Leigh, Gable, Taylor, Tracy, Bogart, Brando, Fonda, and Nicholson followed in the fans' voting.

However, it was individual performances I was seeking more than anything else.

Among actors, the critics rated Gable's role of Rhett Butler in *Gone With the Wind* best, and it was second in the fans' vote. The fans voted Brando's Stanley Kowalski in *A Streetcar Named Desire* best. It was seventh in the critics' vote. In any event, neither won an Oscar.

It is noteworthy that eight of the top ten choices of the critics and seven of the top ten choices of the fans did not win Oscars.

The critics' second choice, Brando's *On the Waterfront*, and fifth, Bogart's *The African Queen*, won. But Fonda's *The Grapes of Wrath*, Welles' *Citizen Kane*, Clift's *From Here to Eternity*, Brando's *Streetcar*, Hoffman's *Midnight Cowboy*, Bogart's *Casablanca*, and Dean's *East of Eden* did not.

The fans' third choice, Bogart's *African Queen*; sixth, Nicholson's *One Flew over the Cuckoo's Nest*, and Wayne's *True Grit* won Oscars, but Dean's *Eden*, Hoffman's *Cowboy*, Clift's *Eternity*, Paul Newman's *Butch Cassidy and the Sundance Kid*, and Jack Lemmon's *The Apartment* did not.

Other noteworthy favorites on one list or the other that went without Academy Awards were Richard Burton's *Who's Afraid of Virginia Woolf?*, Charles Laughton's *Mutiny on the Bounty*, and Rod Steiger's *The Pawnbroker*.

Among actresses, Katharine Hepburn's *The African Queen* and Bette Davis' *All About Eve* were the critics' one-two choices and neither won Oscars. The fans' first choice, Vivien Leigh's *Gone With the Wind* won, but their second choice, Davis' *Eve*, did not.

There was a tie for tenth in the critics' vote. Six of the top eleven did not win Oscars. In the fans' vote, five of the top ten did not.

The critics' third choice, Jane Fonda's *Klute*; fourth, Leigh's *Gone With the Wind*; sixth, Leigh's *Streetcar*; eighth, Taylor's *Woolf*, and tenth, Bancroft's *The Miracle Worker* won. Garland's *Wizard of Oz*, Bergman's *Casablanca*, Deborah Kerr's *From Here to Eternity*, and Fonda's *They Shoot Horses, Don't They?* did not.

The fans' third choice, Taylor's *Woolf*; fourth, Fonda's *Klute*; fifth, Judy Holliday's *Born Yesterday*; and seventh, Anne Bancroft's *Miracle Worker*, won Oscars. Hepburn's *The African Queen* and *The Phila-*

delphia Story, Garland's *Oz*, and Swanson's *Sunset Boulevard* did not.

Other noteworthy non-winners on one list or the other were Olivia De Havilland's *Heiress*, Roz Russell's *Auntie Mame*, Garland's *A Star Is Born*, Garbo's *Camille*, Bergman's *Casablanca*, Kerr's *Sundowners*, and MacLaine's and Bancroft's *The Turning Point*.

Oscar.

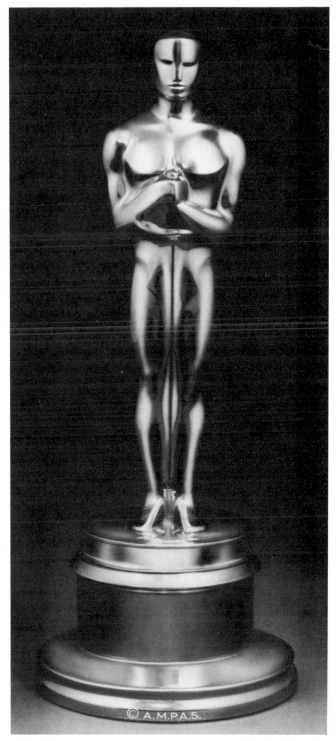

ACADEMY AWARD NOMINEES AND WINNERS
(Winners in CAPS)

FILM	ACTOR	ACTRESS	DIRECTION
1927-28 *The Last Command* *The Racket* *Seventh Heaven* *The Way of All Flesh* WINGS	Richard Barthelmess *(The Noose)* Charles Chaplin *(The Circus)* EMIL JANNINGS *(The Last Command* and *The Way of All Flesh)*	Louise Dresser *(A Ship Comes In)* JANET GAYNOR *(Seventh Heaven* and *Sunrise)* Gloria Swanson *(Sadie Thompson)*	FRANK BORZAGE *(Seventh Heaven)* Herbert Brenon *(Sorrell and Son)* King Vidor *(The Crowd)*

COMEDY DIRECTION
1927-28 (Only year)

Charles Chaplin
(The Circus)
LEWIS MILESTONE
(Two Arabian Nights)
Ted Wilde
(Speedy)

FILM	ACTOR	ACTRESS	DIRECTION
1928-29 *Alibi* THE BROADWAY MELODY *The Hollywood Revue* *In Old Arizona* *The Patriot*	George Bancroft *(Thunderbolt)* WARNER BAXTER *(In Old Arizona)* Chester Morris *(Alibi)* Paul Muni *(The Valiant)* Lewis Stone *(The Patriot)*	Ruth Chatterton *(Madame X)* Betty Compson *(The Barker)* Jeanne Eagels *(The Letter)* Bessie Love *(The Broadway Melody)* MARY PICKFORD *(Coquette)*	Lionel Barrymore *(Madame X)* Harry Beaumont *(Broadway Melody)* Irving Cummings *(In Old Arizona)* FRANK LLOYD *(Drag, Weary River,* and *Divine Lady)* Ernst Lubitsch *(The Patriot)*
1929-30 ALL QUIET ON THE WESTERN FRONT *The Big House* *Disraeli* *The Divorcee* *The Love Parade*	GEORGE ARLISS *(Disraeli* and *The Green* *Goddess)* Wallace Beery *(The Big House)* Maurice Chevalier *(The Love Parade* and *The Big* *Pond)* Ronald Colman *(Bulldog Drummond* and *Condemned)* Lawrence Tibbett *(The Rogue Song)*	Nancy Carroll *(The Devil's Holiday)* Ruth Chatterton *(Sarah and Son)* Greta Garbo *(Anna Christie* and *Romance)* NORMA SHEARER *(The Divorcee* and *Their Own* *Desire)* Gloria Swanson *(The Trespasser)*	Clarence Brown *(Anna Christie)* Robert Leonard *(The Divorcee)* Ernst Lubitsch *(The Love Parade)* LEWIS MILESTONE *(All Quiet on the Western Front)* King Vidor *(Hallelujah)*

FILM	ACTOR	ACTRESS	DIRECTION
1930–31 *CIMARRON* *East Lynne* *The Front Page* *Skippy* *Trader Horn*	LIONEL BARRYMORE *(A Free Soul)* Jackie Cooper *(Skippy)* Richard Dix *(Cimarron)* Fredric March *(The Royal Family)* Adolphe Menjou *(The Front Page)*	Marlene Dietrich *(Morocco)* MARIE DRESSLER *(Min and Bill)* Irene Dunne *(Cimarron)* Ann Harding *(Holiday)* Norma Shearer *(A Free Soul)*	Clarence Brown *(A Free Soul)* Lewis Milestone *(The Front Page)* Wesley Ruggles *(Cimarron)* NORMAN TAUROG *(Skippy)* Josef von Sternberg *(Morocco)*
1931–32 *Arrowsmith* *Bad Girl* *The Champ* *Five Star Final* *GRAND HOTEL* *One Hour with You* *Shanghai Express* *The Smiling Lieutenant*	WALLACE BEERY *(The Champ)* Alfred Lunt *(The Guardsman)* FREDRIC MARCH *(Dr. Jekyll and Mr. Hyde)*	Marie Dressler *(Emma)* Lynne Fontanne *(The Guardsman)* HELEN HAYES *(The Sin of Madelon Claudet)*	FRANK BORZAGE *(Bad Girl)* King Vidor *(The Champ)* Josef von Sternberg *(Shanghai Express)*
1932–33 *CAVALCADE* *A Farewell to Arms* *42nd Street* *I Am a Fugitive from a Chain Gang* *Lady for a Day* *Little Women* *The Private Life of Henry VIII* *She Done Him Wrong* *Smilin' Through* *State Fair*	Leslie Howard *(Berkeley Square)* CHARLES LAUGHTON *(The Private Life of Henry VIII)* Paul Muni *(I Am a Fugitive from a Chain Gang)*	KATHARINE HEPBURN *(Morning Glory)* May Robson *(Lady for a Day)* Diana Wynyard *(Cavalcade)*	Frank Capra *(Lady for a Day)* George Cukor *(Little Women)* FRANK LLOYD *(Cavalcade)*
1934 *The Barretts of Wimpole Street* *Cleopatra* *Flirtation Walk* *The Gay Divorcee* *Here Comes the Navy* *The House of Rothschild* *Imitation of Life* *IT HAPPENED ONE NIGHT* *One Night of Love* *The Thin Man* *Viva Villa* *The White Parade*	CLARK GABLE *(It Happened One Night)* Frank Morgan *(Affairs of Cellini)* William Powell *(The Thin Man)*	CLAUDETTE COLBERT *(It Happened One Night)* Grace Moore *(One Night of Love)* Norma Shearer *(The Barretts of Wimpole Street)*	FRANK CAPRA *(It Happened One Night)* Victor Schertzinger *(One Night of Love)* W. S. Van Dyke *(The Thin Man)*
1935 *Alice Adams* *Broadway Melody of 1936* *Captain Blood* *David Copperfield* *The Informer* *Les Miserables* *The Lives of a Bengal Lancer* *A Midsummer Night's Dream* *MUTINY ON THE BOUNTY* *Naughty Marietta* *Ruggles of Red Gap* *Top Hat*	Clark Gable *(Mutiny on the Bounty)* Charles Laughton *(Mutiny on the Bounty)* VICTOR McLAGLEN *(The Informer)* Franchot Tone *(Mutiny on the Bounty)*	Elisabeth Bergner *(Escape Me Never)* Claudette Colbert *(The Private Worlds)* BETTE DAVIS *(Dangerous)* Katharine Hepburn *(Alice Adams)* Miriam Hopkins *(Becky Sharpe)* Merle Oberon *(The Dark Angel)*	JOHN FORD *(The Informer)* Henry Hathaway *(Lives of a Bengal Lancer)* Frank Lloyd *(Mutiny on the Bounty)*

	FILM	ACTOR	ACTRESS
1936	Anthony Adverse	Gary Cooper	Irene Dunne
	Dodsworth	(Mr. Deeds Goes to Town)	(Theodora Goes Wild)
	THE GREAT ZIEGFELD	Walter Huston	Gladys George
	Libeled Lady	(Dodsworth)	(Valiant Is the Word for Carrie)
	Mr. Deeds Goes to Town	PAUL MUNI	Carole Lombard
	Romeo and Juliet	(The Story of Louis Pasteur)	(My Man Godfrey)
	San Francisco	William Powell	LUISE RAINER
	The Story of Louis Paeteur	(My Man Godfrey)	(The Great Ziegfeld)
	A Tale of Two Cities	Spencer Tracy	Norma Shearer
		(San Francisco)	(Romeo and Juliet)
1937	The Awful Truth	Charles Boyer	Irene Dunne
	Captains Courageous	(Conquest)	(The Awful Truth)
	Dead End	Fredric March	Greta Garbo
	The Good Earth	(A Star Is Born)	(Camille)
	In Old Chicago	Robert Montgomery	Janet Gaynor
	THE LIFE OF EMILE ZOLA	(Night Must Fall)	(A Star Is Born)
	Lost Horizon	Paul Muni	LUISE RAINER
	100 Men and a Girl	(The Life of Emile Zola)	(The Good Earth)
	Stage Door	SPENCER TRACY	Barbara Stanwyck
	A Star Is Born	(Captains Courageous)	(Stella Dallas)
1938	The Adventures of Robin Hood	Charles Boyer	Fay Bainter
	Alexander's Ragtime Band	(Algiers)	(White Banners)
	Boys Town	James Cagney	BETTE DAVIS
	The Citadel	(Angels with Dirty Faces)	(Jezebel)
	Four Daughters	Robert Donat	Wendy Hiller
	Grand Illusion	(The Citadel)	(Pygmalion)
	Jezebel	Leslie Howard	Norma Shearer
	Pygmalion	(Pygmalion)	(Marie Antoinette)
	Test Pilot	SPENCER TRACY	Margaret Sullavan
	YOU CAN'T TAKE IT WITH YOU	(Boys Town)	(Three Comrades)
1939	Dark Victory	ROBERT DONAT	Bette Davis
	GONE WITH THE WIND	(Goodbye, Mr. Chips)	(Dark Victory)
	Goodbye, Mr. Chips	Clark Gable	Irene Dunne
	Love Affair	(Gone With the Wind)	(Love Affair)
	Mr. Smith Goes to Washington	Laurence Olivier	Greta Garbo
	Ninotchka	(Wuthering Heights)	(Ninotchka)
	Of Mice and Men	Mickey Rooney	Greer Garson
	Stagecoach	(Babes in Arms)	(Goodbye, Mr. Chips)
	The Wizard of Oz	James Stewart	VIVIEN LEIGH
	Wuthering Heights	(Mr. Smith Goes to Washington)	(Gone With the Wind)
1940	All This and Heaven Too	Charles Chaplin	Bette Davis
	Foreign Correspondent	(The Great Dictator)	(The Letter)
	The Grapes of Wrath	Henry Fonda	Joan Fontaine
	The Great Dictator	(The Grapes of Wrath)	(Rebecca)
	Kitty Foyle	Raymond Massey	Katharine Hepburn
	The Letter	(Abe Lincoln in Illinois)	(The Philadelphia Story)
	The Long Voyage Home	Laurence Olivier	GINGER RODGERS
	Our Town	(Rebecca)	(Kitty Foyle)
	The Philadelphia Story	JAMES STEWART	Martha Scott
	REBECCA	(The Philadelphia Story)	(Our Town)

	SUPPORTING ACTOR	SUPPORTING ACTRESS	DIRECTOR
1936	Mischa Auer (My Man Godfrey) WALTER BRENNAN (Come and Get It) Stuart Erwin (Pigskin Parade) Basil Rathbone (Romeo and Juliet) Akim Tamiroff (The General Died at Dawn)	Beulah Bondi (The Gorgeous Hussy) Alice Brady (My Man Godfrey) Bonita Granville (These Three) Maria Ouspenskaya (Dodsworth) GALE SONDERGAARD (Anthony Adverse)	FRANK CAPRA (Mr. Deeds Goes to Town) Gregory La Cava (My Man Godfrey) Robert Leonard (The Great Ziegfeld) W. S. Van Dyke (San Francisco) William Wyler (Dodsworth)
1937	Ralph Bellamy (The Awful Truth) Thomas Mitchell (Hurricane) JOSEPH SCHILDKRAUT (Emile Zola) H. B. Warner (Lost Horizon) Roland Young (Topper)	ALICE BRADY (In Old Chicago) Andrea Leeds (Stage Door) Anne Shirley (Stella Dallas) Claire Trevor (Dead End) Dame May Whitty (Night Must Fall)	William Dieterle (Emile Zola) Sidney Franklin (The Good Earth) Gregory La Cava (Stage Door) LEO McCAREY (The Awful Truth) William Wellman (A Star Is Born)
1938	WALTER BRENNAN (Kentucky) John Garfield (Four Daughters) Gene Lockhart (Algiers) Robert Morley (Marie Antoinette) Basil Rathbone (If I Were King)	FAY BAINTER (Jezebel) Beulah Bondi (Of Human Hearts) Billie Burke (Merrily We Live) Spring Byington (You Can't Take It with You) Miliza Korjus (The Great Waltz)	FRANK CAPRA (You Can't Take It with You) Michael Curtiz (Angels with Dirty Faces) Norman Taurog (Boys Town) King Vidor (The Citadel) Michael Curtiz (Four Daughters)
1939	Brian Aherne (Juarez) Harry Carey (Mr. Smith Goes to Washington) Brian Donlevy (Beau Geste) THOMAS MITCHELL (Stagecoach) Claude Rains (Mr. Smith Goes to Washington)	Olivia De Havilland (Gone With the Wind) Geraldine Fitzgerald (Wuthering Heights) HATTIE McDANIEL (Gone With the Wind) Edna May Oliver (Drums Along the Mohawk) Maria Ouspenskaya (Love Affair)	Frank Capra (Mr. Smith Goes to Washington) VICTOR FLEMING (Gone With the Wind) John Ford (Stagecoach) Sam Wood (Goodbye, Mr. Chips) William Wyler (Wuthering Heights)
1940	Albert Basserman (Foreign Correspondent) WALTER BRENNAN (The Westerner) William Gargan (They Knew What They Wanted) Jack Oakie (The Great Dictator) James Stephenson (The Letter)	Judith Anderson (Rebecca) JANE DARWELL (Grapes of Wrath) Ruth Hussey (The Philadelphia Story) Barbara O'Neil (All This and Heaven Too) Marjorie Rambeau (Primrose Path)	George Cukor (The Philadelphia Story) JOHN FORD (The Grapes of Wrath) Alfred Hitchcock (Rebecca) Sam Wood (Kitty Foyle) William Wyler (The Letter)

FILM	ACTOR	ACTRESS

1941 Blossoms in the Dust
Citizen Kane
Here Comes Mr. Jordan
Hold Back the Dawn
HOW GREEN WAS MY
    VALLEY
The Little Foxes
The Maltese Falcon
One Foot in Heaven
Sergeant York
Suspicion
	GARY COOPER
	  (Sergeant York)
	Cary Grant
	  (Penny Serenade)
	Walter Huston
	  (All That Money Can Buy)
	Robert Montgomery
	  (Here Comes Mr. Jordan)
	Orson Welles
	  (Citizen Kane)
		Bette Davis
		  (The Little Foxes)
		JOAN FONTAINE
		  (Suspicion)
		Greer Garson
		  (Blossoms in the Dust)
		Olivia De Havilland
		  (Hold Back the Dawn)
		Barbara Stanwyck
		  (Ball of Fire)

1942 The Invaders
Kings Row
The Magnificent Ambersons
MRS. MINIVER
The Pied Piper
The Pride of the Yankees
Random Harvest
The Talk of the Town
Wake Island
Yankee Doodle Dandy
	JAMES CAGNEY
	  (Yankee Doodle Dandy)
	Ronald Colman
	  (Random Harvest)
	Gary Cooper
	  (The Pride of the Yankees)
	Walter Pidgeon
	  (Mrs. Miniver)
	Monty Woolley
	  (The Pied Piper)
		Bette Davis
		  (Now Voyager)
		GREER GARSON
		  (Mrs. Miniver)
		Katharine Hepburn
		  (Woman of the Year)
		Rosalind Russell
		  (My Sister Eileen)
		Teresa Wright
		  (The Pride of the Yankees)

1943 CASABLANCA
For Whom the Bell Tolls
Heaven Can Wait
In Which We Serve
Madame Curie
The More the Merrier
The Ox-Bow Incident
The Song of Bernadette
Watch on the Rhine
	Humphrey Bogart
	  (Casablanca)
	Gary Cooper
	  (For Whom the Bell Tolls)
	PAUL LUKAS
	  (Watch on the Rhine)
	Walter Pidgeon
	  (Madame Curie)
	Mickey Rooney
	  (The Human Comedy)
		Jean Arthur
		  (The More the Merrier)
		Ingrid Bergman
		  (For Whom the Bell Tolls)
		Joan Fontaine
		  (The Constant Nymph)
		Greer Garson
		  (Madame Curie)
		JENNIFER JONES
		  (The Song of Bernadette)

1944 Double Indemnity
Gaslight
GOING MY WAY
Since You Went Away
Wilson
	Charles Boyer
	  (Gaslight)
	BING CROSBY
	  (Going My Way)
	Barry Fitzgerald
	  (Going My Way)
	Cary Grant
	  (None But the Lonely Heart)
	Alexander Knox
	  (Wilson)
		INGRID BERGMAN
		  (Gaslight)
		Claudette Colbert
		  (Since You Went Away)
		Bette Davis
		  (Mr. Skeffington)
		Greer Garson
		  (Mrs. Parkington)
		Barbara Stanwyck
		  (Double Indemnity)

1945 Anchors Aweigh
The Bells of St. Mary's
THE LOST WEEKEND
Mildred Pierce
Spellbound
	Bing Crosby
	  (The Bells of St. Mary's)
	Gene Kelly
	  (Anchors Aweigh)
	RAY MILLAND
	  (The Lost Weekend)
	Gregory Peck
	  (The Keys of the Kingdom)
	Cornell Wilde
	  (A Song to Remember)
		Ingrid Bergman
		  (The Bells of St. Mary's)
		JOAN CRAWFORD
		  (Mildred Pierce)
		Greer Garson
		  (The Valley of Decision)
		Jennifer Jones
		  (Love Letters)
		Gene Tierney
		  (Leave Her to Heaven)

	SUPPORTING ACTOR	SUPPORTING ACTRESS	DIRECTOR
1941	Walter Brennan (*Sergeant York*) Charles Coburn (*The Devil and Miss Jones*) DONALD CRISP (*How Green Was My Valley*) James Gleason (*Here Comes Mr. Jordan*) Sydney Greenstreet (*The Maltese Falcon*)	Sara Allgood (*How Green Was My Valley*) MARY ASTOR (*The Great Lie*) Patricia Collinge (*The Little Foxes*) Teresa Wright (*The Little Foxes*) Margaret Wycherly (*Sergeant York*)	JOHN FORD (*How Green Was My Valley*) Alexander Hall (*Here Comes Mr. Jordan*) Howard Hawks (*Sergeant York*) Orson Welles (*Citizen Kane*) William Wyler (*The Little Foxes*)
1942	William Bendix (*Wake Island*) VAN HEFLIN (*Johnny Eager*) Walter Huston (*Yankee Doodle Dandy*) Frank Morgan (*Tortilla Flat*) Henry Travers (*Mrs. Miniver*)	Gladys Cooper (*Now Voyager*) Agnes Moorehead (*The Magnificent Ambersons*) Susan Peters (*Random Harvest*) Dame May Whitty (*Mrs. Miniver*) TERESA WRIGHT (*Mrs. Miniver*)	Michael Curtiz (*Yankee Doodle Dandy*) John Farrow (*Wake Island*) Mervyn LeRoy (*Random Harvest*) Sam Wood (*Kings Row*) WILLIAM WYLER (*Mrs. Miniver*)
1943	Charles Bickford (*The Song of Bernadette*) CHARLES COBURN (*The More the Merrier*) J. Carroll Naish (*Sahara*) Claude Rains (*Casablanca*) Akim Tamiroff (*For Whom the Bell Tolls*)	Gladys Cooper (*The Song of Bernadette*) Paulette Goddard (*So Proudly We Hail*) KATINA PAXINOU (*For Whom the Bell Tolls*) Anne Revere (*The Song of Bernadette*) Lucille Watson (*Watch on the Rhine*)	Clarence Brown (*The Human Comedy*) MICHAEL CURTIZ (*Casablanca*) Henry King (*The Song of Bernadette*) Ernst Lubitsch (*Heaven Can Wait*) George Stevens (*The More the Merrier*)
1944	Hume Cronyn (*Seventh Cross*) BARRY FITZGERALD (*Going My Way*) Claude Rains (*Mr. Skeffington*) Clifton Webb (*Laura*) Monty Woolley (*Since You Went Away*)	ETHEL BARRYMORE (*None But the Lonely Heart*) Jennifer Jones (*Since You Went Away*) Angela Lansbury (*Gaslight*) Aline MacMahon (*Dragon Seed*) Agnes Moorehead (*Mrs. Parkington*)	Alfred Hitchcock (*Lifeboat*) Henry King (*Wilson*) LEO McCAREY (*Going My Way*) Otto Preminger (*Laura*) Billy Wilder (*Double Indemnity*)
1945	Michael Chekhov (*Spellbound*) John Dall (*The Corn Is Green*) JAMES DUNN (*A Tree Grows in Brooklyn*) Robert Mitchum (*The Story of GI Joe*) J. Carroll Naish (*A Medal for Benny*)	Eve Arden (*Mildred Pierce*) Ann Blyth (*Mildred Pierce*) Angela Lansbury (*The Picture of Dorian Gray*) Joan Lorring (*The Corn Is Green*) ANNE REVERE (*National Velvet*)	Clarence Brown (*National Velvet*) Alfred Hitchcock (*Spellbound*) Leo McCarey (*The Bells of St. Mary's*) Jean Renoir (*The Southerner*) BILLY WILDER (*The Lost Weekend*)

	FILM	ACTOR	ACTRESS
1946	THE BEST YEARS OF OUR LIVES *Henry V* *It's a Wonderful Life* *The Razor's Edge* *The Yearling*	FREDRIC MARCH *(The Best Years of Our Lives)* Laurence Olivier *(Henry V)* Larry Parks *(The Jolson Story)* Gregory Peck *(The Yearling)* James Stewart *(It's a Wonderful Life)*	OLIVIA DE HAVILLAND *(To Each His Own)* Celia Johnson *(Brief Encounter)* Jennifer Jones *(Duel in the Sun)* Rosalind Russell *(Sister Kenny)* Jane Wyman *(The Yearling)*
1947	*The Bishop's Wife* *Crossfire* GENTLEMAN'S AGREEMENT *Great Expectations* *Miracle on 34th Street*	RONALD COLMAN *(A Double Life)* John Garfield *(Body and Soul)* Gregory Peck *(Gentleman's Agreement)* William Powell *(Life with Father)* Michael Redgrave *(Mourning Becomes Electra)*	Joan Crawford *(Possessed)* Susan Hayward *(Smash Up)* Dorothy McGuire *(Gentleman's Agreement)* Rosalind Russell *(Mourning Becomes Electra)* LORETTA YOUNG *(The Farmer's Daughter)*
1948	HAMLET *Johnny Belinda* *The Red Shoes* *The Snake Pit* *The Treasure of the Sierra Madre*	Lew Ayres *(Johnny Belinda)* Montgomery Clift *(The Search)* Dan Dailey *(When My Baby Smiles at Me)* LAURENCE OLIVIER *(Hamlet)* Clifton Webb *(Sitting Pretty)*	Ingrid Bergman *(Joan of Arc)* Olivia De Havilland *(The Snake Pit)* Irene Dunne *(I Remember Mama)* Barbara Stanwyck *(Sorry, Wrong Number)* JANE WYMAN *(Johnny Belinda)*
1949	ALL THE KING'S MEN *Battleground* *The Heiress* *A Letter to Three Wives* *12 O'Clock High*	BRODERICK CRAWFORD *(All the King's Men)* Kirk Douglas *(Champion)* Gregory Peck *(12 O'Clock High)* Richard Todd *(The Hasty Heart)* John Wayne *(Sands of Iwo Jima)*	Jeanne Crain *(Pinky)* OLIVIA DE HAVILLAND *(The Heiress)* Susan Hayward *(My Foolish Heart)* Deborah Kerr *(Edward, My Son)* Loretta Young *(Come to the Stable)*
1950	ALL ABOUT EVE *Born Yesterday* *Father of the Bride* *King Solomon's Mines* *Sunset Boulevard*	Louis Calhern *(The Magnificent Yankee)* JOSE FERRER *(Cyrano de Bergerac)* William Holden *(Sunset Boulevard)* James Stewart *(Harvey)* Spencer Tracy *(Father of the Bride)*	Anne Baxter *(All About Eve)* Bette Davis *(All About Eve)* JUDY HOLLIDAY *(Born Yesterday)* Eleanor Parker *(Caged)* Gloria Swanson *(Sunset Boulevard)*

	SUPPORTING ACTOR	SUPPORTING ACTRESS	DIRECTION
1946	Charles Coburn *(The Green Years)* William Demarest *(The Jolson Story)* Claude Rains *(Notorious)* HAROLD RUSSELL *(The Best Years of Our Lives)* Clifton Webb *(The Razor's Edge)*	Ethel Barrymore *(Spiral Staircase)* ANNE BAXTER *(The Razor's Edge)* Lillian Gish *(Duel in the Sun)* Flora Robson *(Saratoga Trunk)* Gale Sondergaard *(Anna)*	Clarence Brown *(The Yearling)* Frank Capra *(It's a Wonderful Life)* David Lean *(Brief Encounter)* Robert Siodmak *(The Killers)* WILLIAM WYLER *(The Best Years of Our Lives)*
1947	Charles Bickford *(The Farmer's Daughter)* Thomas Gomez *(Ride the Pink Horse)* EDMUND GWENN *(Miracle on 34th Street)* Robert Ryan *(Crossfire)* Richard Widmark *(Kiss of Death)*	Ethel Barrymore *(The Paradine Case)* Gloria Grahame *(Crossfire)* CELESTE HOLM *(Gentleman's Agreement)* Marjorie Main *(The Egg and I)* Anne Revere *(Gentleman's Agreement)*	George Cukor *(A Double Life)* Edward Dmytryk *(Crossfire)* ELIA KAZAN *(Gentleman's Agreement)* Henry Koster *(The Bishop's Wife)* David Lean *(Great Expectations)*
1948	Charles Bickford *(Johnny Belinda)* Jose Ferrer *(Joan of Arc)* Oscar Homolka *(I Remember Mama)* WALTER HUSTON *(The Treasure of the Sierra Madre)* Cecil Kellaway *(Luck of the Irish)*	Barbara Bel Geddes *(I Remember Mama)* Ellen Corby *(I Remember Mama)* Agnes Moorehead *(Johnny Belinda)* Jean Simmons *(Hamlet)* CLAIRE TREVOR *(Key Largo)*	JOHN HUSTON *(The Treasure of the Sierra Madre)* Anatole Litvak *(The Snake Pit)* Jean Neguleso *(Johnny Belinda)* Laurence Olivier *(Hamlet)* Fred Zinnemann *(The Search)*
1949	John Ireland *(All the King's Men)* DEAN JAGGER *(12 O'Clock High)* Arthur Kennedy *(Champion)* Ralph Richardson *(The Heiress)* James Whitmore *(Battleground)*	Ethel Barrymore *(Pinky)* Celeste Holm *(Come to the Stables)* Elsa Lanchester *(Come to the Stables)* MERCEDES McCAMBRIDGE *(All the King's Men)* Ethel Waters *(Pinky)*	JOSEPH MANKIEWICZ *(A Letter to Three Wives)* Carol Reed *(The Fallen Idol)* Robert Rossen *(All the King's Men)* William Wellman *(Battleground)* William Wyler *(The Heiress)*
1950	Jeff Chandler *(Broken Arrow)* Edmund Gwenn *(Mr. 880)* Sam Jaffe *(The Asphalt Jungle)* GEORGE SANDERS *(All About Eve)* Erich Von Stroheim *(Sunset Boulevard)*	Hope Emerson *(Caged)* Celeste Holm *(All About Eve)* JOSEPHINE HULL *(Harvey)* Nancy Olson *(Sunset Boulevard)* Thelma Ritter *(All About Eve)*	George Cukor *(Born Yesterday)* John Huston *(The Asphalt Jungle)* JOSEPH MANKIEWICZ *(All About Eve)* Carol Reed *(The Third Man)* Billy Wilder *(Sunset Boulevard)*

FILM	ACTOR	ACTRESS

1951   *AN AMERICAN IN PARIS*
Decision Before Dawn
A Place in the Sun
Quo Vadis
A Streetcar Named Desire
	HUMPHREY BOGART
	  (*The African Queen*)
	Marlon Brando
	  (*A Streetcar Named Desire*)
	Montgomery Clift
	  (*A Place in the Sun*)
	Arthur Kennedy
	  (*Bright Victory*)
	Fredric March
	  (*Death of a Salesman*)
		Katharine Hepburn
		  (*The African Queen*)
		VIVIEN LEIGH
		  (*A Streetcar Named Desire*)
		Eleanor Parker
		  (*Detective Story*)
		Shelley Winters
		  (*A Place in the Sun*)
		Jane Wyman
		  (*The Blue Veil*)

1952   *THE GREATEST SHOW ON*
    EARTH
High Noon
Ivanhoe
Moulin Rouge
The Quiet Man
	Marlon Brando
	  (*Viva Zapata!*)
	GARY COOPER
	  (*High Noon*)
	Kirk Douglas
	  (*The Bad and the Beautiful*)
	Jose Ferrer
	  (*Moulin Rouge*)
	Alec Guinness
	  (*The Lavender Hill Mob*)
		SHIRLEY BOOTH
		  (*Come Back, Little Sheba*)
		Joan Crawford
		  (*Sudden Fear*)
		Bette Davis
		  (*The Star*)
		Julie Harris
		  (*The Member of the Wedding*)
		Susan Hayward
		  (*With a Song in My Heart*)

1953   *FROM HERE TO ETERNITY*
Julius Caesar
The Robe
Roman Holiday
Shane
	Marlon Brando
	  (*Julius Caesar*)
	Richard Burton
	  (*The Robe*)
	Montgomery Clift
	  (*From Here to Eternity*)
	WILLIAM HOLDEN
	  (*Stalag 17*)
	Burt Lancaster
	  (*From Here to Eternity*)
		Leslie Caron
		  (*Lili*)
		Ava Gardner
		  (*Mogambo*)
		AUDREY HEPBURN
		  (*Roman Holiday*)
		Deborah Kerr
		  (*From Here to Eternity*)
		Maggie McNamara
		  (*The Moon Is Blue*)

1954   *The Caine Mutiny*
The Country Girl
ON THE WATERFRONT
Seven Brides for Seven Brothers
Three Coins in the Fountain
	Humphrey Bogart
	  (*The Caine Mutiny*)
	MARLON BRANDO
	  (*On the Waterfront*)
	Bing Crosby
	  (*The Country Girl*)
	James Mason
	  (*A Star Is Born*)
	Dan O'Herlihy
	  (*The Adventures of Robinson Crusoe*)
		Dorothy Dandridge
		  (*Carmen Jones*)
		Judy Garland
		  (*A Star Is Born*)
		Audrey Hepburn
		  (*Sabrina*)
		GRACE KELLY
		  (*The Country Girl*)
		Jane Wyman
		  (*The Magnificent Obsession*)

1955   *Love Is a Many-Splendored Thing*
MARTY
Mister Roberts
Picnic
The Rose Tattoo
	ERNEST BORGNINE
	  (*Marty*)
	James Cagney
	  (*Love Me or Leave Me*)
	James Dean
	  (*East of Eden*)
	Frank Sinatra
	  (*The Man with the Golden Arm*)
	Spencer Tracy
	  (*Bad Day at Black Rock*)
		Susan Hayward
		  (*I'll Cry Tomorrow*)
		Katharine Hepburn
		  (*Summertime*)
		Jennifer Jones
		  (*Love Is a Many-Splendored Thing*)
		ANNA MAGNANI
		  (*The Rose Tattoo*)
		Eleanor Parker
		  (*Interrupted Melody*)

SUPPORTING ACTOR	SUPPORTING ACTRESS	DIRECTION
1951		
Leo Genn	Joan Blondell	John Huston
(Quo Vadis)	*(The Blue Veil)*	*(The African Queen)*
KARL MALDEN	Mildred Dunnock	Elia Kazan
(A Streetcar Named Desire)	*(Death of a Salesman)*	*(A Streetcar Named Desire)*
Kevin McCarthy	Lee Grant	Vincente Minnelli
(Death of a Salesman)	*(Detective Story)*	*(An American in Paris)*
Peter Ustinov	KIM HUNTER	GEORGE STEVENS
(Quo Vadis)	*(A Streetcar Named Desire)*	*(A Place in the Sun)*
Gig Young	Thelma Ritter	William Wyler
(Come Fill the Cup)	*(The Mating Season)*	*(Dectective Story)*
1952		
Richard Burton	GLORIA GRAHAME	Cecil B. DeMille
(My Cousin Rachel)	*(The Bad and the Beautiful)*	*(The Greatest Show*
Arthur Hunnicutt	Jean Hagen	*on Earth)*
(The Big Sky)	*(Singin' in the Rain)*	JOHN FORD
Victor McLaglen	Colette Marchand	*(The Quiet Man)*
(The Quiet Man)	*(Moulin Rouge)*	John Huston
Jack Palance	Terry Moore	*(Moulin Rouge)*
(Sudden Fear)	*(Come Back, Little Sheba)*	Joseph Mankiewicz
ANTHONY QUINN	Thelma Ritter	*(Five Fingers)*
(Viva Zapata!)	*(With a Song in My Heart)*	Fred Zinneman
		(High Noon)
1953		
Eddie Albert	Grace Kelly	George Stevens
(Roman Holiday)	*(Mogambo)*	*(Shane)*
Brando De Wilde	Geraldine Page	Charles Walters
(Shane)	*(Hondo)*	*(Lili)*
Jack Palance	Marjorie Rambeau	Billy Wilder
(Shane)	*(Torch Song)*	*(Stalag 17)*
FRANK SINATRA	DONNA REED	William Wyler
(From Here to Eternity)	*(From Here to Eternity)*	*(Roman Holiday)*
Robert Strauss	Thelma Ritter	FRED ZINNEMANN
(Stalag 17)	*(Pickup on South Street)*	*(From Here to Eternity)*
1954		
Lee J. Cobb	Nina Foch	Alfred Hitchcock
(On the Waterfront)	*(Executive Suite)*	*(Rear Window)*
Karl Malden	Katy Jurado	ELIA KAZAN
(On the Waterfront)	*(Broken Lance)*	*(On the Waterfront)*
EDMOND O'BRIEN	EVA MARIE SAINT	George Seaton
(The Barefoot Contessa)	*(On the Waterfront)*	*(The Country Girl)*
Rod Steiger	Jan Sterling	William Wellman
(On the Waterfront)	*(The High and the Mighty)*	*(The High and the Mighty)*
Tom Tully	Claire Trevor	Billy Wilder
(The Caine Mutiny)	*(The High and the Mighty)*	*(Sabrina)*
1955		
Arthur Kennedy	Betsy Blair	Elia Kazan
(Trial)	*(Marty)*	*(East of Eden)*
JACK LEMMON	Peggy Lee	David Lean
(Mister Roberts)	*(Pete Kelly's Blues)*	*(Summertime)*
Joe Mantell	Marisa Pavan	Joshua Logan
(Marty)	*(The Rose Tattoo)*	*(Picnic)*
Sal Mineo	JO VAN FLEET	DELBERT MANN
(Rebel Without a Cause)	*(East of Eden)*	*(Marty)*
Arthur O'Connell	Natalie Wood	John Sturges
(Picnic)	*(Rebel Without a Cause)*	*(Bad Day at Black Rock)*

	FILM	ACTOR	ACTRESS
1956	AROUND THE WORLD IN 80 DAYS	YUL BRYNNER *(The King and I)*	Carroll Baker *(Baby Doll)*
	Friendly Persuasion	James Dean *(Giant)*	INGRID BERGMAN *(Anastasia)*
	Giant	Kirk Douglas *(Lust for Life)*	Katharine Hepburn *(The Rainmaker)*
	The King and I	Rock Hudson *(Giant)*	Nancy Kelly *(The Bad Seed)*
	The Ten Commandments	Laurence Olivier *(Richard III)*	Deborah Kerr *(The King and I)*
1957	THE BRIDGE ON THE RIVER KWAI	Marlon Brando *(Sayonara)*	Deborah Kerr *(Heaven Knows Mr. Allison)*
	Peyton Place	Anthony Franciosa *(A Handful of Rain)*	Anna Magnani *(Wild Is the Wind)*
	Sayonara	ALEC GUINNESS *(The Bridge on the River Kwai)*	Elizabeth Taylor *(Raintree County)*
	12 Angry Men	Charles Laughton *(Witness for the Prosecution)*	Lana Turner *(Peyton Place)*
	Witness for the Prosecution	Anthony Quinn *(Wild Is the Wind)*	JOANNE WOODWARD *(The Three Faces of Eve)*
1958	*Auntie Mame*	Tony Curtis *(The Defiant Ones)*	SUSAN HAYWARD *(I Want to Live!)*
	Cat on a Hot Tin Roof	Paul Newman *(Cat on a Hot Tin Roof)*	Deborah Kerr *(Separate Tables)*
	The Defiant Ones	DAVID NIVEN *(Separate Tables)*	Shirley MacLaine *(Some Came Running)*
	GIGI	Sidney Poitier *(The Defiant Ones)*	Rosalind Russell *(Auntie Mame)*
	Separate Tables	Spencer Tracy *(The Old Man and the Sea)*	Elizabeth Taylor *(Cat on a Hot Tin Roof)*
1959	*Anatomy of a Murder*	Laurence Harvey *(Room at the Top)*	Doris Day *(Pillow Talk)*
	BEN-HUR	CHARLTON HESTON *(Ben-Hur)*	Audrey Hepburn *(The Nun's Story)*
	The Diary of Anne Frank	Jack Lemmon *(Some Like It Hot)*	Katharine Hepburn *(Suddenly Last Summer)*
	The Nun's Story	Paul Muni *(The Last Angry Man)*	SIMONE SIGNORET *(Room at the Top)*
	Room at the Top	James Stewart *(Anatomy of a Murder)*	Elizabeth Taylor *(Suddenly, Last Summer)*
1960	*The Alamo*	Trevor Howard *(Sons and Lovers)*	Greer Garson *(Sunrise at Campobello)*
	THE APARTMENT	BURT LANCASTER *(Elmer Gantry)*	Deborah Kerr *(The Sundowners)*
	Elmer Gantry	Jack Lemmon *(The Apartment)*	Shirley MacLaine *(The Apartment)*
	Sons and Lovers	Laurence Olivier *(The Entertainer)*	Melina Mercouri *(Never on Sunday)*
	The Sundowners	Spencer Tracy *(Inherit the Wind)*	ELIZABETH TAYLOR *(Butterfield 8)*

SUPPORTING ACTOR	SUPPORTING ACTRESS	DIRECTION
1956 Don Murray *(Bus Stop)* Anthony Perkins *(Friendly Persuasion)* ANTHONY QUINN *(Lust for Life)* Mickey Rooney *(Bold and the Brave)* Robert Stack *(Written on the Wind)*	Mildred Dunnock *(Baby Doll)* Eileen Heckart *(The Bad Seed)* Mercedes McCambridge *(Giant)* Patty McCormack *(The Bad Seed)* DOROTHY MALONE *(Written on the Wind)*	Michael Anderson *(Around the World in 80 Days)* Walter Lang *(The King and I)* GEORGE STEVENS *(Giant)* King Vidor *(War and Peace)* William Wyler *(Friendly Persuasion)*
1957 RED BUTTONS *(Sayonara)* Vittorio De Sica *(A Farewell to Arms)* Sessue Hayakawa *(The Bridge on the River Kwai)* Arthur Kennedy *(Peyton Place)* Russ Tamblyn *(Peyton Place)*	Carolyn Jones *(The Bachelor Party)* Elsa Lanchester *(Witness for the Prosecution)* Hope Lange *(Peyton Place)* MIYOSHI UMEKI *(Sayonara)* Diane Varsi *(Peyton Place)*	DAVID LEAN *(The Bridge on the River Kwai)* Joshua Logan *(Sayonara)* Sidney Lumet *(12 Angry Men)* Mark Robson *(Peyton Place)* Billy Wilder *(Witness for the Prosecution)*
1958 Theodore Bikel *(The Defiant Ones)* Lee J. Cobb *(Brothers Karamazov)* BURL IVES *(The Big Country)* Arthur Kennedy *(Some Came Running)* Gig Young *(Teacher's Pet)*	Peggy Cass *(Auntie Mame)* WENDY HILLER *(Separate Tables)* Martha Hyer *(Some Came Running)* Maureen Stapleton *(Lonelyhearts)* Cara Williams *(The Defiant Ones)*	Richard Brooks *(Cat on a Hot Tin Roof)* Stanley Kramer *(The Defiant Ones)* VINCENTE MINNELLI *(Gigi)* Mark Robson *(The Inn of the Sixth Happiness)* Robert Wise *(I Want to Live!)*
1959 HUGH GRIFFITH *(Ben-Hur)* Arthur O'Connell *(Anatomy of a Murder)* George C. Scott *(Anatomy of a Murder)* Robert Vaughn *(The Young Philadelphians)* Ed Wynn *(The Diary of Anne Frank)*	Hermione Baddeley *(Room at the Top)* Susan Kohner *(Imitation of Life)* Juanita Moore *(Imitation of Life)* Thelma Ritter *(Pillow Talk)* SHELLEY WINTERS *(The Diary of Anne Frank)*	Jack Clayton *(Room at the Top)* George Stevens *(The Diary of Anne Frank)* Billy Wilder *(Some Like It Hot)* WILLIAM WYLER *(Ben-Hur)* Fred Zinnemann *(The Nun's Story)*
1960 Peter Falk *(Murder Inc.)* Jack Kruschen *(The Apartment)* Sal Mineo *(Exodus)* PETER USTINOV *(Spartacus)* Chill Wills *(The Alamo)*	Glynis Johns *(The Sundowners)* SHIRLEY JONES *(Elmer Gantry)* Shirley Knight *(Top of the Stairs)* Janet Leigh *(Psycho)* Mary Ure *(Sons and Lovers)*	Jack Cardiff *(Sons and Lovers)* Jules Dassin *(Never on Sunday)* Alfred Hitchcock *(Psycho)* BILLY WILDER *(The Apartment)* Fred Zinnemann *(The Sundowners)*

33

	FILM	ACTOR	ACTRESS
1961	*Fanny* *The Guns of Navarone* *The Hustler* *Judgment at Nuremberg* *WEST SIDE STORY*	Charles Boyer *(Fanny)* Paul Newman *(The Hustler)* MAXIMILIAN SCHELL *(Judgment at Nuremberg)* Spencer Tracy *(Judgment at Nuremberg)* Stuart Whitman *(The Mark)*	Audrey Hepburn *(Breakfast at Tiffany's)* Piper Laurie *(The Hustler)* SOPHIA LOREN *(Two Women)* Geraldine Page *(Summer and Smoke)* Natalie Wood *(Splendor in the Grass)*
1962	*LAWRENCE OF ARABIA* *The Longest Day* *The Music Man* *Mutiny on the Bounty* *To Kill a Mockingbird*	Burt Lancaster *(Bird Man of Alcatraz)* Jack Lemmon *(Days of Wine and Roses)* Marcello Mastroianni *(Divorce—Italian Style)* Peter O'Toole *(Lawrence of Arabia)* GREGORY PECK *(To Kill a Mockingbird)*	ANNE BANCROFT *(The Miracle Worker)* Bette Davis *(What Ever Happened to Baby Jane?)* Katharine Hepburn *(Long Day's Journey into Night)* Geraldine Page *(Sweet Bird of Youth)* Lee Remick *(Days of Wine and Roses)*
1963	*America, America* *Cleopatra* *How the West Was Won* *Lilies of the Field* *TOM JONES*	Albert Finney *(Tom Jones)* Richard Harris *(This Sporting Life)* Rex Harrison *(Cleopatra)* Paul Newman *(Hud)* SIDNEY POITIER *(Lilies of the Field)*	Leslie Caron *(The L-Shaped Room)* Shirley MacLaine *(Irma La Douce)* PATRICIA NEAL *(Hud)* Rachel Roberts *(This Sporting Life)* Natalie Wood *(Love with the Proper Stranger)*
1964	*Becket* *Dr. Strangelove* *Mary Poppins* *MY FAIR LADY* *Zorba the Greek*	Richard Burton *(Becket)* REX HARRISON *(My Fair Lady)* Peter O'Toole *(Becket)* Anthony Quinn *(Zorba the Greek)* Peter Sellers *(Dr. Strangelove)*	JULIE ANDREWS *(Mary Poppins)* Anne Bancroft *(The Pumpkin Eater)* Sophia Loren *(Marriage Italian Style)* Debbie Reynolds *(The Unsinkable Molly Brown)* Kim Stanley *(Seance on a Wet Afternoon)*
1965	*Darling* *Doctor Zhivago* *Ship of Fools* *THE SOUND OF MUSIC* *A Thousand Clowns*	Richard Burton *(The Spy Who Came in from the Cold)* LEE MARVIN *(Cat Ballou)* Laurence Olivier *(Othello)* Rod Steiger *(The Pawnbroker)* Oskar Werner *(Ship of Fools)*	Julie Andrews *(The Sound of Music)* JULIE CHRISTIE *(Darling)* Samantha Eggar *(The Collector)* Elizabeth Hartman *(A Patch of Blue)* Simone Signoret *(Ship of Fools)*

	SUPPORTING ACTOR	SUPPORTING ACTRESS	DIRECTION
1961	GEORGE CHAKIRIS *(West Side Story)* Montgomery Clift *(Judgment at Nuremberg)* Peter Falk *(Pocketful of Miracles)* Jackie Gleason *(The Hustler)* George C. Scott *(The Hustler)*	Fay Bainter *(The Children's Hour)* Judy Garland *(Judgment at Nuremberg)* Lotte Lenya *(The Roman Spring)* Una Merkel *(Summer and Smoke)* RITA MORENO *(West Side Story)*	Federico Fellini *(La Dolce Vita)* Stanley Kramer *(Judgment at Nuremberg)* Robert Rossen *(The Hustler)* J. Lee Thompson *(The Guns of Navarone)* ROBERT WISE/JEROME ROBBINS *(West Side Story)*
1962	ED BEGLEY *(Sweet Bird of Youth)* Victor Buono *(What Ever Happened to Baby Jane?)* Telly Savalas *(Bird Man of Alcatraz)* Omar Sharif *(Lawrence of Arabia)* Terence Stamp *(Billy Budd)*	Mary Badham *(To Kill a Mockingbird)* PATTY DUKE *(The Miracle Worker)* Shirley Knight *(Sweet Bird of Youth)* Angela Lansbury *(The Manchurian Candidate)* Thelma Ritter *(Bird Man of Alcatraz)*	Pietro Germi *(Divorce—Italian Style)* DAVID LEAN *(Lawrence of Arabia)* Robert Mulligan *(To Kill a Mockingbird)* Arthur Penn *(The Miracle Worker)* Frank Perry *(David and Lisa)*
1963	Nick Adams *(Twilight of Honor)* Bobby Darin *(Captain Newman)* MELVYN DOUGLAS *(Hud)* Hugh Griffith *(Tom Jones)* John Huston *(The Cardinal)*	Diane Cilento *(Tom Jones)* Dame Edith Evans *(Tom Jones)* Joyce Redman *(Tom Jones)* MARGARET RUTHERFORD *(The VIPs)* Lilia Skala *(Lilies of the Field)*	Federico Fellini *(8½)* Elia Kazan *(America, America)* Otto Preminger *(The Cardinal)* TONY RICHARDSON *(Tom Jones)* Martin Ritt *(Hud)*
1964	John Gielgud *(Becket)* Stanley Holloway *(My Fair Lady)* Edmond O'Brien *(Seven Days in May)* Lee Tracy *(The Best Man)* PETER USTINOV *(Topkapi)*	Gladys Cooper *(My Fair Lady)* Dame Edith Evans *(The Chalk Garden)* Grayson Hall *(Night of the Iguana)* LILA KEDROVA *(Zorba the Greek)* Agnes Moorehead *(Hush...Hush, Sweet Charlotte)*	Michael Cacoyannis *(Zorba the Greek)* GEORGE CUKOR *(My Fair Lady)* Peter Glenville *(Becket)* Stanley Kubrick *(Dr. Strangelove)* Robert Stevenson *(Mary Poppins)*
1965	MARTIN BALSAM *(A Thousand Clowns)* Ian Bannen *(The Flight of the Phoenix)* Tom Courtenay *(Doctor Zhivago)* Michael Dunn *(Ship of Fools)* Frank Finlay *(Othello)*	Ruth Gordon *(Inside Daisy Clover)* Joyce Redman *(Othello)* Maggie Smith *(Othello)* SHELLEY WINTERS *(A Patch of Blue)* Peggy Wood *(The Sound of Music)*	David Lean *(Doctor Zhivago)* John Schlesinger *(Darling)* Hiroshi Teshigahara *(Woman in the Dunes)* ROBERT WISE *(The Sound of Music)* William Wyler *(The Collector)*

FILM	ACTOR	ACTRESS

1966
Alfie
A MAN FOR ALL SEASONS
The Russians Are Coming, The Russians Are Coming
The Sand Pebbles
Who's Afraid of Virginia Woolf?

Alan Arkin
  (The Russians Are Coming, The Russians Are Coming)
Richard Burton
  (Who's Afraid of Virginia Woolf?)
Michael Caine
  (Alfie)
Steve McQueen
  (The Sand Pebbles)
PAUL SCOFIELD
  (A Man for All Seasons)

Anouk Aimee
  (A Man and a Woman)
Ida Kaminska
  (The Shop in Main Street)
Lynn Redgrave
  (Georgy Girl)
Vanessa Redgrave
  (Morgan)
ELIZABETH TAYLOR
  (Who's Afraid of Virginia Woolf?)

1967
Bonnie and Clyde
Doctor Doolittle
The Graduate
Guess Who's Coming to Dinner
IN THE HEAT OF THE NIGHT

Warren Beatty
  (Bonnie and Clyde)
Dustin Hoffman
  (The Graduate)
Paul Newman
  (Cool Hand Luke)
ROD STEIGER
  (In the Heat of the Night)
Spencer Tracy
  (Guess Who's Coming to Dinner)

Anne Bancroft
  (The Graduate)
Faye Dunaway
  (Bonnie and Clyde)
Edith Evans
  (The Whisperers)
Audrey Hepburn
  (Wait Until Dark)
KATHARINE HEPBURN
  (Guess Who's Coming to Dinner)

1968
Funny Girl
The Lion in Winter
OLIVER!
Rachel, Rachel
Romeo and Juliet

Alan Arkin
  (The Heart Is a Lonely Hunter)
Alan Bates
  (The Fixer)
Ron Moody
  (Oliver!)
Peter O'Toole
  (The Lion in Winter)
CLIFF ROBERTSON
  (Charly)

KATHARINE HEPBURN
  (The Lion in Winter)
Patricia Neal
  (The Subject Was Roses)
Vanessa Redgrave
  (Isadora)
BARBRA STREISAND
  (Funny Girl)
Joanne Woodward
  (Rachel, Rachel)

1969
Anne of the Thousand Days
Butch Cassidy and the Sundance Kid
Hello, Dolly!
MIDNIGHT COWBOY
Z (non-winner)

Richard Burton
  (Anne of the Thousand Days)
Dustin Hoffman
  (Midnight Cowboy)
Peter O'Toole
  (Goodbye, Mr. Chips)
John Voight
  (Midnight Cowboy)
JOHN WAYNE
  (True Grit)

Genevieve Bujold
  (Anne of the Thousand Days)
Jane Fonda
  (They Shoot Horses, Don't They?)
Liza Minnelli
  (The Sterile Cuckoo)
Jean Simmons
  (The Happy Ending)
MAGGIE SMITH
  (The Prime of Miss Jean Brodie)

1970
Airport
Five Easy Pieces
Love Story
*M*A*S*H (non-winner)*
PATTON

Melvyn Douglas
  (I Never Sang for My Father)
James Earl Jones
  (The Great White Hope)
Jack Nicholson
  (Five Easy Pieces)
Ryan O'Neal
  (Love Story)
GEORGE C. SCOTT
  (Patton)

Jane Alexander
  (The Great White Hope)
GLENDA JACKSON
  (Women in Love)
Ali MacGraw
  (Love Story)
Sarah Miles
  (Ryan's Daughter)
Carrie Snodgrass
  (Diary of a Mad Housewife)

SUPPORTING ACTOR	SUPPORTING ACTRESS	DIRECTION
1966 Mako *(The Sand Pebbles)* James Mason *(Georgy Girl)* **WALTER MATTHAU** *(Fortune Cookie)* George Segal *(Who's Afraid of Virginia Woolf?)* Robert Shaw *(A Man for All Seasons)*	SANDY DENNIS *(Who's Afraid of Virginia Woolf?)* Wendy Hiller *(A Man for All Seasons)* Jocelyne Lagarde *(Hawaii)* Vivien Merchant *(Alfie)* Geraldine Page *(You're a Big Boy)*	Michelangelo Antonioni *(Blow-Up)* Richard Brooks *(The Professionals)* Claude Lelouche *(A Man and a Woman)* Mike Nichols *(Who's Afraid of Virginia Woolf?)* **FRED ZINNEMANN** *(A Man for All Seasons)*
1967 John Cassavetes *(The Dirty Dozen)* Gene Hackman *(Bonnie and Clyde)* Cecil Kellaway *(Guess Who's Coming to Dinner)* **GEORGE KENNEDY** *(Cool Hand Luke)* Michael Pollard *(Bonnie and Clyde)*	Carol Channing *(Thoroughly Modern Millie)* Mildred Natwick *(Barefoot in the Park)* **ESTELLE PARSONS** *(Bonnie and Clyde)* Beah Richards *(Guess Who's Coming to Dinner)* Katharine Ross *(The Graduate)*	Richard Brooks *(In Cold Blood)* Norman Jewison *(In the Heat of the Night)* Stanley Kramer *(Guess Who's Coming to Dinner)* **MIKE NICHOLS** *(The Graduate)* Arthur Penn *(Bonnie and Clyde)*
1968 **JACK ALBERTSON** *(The Subject Was Roses)* Seymour Cassel *(Faces)* Daniel Massey *(Star)* Jack Wild *(Oliver!)* Gene Wilder *(The Producers)*	Lynn Carlin *(Faces)* **RUTH GORDON** *(Rosemary's Baby)* Sondra Locke *(The Heart Is a Lonely Hunter)* Key Medford *(Funny Girl)* Estelle Parsons *(Rachel, Rachel)*	Anthony Harvey *(The Lion in Winter)* Stanley Kubrick *(2001: A Space Odyssey)* Gillo Pontecorvo *(The Battle of Algiers)* **CAROL REED** *(Oliver!)* Franco Zeffirelli *(Romeo and Juliet)*
1969 Rupert Crosse *(The Reivers)* Elliott Gould *(Bob & Carol & Ted & Alice)* Jack Nicholson *(Easy Rider)* Anthony Quayle *(Anne of the Thousand Days)* **GIG YOUNG** *(They Shoot Horses, Don't They?)*	Catherine Burns *(Last Summer)* Dyan Cannon *(Bob & Carol & Ted & Alice)* **GOLDIE HAWN** *(Cactus Flower)* Sylvia Miles *(Midnight Cowboy)* Susannah York *(They Shoot Horses, Don't They?)*	Costa-Gavras *(Z)* George Roy Hill *(Butch Cassidy and the Sundance Kid)* Arthur Penn *(Alice's Restaurant)* Sidney Pollack *(They Shoot Horses, Don't They?)* **JOHN SCHLESINGER** *(Midnight Cowboy)*
1970 Richard Castellano *(Lovers and Strangers)* Chief Dan George *(Little Big Man)* Gene Hackman *(I Never Sang for My Father)* John Marley *(Love Story)* **JOHN MILLS** *(Ryan's Daughter)*	Karen Black *(Five Easy Pieces)* Lee Grant *(The Landlord)* **HELEN HAYES** *(Airport)* Sally Kellerman *(M*A*S*H)* Maureen Stapleton *(Airport)*	Robert Altman *(M*A*S*H)* Federico Fellini *(Satyricon)* Arthur Hiller *(Love Story)* Ken Russell *(Women in Love)* **FRANKLIN SCHAFFNER** *(Patton)*

FILM	ACTOR	ACTRESS
1971 A Clockwork Orange Fiddler on the Roof THE FRENCH CONNECTION The Last Picture Show Nicholas and Alexandra	Peter Finch (Sunday Bloody Sunday) GENE HACKMAN (The French Connection) Walter Matthau (Kotch) George C. Scott (The Hospital) Topol (Fiddler on the Roof)	Julie Christie (McCabe and Mrs. Miller) JANE FONDA (Klute) Glenda Jackson (Sunday Bloody Sunday) Vanessa Redgrave (Mary Queen of Scots) Janet Suzman (Nicholas and Alexandra)
1972 Cabaret Deliverance The Emigrants THE GODFATHER Sounder	MARLON BRANDO (The Godfather) Michael Caine (Sleuth) Laurence Olivier (Sleuth) Peter O'Toole (The Ruling Class) Paul Winfield (Sounder)	LIZA MINNELLI (Cabaret) Diana Ross (Lady Sings the Blues) Maggie Smith (Travels with My Aunt) Cicely Tyson (Sounder) Liv Ullmann (The Emigrants)
1973 American Graffiti Cries and Whispers The Exorcist THE STING A Touch of Class	Marlon Brando (Last Tango in Paris) JACK LEMMON (Save the Tiger) Jack Nicholson (The Last Detail) Al Pacino (Serpico) Robert Redford (The Sting)	Ellen Burstyn (The Exorcist) GLENDA JACKSON (A Touch of Class) Marsha Mason (Cinderella Liberty) Barbra Streisand (The Way We Were) Joanne Woodward (Summer Wishes, Winter Dreams)
1974 Chinatown The Conversation THE GODFATHER PART II Lenny The Towering Inferno	ART CARNEY (Harry and Tonto) Albert Finney (Murder on the Orient Express) Dustin Hoffman (Lenny) Jack Nicholson (Chinatown) Al Pacino (The Godfather Part II)	ELLEN BURSTYN (Alice Doesn't Live Here Anymore) Diahann Carroll (Claudine) Faye Dunaway (Chinatown) Valerie Perrine (Lenny) Gena Rowlands (A Woman Under the Influence)
1975 Barry Lyndon Dog Day Afternoon Jaws Nashville ONE FLEW OVER THE CUCKOO'S NEST	Walter Matthau (The Sunshine Boys) JACK NICHOLSON (One Flew over the Cuckoo's Nest) Al Pacino (Dog Day Afternoon) Maximilian Schell (The Man in the Glass Booth) James Whitmore (Give 'em Hell, Harry!)	Isabelle Adjani (The Story of Adele H) Ann-Margret (Tommy) LOUISE FLETCHER (One Flew over the Cuckoo's Nest) Glenda Jackson (Hedda) Carol Kane (Hester Street)

	SUPPORTING ACTOR	SUPPORTING ACTRESS	DIRECTION
1971	Jeff Bridges (The Last Picture Show) Leonard Frey (Fiddler on the Roof) Richard Jaeckel (Sometimes a Great Notion) BEN JOHNSON (The Last Picture Show) Roy Scheider (The French Connection)	Ellen Burstyn (The Last Picture Show) Barbara Harris (Harry Kellerman) CLORIS LEACHMAN (The Last Picture Show) Margaret Leighton (The Go-Between) Ann-Margret (Carnal Knowledge)	Peter Bogdanovich (The Last Picture Show) WILLIAM FRIEDKIN (The French Connection) Norman Jewison (Fiddler on the Roof) Stanley Kubrick (A Clockwork Orange) John Schlesinger (Sunday Bloody Sunday)
1972	Eddie Albert (The Heartbreak Kid) James Caan (The Godfather) Robert Duvall (The Godfather) JOEL GREY (Cabaret) Al Pacino (The Godfather)	Jeannie Berlin (The Heartbreak Kid) EILEEN HECKART (Butterflies Are Free) Geraldine Page (Pete 'n Tillie) Susan Tyrell (Fat City) Shelley Winters (The Poseidon Adventure)	John Boorman (Deliverance) Francis Ford Coppola (The Godfather) BOB FOSSE (Cabaret) Joseph Mankiewicz (Sleuth) Jan Troell (The Emigrants)
1973	Vincent Gardenia (Bang the Drum Slowly) Jack Gilford (Save the Tiger) JOHN HOUSEMAN (Paper Chase) Jason Miller (The Exorcist) Randy Quaid (The Last Detail)	Linda Blair (The Exorcist) Candy Clark (American Graffiti) Madeline Kahn (Paper Moon) TATUM O'NEAL (Paper Moon) Sylvia Sidney (Summer Wishes, Winter Dreams)	Ingmar Bergman (Cries and Whispers) Bernardo Bertolucci (Last Tango in Paris) William Friedkin (The Exorcist) GEORGE ROY HILL (The Sting) George Lucas (American Graffiti)
1974	Fred Astaire (The Towering Inferno) Jeff Bridges (Thunderbolt) ROBERT DE NIRO (The Godfather Part II) Michael Gazzo (The Godfather Part II) Lee Strasberg (The Godfather Part II)	INGRID BERGMAN (Murder on the Orient Express) Valentina Cortese (Day for Night) Madeline Kahn (Blazing Saddles) Diane Ladd (Alice Doesn't Live Here Anymore) Talia Shire (The Godfather Part II)	John Cassavetes (A Woman Under the Influence) FRANCIS FORD COPPOLA (The Godfather Part II) Bob Fosse (Lenny) Roman Polanski (Chinatown) Francois Truffaut (Day for Night)
1975	GEORGE BURNS (The Sunshine Boys) Brad Dourif (One Flew over the Cuckoo's Nest) Burgess Meredith (The Day of the Locust) Chris Sarandon (Dog Day Afternoon) Jack Warden (Shampoo)	Ronee Blakley (Nashville) LEE GRANT (Shampoo) Sylvia Miles (Farewell, My Lovely) Lily Tomlin (Nashville) Brenda Vaccaro (Once Is Not Enough)	Robert Altman (Nashville) Federico Fellini (Amarcord) MILOS FORMAN (One Flew over the Cuckoo's Nest) Stanley Kubrick (Barry Lyndon) Sidney Lumet (Dog Day Afternoon)

	FILM	ACTOR	ACTRESS
1976	*All the President's Men* *Bound for Glory* *Network* *ROCKY* *Taxi Driver*	Robert DeNiro *(Taxi Driver)* PETER FINCH *(Network)* Giancarlo Giannini *(Seven Beauties)* William Holden *(Network)* Sylvester Stallone *(Rocky)*	Marie-Christine Barrault *(Cousin, Cousine)* FAYE DUNAWAY *(Network)* Talia Shire *(Rocky)* Sissy Spacek *(Carrie)* Liv Ullmann *(Face to Face)*
1977	*ANNIE HALL* *The Goodbye Girl* *Julia* *Star Wars* *The Turning Point*	Woody Allen *(Annie Hall)* Richard Burton *(Equus)* RICHARD DREYFUSS *(The Goodbye Girl)* Marcello Mastroianni *(A Special Day)* John Travolta *(Saturday Night Fever)*	Anne Bancroft *(The Turning Point)* Jane Fonda *(Julia)* DIANE KEATON *(Annie Hall)* Shirley MacLaine *(The Turning Point)* Marsha Mason *(The Goodbye Girl)*
1978	*Coming Home* *THE DEER HUNTER* *Heaven Can Wait* *Midnight Express* *An Unmarried Woman*	Warren Beatty *(Heaven Can Wait)* Gary Busey *(The Buddy Holly Story)* Robert DeNiro *(The Deer Hunter)* Laurence Olivier *(The Boys from Brazil)* JON VOIGHT *(Coming Home)*	Ingrid Bergman *(Autumn Sonata)* Ellen Burstyn *(Same Time, Next Year)* Jill Clayburgh *(An Unmarried Woman)* JANE FONDA *(Coming Home)* Geraldine Page *(Interiors)*
1979	*All That Jazz* *Apocalypse Now* *Breaking Away* *KRAMER VS. KRAMER* *Norma Rae*	DUSTIN HOFFMAN *(Kramer vs. Kramer)* Jack Lemmon *(The China Syndrome)* Al Pacino *(And Justice for All)* Roy Scheider *(All That Jazz)* Peter Sellers *(Being There)*	Jill Clayburgh *(Starting Over)* SALLY FIELD *(Norma Rae)* Jane Fonda *(China Syndrome)* Marsha Mason *(Chapter Two)* Bette Midler *(The Rose)*

	SUPPORTING ACTOR	SUPPORTING ACTRESS	DIRECTION
1976	Ned Beatty (Network) Burgess Meredith (Rocky) Laurence Olivier (Marathon Man) JASON ROBARDS (All the President's Men) Burt Young (Rocky)	Jane Alexander (All the President's Men) Jodie Foster (Taxi Driver) Lee Grant (Voyage of the Damned) Piper Laurie (Carrie) BEATRICE STRAIGHT (Network)	JOHN AVILDSEN (Rocky) Ingmar Bergman (Face to Face) Sidney Lumet (Network) Alan J. Paukla (All the President's Men) Lina Wertmuller (Seven Beauties)
1977	Mikhail Baryshnikov (The Turning Point) Peter Firth (Equus) Alec Guinness (Star Wars) JASON ROBARDS (Julia) Maximilian Schell (Julia)	Leslie Browne (The Turning Point) Quinn Cummings (The Goodbye Girl) Melinda Dillon (Close Encounters of the Third Kind) VANESSA REDGRAVE (Julia) Tuesday Weld (Looking for Mr Goodbar)	WOODY ALLEN (Annie Hall) George Lucas (Star Wars) Herbert Ross (The Turning Point) Steven Spielberg (Close Encounters of the Third Kind) Fred Zinnemann (Julia)
1978	Bruce Dern (Coming Home) Richard Farnsworth (Comes a Horseman) John Hurt (Midnight Express) CHRISTOPHER WALKEN (The Deer Hunter) Jack Warden (Heaven Can Wait)	Dyan Cannon (Heaven Can Wait) Penelope Milford (Coming Home) MAGGIE SMITH (California Suite) Maureen Stapleton (Interiors) Meryl Streep (The Deer Hunter)	Hal Ashby (Coming Home) MICHAEL CIMINO (The Deer Hunter) Woody Allen (Interiors) Warren Beatty, Buck Henry (Heaven Can Wait) Alan Parker (Midnight Express)
1979	MELVYN DOUGLAS (Being There) Robert Duvall (Apocalypse Now) Fredric Forrest (The Rose) Justin Henry (Kramer vs. Kramer) Mickey Rooney (The Black Stallion)	Jane Alexander (Kramer vs. Kramer) Barbara Barrie (Breaking Away) Candice Bergen (Starting Over) Mariel Hemingway (Manhattan) MERYL STREEP (Kramer vs. Kramer)	ROBERT BENTON (Kramer vs. Kramer) Bob Fosse (All That Jazz) Francis Ford Coppola (Apocalypse Now) Edouward Moinaro (La Cage Aux Folles) Peter Yates (Breaking Away)

FANS' 100 FAVORITE FILMS
(Selected in 1978 by *Los Angeles Times* readers with "ten-best" lists)
(Oscar-winners in caps)

1. *GONE WITH THE WIND*
2. *CASABLANCA*
3. *Citizen Kane*
4. *The Wizard of Oz*
5. *The African Queen*
6. *THE SOUND OF MUSIC*
7. *ONE FLEW OVER THE CUCKOO'S NEST*
8. *The Grapes of Wrath*
9. *THE GODFATHER*
10. *Star Wars*
11. *2001: A Space Odyssey*
12. *Singin' in the Rain*
13. *ROCKY*
14. *The Graduate*
15. *Fantasia*
16. *BEN-HUR*
17. *IT HAPPENED ONE NIGHT*
18. *The Treasure of the Sierra Madre*
19. *THE BEST YEARS OF OUR LIVES*
20. *ON THE WATERFRONT*
21. *Wuthering Heights*
22. *To Kill a Mockingbird*
23. *THE STING*
24. *Butch Cassidy and the Sundance Kid*
25. *THE BRIDGE ON THE RIVER KWAI*
26. *Cabaret*
27. *MIDNIGHT COWBOY*
28. *Sunset Boulevard*
29. *Dr. Strangelove*
30. *WEST SIDE STORY*
31. *LAWRENCE OF ARABIA*
32. *High Noon*
33. *ALL ABOUT EVE*
34. *The Maltese Falcon*
35. *Snow White and the Seven Dwarfs*
36. *THE GODFATHER PART II*
37. *Chinatown*
38. *All the President's Men*
39. *A Streetcar Named Desire*
40. *King Kong (original)*
41. *ALL QUIET ON THE WESTERN FRONT*
42. *Jaws*
43. *Psycho*
44. *It's a Wonderful Life*
45. *Modern Times*
46. *The Birth of a Nation*
47. *Shane*
48. *The Philadelphia Story*
49. *Stagecoach*
50. *Mr. Smith Goes to Washington*
51. *City Lights*
52. *ANNIE HALL*
53. *Some Like It Hot*
54. *Nashville*
55. *Dr. Zhivago*
56. *North by Northwest*
57. *Lost Horizon (original)*
58. *Who's Afraid of Virginia Woolf?*
59. *The Gold Rush*
60. *Yankee Doodle Dandy*
61. *The General*
62. *Red River*
63. *PATTON*
64. *FROM HERE TO ETERNITY*
65. *Top Hat*
66. *Harold and Maude*
67. *The Searchers*
68. *AN AMERICAN IN PARIS*
69. *American Graffiti*
70. *Intolerance*
71. *M*A*S*H (non-winner)*
72. *Close Encounters of the Third Kind*
73. *Funny Girl*
74. *MY FAIR LADY*
75. *Vertigo*
76. *MARTY*
77. *Giant*
78. *A Place in the Sun*
79. *Bonnie and Clyde*
80. *Five Easy Pieces*
81. *REBECCA*
82. *Music Man*
83. *Bringing Up Baby*
84. *GIGI*
85. *McCabe & Mrs. Miller*
86. *Mr. Roberts*
87. *The Quiet Man*
88. *A Night at the Opera*
89. *Miracle on 34th Street*
90. *A Star Is Born (Judy Garland & James Mason, 1954)*
91. *East of Eden*
92. *Easy Rider*
93. *Duck Soup*
94. *The Exorcist*
95. *Gunga Din*
96. *Little Big Man*
97. *Meet Me in St. Louis*
98. *Paths of Glory*
99. *Taxi Driver*
100. *Laura*

THE GREATEST AMERICAN FILMS
(As selected by The American Film Institute membership)
(Oscar winners in caps)

THE TOP TEN

Number One

GONE WITH THE WIND

Others in Top Ten (In Alphabetical Order)

The African Queen
CASABLANCA
Citizen Kane
The Grapes of Wrath
ONE FLEW OVER THE CUCKOO'S NEST
Singin' in the Rain
Star Wars
2001: A Space Odyssey
The Wizard of Oz

OTHERS

(In Alphabetical Order)

ALL ABOUT EVE
ALL QUIET ON THE WESTERN FRONT
THE BEST YEARS OF OUR LIVES
The Birth of a Nation
THE BRIDGE ON THE RIVER KWAI
Butch Cassidy and the Sundance Kid
Cabaret
Chinatown
Dr. Strangelove
Fantasia
The General
THE GODFATHER
THE GODFATHER PART II
The Graduate
High Noon
Intolerance
IT HAPPENED ONE NIGHT
It's a Wonderful Life
MIDNIGHT COWBOY
Modern Times
Nashville
ON THE WATERFRONT
Psycho
ROCKY
Snow White and the Seven Dwarfs
THE SOUND OF MUSIC
THE STING
A Streetcar Named Desire
Sunset Boulevard
To Kill a Mockingbird
The Treasure of the Sierra Madre
WEST SIDE STORY
Wuthering Heights

50 MOST SIGNIFICANT FILMS
(Milestone movies which advanced the art—Selected in 1972 by USC Performing Arts Council Poll of film producers & critics)
(Oscar winners in caps)

1. Citizen Kane (tie)
   GONE WITH THE WIND
3. The Birth of a Nation
4. ALL QUIET ON THE WESTERN FRONT
5. THE BEST YEARS OF OUR LIVES
   MIDNIGHT COWBOY
   Stagecoach
8. ON THE WATERFRONT
   High Noon
10. 2001: A Space Odyssey
11. The Treasure of the Sierra Madre
12. The Jazz Singer
    The Informer
    WEST SIDE STORY
    The Grapes of Wrath
16. IT HAPPENED ONE NIGHT
    The Gold Rush

18. CASABLANCA
    The Big Parade
    Fantasia
21. Greed
    Intolerance
    King Kong
24. Who's Afraid of Virginia Woolf?
    The Great Train Robbery
    Sunset Boulevard
    The Wizard of Oz
    The Graduate
29. THE BRIDGE ON THE RIVER KWAI
    THE SOUND OF MUSIC
    Nanook of the North
    Little Caesar
33. 42nd Street
    City Lights
    Ben-Hur (1925)
    Public Enemy

The Maltese Falcon
Dr. Strangelove
39. BEN-HUR (1959)
    AN AMERICAN IN PARIS
    THE LOST WEEKEND
    I Am a Fugitive from a Chain Gang
    The Robe
    A Streetcar Named Desire
    The Lost Weekend
    Easy Rider
    Bonnie and Clyde
48. THE GODFATHER
    The 39 Steps
    Lost Horizon (1937)
    Snow White and the Seven Dwarfs
    The General
    Shane
    Covered Wagon

Jane Fonda
(2 Oscars)·
They Shoot Horses, Don't They?, 1969
*Klute, 1971
Julia, 1977
*Coming Home, 1978
The China Syndrome, 1979

Susan Hayward
(1 Oscar)
Smash Up, 1947
My Foolish Heart, 1949
With a Song in My Heart, 1952
I'll Cry Tomorrow, 1955
*I Want to Live!, 1958

Audrey Hepburn
(1 Oscar)
*Roman Holiday, 1953
Sabrina, 1954
The Nun's Story, 1959
Breakfast at Tiffany's, 1961
Wait Until Dark, 1967

Jennifer Jones
(1 Oscar)
*The Song of Bernadette, 1943
Since You Went Away, 1944 #
Love Letters, 1945
Duel in the Sun, 1946
Love Is a Many-Splendored Thing, 1955

Fredric March
(2 Oscars)
The Royal Family, 1930–31
*Dr. Jekyll and Mr. Hyde, 1931–32
A Star Is Born, 1937
*The Best Years of Our Lives, 1946
Death of a Salesman, 1951

Paul Muni
(1 Oscar)
The Valiant, 1928–29
I Am a Fugitive from a Chain Gang, 1932–33
*The Story of Louis Pasteur, 1936
The Life of Emile Zola, 1937
The Last Angry Man, 1959

Jack Nicholson
(1 Oscar)
Easy Rider, 1969 #
Five Easy Pieces, 1970
The Last Detail, 1973
Chinatown, 1974
*One Flew over the Cuckoo's Nest, 1975

Peter O'Toole
(0 Oscars)
Lawrence of Arabia, 1962
Becket, 1964
The Lion in Winter, 1968
Goodbye, Mr. Chips, 1969
The Ruling Class, 1972

Geraldine Page
(0 Oscars)
Hondo, 1953 #
Summer and Smoke, 1961
Sweet Bird of Youth, 1962
You're a Big Boy Now, 1966 #
Pete 'n' Tillie, 1972 #

Gregory Peck
(1 Oscar)
The Keys of the Kingdom, 1945
The Yearling, 1946
Gentleman's Agreement, 1947
12 O'Clock High, 1949
*To Kill a Mockingbird, 1962

Norma Shearer
(1 Oscar)
*The Divorcee and *Their Own Desire*, 1929–30
A Free Soul, 1931
The Barretts of Wimpole Street, 1934
Romeo and Juliet, 1936
Marie Antoinette, 1938

James Stewart
(1 Oscar)
Mr. Smith Goes to Washington, 1939
*The Philadelphia Story, 1940
It's a Wonderful Life, 1946
Harvey, 1950
Anatomy of a Murder, 1959

Elizabeth Taylor
(2 Oscars)
Raintree County, 1957
Cat on a Hot Tin Roof, 1958
Suddenly Last Summer, 1959
*Butterfield 8, 1960
*Who's Afraid of Virginia Woolf?, 1966

4
Ethel Barrymore
(1 Oscar)
*None But the Lonely Heart, 1944 #
The Spiral Staircase, 1946 #
The Paradine Case, 1947 #
Pinky, 1949 #

Charles Boyer
(0 Oscars)
Conquest, 1937
Algiers, 1938
Gaslight, 1944
Fanny, 1961

Walter Brennan
(3 Oscars)
Come and Get It, 1936 #
Kentucky, 1938 #
The Westerner, 1940 #
Sergeant York, 1941 #

Montgomery Clift
(0 Oscars)
The Search, 1948
A Place in the Sun, 1951
From Here to Eternity, 1953
Judgment at Nuremberg, 1961 #

Dustin Hoffman
(1 Oscar)
The Graduate, 1967
Midnight Cowboy, 1969
Lenny, 1974
Kramer vs. Kramer, 1979

Walter Huston
(1 Oscar)
Dodsworth, 1936
All that Money Can Buy, 1941
Yankee Doodle Dandy, 1942 #
The Treasure of the Sierra Madre, 1948 #

Arthur Kennedy
(0 Oscars)
Champion, 1949 #
Bright Victory, 1951
Peyton Place, 1958 #
Some Came Running, 1958 #

Shirley MacLaine
(0 Oscars)
Some Came Running, 1958
The Apartment, 1960
Irma La Douce, 1963
The Turning Point, 1977

Agnes Moorehead
(0 Oscars)
The Magnificent Ambersons, 1942 #
Mrs. Parkington, 1944 #
Johnny Belinda, 1948 #
Hush...Hush, Sweet Charlotte, 1964 #

Paul Newman
(0 Oscars)
Cat on a Hot Tin Roof, 1958
The Hustler, 1961
Hud, 1963
Cool Hand Luke, 1967

Anthony Quinn
(2 Oscars)
Viva Zapata, 1952 #
Lust for Life, 1956 #
Wild Is the Wind, 1957
Zorba the Greek, 1964

Claude Rains
(0 Oscars)
Mr. Smith Goes to Washington, 1939 #
Casablanca, 1943 #
Mr. Skeffington, 1944 #
Notorious, 1946 #

Rosalind Russell
(0 Oscars)
My Sister Eileen, 1942
Sister Kenny, 1946
Mourning Becomes Electra, 1947
Auntie Mame, 1958

Barbara Stanwyck
(0 Oscars)
Stella Dallas, 1937
Ball of Fire, 1941
Double Indemnity, 1944
Sorry, Wrong Number, 1948

Jane Wyman
(1 Oscar)
The Yearling, 1946
Johnny Belinda, 1948
The Blue Veil, 1951
The Magnificent Obsession, 1954

THE GREATEST PERFORMANCES
(Results of our 1978-79 poll. Oscar winners—*)

MALE PERFORMANCES

Fans' Choices

1. Marlon Brando
   (*A Streetcar Named Desire*, 1951)
2. Clark Gable
   (*Gone With the Wind*, 1939)
3. *Humphrey Bogart
   (*The African Queen*, 1951)
4. James Dean
   (*East of Eden*, 1955)
5. Dustin Hoffman
   (*Midnight Cowboy*, 1969)
6. *Jack Nicholson
   (*One Flew over the Cuckoo's Nest*, 1975)
7. Montgomery Clift
   (*From Here to Eternity*, 1953)
8. *John Wayne
   (*True Grit*, 1969)
9. Paul Newman
   (*Butch Cassidy and the Sundance Kid*, 1969)
10. Jack Lemmon
    (*The Apartment*, 1960)
11. *George C. Scott
    (*Patton*, 1970)
12. Richard Burton
    (*Who's Afraid of Virginia Woolf?*, 1966)
13. Charles Laughton
    (*Mutiny on the Bounty*, 1935)
14. Al Pacino
    (*The Godfather Part II*, 1974)
15. Orson Welles
    (*Citizen Kane*, 1941)
16. Humphrey Bogart
    (*Casablanca*, 1943)
17. *Marlon Brando
    (*The Godfather*, 1972)
18. Cary Grant
    (*Suspicion*, 1941)
    Humphrey Bogart
    (*The Treasure of the Sierra Madre*, 1945)
    James Dean
    (*Rebel Without a Cause*, 1955)
21. Robert Redford
    (*Butch Cassidy and the Sundance Kid*, 1969)
22. *Jon Voight
    (*Coming Home*, 1978)
    *Marlon Brando
    (*On the Waterfront*, 1954)
    Paul Newman
    (*Hud*, 1963)
25. Laurence Olivier
    (*Wuthering Heights*, 1939)
    James Stewart
    (*Mr. Smith Goes to Washington*, 1939)
    *Rod Steiger
    (*In the Heat of the Night*, 1967)
    *James Cagney
    (*Yankee Doodle Dandy*, 1942)
    Henry Fonda
    (*The Grapes of Wrath*, 1940)
    *Spencer Tracy
    (*Captains Courageous*, 1937)

Newspaper Critics' Choices

1. Clark Gable
   (*Gone With the Wind*, 1939)
2. *Marlon Brando
   (*On the Waterfront*, 1954)
3. Henry Fonda
   (*The Grapes of Wrath*, 1940)
4. Orson Welles
   (*Citizen Kane*, 1941)
5. *Humphrey Bogart
   (*The African Queen*, 1951)
6. Montgomery Clift
   (*From Here to Eternity*, 1953)
7. Marlon Brando
   (*A Streetcar Named Desire*, 1951)
8. Dustin Hoffman
   (*Midnight Cowboy*, 1969)
9. Humphrey Bogart
   (*Casablanca*, 1943)
10. James Dean
    (*East of Eden*, 1955)
11. *Jack Nicholson
    (*One Flew over the Cuckoo's Nest*, 1975)
12. *George C. Scott
    (*Patton*, 1970)
13. Rod Steiger
    (*The Pawnbroker*, 1965)
14. Charles Laughton
    (*Mutiny on the Bounty*, 1935)
15. *Paul Muni
    (*The Story of Louis Pasteur*, 1936)
    *Spencer Tracy
    (*Captains Courageous*, 1937)
17. Charles Chaplin
    (*City Lights*, 1932)
18. Buster Keaton
    (*The General*, 1927)

19. Paul Muni
(*I Was a Fugitive from a Chain Gang,* 1932)
20. Spencer Tracy
(*Judgment at Nuremberg,* 1961)
21. Jon Voight
(*Midnight Cowboy,* 1969)
Paul Newman
(*The Hustler,* 1961)
23. Jack Lemmon
(*The Apartment,* 1960)
Anthony Perkins
(*Psycho,* 1960)
25. Montgomery Clift
(*A Place in the Sun,* 1951)
Alan Arkin
(*The Heart Is a Lonely Hunter,* 1968)
Jason Robards
(*A Thousand Clowns,* 1965)

Paul Muni
(*The Life of Emile Zola,* 1937)
Spencer Tracy
(*Inherit the Wind,* 1961)
James Stewart
(*Mr. Smith Goes to Washington,* 1939)
Robert DeNiro
(*Taxi Driver,* 1976)
*Burt Lancaster
(*Elmer Gantry,* 1965)
*Jack Lemmon
(*Save the Tiger,* 1973)
Laurence Olivier
(*Wuthering Heights,* 1939)
Richard Burton
(*Who's Afraid of Virginia Woolf?,* 1966)
Jose Ferrer
(*Moulin Rouge,* 1952)

Most Nominations—Fans (Different Performances)	*Most Nominations—Critics (Different Performances)*	*Most Votes—Fans (All Performances)*	*Most Votes—Critics (All Performances)*
12 Cary Grant	6 Spencer Tracy	1. Clark Gable	1. Marlon Brando
11 Spencer Tracy	5 Laurence Olivier	2. Spencer Tracy	2. Humphrey Bogart
9 John Wayne	Paul Muni	3. Humphrey Bogart	3. Spencer Tracy
8 Laurence Olivier	Montgomery Clift	4. Marlon Brando	4. Montgomery Clift
Marlon Brando	4 James Stewart	5. Jack Nicholson	5. Laurence Olivier
7 James Stewart	Jack Nicholson	6. Montgomery Clift	6. Dustin Hoffman
Fredric March	Marlon Brando	7. Dustin Hoffman	7. Jack Nicholson
James Cagney	Paul Newman	8. James Dean	8. Paul Muni
6 Clark Gable	Humphrey Bogart	9. Paul Newman	9. George C. Scott
Gary Cooper	Dustin Hoffman	10. John Wayne	10. Clark Gable
Humphrey Bogart	3 Richard Burton	11. Cary Grant	11. Henry Fonda
Montgomery Clift	Jack Lemmon	12. Jack Lemmon	12. James Stewart
5 Gregory Peck	Fredric March	13. Laurence Olivier	13. Charles Laughton
Jack Lemmon	George C. Scott	14. Gary Cooper	Charles Chaplin
Walter Huston	Rod Steiger	15. James Cagney	15. Paul Newman
Henry Fonda	Clark Gable		Rod Steiger
Kirk Douglas	James Dean		James Dean
4 Jack Nicholson	Henry Fonda		
Paul Muni	Jon Voight		
Charles Laughton	James Cagney		
Burt Lancaster	Gary Cooper		
William Holden	Peter O'Toole		
Paul Newman	Robert DeNiro		
Dustin Hoffman	Cary Grant		
3 James Dean	Charles Laughton		
George C. Scott	Burt Lancaster		
Richard Burton	Charles Chaplin		
Al Pacino	John Wayne		
Robert Redford			
Jon Voight			
Robert DeNiro			
Rod Steiger			
James Cagney			
John Wayne			

FEMALE PERFORMANCES

Fans' Choices

1. *Vivien Leigh
   (*Gone With the Wind*, 1939)
2. Bette Davis
   (*All About Eve*, 1950)
3. *Elizabeth Taylor
   (*Who's Afraid of Virginia Woolf?*, 1966)
4. *Jane Fonda
   (*Klute*, 1971)
5. *Judy Holliday
   (*Born Yesterday*, 1950)
6. Katharine Hepburn
   (*The African Queen*, 1951)
7. *Anne Bancroft
   (*The Miracle Worker*, 1962)
8. Judy Garland
   (*The Wizard of Oz*, 1939)
9. Katharine Hepburn
   (*The Philadelphia Story*, 1940)
10. Gloria Swanson
    (*Sunset Boulevard*, 1950)
11. Olivia De Havilland
    (*The Heiress*, 1949)
12. Rosalind Russell
    (*Auntie Mame*, 1958)
13. *Vivien Leigh
    (*A Streetcar Named Desire*, 1951)
14. Judy Garland
    (*A Star Is Born*, 1954)
15. *Joanne Woodward
    (*Three Faces of Eve*, 1957)
    *Barbra Streisand
    (*Funny Girl*, 1968)
17. Greta Garbo
    (*Camille*, 1937)
    Ingrid Bergman
    (*Casablanca*, 1943)
19. *Jane Fonda
    (*Coming Home*, 1978)
    Shirley MacLaine
    (*The Turning Point*, 1977)
21. Olivia De Havilland
    (*The Snake Pit*, 1948)
22. Bette Davis
    (*What Ever Happened to Baby Jane?*, 1962)
23. Anne Bancroft
    (*The Turning Point*, 1977)
    Greta Garbo
    (*Ninotchka*, 1939)
25. *Liza Minnelli
    (*Cabaret*, 1972)
    *Shirley Booth
    (*Come Back Little Sheba*, 1952)
    Marsha Mason
    (*The Goodbye Girl*, 1977)
    *Diane Keaton
    (*Annie Hall*, 1977)

Critics' Choices

1. Katharine Hepburn
   (*The African Queen*, 1951)
2. Bette Davis
   (*All About Eve*, 1950)
3. *Jane Fonda
   (*Klute*, 1971)
4. *Vivien Leigh
   (*Gone With the Wind*, 1939)
5. Judy Garland
   (*The Wizard of Oz*, 1939)
6. Ingrid Bergman
   (*Casablanca*, 1943)
   *Vivien Leigh
   (*A Streetcar Named Desire*, 1951)
8. *Elizabeth Taylor
   (*Who's Afraid of Virginia Woolf?*, 1966)
   Deborah Kerr
   (*From Here to Eternity*, 1953)
10. Jane Fonda
    (*They Shoot Horses, Don't They?*, 1969)
    *Anne Bancroft
    (*The Miracle Worker*, 1962)
12. *Katharine Hepburn
    (*The Philadelphia Story*, 1940)
13. Olivia De Havilland
    (*The Heiress*, 1949)
14. *Diane Keaton
    (*Annie Hall*, 1977)
15. Jane Darwell
    (*Grapes of Wrath*, 1940)
    *Liza Minnelli
    (*Cabaret*, 1972)
    *Judy Holliday
    (*Born Yesterday*, 1950)
18. Gloria Swanson
    (*Sunset Boulevard*, 1950)
19. Patricia Neal
    (*Hud*, 1963)
20. Deborah Kerr
    (*The Sundowners*, 1960)
    Anne Bancroft
    (*The Turning Point*, 1977)
22. Bette Davis
    (*Of Human Bondage*, 1934)
    Joanne Woodward
    (*Rachel, Rachel*, 1968)
    *Glenda Jackson
    (*A Touch of Class*, 1973)
25. Anne Bancroft
    (*The Graduate*, 1963)
    *Ingrid Bergman
    (*Anastasia*, 1956)
    Shirley MacLaine
    (*The Turning Point*, 1977)
    Shirley MacLaine
    (*The Apartment*, 1960)
    *Audrey Hepburn
    (*Roman Holiday*, 1953)
    Gena Rowlands
    (*A Woman Under the Influence*, 1974)

Most Nominations—Fans (Different Performances)	Most Nominations—Critics (Different Performances)	Most Votes—Fans (All Performances)	Most Votes—Critics (All Performances)
18 Katharine Hepburn	8 Katharine Hepburn	1. Katharine Hepburn	1. Katharine Hepburn
11 Bette Davis	7 Bette Davis	2. Bette Davis	2. Bette Davis
9 Ingrid Bergman	6 Judy Garland	3. Vivien Leigh	3. Vivien Leigh
8 Elizabeth Taylor	Jane Fonda	4. Elizabeth Taylor	4. Jane Fonda
7 Audrey Hepburn	5 Ingrid Bergman	5. Jane Fonda	5. Ingrid Bergman
Joan Crawford	Deborah Kerr	6. Ingrid Bergman	6. Judy Garland
Marilyn Monroe	Audrey Hepburn	Judy Garland	7. Deborah Kerr
6 Greta Garbo	Anne Bancroft	8. Olivia De Havilland	8. Elizabeth Taylor
Judy Garland	4 Vivien Leigh	9. Greta Garbo	9. Anne Bancroft
Susan Hayward	Olivia De Havilland	10. Audrey Hepburn	10. Olivia De Havilland
5 Olivia De Havilland	Marilyn Monroe	11. Marilyn Monroe	11. Judy Holliday
Claudette Colbert	Shirley MacLaine	12. Judy Holliday	12. Shirley MacLaine
Barbara Stanwyck	Joanne Woodward	13. Susan Hayward	13. Joanne Woodward
Barbra Streisand	Rosalind Russell	14. Rosalind Russell	14. Rosalind Russell
Carole Lombard	Greer Garson	15. Claudette Colbert	15. Marilyn Monroe
Shirley MacLaine	Irene Dunne	Barbra Streisand	
Rosalind Russell	Joan Fontaine		
4 Jennifer Jones	Ginger Rogers		
Deborah Kerr	Anne Baxter		
Joanne Woodward			
Marlene Dietrich			
Anne Bancroft			
Jane Fonda			
Doris Day			
Faye Dunaway			
Dorothy McGuire			
Grace Kelly			
Jean Arthur			

MOST TOTAL VOTES
(Combined Male & Female)

Fans' Choice	Critics' Choice
1. Katharine Hepburn	1. Katharine Hepburn
2. Bette Davis	2. Bette Davis
3. Vivien Leigh	3. Marlon Brando
4. Clark Gable	4. Vivien Leigh
5. Elizabeth Taylor	5. Humphrey Bogart
6. Spencer Tracy	6. Spencer Tracy
7. Humphrey Bogart	7. Montgomery Clift
8. Marlon Brando	8. Laurence Olivier
9. Jane Fonda	9. Dustin Hoffman
10. Jack Nicholson	10. Jack Nicholson
11. Ingrid Bergman	11. Jane Fonda
Judy Garland	12. Ingrid Bergman
	Paul Muni

THREE

The Actors

IN MORE THAN fifty years of "talkies," only a few performances stand out. Often they are not the ones that won Oscars. One of these is Charles Laughton's portrayal of Captain Bligh in *Mutiny on the Bounty* in 1935. More than forty years later, it still packs a potent punch.

Many of Hollywood's finest films have been remade, some of them more than once. Few of these remakes can bear being compared to the original. One sometimes wonders why filmmakers bother. Why not re-issue the original, rather than remake it? It might be better to remake flops. Many had the potential to be hits. A change in directors or actors might make hits of flops.

The version of *Mutiny on the Bounty* released in 1962 is an excellent example of a remake that fell far short of the original. Marlon Brando's temperamental excesses sent the film far over budget and made production rocky. A superior performer, Brando was less Fletcher Christian than Clark Gable had been. Though an outstanding actor, Trevor Howard was less Captain Bligh than Laughton had been.

Bounty was based on the novel by Charles Nordhoff and James Norman Hall, about a true episode of British Naval history in the late 1700s. The HMS *Bounty* sailed from England on a scientific expedition to take breadfruit trees from the South Seas to the British West Indies as cheap food for slave labor. The crew rebelled against a tyrannical captain, cast him adrift in an open boat, and settled in the Tahitian Islands. While liberties were taken, the book and film remained remarkably true to history.

An earlier version of the incident was made in 1933 in Australia. It was titled *In the Wake of the Bounty* and starred Errol Flynn, not yet an American film star, as Christian. Director Frank Lloyd bought American rights to the book for a mere $12,500 and tried to sell them to MGM. Producer Walter Wanger wanted to buy it as a starring vehicle for Robert Montgomery. Producer Irving Thalberg wanted it as a starring vehicle for Gable.

Louis B. Mayer, the boss of MGM, didn't want it at all. This was before the days of anti-heroes and he didn't think that a film featuring mutineers as heroes could be successful. But Irving Thalberg, who was production head at the studio, fought for the film and won Mayer's reluctant permission to purchase it. Gable didn't want the role of Christian but the studio was insistent. For it he had to shave off his mustache and wear pigtails and knickers. He felt that he looked sissified, as did Brando later.

Christian has been considered the key role in every version of *Mutiny on the Bounty*. Gable carried off the part so well that it established him as a dramatic actor of sensitivity. Both he and Franchot Tone, playing a lesser seaman, earned nominations for Academy Awards. So did Laughton. It is the only time that three actors from one film were nominated for featured roles. This divided vote may have cost Laughton the Oscar, which went to Victor McLaglen, one of only four Oscar nominees, for *The Informer*. Laughton stole *Bounty*. He gave the picture its punch.

Laughton was thirty-six when *Mutiny on the Bounty* was released. Self-conscious about his hefty, homely

Captain Bligh, Charles Laughton, is confronted by Mr. Christian, Clark Gable, as Donald Crisp looks on in Mutiny on the Bounty.

appearance, he was a character actor almost from the start of his career. Also, he was a homosexual, but made a successful marriage of convenience with the actress Elsa Lanchester. A British stage actor, he came to the United States to appear on Broadway in 1931. He won his only Academy Award for his memorable performance in *The Private Life of Henry VIII* in 1933. He was called "a fat slob" by the drunken actress Tallulah Bankhead in an earlier film, and no one ever tore into a bird the way he did in the infamous eating scene in *Henry VIII*.

Lloyd wanted to star in as well as direct *Bounty*, but was persuaded by Thalberg to let Laughton play Bligh. A perfectionist, Laughton researched Bligh extensively, discovered where he had his uniforms tailored, went to the old shop, found that they still had the order on file, and had it duplicated to his size. A replica of the *Bounty* was constructed and the movie was filmed in the original locales of Tahiti and Pitcairn Islands, as well as at Catalina Island.

Three years in the making, at an extravagant Depression days' cost of $2 million, *Bounty* is one of the great sea stories of all time. The original *New York Times* review referred to it as "magnificent... savagely exciting, rousingly dramatic." It said Laughton "has the perfect role and he plays it perfectly."

Laughton and Gable feuded throughout the film. Laughton was stealing the film from him, and Gable saw it. He called Laughton "a ham" and threatened to quit. Thalberg had to step in to hold things together several times. When Laughton called, "Miss-ter Christchun...come here," as he did so often, and so unforgettably, it had very real venom to it.

Laughton fought sea sickness throughout the several rolling-stage, water-drenched scenes he had to shoot. It took a week to shoot the stormy scenes in the open boat, and then they had to be re-shot when they found an actor on board who didn't belong. After he delivered the triumphant line, "We have beaten the sea itself," Laughton broke down in tears, and others on the set wept with him, moved deeply by his performance.

It was perhaps the most memorable performance in movie history, though it did not win an Oscar. However, it was through his depiction of the sadistic captain that the film did win that year's Award. He had given great performances in *The Private Life of Henry VIII* in 1933 and as the relentless Javert in *Les Miserables* in 1935, and he would give others in *The Hunchback of Notre Dame* in 1940 and *Witness for the Prosecution* in 1957 in a thirty-three-year career of almost fifty films. But, nothing he ever did beat Bligh.

The real William Bligh may or may not have been as bad as Laughton played him. However, when Bligh later became Governor of New South Wales, he was so tyrannical that a second mutiny was massed against him, by the Australian army. In both instances, courts found the mutineers guilty, not Bligh. Bligh was a hero of several naval battles and his skippering of an open boat and eighteen men safely over 3,600 miles of ocean is considered classic seamanship.

Christian actually was Bligh's constant companion until he clashed with his captain in an effort to return to a woman with whom he had fallen in love on Tahiti. Many of the *Bounty*'s crew had fallen in love on or with Tahiti. Life for an English seaman was not easy in those days. They sought refuge on the remote, tiny Pitcairn Island and sank their ship. They fought over the few available women and within four years all but a handful were slain by natives. Several drowned in drink. Only one endured as many as fifteen years, John Adams. About a hundred descendants still live there, including one named Fletcher Christian.

Gable was as handsome as Laughton was homely, as masculine as Laughton was feminine. Gable was less a performer and more a personality. According to

him, "I'm no actor and I never have been. What people see on the screen is me." He won one Academy Award for his portrayal of a fun-loving ladies' man a lot like himself in *It Happened One Night* in 1934. But he became an actor of accomplishment in his thirtieth film, *Bounty*. He earned a third and last nomination in his fortieth film, *Gone With the Wind*, in 1939. His portrayal of the romantic rogue Rhett Butler is about as perfect as a part can be played, possibly because his personality so perfectly fit the role.

Ironically, he almost didn't get the part. A story editor for Selznick International, Kay Brown, read an advance copy of Margaret Mitchell's book and sent a synopsis to David Selznick, practically ordering him to buy it, available prior to publication for $50,000. He liked it, but thought the price too high. He felt that the book, 1,037 pages, was too long to fit into a film and that Civil War films died on the battlefield of the box office. She turned to the chairman of the board, Jock Whitney, who offered to produce it himself. Selznick then had second thoughts and bought it for a fraction of the $75 million the film grossed. At higher ticket prices, other movies have made more money, but none has been seen in theaters by as many people. More than 300 million moviegoers have seen it, to say nothing of television viewers.

More than 1.5 million people bought the book at its original $3 hard-cover price in its first year of publication. It was one of the surprise publishing success stories of all time and every reader eagerly awaited the movie version. Almost all saw Gable as Rhett Butler. But Selznick did not want to deal with MGM and his father-in-law, Louis B. Mayer, for the loan of Gable. Instead, he tried to deal with Sam Goldwyn for the loan of Gary Cooper. The strong, shy, gangling Cooper might not seem the sort to play Rhett Butler, but privately in Hollywood, off the screen, he was considered the town's greatest lover. He was offered the part first, but turned it down. He said later, "I just thought the part was too dashing for me. When I saw Gable in it, I knew I was right." Then, Selznick tried to deal with Jack Warner for Errol Flynn, but was unsuccessful. Actually, Warner did offer Flynn and Bette Davis, to play Scarlett O'Hara, as a package deal, and Selznick was agreeable, but Davis refused. She wanted better parts than she was getting and was about to sue to break her contract with Warner. As she left his office after an argument, he told her she shouldn't go, that he had the best part of her life for her. She said, "I bet it's a pip," and slammed the door behind her. She assumed he was stalling. She didn't even ask what the part was. It was Scarlett. Years later, she said she wouldn't have wanted to play Scarlett opposite Flynn, anyway, but would have loved to play her opposite Gable. In the end, Gable was the third choice.

Selznick finally got Gable and half the estimated production cost of $2.5 million in exchange for giving release rights and half the profits to Mayer and MGM. Gable was so right for Rhett Butler that this incredible cost was well worth it. Many critics have called his casting the most perfect fit of person and part, personality and performance, in film history. Yet, he feared it. He thought it too much for him, and he had recently had a bad experience in another costume drama, *Parnell*. He took it only for a $100,000 bonus he needed to pay a $300,000 settlement to his wife, Rhea, so he could get a divorce and marry Carole Lombard.

Selznick still needed a Scarlett. Katharine Hepburn wanted it. She told David, "The part practically was written for me." He told her, "I can't imagine him chasing *you* for ten years." He wanted Norma Shearer. She didn't want it, feeling she was too much a lady to play the unlady-like Scarlett. Selznick considered Carole Lombard, Claudette Colbert, Joan Crawford, Joan Bennett, Ann Sheridan, even Tallulah Bankhead. He tested many young actresses, including Susan Hayward. He had others read the part, including Lucille Ball. He almost gave it to the beautiful Paulette Goddard, but when she did not produce a marriage license to prove she was married to, and not merely having an affair with, Charlie Chaplin, Selznick backed down.

At the advice of publicist Russell Birdwell, he conducted a nationwide search for an unknown to play the part. Some 150,000 feet of film were shot of 14,000 applicants. The picture got publicity, but no unknown got the part. Finally, Selznick's brother Myron, an agent and a stockholder in Selznick International, brought Vivien Leigh to David. He had brought his brother others, but David was taken by this one.

She was an accomplished, if young, actress. She was British, but spoke well with a Southern accent in three screen tests she took. Her blue eyes could be turned to Scarlett's green with the use of a yellow spotlight. She had recently lost the part of Cathy opposite Laurence Olivier's Heathcliff in *Wuthering Heights*, and her passion to play Scarlett gave her test tremendous fire. She was having an affair with Olivier—was later to marry him—and infuriated him by accepting a seven-year contract with Selznick in order to get the part of Scarlett. The picture was already in production when she was signed.

She was as perfect in her part as Gable was in his. Without her passionate performance, his colorful portrayal might not have been nearly as effective. The production, however, was not without its problems. George Cukor began as director, but was fired after three weeks. Gable felt his part was being neglected. Selznick felt the film's grandeur was being neglected. Victor Fleming was brought in. He had never read the book but demanded a rewrite of the script. Later, he was fired. Leigh thought her part was being neglected. Sam Wood was brought in. He was fired. Fleming was rehired. He finished the film. It captured the Oscar, as did he, as its director of record.

The saga of the old South in the midst of the Civil War was given grand treatment in Technicolor. Near the end of the film came the classic line. As Scarlett turns to Rhett at last, he turns from her, finally. At the door, she asks, "If you leave me, what shall I do?" He turns and says, "Frankly, my dear, I don't give a damn." The use of that last word on the screen caused a commotion at the time, but it is a line that has lasted in the memory of moviegoers.

Most think it is the last line in the film. It is not. Scarlett turns away from the door and goes to the stairway. She tries to take her disappointment in stride. The Civil War and Rhett Butler may have been lost, but she is not yet beaten. "Tomorrow, I'll think of some way to get him back," she announces to herself. "After all, tomorrow is another day."

That is the last line. It was also the title of the book until the publisher, Macmillan, asked that it be changed because the word "tomorrow" had been in too many other book titles. Margaret Mitchell found her new title in a poem, *Cynara*, by Ernest Dowson.

Margaret Mitchell wanted nothing to do with writing the film script. It was written and rewritten by a dozen different writers, including such famous ones as Sidney Howard, John Van Druten, Charles MacArthur, and F. Scott Fitzgerald. She made little money from the film—only the small sum paid her for rights—and never wrote anything of consequence afterward.

Gone With the Wind ran three hours and thirty-nine minutes, making it the longest movie of its time and the only one with an intermission. It is a beautiful film which has maintained audience interest for forty years. It has been acclaimed the classic motion picture of all time in more polls than any other, although many purists prefer *Citizen Kane*. In our poll of most memorable performances, the fans selected Leigh's Scarlett O'Hara first among females and Gable's Rhett Butler second among males. Perhaps surprisingly, the critics voted Gable's Rhett Butler the best single performance ever.

Gone With the Wind captured more Oscars than any picture to that time, ten. Vivien Leigh won the Oscar as Best Actress. Hattie McDaniel won one as

Marlon Brando, as Stanley Kowalski, tells Vivien Leigh what she doesn't want to hear in A Streetcar Named Desire.

Best Supporting Actress. But Gable did not win, beaten out by Robert Donat's touching but far less lasting performance in *Goodbye, Mr. Chips*.

Ironically, the one picture that won three acting Academy Awards—*A Streetcar Named Desire* in 1951—did not win for the one performer who created the most unforgettable part and who made the play and the picture the blockbusters they were—Marlon Brando. Vivien Leigh was voted Best Actress, Kim Hunter Best Supporting Actress, and Karl Malden Best Supporting Actor, but Brando, while nominated, did not win. Miss Leigh won her second Oscar while for the second time her costar was denied. In no way would anyone want to put down her portrayal of Blanche DuBois but without the counterpart portrayal of Bran-

do's Stanley Kowalski she would not have been nearly as effective. In our poll, her portrayal was voted one of the best of all time by both fans and critics, but the fans picked his as the best ever by any actor.

In our poll, Brando emerges as one of the greatest American movie actors of all time. Following *Streetcar*, he won Oscars for roles in *On the Waterfront* in 1954 and *The Godfather* in 1972, and he had given many superb performances in a checkered and controversial career. But it was in *Streetcar* that he lit up the screen with incredible brilliance, as Stanley Kowalski, a basic man in a torn T-shirt. It is this role that remains among the most memorable portrayals in the history of movies.

Marlon's mother, Dorothy, was an artistic type, an

amateur actress, and a power in the Omaha Playhouse. She acted with and encouraged such hometown talents as Henry Fonda and Dorothy McGuire, as well as son Marlon. When he was only six they moved to Evanston, Illinois. There he struck up a friendship with an actor-to-be of a different dimension, Wally Cox. The family moved about and "Bud," as he was known, became a rebellious boy who was kicked out of several schools, including military school.

His sister, Jocelyn, who became an actress, was in acting school in New York and, at nineteen, he joined her at the radical New School for Social Research, where the skilled Stella Adler predicted he'd be the best actor on Broadway within a year. His mother came east to keep house for her children. Wally Cox moved in, too. His mother's drinking drove Marlon and Cox to move out and find a place of their own.

At twenty, Marlon was playing Nels in *I Remember Mama*. Following that, he was in a succession of plays that failed but brought him in contact with other great talents, including director Elia Kazan. In 1947, Kazan started the Tennessee Williams play *A Streetcar Named Desire* with Jessica Tandy as Blanche DuBois and John Garfield as Stanley Kowalski. Garfield's movie *Body and Soul* was a hit at that time and he worried about returning to Broadway. He thought Tandy's Blanche was bigger than his Stanley and wanted the parts rewritten. Kazan refused and Garfield withdrew. The part was offered to Burt Lancaster but he declined. It was then offered to Brando, who thought it too big for him but reluctantly agreed to give it a try.

Brando was rebellious, reluctant to rehearse, moody, antagonistic to his fellow actors, but of such natural talent as to be awesome. He was animalistic as Stanley. Ridiculed by some as a "mumbler," his inner intensity captured the spirit of the part perfectly. While Tandy got most of the raves when the play opened, John Chapman of *The Daily News* said that Marlon was "magnificent." He endured the long run of the hit play only through relief of hijinks, often at the expense of his roommate Karl Malden or buddy Wally Cox. He went to Hollywood with the play but first played a paraplegic in *The Men*, in a performance and picture every bit as effective as the later Jon Voight film, *Coming Home*.

Kazan brought *Streetcar* to the screen in 1951, when Brando was twenty-seven. Brando, Kim Hunter, and Malden repeated their roles from Broadway, but Vivien Leigh was brought in to play Blanche. The director, picture, and three stars won Oscars, but Brando did not.

American movie acting would never be the same again. Brando's naturalistic method of acting was accepted as a model by Montgomery Clift, Jimmy Dean, Dustin Hoffman, Robert DeNiro, and other great actors who followed in his footsteps. John Garfield may have been the first of his sort, but Brando's method was superior and seriously set the style. Kazan called his Stanley "as perfectly realized a part as anyone ever played" and it remains more than twenty-five years later a vivid, electrifying characterization.

Yet Brando lost the Academy Award race to Humphrey Bogart for his cynical seaman Charles Allnutt, played opposite Katharine Hepburn's spiritualistic and spirited Rose Sayer in *The African Queen*. The favorite film of all time for many, *The African Queen* was not even nominated for a Best Picture Oscar. Hepburn's performance may have been the best she ever gave, but it did not win her one of her three Oscars. Bogart won his only one, but it may not have been better than other performances he gave. Many believe he won only because he was a popular part of the Hollywood community, overdue for an Award at the age of fifty, after more than sixty films, while Brando was an unorthodox and unpopular newcomer.

Bogart was brilliant in his part. He had been brilliant in the similar part of Dobbs in *The Treasure of the Sierra Madre* in 1948, for which he was not even nominated. He was underrated as an actor and received only three nominations in his twenty-seven-year career of seventy-one films. He was nominated for Rick in *Casablanca* in 1942, for Charles in *The African Queen* in 1951, and for Captain Queeg in *The Caine Mutiny* in 1954. Bogie may be best remembered for Rick in *Casablanca*, another all-time favorite of many, and if he was to win only one Award it probably should have been for this role.

Jack Warner bought an unproduced play, *Everybody Comes to Rick's*, because he saw it as another *Algiers*, a successful 1948 film set in the same exotic locale and starring Charles Boyer and Hedy Lamarr. In fact, Warner originally wanted to star George Raft with Lamarr, but both turned it down because they didn't think it would be a good movie. Then he was ready to lower his sights and cast Dennis Morgan and Ann Sheridan in the key roles, with Ronald Reagan playing the part that eventually went to Paul Henreid. It would have been a "B" movie, filling the lower half of double features in those wartime days.

It was upgraded to "A" status when Bogart accepted it as his first romantic lead, after having achieved stardom only the year before in *The Maltese Falcon*, and Ingrid Bergman was borrowed for the role of Ilsa, opposite him. Henreid, Claude Rains, and Peter Lorre

Humphrey Bogart with Tim Holt in The Treasure of the Sierra Madre.

Humphrey Bogart is confronted by Claude Rains while Paul Henreid and Ingrid Bergman watch in Casablanca.

joined the cast. Howard Koch rewrote the original script and kept rewriting throughout production. In the story, Ingrid, on the run with European resistance leader Henreid, lands in Casablanca where she rekindles an old romance with Rick at his cafe, while collaborationist Rains studies the scene suspiciously. In the end, the question is, will Ingrid remain with Bogey or fly off with Henreid? She complained that she didn't know how to act opposite her two men because she didn't know which one she'd choose. The scriptwriter told her, "When we know, we'll let you know." No one thought the film would work.

It did work, however. It was sentimental, pure romance, and although its setting was one of wartime intrigue, it had little violence. It got a big boost when the Allies landed in North Africa and the Allied leaders staged a summit meeting in Casablanca just before and after the retitled film opened. The film won the Academy Award that year, 1942. But its success at the time cannot be compared to its success since. It is another of what actually is a small list of favorite films by many fans. It is played at film festivals more than any other film. Critics have written more about it than any other movie except *Citizen Kane*. If it worked, Bogart made it work more than any other player in it. It was so popular with young adults that many came to consider Bogart's Rick the character they would most want to be—world-weary, cynical, yet secretly sentimental.

In the film, Bogart speaks lines that are immortal in our memories. Letting Lorre go to the Nazis, Rick says, "I stick my neck out for nobody." Remembering his affair with Ingrid in Paris, he says, "With the whole world crumbling, we pick this time to fall in love." When she walks back into his life, he says, "Of all the gin joints in all the towns in all the world, she walks into mine." Although it is the way it is remembered, he never says, "Play it again, Sam." She says, "Play it, Sam." Later, lonely in the night and drinking, he says to Sam, his pianist, played by Dooley Wilson, "You played it for her, you can play it for me. If she can stand it, I can. Play it." The song? "As Time Goes By."

In the "final" script, she was to stay with him. Later, however, it was decided that she should leave him, maintaining the integrity of this bittersweet story. Had she not left him, his life would not have been what it was and the movie would not have been what it was. It was not meant to have a happy ending. When he finally lets her go at the airport, he says, "The problems of three little people don't amount to a hill of beans in this crazy world. Someday you'll understand that. Here's looking at you, kid." She boards the plane with Henreid and Bogie shoots a Nazi officer to stop him from stopping them. Rains covers for Bogie. As they walk off together, Bogey says to Rains, "Louie, I think this is the beginning of a beautiful friendship."

Paul Lukas was an excellent actor, but his performance in *Watch on the Rhine* is little remembered, and that it should have gotten the Oscar over Bogart's performance in *Casablanca* is hard to believe. It is Bogart's Rick that is among the most remembered portrayals of all time and for which most Bogart fans would want him remembered. Yet, there also are Bogart fans who would prefer he be remembered for his gangster roles, which were most typical of his screen work.

Bogart began his acting career as a pretty boy on the stage. A critic wrote, "He's a young and handsome Valentino." A little age and a lot of drink contributed character lines to his face. A little lisp contributed character to his speech. He talked tough. He acted tough. His Duke Mantee, holding hostage Bette Davis, Leslie Howard, and others at a roadside cafe in his tenth film, *The Petrified Forest*, in 1936 became the model for tough-guy actors. His Baby Face Martin in *Dead End* in 1937, his Roy Earle in *High Sierra* in 1941, and his Sam Spade in *The Maltese Falcon* in 1941 were superb portrayals of their type, though not one of these won him even a nomination for an Oscar.

Bogart certainly was a better actor than another who played a lot of gangster roles, George Raft, and it is ironic that Bogart's career was built on parts Raft turned down. Raft, a former Broadway hoofer, rejected the roles Bogart made famous in *Casablanca*, *The Maltese Falcon*, *Dead End*, and *High Sierra*. He rejected the latter two because he did not want to die on the screen. Until he turned them down, Raft was the more prominent of the two performers.

The actors who portrayed the best-remembered gangsters have never received their share of accolades. Edward G. Robinson's *Little Caesar* and James Cagney's *Public Enemy*, both in 1931, are classic examples of their kind. Neither was even nominated for an Oscar, but both are remembered vividly.

Cagney's portrayal of Tom Powers, small but tough, a cocky character with a chip on his shoulder, who even stood tough—shoulders back, chest up, arms cocked tight to his side—remains one of the most vivid characterizations in the history of films. Originally a vaudeville hoofer, he copied the character from toughs he'd known on the sidewalks of New York.

When his mistress, Mae Clarke, asks him at breakfast, "Maybe you've found someone you like better?" and he mashes a grapefruit into her face, he created one of the screen's most memorable moments. The grapefruit was Jimmy's idea. Mae never liked it, but director William Wellman wanted it.

On the day the scene was to be shot, Mae came to the set with a cold, asking that the scene be faked. Wellman said it could be and Cagney agreed to make it merely appear that he had hit her with the grapefruit. But when the time came, he not only shoved it full into her face, but twisted it so hard her nose began to bleed. Her scream of anger and her tears were real. She shouted at Cagney, "You son of a bitch!" That was cut. The rest of the scene remained, and remains to this day among our movie memories. Cagney smiled then and smiles now. "It made her a star," he has said.

In the film, he does find someone he likes better, Jean Harlow. But, of course, he comes to a bad end. Following a shootout with a rival mob, he stumbles into a rain-spattered street, seriously wounded, muttering the remembered line, "I ain't so tough." But he does not die so easily. After he is kidnapped from the hospital, his rivals call his mother to tell her he is coming home. The doorbell rings and she opens the door happily. There is the bullet-riddled body of her son, bound in a blanket on a board like a mummy. He stands there for a moment and you do not know if he is alive or dead. Then he topples forward, toward the camera, face first, finished. It is a never-to-be-forgotten scene.

The end of Edward G. Robinson as Rico Bandello in *Little Caesar* is similarly unforgettable. The hoodlum does die of bullets, staggering across the street to some church steps. His unforgettable last line, "Mother of God, is this the end of Rico?" was reshot to become "Mother of Mercy, is this the end of Rico?" in some versions because of complaints over the use of the Lord's name.

Robinson also was small, but tough. Hefty and homely, he lacked Cagney's charm, but his rasping voice added extra threat to his warnings. "Some people have youth, some have beauty, I have menace," he'd say. He was a great stage actor but his appearance limited the roles he received in films. Yet, he was a great movie actor, who loved beauty, collected great art, and was one of the most artistic and intellectual members of the screen community.

Like Laughton, Gable, Brando, and Bogart, Cagney did win one Oscar. Unlike them, he won it for the role

Edward G. Robinson as Little Caesar *shoots it out with the cops.*

for which he is best remembered—the strutting music-man George M. Cohan in the 1942 film *Yankee Doodle Dandy*. He might have won another had he accepted later in life a million-dollar offer from Jack Warner to do the Rex Harrison role in *My Fair Lady*. But *Dandy* is not the most typical of his roles. More typical was the thug he played in *Angels with Dirty Faces*, for which he was nominated, in 1938, or the one in *White Heat*, for which he was not, in 1949. He won the New York Critics Award for *Angels*. Most typical was the hood he portrayed in his fifth film, *Public Enemy*.

Incredibly, Robinson was never even nominated for an Oscar, despite powerful portrayals in *The Sea Wolf* in 1941, *Double Indemnity* in 1944, *All My Sons* in 1948, *The Cincinnati Kid* in 1965, and the picture of which he was proudest, *Dr. Ehrlich's Magic Bullet* in 1940. He is best remembered for his hoods, including the one in *Key Largo* in 1948 and in his eighth film, the first gangster "talkie," *Little Caesar*, in 1931.

Robinson's Rico was modelled after the malevolent Al Capone. So, also, was Paul Muni's *Scarface*, which followed in 1932. It was this great stage actor's first film and one of his most memorable. To soften the title, the sub-title *Shame of a Nation* was added to *Scarface*, but Muni portrayed Scarface powerfully as a sadist without redeeming virtue. In *Public Enemy*, Cagney liked his family. In *Scarface*, Muni liked his sister a little too much. His portrayal hinted incest. When George Raft, as the unforgettable coin-flipping Little Boy, romances Muni's sister, Ann Dvorak, Raft's fate is sealed. Raft copied the coin-flipping from a tough in New York and never topped it.

Howard Hawks, one of the many great directors who never won an Oscar, directed *Scarface* fiercely and superbly with dark moods set by imaginative camera angles. Ben Hecht wrote an excellent script. The film may be less well remembered than some because prints are scarce and it has not had the exposure of others on television or at festivals.

Muni may have been our finest film actor. He may have been our finest actor, period. He was nominated five times for Academy Awards but won only one, for *The Story of Louis Pasteur* in 1936. Had he gotten to

Paul Muni as Scarface.

The Life of Emile Zola *won the Oscar, but Paul Muni as Zola didn't.*

How is he getting by? "I steal," says Paul Muni to Helen Vinson just before he fades into the shadows in I Am a Fugitive from a Chain Gang.

replay his Broadway role in Arthur Miller's film *Death of a Salesman* instead of Fredric March in 1951, Muni may have won another Oscar and made the movie what it should have been. Muni was a magnificent Willy Loman. He was as magnificent in *The Life of Emile Zola* in 1937, for which he won the New York Film Critics Award as he was in *The Story of Louis Pasteur.* He was as magnificent in *I Am a Fugitive from a Chain Gang* in 1933 as he was in *Scarface* in 1932.

In many ways, Muni's portrayal of the fugitive in *Chain Gang* may be his most memorable. It was based on a true case of a man who escapes from prison, makes a respectable life for himself, then is recaptured. Muni portrayed the character's plight with such sensitivity that viewers' sympathies are with him completely. He is one of the most unforgettable characters we have ever met in movies.

After his recapture, Muni's character is promised that because of his redemption he will be released after he is returned to prison. He is not. He escapes again. He returns to see his sweetheart one last time to let her know he is alive. She asks, "How do you live?" As he fades away, forever, into the darkness, he hisses, "I steal." It is the most haunting of all last lines in film history and makes the film a haunting memory.

Originally, the last scene was to be shot in the half-light of a street light. Shot in downtown Los Angeles, a power failure put out the light as the scene was being shot. The last line was so effective spoken as the scene dissolved into darkness that it was left that way.

A performance of lesser stature, but one of the more memorable from the gangster films, was that of Richard Widmark as the sneering, small-time hood Tommy Udo in the 1947 movie *Kiss of Death.* Pushing an old lady in a wheelchair down a flight of stairs, celebrating with a maniacal laugh, Widmark's character is unforgettable. Widmark won a nomination for a Supporting Actor Oscar for the part, but lost to Edmund Gwenn's Santa Claus in *Miracle on 34th Street*. It was Widmark's first film and only nomination, but he has since had a long and interesting career.

Paul Muni's career declined drastically after he refused, as did George Raft, the Bogart role in *High Sierra*. Muni was a great actor, born in Europe, reared on New York's lower east side, educated on the Yiddish stage. He was a perfectionist, who prepared carefully for each role. When he played historical characters, the makeup and costumes had to be exactly right, and the little touches he gave to the personalities brought them dramatically to life. But he was not big at the box office and Warners released him at the peak of his prowess. Muni later did have great stage success with *Death of a Salesman* (as successor to Lee J. Cobb) and *Inherit the Wind* before his death in his early seventies in 1967.

If Muni had a rival as the finest film actor of the golden age of Hollywood, it was Spencer Tracy, but Tracy was more versatile, more personally appealing, and attracted larger audiences. Where most of Muni's twenty-two movies were done in a mere ten-year heyday, Tracy made more than seventy movies in a career that endured more than thirty-five years before he died in his late sixties, also in 1967.

The supposedly incomparable Laurence Olivier once said, "I learned more from Spencer Tracy's movies than from any other actor. There was great truth in everything he did. And he did everything well." Tracy's pal, Clark Gable, said, "There's nobody in the business who can touch him, and you're a fool to try. And the bastard knows it, so don't fall for that humble stuff."

Tracy acted humble. He said, "This mug of mine is as plain as a barn door. Why should people pay thirty-five cents to see it?" But Katharine Hepburn remembers that when they met to make their first movie and she said, "I'm afraid I'm too tall for you, Mr. Tracy," he said, "Don't worry, I'll soon cut you down to my size."

Their off-screen romance endured many years, despite his troubled marriage. She once said, "He's like an old oak tree, or the summer, or the wind. He belonged to an era when men were men." Bogie said, "Spence is the best because you don't see the mechanism at work." Spence said, "There is no mechanism, there's only me."

Like Muni, Tracy played gangster roles early in his career. A memorable 1935 movie, *20,000 Years in Sing Sing*, also closed with a memorable line. Based on true events, it told the story of a hardened criminal softened by his girlfriend, played by Bette Davis, and a warden, who in real life was Louis E. Lawes. At the end, Tracy's death, in the electric chair, is announced in a newsbreak on radio. Then the station switches back to Ted Lewis, the famous musician, closing with his famous farewell, "Is everybody happy?" The irony of it was enormously effective.

Tracy and Pat O'Brien were boyhood friends in Milwaukee and both at one time wanted to study for the priesthood. Together, they attended military school, went into the navy, and came out to attend dramatic school in New York. O'Brien has had a long and distinguished career, memorable mainly for the title role in *Knute Rockne—All American* in 1940. His portrayal of the inspirational, pep-talking football coach endures as one of the most vivid in movie history, but it was not even nominated for an Oscar. O'Brien was never nominated for an Oscar.

Tracy was nominated nine times for Academy Awards and took two—for *Captains Courageous* in 1937 and *Boys Town* in 1938. He was as equally effective as a minister in *San Francisco* in 1936 as in *Boys Town*; in *The Old Man and the Sea* in 1958 as in *Captains Courageous*. Late in his career he produced powerful performances in *Bad Day at Black Rock* in 1955, *Inherit the Wind* in 1960, and *Judgment at Nuremberg* in 1961. He was as clever in comedy as he was adept at drama. He was superb in *Father of the Bride* with Elizabeth Taylor in 1950 and *Guess Who's Coming to Dinner* with Katharine Hepburn in 1967, for which he was nominated, and *Adam's Rib*, with longtime flame Hepburn, in 1949, for which he was not nominated. Tracy was so versatile that he could have won for any one of a dozen portrayals of different types. No one stands out, though he took two Oscars. Since no other actor ever won more, presumably he was sufficiently rewarded.

Jack Lemmon also took two—as a supporting actor in *Mister Roberts* in 1955 and as a starring actor in *Save the Tiger* in 1933. Yet it is his performance in *The Apartment* in 1960, a comedic classic, in which he plays a flunky who loans his pad to his bosses, that is his best-remembered role according to both the critics and fans who participated in our poll. The fans, in fact, fit it into the all-time top ten performances. It was nominated in 1960, but lost to Burt Lancaster's *Elmer Gantry*.

James Stewart won one Oscar—for his light-hearted part in *The Philadelphia Story* in 1940. He is best remembered, however, for the first of his five nominations, *Mr. Smith Goes to Washington* in 1939. Many

James Stewart in his famous filibuster scene in Mr. Smith Goes to Washington.

Pat O'Brien became the great coach in Knute Rockne—All American. Here he's with Nick Lukats, who played Harry Stduhldreher, one of the "Four Horsemen of Notre Dame."

feel he won for *The Philadelphia Story* only because he lost for *Mr. Smith*. Like Clark Gable's performance in *Gone With the Wind* and Laurence Olivier's in *Wuthering Heights*, it lost out to Robert Donat's *Goodbye, Mr. Chips* in that memorable movie year of 1939. Yet, in more than forty years and eighty films, Stewart never gave a greater performance, nor one that suited his sincere, low-key style better, nor one that moved movie audiences more.

Stewart was thirty-one when he played Jefferson Smith, an idealistic, naive young man who goes to Washington to fill an unexpired term in Congress. He runs into crooked politics and decides to expose the fraud. In what has come to be considered one of the great virtuoso scenes, Stewart, as Smith, filibusters to force the Senate to listen to him. He speaks for what is supposed to be almost twenty-four hours. He speaks until he is exhausted. He says, "You think I'm licked. Well, I'm not licked. I'm going to stay right here and fight for the lost cause. Somebody will listen to me," he says. And he faints. His emotionally moving performance won him the New York Film Critics best actor award for that year, if not the Oscar.

Stewart, Henry Fonda, and Gary Cooper were a lot alike in that they were slender fellows, small-town types, who portrayed simple, sincere people and who all but stuttered when they spoke. Stewart was active in amateur theatrics with the Princeton Triangle Club but aimed at a career in architecture until persuaded by classmate Josh Logan to join Fonda and Margaret Sullavan in summer theater in New England. Stewart roomed with Fonda when both were trying to break onto Broadway. Fonda later had his greatest stage success on Broadway in Logan's *Mister Roberts*. Stewart and Fonda were friends with Cooper in Hollywood.

The role of Jefferson Smith was first offered to Cooper as the logical follow-up to his successful film *Mr. Deeds Goes to Town* of three years earlier. In that one, a small-town young man inherits a fortune and runs afoul of big-town sharpies while trying to give his money to the needy. Had he been free to do it, it would have been done as *Mr. Deeds Goes to Washington*.

The two pictures were a lot alike. Both were directed by Frank Capra, who specialized in these heartwarming message films. Both had the delightful Jean Arthur as the love interest. The characters of Longfellow Deeds as played by Cooper and Jefferson Smith as played by Stewart were remarkably close. *Mr. Smith* probably benefited by not being merely a sequel to *Mr. Deeds*.

Cooper did do a sort of sequel to *Mr. Deeds* in *Meet John Doe* in 1941. This one also was directed by Capra. As in *Mr. Deeds*, his sidekick was portrayed by Walter Brennan. In this one, however, the love interest was played by Barbara Stanwyck. A washed-up ballplayer, a drifter, is corrupted by an offer to become a political candidate, portraying a "man of the people." Exposed, he is guilt-stricken and tempted to commit suicide by leaping from a skyscraper on Christmas Eve.

The scene in which John Doe is shouted down by the ballpark crowd as he confesses his guilt and the one in which he is talked out of jumping from high atop the Big City are among the best remembered in movie history. I can still feel the rain and anger in the ball park, the chill and gloom atop Big Town. *Meet John Doe* was a more powerful film than *Mr. Deeds Goes to Town* and, while both roles typified his personality perfectly, the Doe role probably was better. Cooper was not even nominated for *John Doe*, but was nominated and won his first Oscar for *Sergeant York* that same year, 1941. He later received a second Oscar for *High Noon* in 1952.

Cooper had a powerful personality as an actor, but he was the sort of man that women wanted to mother. Although his marriage survived almost thirty tumultuous years, he had a series of often fiery romances with Clara Bow, Lupe Velez, Tallulah Bankhead, Carole Lombard, Marlene Dietrich, Ingrid Bergman, Patricia Neal, and others. Tallulah once said, "Gary and John Barrymore were the two most beautiful men I ever looked upon." The classic quote on Cooper, however, came from the free soul, Bow, the "It" girl, who told gossip columnist Hedda Hopper, "he's hung like a horse and he can go all night."

Cooper was natural, in or out of bed. Early in his career he had one big scene in the first Oscar winner, *Wings*. He asked the director to reshoot it because he had picked his nose in it. Bill Wellman said, "You keep right on picking your nose and you'll pick your nose into a fortune."

Cooper, who broke into films as an extra in westerns, made more than eighty movies in close to forty years. He received five nominations for Oscars, including one for his portrayal of baseball great Lou Gehrig in *Pride of the Yankees* and one for *Mr. Deeds*, but not one for *John Doe*, which may be his most typical and moving characterization. He received a special Oscar in the 1961 Academy Award ceremonies, but it was received for him by his pal Jimmy Stewart. Accepting it, Stewart all but broke down. He had just learned Cooper was incurably ill with cancer. At that moment the world learned it. Headlines blared cruelly, "Gary Cooper Dying." Within one month, Cooper died at the age of sixty.

Henry Fonda in The Grapes of Wrath *with two of his "family" framed in the mirror.*

Stewart, who again won the New York Film Critics Award for *Anatomy of a Murder* in 1959, but not the Oscar, still was active in his late seventies in the early 1980s. When someone asked him where the new Jimmy Stewart might be found, he asked, "How about me?"

Henry Fonda, who has made more than eighty films in more than forty years, also was still active as he approached the age of seventy-five in the early 1980s. Unlike Cooper and Stewart, he not only never won an Oscar, but has had only one nomination.

He may have been underrated because he underplayed his roles, but he deserved an Award for his one nomination, *The Grapes of Wrath* in 1940, and

deserved at least nominations for *The Lady Eve* in 1941, *The Male Animal* in 1942, *The Ox-Bow Incident* in 1943, *Mister Roberts* in 1955, *12 Angry Men* in 1957, and several cowboy characterizations he performed in John Ford films.

By the time *Mister Roberts* went before the cameras, Fonda had given 1,700 Award winning quality performances of *Mister Roberts* on Broadway. Yet the producers offered the role to Marlon Brando and Bill Holden before director John Ford insisted that Fonda deserved it. Ironically, Ford and Fonda did not get along on the set and Mervyn LeRoy replaced Ford before the film was finished.

Typically, Fonda was not fully appreciated. His lack

of Oscars or even nominations has caused his career to be underrated. Olivia De Havilland has admitted that when they played together in the play *A Gift of Time* she was outraged when he suggested six changes in her performance. She says, "I wanted to say, how dare you? I have two Academy Awards. Where are yours? But the first night I put five of the changes in and the second night the sixth, they all worked, and all I could do was thank him. But I was so mad at myself I kicked a wall and almost broke my foot."

She says, "Fonda always did little things to make a portrayal right. Sometimes you didn't see them, but they always were there." He says, "Heck, I never wanted anyone to see anything I did. I always under-played my parts if possible. I wanted to be the part, I didn't want to show through the part."

Writing in the *Los Angeles Times*, critic Dan Sullivan says, "Some people say, 'You can always tell it's Henry Fonda'.... The statement suggests that acting is basically a matter of pretending to be somebody else. I've come to suspect that it's basically the opposite, a process of revealing yourself under a series of transparent masks, known as character.... With a great mimic like Olivier, there's enormous pleasure in the mask work ... But underneath we know it's Olivier.... With John Wayne there was very little mask work.... If Wayne was an actor, Fonda certainly is one. He can project his character two inches to the

Mr. Roberts teamed top talents with, left to right, Henry Fonda, James Cagney, William Powell, and Jack Lemmon.

camera or 100 feet to the back of a theater.... Audiences trust Fonda. We don't love him but we respect him, more than any other living American actor." Playwright William Gibson says, "He has such star quality, other actors that stand near him seem to shrink in size."

Introduced to the theater by Dorothy Brando in Omaha when her son Marlon was but an infant in 1925, Fonda developed as an actor in New England summer theater in the late 1920s and shifted to Hollywood films in the middle 1930s. *The Grapes of Wrath* was his twenty-first film and he was twenty-five. It lost to *Rebecca* and·he lost to his pal Stewart's *Philadelphia Story* in the Academy Award balloting. Time, however, has made it clear that Fonda's film and his performance in it were far superior and among the most outstanding of all time.

John Ford did win an Oscar as director of *Wrath* and Jane Darwell won the supporting actress Award. This John Steinbeck story of a migrant family driven from Oklahoma's "Dust Bowl," landing where they were not wanted, in California's land of milk and honey, was a superb picture, deeply enriched by Fonda's sensitive performance as young Tom Joad. He has said, "I like

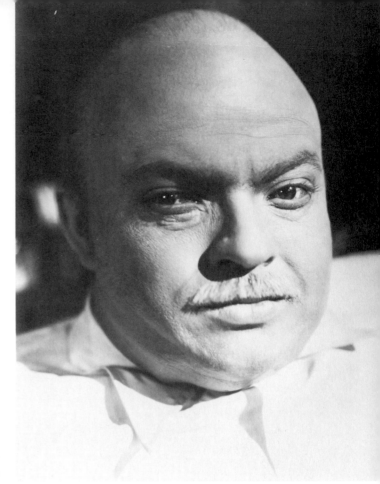

Orson Welles, aged by makeup for his classic Citizen Kane.

Jose Ferrer was unforgettable as Toulouse Lautrec in Moulin Rouge.

Rod Steiger was outstanding as The Pawnbroker.

to think I have grown as an actor in the years since, but that movie was so good and that role so right I suppose you could say it was my best."

In our poll, critics considered it the third best acting performance of all time. In displaying frustration and anger without histrionics, Fonda gave a controlled performance that fit the character as perfectly as possible. That he was not honored for it, nor for any of his other roles of merit, is sad.

Competition for Oscars was staggering in the late 1930s and early 1940s. There remains little justification for *The Grapes of Wrath* losing to *Rebecca* in 1940, although one might accept *Mr. Smith Goes to Washington* and others losing to *Gone With the Wind* in 1939 and *Citizen Kane* and others losing to *How Green Was My Valley* in 1941. Is there justification for Robert Donat's Mr. Chips beating Gable's Rhett Butler, Stewart's Mr. Smith, and Olivier's Heathcliff in 1939, Stewart's Mike Connor (in *Philadelphia Story*) beating out Fonda's Tom Joad in 1940, or Cooper's Sergeant York beating out his own John Doe or Orson Welles' Citizen Kane in 1941?

Olivier may have been the greatest of modern actors. That he has been nominated ten times and won

Kirk Douglas soared to stardom in Champion. *Here he's with Paul Stewart.*

only one Oscar seems on the surface ridiculous. However, most of his movies have been British and so, sentimentally, not as significant to American voters. His *Hamlet* in 1948 could not be denied. In retrospect, it is surprising his Heathcliff in 1939's *Wuthering Heights* was denied. It is said that he was young—he was thirty-two at the time—and overacted. Merle Oberon, his costar as Cathy, said he spit on her when he spoke to her. Yet, his role as the brooding, romantic young man who pursues his love over fog-swept moors remains a highlight in the history of films.

Orson Welles was given to overacting, especially later in his checkered career, but it was not only his staging and directing of the revolutionary *Citizen Kane* but his performance in the part of Charles Kane that made this movie a masterpiece. He made Kane come alive as a charming and commanding figure, as well as a vain and vicious one full of enthusiasms and frustrations. It was a rich characterization by the twenty-six-year-old genius from radio ranks, and he has not topped it in forty years of extreme efforts. In our poll, the critics rated it the fourth finest performance. It was his one nomination for an acting Academy Award.

Many feel, however, that Welles' finest performance was as Rochester in *Jane Eyre* in 1944. He gave other powerful performances in *The Stranger* in 1946, *Touch of Evil* in 1958, *MacBeth* in 1948, *Othello* in 1952, *Tomorrow Is Forever* in 1946, and *The Third Man* in 1949.

Jose Ferrer is another of those who received one Oscar, but maybe not for his best movie role. He was nominated three times, as a supporting actor for *Joan of Arc* in 1948 and as a starring actor for *Cyrano De Bergerac* in 1950 and *Moulin Rouge* in 1952. He won for the classical Cyrano, and it was a splendid performance he gave. But he is better remembered for his playing of the tortured Toulouse-Lautrec in the magnificent *Moulin Rouge*. The Puerto-Rican born Ferrer gave great depth to his portrayal of the crippled artist and deserved more recognition for it. He has received few outstanding opportunities in the years since.

Another who received an Oscar, but not for his top performance, is Rod Steiger. Honored for *In the Heat of the Night* in 1967, he should have been honored for *The Pawnbroker* in 1965. His performance as a Jewish refugee from the Nazi concentration camps trying to come to grips with life in modern New York is one of the most powerful the screen has had. He was nominated for it but did not win. It was not a "big" picture, but it was a giant portrayal.

Rod Steiger is a leading proponent of the "method" style of acting and has been given to overacting at times. He won a nomination earlier in his career as supporting actor to Brando in *On the Waterfront* in 1954, but has had few roles superior to and none to match his part of Sol Nazerman in *The Pawnbroker*. Boston critic David Rosenbaum called Steiger's loss to Lee Marvin, who won for *Cat Ballou* that year, "the greatest miscarriage of justice" in Oscar history. Kirk Douglas, incidentally, first was offered the drunken cowboy part in *Cat Ballou*, but his agent talked him out of taking it.

Curiously, some consider winning an Oscar a curse. Steiger's Award-winning performance was his fortieth in films, but his career careened downhill after that. He got to play Napoleon, Mussolini, and W. C. Fields, but he got bad reviews, his health went bad, and his life went bad. He has been trying to recover. Gig Young made only two minor films after winning his Oscar. Rita Moreno is the only actress to have won the movies' Oscar, the theater's Tony, and television's Emmy, but after she won her Oscar in *West Side Story*, she did not step on a Hollywood stage for seven years. "All they offered me was more 'Spanish Spitfire' roles," she says. Fortunately, she had the singing and dancing ability to build another career for herself. After winning two straight Oscars in the 1930s, Luise Rainer, on the advice of her husband, playwright Clifford Odets, held out for major roles. She never got another one, left Hollywood, and soon was retired.

Oscar does pay off financially. Steiger went from $100,000 a film before Oscar to $350,000 a film immediately after. Marlon Brando went from $75,000 before Oscar to $1.2 million immediately after. Bill Holden went from $250,000 to $1 million. Joan Fontaine's contract was owned by a studio. Her fee for a film went from $25,000 to $125,000, but she still only got $12,500 per picture. Julie Andrews went from $125,000 to $750,000, but she made some flops and soon was out of demand.

Kirk Douglas joins Henry Fonda, Edward G. Robinson, and so many other actors of great ability who never won an Oscar, as well as those who gave one of the great single performances in screen history. He was nominated for *Champion* in 1959, *The Bad and the Beautiful* in 1952, and *Lust for Life* in 1956. He won the New York Film Critics Award for his portrayal of the passionate artist Van Gogh in *Lust for Life*. It is, however, his portrayal of the ambitious boxer Midge Kelly in *Champion* that endures. This was the type of part—cocky and ruthless—for which he was so well fitted. Born Issur Danielovitch in upstate New York of Russian immigrant parents, he changed his name to

Isidore Demskey before he became Kirk Douglas. He was thirty-two when he charged to the top in *Champion*.

Maybe the most notable of the non-winners is Richard Burton, who has had more nominations, seven, than any actor or actress who never won the Oscar. Although a Briton, many of his nominations came in American films. He was nominated for *My Cousin Rachel* in 1952, *The Robe* in 1953, *Becket* in 1954, *The Spy Who Came in from the Cold* in 1965, *Who's Afraid of Virginia Woolf?* in 1966, *Anne of a Thousand Days* in 1969, and *Equus* in 1977.

His part as George opposite Elizabeth Taylor's Martha in that story of a venomous marriage, *Who's Afraid of Virginia Woolf?*, was probably the capper of his considerable career. Elizabeth won, but he did not. He was her equal in this one—together, they gave off sparks that caught fire. Some believe the notoriety he has had in real life has dimmed his image on the silver screen. Yet, he has had the nominations. One of the classic actors, he is another who never won the Oscar.

Charlie Chaplin in his City Lights.

FOUR

The Actors, Part II

FROM THE FIRST Academy Award presentations to the last, many of film's finest actors have been neglected. Although the first Awards, spanning the 1927–28 period, came at the time of the transition from silents to talkies, there still was time to honor Charlie Chaplin and Buster Keaton for roles of unusual merit, but the opportunity was not taken.

Harold Lloyd, Chaplin, and Keaton formed "The Big Three" of silent comedians. Lloyd's zany "everyman" was a classic character. His films outdrew Chaplin's and Keaton's in the 1920s. Like them, he faded fast in the 1930s. Unlike them, he had no classic films left in him. Chaplin had *The Circus* in 1928, *City Lights* in 1931, and *Modern Times* in 1936. Keaton had *The General* in 1927 and *The Cameraman* in 1928. Of these, only Chaplin's role in *The Circus* was even nominated.

Chaplin may have been the first genius of films. It has been said that he was the only comic actor who could make you cry. W. C. Fields called him "the best ballet dancer who ever lived." Enviously, he admitted, "If I get a good chance, I'll strangle him with my bare hands." Chaplin's characterization of "The Tramp" probably is the best loved and most remembered in film history. "The Little Fellow" told funny-sad stories that will never be forgotten.

His *City Lights* and *Modern Times* are, like Keaton's *The General*, among our greatest comedies. His performances in these are among the classic portrayals. It seems as if, in its sudden sophistication, Hollywood simply would not honor silents once the era of talkies came in.

Chaplin returned with *The Great Dictator* in 1940 and *Monsieur Verdoux* in 1952, as well as with a couple of less successful later films. He was nominated for his performance as a comic Hitler in *Dictator* but did not win. He did win the New York Film Critics Award for it. He won nothing, not even a nomination, for *Verdoux*, in which he portrayed "Bluebeard," killer of ladies. Yet, he once said, "It was the only film I ever made with which I was satisfied." It was one of the first black comedies. Film historian Arthur Knight calls it, "the most nonconformist movie ever made." In it, Chaplin points a finger at munitions makers and military leaders, and says, "One murder makes a villain. Millions sanctify."

Buster Keaton's stone-faced, depressed character with the porkpie hat atop his head is almost as well loved and well remembered as Chaplin's little tramp with the small mustache and waddling walk. The critic James Agee called Keaton's performance a juggling act in which the entire universe seems in motion, with the juggler the one point of repose. Athletic and acrobatic, Keaton's portrayal of a Union spy who captures a Confederate train during the Civil War is charged with energy and enormous comic invention. It is sad that it was not so seen in its time. He faded from fashion, took to drink, and almost succumbed to melancholia. He came back a bit in later years, especially in television, but was misused by that medium, too.

There really never has seemed to be a place in the Academy Awards for pure comedy and comedians like W. C. Fields, the Marx Brothers, Laurel and Hardy, Woody Allen, and Mel Brooks. Apparently, people hesitate to put a comic performance by a Fields or a Groucho Marx in the same class with a dramatic part. Yet, many admit that comedy is more difficult to do successfully than drama. There certainly have been fewer great comic actors than dramatic actors. On his deathbed, Edmund Gwenn, a versatile character actor, admitted to a friend that dying was difficult, "But comedy is harder."

There probably should have been a category for comedies, or at least variety, which would also include musicals. Certainly the characterizations of Fields as a cynical dissipate and Groucho as a zany irreverent in countless films meant as much to the industry as any others. Fields, ripping society in his raspy voice, and Groucho, stinging it with wisecracks, suited talkies, too. Both were visual masters, but verbal geniuses. Neither won even one nomination, though Fields did win critical acclaim for his one serious role, as Micawber in *David Copperfield* in 1935.

Only a small place has been allotted for the sophisticated actors of comedy, such as Cary Grant or William Powell. There have been few greater subtle comedians than Grant, but his two Oscar nominations came for serious roles, in *Penny Serenade* in 1941 and

Cary Grant is concerned as Irene Dunne hands his hat to her dog in The Awful Truth.

Cary Grant romances Katharine Hepburn in The Philadelphia Story.

None But the Lonely Heart in 1944. It is difficult to believe that he was not nominated and did not win at least once for *The Awful Truth* in 1937, *Bringing Up Baby* in 1938, *His Girl Friday* in 1940, *The Philadelphia Story* or *Suspicion* in 1941, *The Talk of the Town* in 1942, *To Catch a Thief* in 1955, or *North by Northwest* in 1959. A master of mugging with perfect timing, sophisticated Cary, maybe the movies' quintessential "dream man," made more than seventy films over thirty-five years until his retirement at the age of sixty-two in 1966. He deserved an Oscar if anyone did. It is due to snobbery that he was denied one.

Another master of light comedy, William Powell, was nominated for *The Thin Man* in 1934, *My Man Godfrey* in 1936, and *Life with Father* in 1947, but never won. He might well have received Oscar for any of these fine films, as well as for *The Great Ziegfeld* in 1936, *The Senator Was Indiscreet* in 1948, or *Mister*

Roberts in 1955. He did not have the appeal or opportunities of Grant, but Bill Powell was a superb performer of sophisticated comedy and rates more recognition than he ever was given.

Robert Young originally made his mark in light comedies in a career that began in 1931, but proved himself a versatile and dramatic actor in such movies as *Three Comrades* in 1938, *The Mortal Storm* and *Northwest Passage* in 1939, *Joe Smith American* in 1942, *Claudia* in 1943, and *The Enchanted Cottage* in 1945. A fine professional, he made more than a hundred movies, but never won even one nomination for an Oscar. His screen career ended in 1954, but he has since starred on television in *Father Knows Best* in the 1960s and *Marcus Welby, M.D.* in the 1970s as a wise, solid citizen. This he has been in real life as husband to the same woman since 1933 and father of five daughters.

Don Ameche is another who made his mark in light

comedies and musicals, in a career that commenced in 1936 and ran through 1970. Among his major films were *In Old Chicago* and *Alexander's Ragtime Band* in 1938 and *Heaven Can Wait* in 1943. He was best known for the title role in *The Story of Alexander Graham Bell* in 1939. He became so well known for this role that for a while a telephone was called "an Ameche." But he was not nominated for this or any other part. He also was prominent as a radio announcer.

Eddie Albert was wasted for years as a second lead in light comedies, but the veteran actor, born Edward Albert Himbrayer, who debuted in *Brother Rat* in 1938, deserved one or two nominations for *The Wagons Roll at Night* in 1941, *Smash-Up* in 1947, *Roman Holiday* in 1955, *I'll Cry Tomorrow* in 1955, *The Sun Also Rises* in 1957, *The Roots of Heaven* in 1958, and *Orders to Kill*, a marvelous little drama hardly noticed when it came out in 1959.

Robert Walker was a boyish, charming actor, who developed as a light comedian in such films as *See Here Private Hargrove* in 1944 and *The Clock* in 1945 but turned in impressive dramatic portrayals in *Since You Went Away* in 1944 and *Strangers on a Train* in 1951. He was never nominated for an Award, but was worthy. Jennifer Jones was his wife before they became stars. The breakup of that marriage when she turned to David O. Selznick hurt terribly. A later marriage to John Ford's daughter Barbara lasted only six weeks. Depressed, Walker drank heavily, suffered nervous breakdowns, and died of an overdose of sedatives in 1951 at the age of thirty-two.

Tony Curtis came to prominence in the lightest of comedies and the silliest of films, but he was convincing in the comedy *Some Like It Hot* in 1959 and compelling in the dramas *Sweet Smell of Success* in 1957, and *The Defiant Ones* in 1958, for which he won nominations for Oscars but did not win. Born Bernard Schwartz in the Bronx, he has proven to be more than a "pretty boy."

More recently, Burt Reynolds has been trying to establish himself in madcap comedies as a light comedian comparable to Cary Grant and William Powell. He was especially effective in *The Longest Yard* in 1974, *The End* in 1978, and *Starting Over* in 1979 and has had a string of money-making hits. He was persuasive in a powerful dramatic part in *Deliverance* in 1972, but he has yet to win nomination for an Oscar.

Recently, Woody Allen starred in and developed a series of inventive comedies, but earned a nomination as an actor only when he turned to a somewhat more sophisticated effort in *Annie Hall* in 1977. He did not win, but his co-star Diane Keaton and the film itself did. He was also nominated as director. His *Interiors* in 1978 gained some laurels. When his *Manhattan* was denied major nominations in 1979, many critics complained bitterly.

Mel Brooks has deserved but been denied nominations for a series of inspired comedies. It seems as though the Academy Award voters do not yet recognize the place laughter has in our lives or in the medium of movies.

Clark Gable won for *It Happened One Night* in 1934, James Stewart for *The Philadelphia Story* in 1940, and Richard Dreyfuss for *The Goodbye Girl* in 1977. That's it for Oscars as far as even sophisticated comedy performances by actors go. Furthermore, the slapstick clan, the outrageous comedians, are left out entirely.

Fred Astaire won a nomination only late in his career for *The Towering Inferno* in 1974. It was as though his incomparable dancing in so many marvelous musicals went unnoticed, although two, *The Gay Divorcee* in 1934 and *Top Hat* in 1935, were themselves nominated. More than a dynamic dancer, Astaire was a singer and romantically effective. He was distinguished as a sophisticated player of light parts and became the role model for many college lads of the 1930s.

Gene Kelly was nominated for his more acrobatic dancing and light comedy style in *Anchors Aweigh* in 1945, but unbelievably, not for his *An American in Paris*, which won the Best Picture Oscar in 1951. If he did not make that fine film what it was, who did? Nor was he nominated for his even better remembered *Singin' in the Rain* in 1952. A classic choreographer, Kelly stands (if ever he stands) as a classic case of a neglected performer in the annals of Oscars.

Like comedies, musicals were the stuff of life in Hollywood film history, yet were denied deserved Awards. An Astaire and a Kelly merited more than honorary Oscars. Furthermore, the great singers of films were entirely forgotten. In the early years, a Maurice Chevalier or Lawrence Tibbett might win a nomination, but not an Award. Later on, none would even be nominated though Bing Crosby did win for an essentially non-singing role in *Going My Way* in 1944 and Rex Harrison, though perhaps not for his singing, in *My Fair Lady* in 1964. Dan Dailey was nominated for a dancing part in *When My Baby Smiles at Me* in 1948, but dancers and singers are among the greatly neglected of Hollywood history.

Dick Powell's early career consisted of light comedy and romantic singing in musicals, but he did develop late in life dramatically in such films as *Murder My*

Sweet and *The Bad and the Beautiful.* Eventually he became one of the most respected men in Hollywood as a producer and director for films and televisions, but he never won a nomination for any of his abilities.

Mickey Rooney was the biggest star at the box office in the late 1930s and early 1940s. Maybe you remember him best as the All-American, mugging teenager in the fifteen *Andy Hardy* films, but he had a great, versatile talent. He was nominated for *Babes in Arms* in 1939 and *The Human Comedy* in 1943 but not for *Captains Courageous* in 1937 or his *Boys Town* in 1938. He never won although each nomination was worthy of winning. He was nominated again in 1979 for *The Black Stallion*, and his loss was surprising and disappointing. Rooney, whose father, Joe Yule, was a vaudevillian, was a year old when he made his first appearance on stage and six when he made his first movie. He went from *Our Gang* shorts to star in a

Mickey Rooney mourns a fallen friend in Boys Town.

John Barrymore, "the Great Profile," toasts a friend in Dinner at Eight.

series of *Mickey McGuire* shorts and even used that name for awhile. As an adolescent, age fourteen, he was superb as Puck in *Midsummer Night's Dream* in 1935. His musicals with Judy Garland are remembered fondly. Balding and bulging at almost sixty, this pint-sized dynamo returned to stardom with *Sugar Babies* on Broadway in 1979 and was nominated for a Tony, but lost. These two losses in one year, late in his career, must have been tough to take, but he took them well. He'd been down a long time and said, "The saddest thing is to be an actor without an audience."

Mickey merited an Oscar somewhere along the way. Bette Davis says, "No doubt about it, Rooney was, is, and always will be one of Hollywood's great acting talents."

Over the years, the most popular leading men of movies often were not considered worthy of Awards for acting. These include Grant, Tyrone Power, Robert Taylor, Errol Flynn, and Charles Boyer. John Barrymore was worthy. He was successful in the silents and early talkies, but the talkies came too late to take full advantage of his rich speech and deep acting talent. Late in his career, he was but a drunken caricature of himself. He was not nominated for but did excell in *A Bill of Divorcement* in 1932, in which Katharine Hepburn made a brilliant screen debut, and *Twentieth Century* in 1934, in which Carole Lombard captivated audiences.

Neither Power nor Taylor were ever nominated even though Power provided persuasive performances in *Blood and Sand* in 1941, *The Razor's Edge* in 1946, *Nightmare Alley* in 1947, and *The Sun Also Rises* in 1957, and Taylor was effective in *Camille* in 1937, *Three Comrades* in 1938, *Waterloo Bridge* in 1940, and *Johnny Eager* in 1942. Power worked hard to gain stature as an actor, but Taylor always was amused by his profession and did not take himself seriously.

Recent writings have brought notoriety to Tyrone Power and Errol Flynn as "bisexuals." While Power was married to actresses Annabella, Linda Christian, and Deborah Minardos, and had romances with Janet Gaynor, Judy Garland, Doris Day, Lana Turner, and Sonja Henie, and had two daughters and a son, he reportedly had homosexual affairs with Charles Laughton, Flynn, and many others.

Flynn was married to actresses Lila Damita, Nora Eddington, and Patrice Wymore, and had romances with Joan Bennett, Lupe Velez, Eva Peron, and many others, including teenager Beverly Aadland. It was because of his romance with Aadland and other young girls that he was disqualified from the James Mason role in *Lolita*. Flynn had a son and three daughters. He supposedly had homosexual affairs with Power, Truman Capote, Howard Hughes, and others.

Flynn was accepted as a modern-day successor to Douglas Fairbanks, as a roguish daredevil and ladies'

Matador Tyrone Power visits a sick friend, a young John Carradine, felled by the bulls in Blood and Sand.

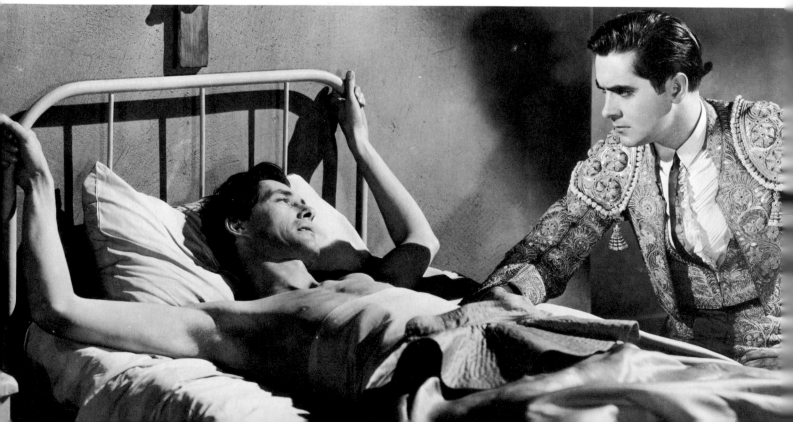

Charles Boyer, as Pepe LeMoko, says it all with a look at Hedy Lamarr in Algiers.

man in *Captain Blood* in 1935, *The Adventures of Robin Hood* in 1938, and *The Sea Hawk* in 1940. He never won a nomination but he put a vitality into these roles that never received its just recognition. His reputation as a ladies' man off the screen clouded his performance in these parts on the screen. Late in his life, his heavy drinking may have added reality to his portrayal of the dissipated Mike Campbell in *The Sun Also Rises* in 1957 and of another dissipate in the underrated *The Roots of Heaven* in 1958.

Charles Boyer's image as a screen lover, with his thick French accent, clouded assessments of his acting ability. He is best known for a line he never spoke, "Come wiz me to ze casbah," supposedly said to Hedy Lamarr in *Algiers*. There was a moment in that film, where Boyer reached across a table at a sidewalk cafe and lightly touched her hand, that said more than all the words he might have spoken. It is more erotic than most scenes provided by today's explicit dialogue films.

Never nominated for an Award, the charming Gallic

figure was an accomplished actor, whose role as Pepe LeMoko in *Algiers* in 1938, as well as roles in *All This and Heaven Too* in 1940, *Hold Back the Dawn* in 1941, *Gaslight* in 1944, and *Fanny* in 1962 were worthy of wider recognition.

Boyer, in French films for ten years before he even came to Hollywood in 1931, may have been at his best as Gregory Anton, who tries to drive his wife Paula, played by Ingrid Bergman, insane in *Gaslight*. The concluding scene in which he pleads for forgiveness and mercy from her, but is denied it, is dazzling. She won an Oscar for her role but he did not even win a nomination for his.

Boyer and Tyrone Power did receive great recognition for a series of stage readings in the 1950s. While Power was romantically overactive off the screen, Boyer, in contrast to his roles on the screen, was married to the same woman for more than thirty years. Tragically, their only child, a son, committed suicide in 1965. Then, two days after the death of his wife, Pat,

"Where's the rest of me?" asks Ronald Reagan of Ann Sheridan after finding his legs have been amputated in King's Row.

Robert Montgomery is upset and Edward Everett Horton, left, and Claude Rains, right, are amused in Here Comes Mr. Jordan, which was remade years later by Warren Beatty as Heaven Can Wait.

in 1979, Boyer took his own life, at the age of eighty.

Ronald Reagan was regarded as a light leading man and often a second lead. He achieved greater fame as governor of California for eight years and more recently as a top presidential candidate, but in retrospect he was an underrated actor. He was especially effective as Drake McHugh in *Kings Row* in 1941. He played the usual charming rogue until his legs were amputated after an accident. Waking up in bed, he reaches for his legs. "Where's the rest of me?" he pleads in anguish. It was not to be forgotten. He was effective as George Gipp in *Knute Rockne—All American* in 1940 and *The Hasty Heart* in 1950. Yet, he never won a nomination.

Robert Montgomery was typecast for years as a light comedian. He was nominated for an Oscar for his role in the comedy *Here Comes Mr. Jordan* in 1941, but did not win. Earlier, in 1937, he had been nominated for a dramatic part in *Night Must Fall*. His chilling performance as Danny, the demented killer who carries his victim's head in a hatbox, is a screen classic. Sadly, it has been all but forgotten. Montgomery is mostly identified now as the father of television actress Elizabeth Montgomery and as television advisor to President Eisenhower instead of for his great acting talent.

Walter Pidgeon won nominations for *Mrs. Miniver* in 1942 and *Madame Curie* in 1943 but, overshadowed by Greer Garson in the title roles, he never had a chance. He might have been nominated for *How Green Was My Valley*, *Blossoms in the Dust*, or *Man Hunt* in 1941, or many others in an unusual career that has spanned one hundred films in fifty years.

Robert Preston played many light comedy parts, often as second lead. He is another who never even won an Oscar nomination although he contributed commanding performances to *The Macomber Affair* in 1947, The *Sundowners* in 1950, *Dark at the Top of the Stairs* in 1960, and *The Music Man* in 1963. He proved himself an actor of power on Broadway but never received the opportunities or recognition he deserved in Hollywood.

Paul Henreid was typecast as a romantic or second lead. He never won a nomination for an Oscar but played underrated roles superbly in *Now, Voyager* in 1942 and *Casablanca* in 1943.

Glenn Ford, Dana Andrews, Fred MacMurray, Joel McCrea, and Joseph Cotten are other leads or second leads of note who never won nominations. Ford deserved consideration for *Gilda* in 1943 and *The Blackboard Jungle* and *Trial* in 1955. Andrews rates respect for sensitive portrayals in *The Ox-Bow Incident* in 1943, *Laura* in 1944, *The Best Years of Our Lives*

A teacher can feel alone in a courtyard full of cocky kids, as Glenn Ford finds out in Blackboard Jungle.

in 1946, and *Boomerang* in 1947. The son of a concert violinist, Fred MacMurray started out as a band saxophonist. He entered films and played second leads deftly with an occasional major role, such as that of the pilot Eddie Rickenbacker in *Captain Eddy*. Eventually he contributed crackerjack performances to such films as *Double Indemnity*, *The Miracle of the Bells*, *The Caine Mutiny*, and *The Apartment*. He continued as a lead in live comedies for Disney and series for television. He married former actress June Haver, who at one time quit films to become a nun. Investing his money in real estate, he made millions becoming one of Hollywood's wealthiest citizens. An Oscar nomination, however, was never his.

Nor was Joel McCrea ever nominated, despite a long career. A second lead in most of his films, McCrea did turn in fine performances in *These Three, Come and Get It, Dead End, Sullivan's Travels, The More the Merrier, The Tall Stranger,* and *Ride the High Country.*

Robert Taylor, who was never nominated for an Oscar, explains life to Van Heflin, who won in his role in Johnny Eager.

Joseph Cotten is an extreme case of an actor of great talent who never received great rewards. As well as being a distinguished member of Orson Welles' Mercury Theater radio ensemble of the 1930s, he and Van Heflin played the Jimmy Stewart and Cary Grant roles opposite Katharine Hepburn in *The Philadelphia Story* on Broadway in 1937. Cotten's superb performances in such films as Welles' *Citizen Kane* in 1941, *The Magnificent Ambersons* in 1942, *Journey into Fear* in 1943, *Shadow of a Doubt* in 1943, *Portrait of Jenny* in 1948, and *The Third Man* in 1949 were worthy of Awards. He did win the Best Actor Award at the Venice Film Festival in 1948 for *Jenny.*

Like Cotten, Van Heflin played leads but never was considered a classic leading man. He was an accomplished actor who rarely received his due. Heflin did get one nomination and won as a supporting actor for his superb portrait of a drunken hanger-on in the underrated underworld drama *Johnny Eager* in 1942, but he never received the recognition he deserved for *Shane* in 1953 and *Patterns* in 1956 and seldom received film opportunities to exercise his immense skill. He probably was one of our most neglected talents.

Another has been Alan Arkin, though nominated for Oscars for *The Russians Are Coming, The Russians*

Are Coming in 1966 and *The Heart Is a Lonely Hunter* in 1968. His sensitive portrayal of a deaf mute in *Heart* is ranked by the critics who participated in our poll as one of the twenty-five finest of all time. It is rated among the best ten ever by some screen scholars, but his opportunities to shine have been few and far between.

Lew Ayres deserved a nomination for his sensitive portrayal of the young soldier in *All Quiet on the Western Front* in 1930 but did not receive one until his role of the father in *Johnny Belinda* in 1948. In between, he got few quality parts, though he did enjoy a successful series as *Dr. Kildare.* Declaring himself a conscientious objector in World War II, he alienated himself from the studios and public, although he volunteered for and achieved distinguished service as a noncombatant medic under fire. He was offered few roles after the war.

Alan Ladd's was a tragic case. The product of an unhappy childhood, he wound up in Hollywood where his stepfather worked as a painter in the studios. Although self conscious about his size—he grew to only 5'5"—Ladd was an outstanding sprinter, swimmer, and diver in high school. He worked as a laborer on sets until he began to get bit parts. One was as a reporter in *Citizen Kane*. His second wife, agent Sue Carol, pushed his career and he broke through as the icy-eyed killer in *This Gun for Hire* in 1942.

Good-looking, but stone-faced, his cool facade carried him effectively through many tough-guy films, a number of which were with Veronica Lake. For years, he was one of the most popular of stars in Hollywood. His fame faded after World War II, although he continued to make many films and was good in *The Great Gatsby* in 1949 and smashing as the stranger in *Shane* in 1953. He made a mistake when he turned down the part that went to James Dean in *Giant* in 1956. He lacked confidence in himself as an actor and grew depressed when his career went downhill. After almost losing his life in an "accidental" self-inflicted gunshot wound, he died of an overdose of pills and whiskey in 1964. His son married actress Diane Ladd and became a prominent producer, heading 20th Century-Fox through the *Star Wars* years.

Ben Gazzara is another who has had limited opportunities to express an interesting talent and so it is not surprising that he has never been nominated for an Award. Outstanding early portrayals in *The Strange One* in 1957 and *Anatomy of a Murder* in 1959 should have earned him more roles of quality than merely the one his sidekick John Cassavetes provided in *Husbands* in 1970 and *The Killing of a Chinese Bookie* in 1976.

Another of the Cassavetes clan with a unique talent is Peter Falk, nominated for Academy Awards as a supporting actor for *Murder Inc.* in 1960 and *Pocketful of Miracles* in 1961, but impressive as a starring actor only in Cassavetes' *Husbands* in 1970 and *A Woman Under the Influence* in 1974.

Cassavetes himself has been more impressive as a director, but has shown talent as an actor and was nominated for a supporting part in *The Dirty Dozen* in 1967.

Typecast as a heavy, Robert Ryan was nominated only once, for his portrayal of the sadistic anti-semite in 1947's *Crossfire*. He was also superb, however, as the illicit lover in *The Woman on the Beach* in 1947, as the menace in *Act of Violence* in 1949, as a washed-up prizefighter in *The Set-Up* in 1949, as the cynic in *They Clash by Night* in 1952, and as killers in *Bad Day at Black Rock* in 1955 and *The Wild Bunch* in 1969. A former collegiate boxing champion at Dartmouth, Ryan may have been at his best as the boxer in *The Set-Up*, but he was greatly underrated for his roles in many movies.

Also typecast as a heavy, and given to nonchalance toward his career, Robert Mitchum was nominated only as a supporting actor in *The Story of GI Joe* in

A wounded Lew Ayres is comforted by a mute Louis Wolheim in All Quiet on the Western Front.

1945. He was overlooked for his masterfully menacing performances in *Crossfire* in 1947, *The Night of the Hunter* in 1955, and *Cape Fear* in 1962, and for a sensitive and moving performance in *The Sundowners* in 1960.

Another heavy of note was Laird Cregar, whose career endured only five years, but which he made memorable with powerful performances in *Blood and Sand* and *I Wake Up Screaming* in 1941, *This Gun for Hire* in 1942, *Heaven Can Wait* in 1943, *The Lodger* in 1944, and *Hangover Square* in 1945. Never nominated, he should have been. A real-life heavy in terms of weight, he died in 1944 at the age of twenty-eight after a crash diet and surgery.

Although he played leads, Cregar was known mainly as a supporting player. He was a character actor. Among our most neglected actors are the character actors, usually nominated for supporting parts. Noteworthy are Arthur Kennedy and Claude Rains, who have been nominated as many times without winning, four times, as any actor other than Richard Burton.

Arthur Kennedy was nominated for supporting parts in *Champion* in 1949, *Peyton Place* in 1957, and *Some Came Running* in 1958 and for a starring role in

Often a nominee, never a winner, Arthur Kennedy learns how a blind man makes it in Bright Victory, *with John Hudson.*

Bright Victory in 1951. Brought from Broadway by James Cagney to play the second lead in his *City for Conquest* in 1940, Kennedy also gave superlative performances in *Boomerang* in 1947, *The Glass Menagerie* in 1950, *Trial* in 1955, and *Cheyenne Autumn* in 1964.

A thoughtful and sensitive artist, Kennedy scored great successes on the stage in two Arthur Miller masterpieces, *All My Sons* and *Death of a Salesman*, in the 1940s and won a Tony Award for his portrayal of Biff in the latter. For most of his career in Hollywood, however, he was seen as too young to play character parts, yet not quite a leading man type. Concluding his career in Italy in recent years, he now likely will never win an Oscar.

A star on the stage in London and New York,

Claude Rains was in his middle forties by the time he reached Hollywood in the middle 1930s. Small and suave, he primarily played charming heavies. He was nominated for supporting parts in *Mr. Smith Goes to Washington* in 1939, *Casablanca* in 1943, *Mr. Skeffington* in 1944, and *Notorious* in 1946, but was equally effective in *Four Daughters* in 1938, *The Sea Hawk* in 1940, *Kings Row* in 1942, and many other films. He was skilled and sensitive, and never received his due. Bette Davis once called him the most impressive actor with whom she had ever acted. He played many parts opposite her.

Walter Huston was nominated four times—for starring roles in *Dodsworth* in 1936 and *The Devil and Daniel Webster* in 1941 and supporting parts in *Yankee Doodle Dandy* in 1942 and *The Treasure of the Sierra Madre* in 1948. He and his son John, who directed the film, became the only father-and-son winners for one film with *Treasure*. Walter was sixty-four and John was forty-two at the time.

Walter Huston, who died two years later, was long overdue for the Oscar by the time he finally won it. An old vaudevillian, he was on the stage as early as 1906 and once gave up acting because "there was no money in it." A longtime friend of the stage actress Edie Davis, he was known as "Uncle Walter" to her actress-daughter Nancy, who became Mrs. Ronald Reagan. He was acclaimed on Broadway for *Knickerbocker Holiday*, in which he rendered his forever-famous rendition of "September Song" and won the New York Film Critics Award for *Dodsworth*. He was one of the great actors and never received the recognition he rated.

Supporting players nominated three times have been Charles Bickford and Charles Coburn. Bickford did not win, but Coburn did.

Bickford was nominated for *Song of Bernadette* in 1943, *The Farmer's Daughter* in 1947, and *Johnny Belinda* in 1948, but distinguished himself in many other major and minor roles, from the romantic lead opposite Greta Garbo in *Anna Christie* in 1930 to the sympathetic father of Lee Remick in *Days of Wine and Roses* in 1962, five years before his death. He had a commanding presence and strong style and deserved dramatic recognition.

Coburn had a great talent for comedy, but often played hard-crusted characters with soft hearts. Nominated for *The Devil and Miss Jones* in 1941, *The More the Merrier* in 1943, and *The Green Years* in 1946, he won for the middle of these. He could well have won for others, including *Kings Row* in 1942 and *Heaven Can Wait* in 1943.

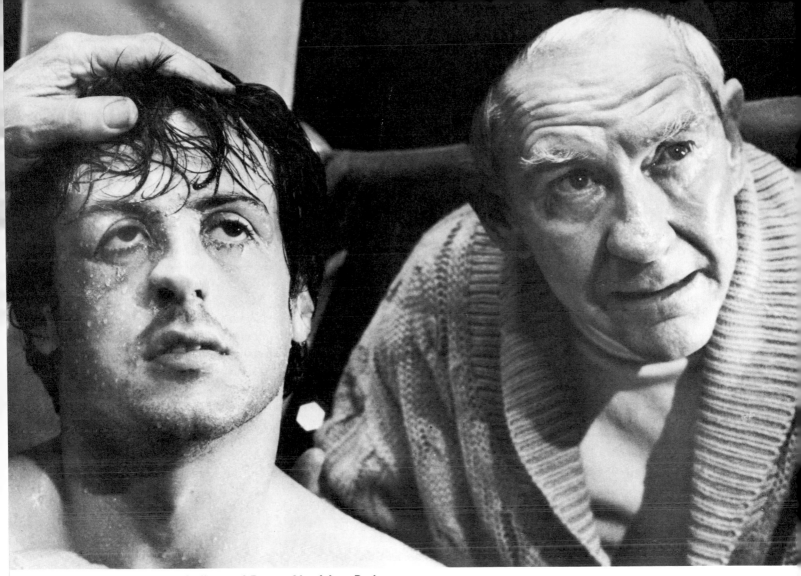

Fighter and manager, Sylvester Stallone and Burgess Meredith, in Rocky.

Among the early supporting stars was Basil Rathbone, who was nominated for *Romeo and Juliet* in 1936 and *If I Were King* in 1938. He did not win but gave many marvelous performances and is most memorable for his depiction of Sherlock Holmes in a dozen films. Another longtime loser was Akim Tamiroff, who won nominations for *The General Died at Dawn* in 1936 and *For Whom the Bell Tolls* in 1943, but never won an Oscar.

Thomas Mitchell was nominated for *Hurricane* in 1937 and won for *Stagecoach* in 1939, but he deserved at least to be nominated for as many as three films in one year—*Only Angels Have Wings, Mr. Smith Goes to Washington,* and *Gone With the Wind* in 1939—as well as *The Long Voyage Home* in 1940, *This Above All* in 1942, and many more. Thomas Mitchell, the brother of Attorney General John Mitchell, was a consummate character actor until his death at seventy in 1962.

Dean Jagger won for his only nomination, *Twelve O'Clock High* in 1949, but merited nominations for *Brigham Young* in 1940, *Sister Kenny* in 1946, *Executive Suite* in 1954, *Bad Day at Black Rock* and *The Eternal Sea* in 1955, *The Nun's Story* in 1959, and *Elmer Gantry* in 1960. In a career that has continued since 1929, he has made the most of limited opportunities and probably rates high among our greatly talented but neglected actors.

Clifton Webb won nominations for his parts in *Laura* in 1944 and *The Razor's Edge* in 1946, but not for his most cherished role as Mr. Belvedere. In the role, he dumps a bowl of hot cereal over the head of a misbehaving child. The film was *Sitting Pretty* in 1948. He was born Webb Parmalee Hollenbeck and became one of the leading ballroom dancers in New York before turning to the stage in 1917. He made three or four silents in the 1920s then went on to movies in his fifties with *Laura*. The acid-tongued actor

role in the movie, it might have been Cobb's greatest triumph and won for him the honors Hollywood denied him.

One of the more solid performers for forty-five years prior to his death in 1963 was Adolphe Menjou. He started in the silents in 1916 and achieved recognition in Chaplin's *A Woman of Paris* in 1923. From then one, with his waxed mustache, stylish dress, and cultured tones, he played suave parts superbly. He received a Best Actor nomination only for *The Front Page* in 1931, but was outstanding in others, including *A Farewell to Arms* in 1932, *A Star Is Born* in 1937, *Golden Boy* in 1939, *Roxie Hart* in 1942, *The Hucksters* in 1947, and *Paths of Glory* in 1957. He was equally effective in serious and comedy roles.

Among the non-winners are a number of character actors especially skilled at comic parts. These include four who were nominated twice for Oscars—Frank Morgan for *The Affairs of Cellini* in 1934 and *Tortilla Flat* in 1942, Monty Woolley for *The Pied Piper* in 1942 and *Since You Went Away* in 1944, J. Carroll Naish for *Sahara* in 1943 and *A Medal for Benny* in 1945, and Robert Morley for *Marie Antoinette* in 1938 and *They're Killing the Great Chefs of Europe* in 1978. The time span between nominations for Morley is noteworthy. Another neglected comic actor was James Gleason, nominated only for *Here Comes Mr. Jordan* in 1941.

Morgan is best remembered for the title role in *The Wizard of Oz* in 1939 and Woolley for the title role in *The Man Who Came to Dinner* in 1942. Morgan also is well remembered as one of Fanny Brice's fathers in radio's "Baby Snooks" series and Naish for television's *Life with Luigi*.

Brian Aherne, Ralph Bellamy, and Melvyn Douglas were masters of sophisticated comedy who played many second leads in romantic roles. Aherne was nominated in 1939 for *Juarez*, Bellamy in 1937 for *The Awful Truth*. They did not win. Douglas won with *Hud* in 1963, lost with *I Never Sang for My Father* in 1970, and won with *Being There* in 1979. Bellamy and Douglas were actors of rich dramatic ability who were wasted in a lot of lightweight parts. Bellamy proved his skills in a series of stage roles on Broadway late in his career, notably winning the New York Drama Critics Award for his Franklin D. Roosevelt in *Sunrise at Campobello*, which he repeated in the film in 1960. Douglas won a Tony Award for his portrayal of a presidential candidate in *The Best Man* on Broadway and a TV Emmy for *Do Not Go Gentle into That Good Night* late in his career. His comic skills in *Theodora Goes Wild* in 1936 and in *Ninotchka* in 1939 matched his dramatic skills.

George Sanders played a sophisticated cad superbly, especially in *The Moon and Sixpence* in 1942 and *All About Eve* in 1950, for which he won nomination and an Oscar. Like the hero of the lightweight detective series "The Saint" and "The Falcon," which he turned over to brother Tom Conway, Sanders was something of a sophisticated cad in real life. He was married to the sisters Zsa Zsa Gabor and Magda Gabor, as well as friend Ronald Colman's widow Benita Hume. He committed suicide at sixty-six in 1972 because he was "bored."

Brian Donlevy, was a bugler in General John Pershing's Mexican expedition against Pancho Villa, a pilot with the famed Lafayette Escadrille in World War I, and a former shirt model. A husky film heavy of note, he won one Oscar nomination for his sadistic sergeant in 1939's *Beau Geste*, but he also was successful in *The Great McGinty* in 1940, *The Glass Key* in 1942, *Two Years Before the Mast* in 1946, and other films.

Sidney Greenstreet, a heavy of enormous menace, won only one nomination, for his incomparable Kasper Gutman in the memorable *The Maltese Falcon* in 1941. He did not win. Equally surprising, Peter Lorre did not even win a nomination for his superb Joel Cairo in the same movie. Lorre never won any nomination, although he was an especially vivid depictor of vile roles. He was unforgettable as the child murderer in the German movie *M*. Greenstreet and Lorre both were incomparable character actors, unrewarded ones.

Ed Begley won one nomination and one Oscar for *Sweet Bird of Youth* in 1962. He repeated television triumphs in the movies *Patterns* in 1956 and *12 Angry Men* in 1957, but did not win nominations for Academy Awards. He did not get to repeat stage triumphs in *All My Sons* or *Inherit the Wind*, or he might have won wider recognition. In the latter, he and Paul Muni created the roles of William Jennings Bryan and Clarence Darrow on Broadway, then swapped parts in mid-run in an incredible display of versatility.

Arthur O'Connell was nominated for *Picnic* in 1955 and *Anatomy of a Murder* in 1959, but did not win, and might well have been nominated for several other roles. His sensitive, spirited performances were superb.

James Whitmore was nominated for *Battleground* in 1949 and again for the one-man movie *Give 'Em Hell, Harry* in 1975, but did not win. Although hailed as a new Spencer Tracy when he began, his career never reached its potential, but he proved his skill in portraying Harry Truman and Teddy Roosevelt in one-man shows in recent years.

Jack Warden was nominated for *Shampoo* in 1975 and *Heaven Can Wait* in 1978. George Segal was nominated for *Who's Afraid of Virginia Woolf?* in 1966, but not for his clever *A Touch of Class* in 1973. Robert Shaw was nominated for *A Man for All Seasons* in 1966, but not for his sensational shark-killer in *Jaws* in 1975. Bruce Dern was nominated for *Coming Home* in 1978, but not for his chilling psychopath in *Black Sunday* in 1977. None of these were winners, but at least they were nominated.

In a forty-year career spanning more than eighty films, including impressive performances in *A Tree Grows in Brooklyn* in 1945 and *A Hatful of Rain* in 1957, the splendid Lloyd Nolan was never nominated for an Academy Award. He won later recognition as an accomplished actor for his portrayal of the neurotic Captain Queeg in the stage and television versions of *The Caine Mutiny Court Martial*, but when Queeg was portrayed in the movies, Humphrey Bogart got the plum.

Strother Martin, who died in 1980, was a fine character actor for over thirty years. He is perhaps best remembered as the warden in 1967's *Cool Hand Luke*, who delivered the memorable line, "What we have here is a failure to communicate." He once said he was always hoping for an important role, but not for an Oscar. He said he wanted to be nominated and to lose, "Then people would say for the rest of my life, 'I think you should have won.'"

It will be interesting to see if Robert Duvall can make it big as he nears fifty. An admiral's son from San Diego, he studied in New York and made a memorable debut as a feeble-minded fellow in *To Kill a Mockingbird* in 1963. He has had great success as a character actor impressively late in his career with nominations for *The Godfather* in 1972 and *Apocalypse Now* in 1979, and was sensational in *The Great Santini* in 1980.

John Garfield's only Oscar nominations were as a supporting actor in *Four Daughters* in 1938 and as a starring actor in *Body and Soul* in 1947, but he was one of the great stars of films who never captured an Award. He was worthy of Awards also for *The Sea Wolf* in 1941, *The Postman Always Rings Twice* in 1946, and *Gentleman's Agreement* in 1947. A product of The Group Theater, which pioneered a naturalistic method of acting, he left for Hollywood when the group denied him the part that was perfect for him, that

John Garfield confronts a bigot in Gentleman's Agreement *as Gregory Peck and Celeste Holm watch.*

of the boxer Joe Bonaparte in Clifford Odets's *Golden Boy*, directed by Elia Kazan. The part went to Luther Adler, who was too old for it. When the movie version was made, it went to Bill Holden, who was too young for it.

Throughout Garfield's screen career he lost important roles to Bill Holden or Jeffrey Lynn or some other young actor who was considered more the star type. Garfield, born Jules Garfinkle on the lower east side of New York, was considered too short, too dark, too Jewish. But he was a forceful performer who was true to type when he played a rebellious young man, cynically outside society, a born loser who knew what he was.

In his first film, *Four Daughters*, in 1938, he played the doomed composer, Mickey, and spoke lines that had the ring of the real truth in his life. Cigarette dangling from his lips, he plays one of his compositions for one of the sisters, played by Priscilla Lane. She says, "It's beautiful." He says, "It stinks. It hasn't got a beginning or an end, only a middle." She says he could give it a beginning and an end. He says, "What for? The fates are against me. They tossed a coin—heads, I'm poor, tails, I'm rich. But they tossed a two-headed coin."

The movie was designed for Errol Flynn, but he rejected it because he didn't like his part. It was offered to Van Heflin, but he was tied up in a Broadway play. Garfield fell into it. It was perfect for him. But it typed him, true to type. He was a rebel, tied to Warner Bros. by contract for years, but several times on suspension from the studio. He was hard to handle.

He had a smouldering sexuality on screen. And off. Despite a troubled marriage that lasted a long time, Garfield liked to take his leading ladies to bed. And other ladies. He had widely publicized affairs with Priscilla Lane during *Dust Be My Destiny*, Hedy Lamarr during *Tortilla Flat*, even an unlikely one with Joan Crawford during *Humoresque*.

When he made *The Postman Always Rings Twice*, he said, "I've had to learn different things to play my characters in different pictures, but I don't have to learn anything for this picture—I play a lover." The lady he loved was Lana Turner. And it was a powerful film version of James M. Cain's powerful novel.

Garfield's best performance probably was that of the ambitious boxer in Robert Rossen's *Body and Soul* in 1947. He gave a one-dimensional character three dimensions. He brought it to life.

That same year he gave a strong supporting performance as Gregory Peck's Jewish friend in *Gentleman's Agreement*. The next year he gave a forceful performance in one of the more underrated films, *Force of Evil*, but turned down Elia Kazan's offer to star on Broadway as Stanley Kowalski in the new play *A Streetcar Named Desire* because he did not feel he was offered enough money. Then he played the Hemingway character Harry Horgan better than Bogie or anyone else, according to Hemingway himself, in *The Breaking Point*, a superior remake of *To Have and Have Not*. No one noticed.

In the early 1950s, Garfield's reputation was smeared by the avid Communist hunt staged by The House Un-American Activities Committee and his career declined. He died of heart failure in his sleep in 1952 at the age of forty-nine. Apparently, he did not die, as was rumored in newspaper gossip columns, in the act of love. However, that was the way many wanted to think of him. Here, after all, was a fellow so sensual that the great French singer Edith Piaf invited him to her room to make love to her after seeing him in a stage production of *Peer Gynt*.

The real legacy Garfield left, however, was an acting style, though unrecognized by Oscar. It is a style that has always been slighted by Oscar. Garfield blazed a trail over which Marlon Brando, Montgomery Clift, James Dean, Paul Newman, and other realistic, sensitive young anti-heroes followed, and among these only Brando won Oscars. Even he did not win for the part that best suited his style, the Stanley Kowalski part in *A Streetcar Named Desire* that Garfield declined. Possibly Clift and Dean had greater range and gave greater depth to their portrayals of rebellious young men, but Garfield led the way.

The sexuality of Clift and Dean was different from Garfield's. Both were bisexual and tortured by it. Both were dissatisfied with success and unhappy in life. Clift, who had platonic love affairs with Elizabeth Taylor and the older Libby Holman, took to drink and drugs, behaved badly many times in his last years, and died at forty-five in 1966 of a heart attack. Dean, despairing over the loss of his love, Pier Angeli, to singer Vic Damone, lived recklessly in his last years, and died at twenty-four in 1955 in the crash of his sports car on the way to a road race. Yet, despite the short, tortured time they had in their aborted careers, both left a legacy of unforgettable roles behind them.

Clift may well have been the finest actor to have been denied an Academy Award. He was nominated for *The Search* in 1948, *A Place in the Sun* in 1951, *From Here to Eternity* in 1953, and *Judgment at Nuremberg* in 1961. He should have been nominated for *Red River* in 1948, *The Heiress* in 1949, and *The Misfits* in 1961. He could have won for any of these

Montgomery Clift gets comfort from Liz Taylor in A Place in the Sun.

films, and should have won for at least one. He was as sensitive as any actor we have had, and each portrayal he gave was close to perfect in the depths to which he took the character.

Clift was another great actor out of Omaha, but with no connection to the Brandos or Henry Fonda. His father was a banker and broker, who moved to New York when his son was five, while the mother travelled about the world with her three children. A serious, studious sort, the young Clift tried amateur theatrics and early on was driven by a desire to be an actor. Although the defection of John Garfield and Franchot Tone had all but destroyed The Group Theater, Clift was influenced greatly by it. One of its leading graduates, Elia Kazan, hesitated to cast Clift in *The Skin of Our Teeth* because of his rumored homosexuality, but met him, took to him, and gave him the part that made him prominent on stage.

Kazan helped form the Actors Studio in the middle 1940s. An offshoot of the group theater, it helped develop Clift, Brando, Karl Malden, Kevin McCarthy, Eli Wallach, David Wayne, Maureen Stapleton, Eva Marie Saint, Mildred Dunnock, and others into accomplished professionals. Clift and Brando developed a curious relationship of mistrust which lasted to Clift's death. They admired one another, but Clift liked to think a part through, while Brando relied on his instincts, and they always were arguing about "the right way" to act. Each had enormous natural acting ability and each would have given a different dimension to a part.

It is difficult to imagine Clift taking Brando's part in *Streetcar*, yet the slightly built Clift had an inner toughness strong enough to stand up to John Wayne in *Red River*. Clift became a nominal star on Broadway, whose talent attracted Hollywood offers. He resisted these offers for a year or more. He'd heard of Garfield's problems with parts. Clift wanted to be free to pick his own roles. Hollywood didn't grant such freedoms to young actors, usually. Clift couldn't resist the costarring part opposite Wayne in *Red River*. Guided by the great director Howard Hawks, Clift played Wayne's rebellious, "sissified" stepson and met the big guy head-on, fight scenes and all. Clift was an excellent actor and his was a superb, sensitive performance.

It was eighteen months before *Red River* was released in 1948. During that time, Clift made *The Search*, which was released first that same year. A low-budget film directed by the young Fred Zinnemann, *The Search* may be one of the most emotionally moving motion pictures ever made, but it never attracted a lot of attention. The film was the heartrending story of the search for each other by a mother and her young son in post-war Europe. More than anyone else, Clift made it the movie it was with his compassionate portrayal of the young soldier who befriends the boy.

The release of these two movies made him a matinee idol. Although neither movie had love scenes, his sensitivity touched teenagers. In reality, he despised his stardom and protected his privacy with a passion. A shy young man, he continued to withdraw more and more from the world. For awhile, he found satisfaction only on the screen. In *The Heiress*, his portrayal of the unscrupulous suitor was a match for Olivia De Havilland's touching title-role performance. Their love scenes were convincing, so much so that she was deluged by mail from fans protesting her shutting the door on him at the end. He worried about how his making love to an older woman might make him look, and dropped out of the role opposite Gloria Swanson in *Sunset Boulevard* that then went to William Holden.

Clift hit his peak playing the ambitious young man who murders his girlfriend, Shelley Winters, so as to be free to marry the boss's daughter, Elizabeth Taylor, in *A Place in the Sun*, the film version of Theodore Dreiser's *An American Tragedy*. His depiction of an awkward lad was so passionate and profound that it left a lasting impression on anyone who saw it.

However, the capper of his career came with his stunning depiction of Prewitt, the private who resists authority in James Jones' *From Here to Eternity*. The role was supposed to go to Aldo Ray or John Derek (the handsome young actor who later achieved greater prominence guiding the careers of beautiful young actresses, notably his wife, Bo, the "perfect ten" of the film, *10*). Director Fred Zinnemann demanded Clift and got him. Clift gave one of the great performances in film history. The critic for *The Saturday Review* wrote, "Clift reveals again his uncanny ability to lend eloquence to an incoherent personality. His eyes, his gestures unfailingly suggest the nuances of feelings that the scriptwriter dare not let him speak." Another critic called it, "*The* classic characterization." In our poll, both critics and fans voted it in the all-time top ten.

Burt Lancaster provided a powerful performance and won a nomination for his part in *From Here to Eternity* and possibly split the votes with Clift. Otherwise it is difficult to understand how the Oscar for 1953 went to Bill Holden for *Stalag 17*, good as he was in it. In any event, Clift's career careened downhill from there. Robert LaGuardia, who wrote *Monty*, his biography, believes that had his career ended there Clift would have had the greatest cult following of any figure in cinema history. However, it went on for thirteen more years, through what one of his acting teachers called "the slowest suicide in show business history."

Early in his career, Monty began leaning heavily on the advice of a lady who taught acting to many young stars at the Actors Studio. She was by his side on his sets and on the set of *The Heiress*, Olivia De Havilland said, "Monty played the part opposite her, not me." Some of his leading ladies objected to this, and she was ordered off his sets at times.

At least one leading lady, Elizabeth Taylor, took to him with understanding, however. Liz was at first infuriated when she found out he did not want to make love to her. With uncommon understanding for a young lady of nineteen, she decided she could be, at least, his friend, which she was to the end.

Clift was a curious individual, difficult to understand. He did not understand himself. But he had a great gift for acting. Some hated him, some loved him. On the set of *Eternity*, Lancaster hated him, Sinatra loved him.

An automobile accident in 1957 scarred and hardened his handsome, sensitive face, and he never really looked the same again. He drifted through disappointing films for years before he rallied with superb performances in three films in one year, 1961—*Wild River*, *The Misfits*, and *Judgment at Nuremberg*. Three ill-fated greats—Clift, Clark Gable, and Marilyn Monroe—all provided superb performances in the underrated and neglected *The Misfits*. Clift and yet another ill-fated great—Judy Garland—were among those who provided superb performances in *Judgment*.

Clift had cataracts removed from both eyes during the filming of *Freud* in 1962. He made only one film afterward, in Europe, before he died, dissipated and depressed, in a drunken stupor one night in 1966.

James Dean was similarly sensitive, talented, and driven. He, too, could show us more about a character with his eyes or hands, with a shrug of the head or movement of body than words could say. When he spoke, it was more the way he spoke than what he said. There was something within him yearning to get out, which he brought out subtly, convincingly, without histrionics. Like Clift, he underacted. Like Clift, he became the part he played. Like Clift, Dean had a haunting quality in his eyes, even in still photos. There is pain there. Life is not easy, his eyes say. He is

sharing that truth with us. Clift and Dean both shared with us.

Clift's smile was engaging, but Dean's was even more engaging. Women wanted to mother both, but men felt closer to Dean. There was sorrow in both, but more fun in Dean. Off the screen, Clift was more difficult to deal with than Dean. Clift was less secure in his profession. Dean dared more. Clift turned all but his truest friends against him, while Dean turned his friends on and off with the many shifts in his moods. He could be engaging and enraging in turn. Although both grew out of Garfield, each nevertheless was distinctly different.

Dean was born and reared in a small town in Indiana, but spent a lot of his youth in southern California. He observed classes at the Actors Studio in New York, broke onto the Broadway stage in the early 1950s, and did some television plays. He was still relatively unknown when a screen test took him to Hollywood. A further screen test with a young Paul Newman won Dean, from Newman, the part of Cal Trask in Elia Kazan's screen adaption of John Steinbeck's *East of Eden*.

Originally, the movie was to co-feature two brothers played by Brando and Clift. Kazan decided to feature one brother, Cal, and wanted an unknown. When he

James Dean confronts Jo Van Fleet in East of Eden.

met Dean and saw his test, he was sold. He took him to Steinbeck, who said, "This is Cal." The other brother became a minor role. Dean's scenes opposite his father, the stern Raymond Massey; his mother, the whore, played by Jo Van Fleet; and his girl, the tender Julie Harris, were remarkable in their varied intensity. Possibly no actor, not even Clift, brought such intensity to the screen.

Massey, Van Fleet, and Harris, all experienced performers of the highest stature, were remarkable in their roles in *East of Eden* but were more than matched by the youthful beginner. Massey, a trained, disciplined actor, did not like Dean, an instinctive, undisciplined actor. Massey was stunned by what Dean did in the birthday scene, but then so was Kazan. "No one, not even Brando, could shake an audience like Dean," the director said.

In that unforgettable scene, Cal has earned some money and he wants to give it to Adam, his father, who needs money. He gives it to him as a gift, wrapped with a ribbon. Adam fumbles with the package, opens it, sees the money, and says, "I don't need the money, Cal. I can't take it. I thank you for it, though."

Desperate, Cal says, "I'll put it away for you. I'll keep it for you."

Sternly, Adam says, "No, I won't ever want it. I would have been so happy if you could have given me . . . well, something like your brother has, something honest and human and good. Money, even clean money, doesn't stack up with that." Seeing Cal's anger, Adam adds, "Don't be angry, son. If you want to give me a present, give me a good life. That would be something I could value. . ."

Despairing, Cal lets the money drop. In the original script, he was to pick up the money, scream, and run out into the night. In the actual performance, Dean let the money flutter down his father's chest, then suddenly throws himself on his horrified father, hits him, hugs him, pleads for love from him in inarticulate despair before running from him, sobbing, from the house.

It is one of the great scenes in film history and conveys clearly that generation gap between father and son which always has existed and always will exist. It is the pivotal point in a powerful motion picture and it was made true by the instinctive invention of the young actor. Kazan said later, "Jimmy always put something into a scene that wasn't in the script. Sometimes it was taken out, sometimes it was left in. In retrospect, too much was taken out. Fortunately, the birthday scene was left in. He had a feel for a character none of us had. He knew what was right better than we did, but we didn't believe it. He was too young."

Dean's performance in *East of Eden* was rated fourth best by the fans and tenth best by critics in our poll. Dean went from *East of Eden* into *Rebel Without a Cause*. This performance was rated in the top twenty by the fans we polled. Again he played a young man alienated from his father and the world, only in modern dress, and at a high school instead of a farm. Here, he is not the only rebel. He is a newcomer at a school full of rebellious young people. Few films have seriously and successfully portrayed high school life with any great degree of depth and reality. No other film ever really captured the feelings of high school youth, as evidenced by the way high school youth admired Dean and this film. Critic Steven Early wrote, "More than any other actor, Dean was the symbol of misunderstood youth, and within weeks young people had transformed him and his screen character into a national cult."

In *Rebel*, Dean's scenes with "the gang," in which he engages one member in a knife fight and in a "chicken run," in which one racing car carries its driver to his death over a cliff, are raw and real, almost sexual. His scenes with Judy, as played by Natalie Wood, are curiously less sexual, the stuff of which romantic dreams are made. His scenes with Plato, as played by Sal Mineo, are the brotherhood of broken dreams. Again, however, it is his scenes with his screen father, here played well by the cartoon *Mr. Magoo*, Jim Backus, that have the most impact.

Following the knife fight, Dean sneaks into his room with a bloody shirt, is found by his father, and confronts his father with his moral dilemma—should he stand up and fight? The father, a coward by nature, says, "Listen, nobody should make a snap decision. This isn't something you just . . . We ought to consider the pros and cons. . ." The son says, "We don't have time." The father says, "We'll make time. Where's some paper? We'll make a list." Furious, the son asks, "What can you do when you have to be a man?" The father is stunned. It is too big a question for him to handle. "What?" he asks.

The son stands before him, suddenly bigger than he is. "You going to stop me, Dad?" he asks. Playing the good guy, his father says, "You know I never stop you from anything." The son knows, suddenly, finally, his father can not help him. Dean's posture makes this painfully clear. Giving up, he starts to dress to go out. His father is saying, "Believe me, you're at a wonderful age. In ten years you'll look back on this and wish you were a kid again. When you're older, you'll laugh at yourself for thinking this is so important. . ."

Dean knows the importance of this turning point in his life. He feels he has to stand up and die if necessary. He grabs his jacket and runs from his stunned father and his house, shouting, "Ten years...ten years... ten years." This painful cry into the night was an invention of Dean's, on the spur of the scene. Originally, he was simply to slam the door behind him. The way he played it impressed the pain of his confusion upon the viewer with shattering impact.

Later, after the "accident" in which the other boy careens over a cliff, Dean confronts his parents with the reality of his "crime" and says he has to confess to the authorities. He does not expect his mother to understand, but he hopes somehow his father will. His mother says, "I don't want him to go to the police. There were other people involved and why should he be the only one involved." Dean says, "But I *am* involved. I was in a crime, Mom. A boy was killed. You don't get out of that by pretending it didn't happen!"

His father says, "You know you did wrong. That's the main thing, isn't it?" The son says, "No! It's nothing. Just nothing." The father, pleading for time, says, "Son, this is all happening so fast..." The son says, out of time and out of patience, "You better give me something, Dad. You better give me something fast. Dad? Aren't you going to stand up for me?" His dad does nothing. He does not know what to do.

Suddenly, Dean screams, "Dad," and leaps at his father with all his searing frustration. He puts his hands around his father's throat and drags him down the stairs. His mother is screaming, "Stop it. You'll kill him, Jim. Do you want to kill your father?" Of course, he does. He wants to strangle him with his bare hands. He wants to get something, at last, out of the old man. But, even this, he cannot get. There is no revenge to be had on a failed father. The son flees once more into the night.

This scene was developed by Dean to its stunning climax. Originally, he was simply to turn from his father. It was Dean's device to fall on his father. Had he not had a real rage within him, he never would have been able to knock down and drag the hefty actor around as he did. Backus was stunned by it, outraged by it, but he went with it, and wound up pleased by it. Director Nicholas Ray said, "Dean did things by instinct that the greatest writers and actors could not reach with all the thought and deliberation in the world."

Biographer David Dalton wrote, "As the adolescent Jim Stark, Jimmy enacted that 'awkward stage' with the intensity of one who has never left it. *Rebel* is

Jimmy's movie. All its currents flow through him....It is his epitaph." It was, in a way, though he made one more movie, *Giant*, the following year. I thought he was miscast as Jett Rink in *Giant*, though others thought otherwise. Costarring with Rock Hudson and Elizabeth Taylor, he did give off sparks. As she had earlier with Montgomery Clift, the sympathetic Taylor became a buddy to Jimmy Dean, but he died within weeks of the finish of the film.

Dean died, in a car crash, at age twenty-four in September of 1955. In the spring of 1956 he became the first actor ever nominated for an Academy Award posthumously, for *Eden*, not for *Rebel*, and again was nominated the following spring for *Giant*, but he did not win either year. It seems almost incredible now, but he lost the first year to Ernest Borgnine's *Marty*. It is difficult to decide which was his better role, Cal Trask or Jim Stark. Some people have made something of the fact that the same five letters are in both last names. Some people have created a cult devoted to the memory of Dean, denying even that he is dead.

In the memory of many, he is more alive today than many who are alive. This, of course, is the miracle of the movies. As long as the film endures, the star endures. For me, the memory of Cal Trask as done by Dean is as vivid as the day I first saw it and no Oscar, however deserved, could make it more memorable.

When Dean died, he was signed to do two films, portraying the outlaw Billy the Kid in *The Left-Handed Gun* and the boxer Rocky Graziano in *Somebody Up There Likes Me*. Paul Newman inherited both parts. The first won him the Cannes Film Festival Best Actor Award and the second made him a star. He won nominations for Oscars for *Cat on a Hot Tin Roof* in 1958, *The Hustler* in 1961, *Hud* in 1963, and *Cool Hand Luke* in 1967. He deserved nominations for *Butch Cassidy and the Sundance Kid* in 1969 and *The Sting* in 1973, but did not get them. He has never won an Oscar, and few actors deserve one more.

Newman was the natural successor to Clift and Dean. He came out of Cleveland, studied dramatics in college, attended the Actors Studio in New York, and vied with Dean, Steve McQueen, and Robert Redford for parts in plays on Broadway and on television. His stage role as the drifter in *Picnic* took him to Hollywood, but the movie part went to William Holden. With his sensitive talents, his rugged good looks, and his expressive blue eyes, he succeeded in becoming a film star, perhaps the dominant star of the 1960s. In addition to acting, his talent extended to directing and producing. He directed his wife, Joanne Woodward,

Hud *with Melvyn Douglas and Paul Newman.*

Paul Newman and Robert Redford in The Sting.

ckie Gleason and Paul Newman prepare to shoot in The
ustler.

exceptionally well in *Rachel, Rachel* in 1968 and has
directed several other films since.

Newman and Woodward were married in 1958.
They have been active politically, primarily for liberal
causes. Perhaps this political activity has hurt his
image with some Academy Award voters. Newman
has been selective about his films and has made more
high quality movies than most actors, but none has
been a really big film or an Academy Award winner

except *The Sting*. Newman did not win for his extraordinary performance in it.

Almost all of his screen performances have been
outstanding, full of good humor and great insight. His
modern-day cowboy in *Hud* and his pool shark in *The
Hustler* are among his best. He may have come closest
to winning an Oscar for his convict in *Cool Hand Luke*,
but Rod Steiger, having been denied for the deserving
Pawnbroker two years earlier, was sentimentally selected for *In the Heat of the Night*.

Unfortunately, Newman had, save for *The Sting*,
few choice parts in the 1970s. Now in his fifties, he has
turned with surprising success to car racing but continues his acting. The combination of his matinee-idol
good looks and his advancing age may have somewhat
curtailed his acting opportunities but his talent has been
too great to have been so long neglected by Oscar and
is too great a talent to be denied further opportunities.

The Jimmy Dean role in *Rebel* was originally
readied for Brando, but he was too old for it by the time
it went to camera. The Paul Newman role in *Butch
Cassidy and the Sundance Kid*, too, originally was
written for Brando. The Robert Redford role was to go
to Jack Lemmon. When Lemmon withdrew, Warren
Beatty was offered it. When Brando and Beatty
rejected the parts, Newman and Redford took them
and made the movie one of the warmest, most charming westerns ever. It was nominated for the Oscar in
1969, but neither Newman nor Redford were. Yet the
story wouldn't have worked without their warmth and
charm. They were a captivating team, reunited four
years later for the Oscar-winning *Sting*. Redford was
nominated for his part this time, but not the neglected
Newman. Newman's performance in *Butch Cassidy*
finished in the top ten and Redford's in the top twenty-
five in our fan vote.

A blue-eyed blond from southern California, Redford's Hollywood looks may have caused the critics to
underrate him. He studied at the American Academy
of Dramatic Arts, starred on Broadway, and from his
first film, the "sleeper" *War Hunt* in 1962, gave a
series of smashing performances. These include the
Sundance Kid in 1969, *The Candidate* and *Jeremiah
Johnson* in 1972, *The Way We Were* in 1973, and *All
the President's Men* in 1976. He was executive producer of the last one. Aside from acting, he is an out-
doorsman and a conservationist.

Redford and Steve McQueen were two of the most
popular and highest-paid performers in films in the
1960s, yet both were denied their due as actors.

A troubled youth, McQueen spent time in reform
school and worked carnivals, lumberjack camps, and
oil fields across the country. He was in and quickly out

of the Marines. He then studied at New York's Neighborhood Playhouse and the Actors Studio and became a star on television with *Wanted, Dead or Alive*. He was nominated for an Oscar for *The Sand Pebbles* in 1966, but also gave meritorious performances in *Love with the Proper Stranger* in 1963, *The Cinncinnati Kid* in 1965, and *The Thomas Crown Affair* and *Bullitt* in 1968. Handsome and magnetic, McQueen, a daredevil motorcyclist and car racer, seemed to have fallen from favor in the 1970s, but he likewise seemed to have lost interest in the Hollywood scene until he began to take roles again late in the decade.

Two actors of great ability and little opportunity have been Richard Kiley and Robert Culp. Kiley made less than ten pictures in thirty years. He won a Tony on Broadway for his unsurpassed *Man of La Mancha*, but made only one movie musical, *The Little Prince*, in 1974. A dramatic actor of rare power, he has had few movie roles of power but played the father in *Looking for Mr. Goodbar* in 1977 powerfully enough to deserve a Supporting Actor Award. He did not even get a nomination. Robert Culp, a skilled, subtle actor, who creates marvelous little touches in his characterizations, has been outrageously neglected on the big screen. His only role of note was in the comedy *Bob & Carol & Ted & Alice* in 1969.

Anthony Perkins, the son of stage and screen actor Osgood Perkins, was sort of a "pretty boy." His exciting talent finally exploded on the screen in his role as maniacal killer Norman Bates in Hitchcock's *Psycho* in 1960. He was not nominated for an Oscar but his performance is one of the best remembered in Hollywood history and has obscured all of his other work. He earlier had been nominated for his part as a young son in *Friendly Persuasion* in 1956. Other excellent performances by Perkins include his characterizations in *Fear Strikes Out* in 1957, *Desire Under the Elms* in 1958, *Pretty Poison* in 1968, *Play It as It Lays* in 1972, and *Lovin' Molly* in 1974. In addition to his American films, he worked in Europe for about ten years.

Also long regarded as a "pretty boy," Warren Beatty proved himself to be a major all-around talent when he produced and starred in *Bonnie and Clyde* in 1967 and *Heaven Can Wait* in 1978. He codirected the latter with Buck Henry and collaborated on the writing of this remake of *Here Comes Mr. Jordan* with Elaine May, formerly of the Elaine and Mike comedy duo. He was nominated in each capacity for both movies.

He also was nominated as coauthor of *Shampoo* in 1975. He could well have won nominations as an actor for *Splendor in the Grass* in 1961, *All Fall Down* in 1962, *Mickey One* in 1965, and *McCabe and Mrs. Miller* in 1971. Known as Shirley MacLaine's brother and regarded as Hollywood's "lover of lovers" off the screen, he has not been appropriately honored for his work on the screen.

Sidney Poitier is the only black actor to have won an Academy Award. In the 1940s and 1950s James Edwards got the good black roles, but was denied nominations for them. More recently, Yaphet Kotto has been a knockout in *Report to the Commissioner* in 1975 and *Brubaker* in 1979 without attracting attention. Maybe the best black actor the movies have had has been James Earl Jones, nominated for *The Great White Hope* in 1970, but not for *Claudine* in 1974. His portrayal of Jack Johnson in *Hope* was as stunning as the screen has seen. His expressive eyes projected smouldering fury more than any words could have. Yet, in recent years the only interesting role he has been offered was to speak the part of Darth Vader, uncredited, in *Star Wars* and *The Empire Strikes Back*. Only on television has he had the chance to use a talent as big as any actor's.

A number of enormously sensitive and skilled young actors have put powerful performances on the small screen that they have not had the opportunity to put on the big screen. Actors like James Dean, Paul Newman, and Steve McQueen made the jump from television to movies in the early years of TV, but that jump has been harder to make recently. There are few more skilled or sensitive actors than Michael Moriarity, but *Bang the Drum Slowly* in 1973 and *Report to the Commissioner* in 1975 have been his sole movie opportunities of note. Alan Alda and Martin Sheen were not even nominated for splendid performances in *The Seduction of Joe Tynan* and *Apocalypse Now*, respectively, in 1979. William Devane is a superb actor who needs only a chance. Carrol O'Connor could by another Wallace Beery, but perhaps having been Archie Bunker is enough.

Hal Holbrook and Dennis Weaver have been television's finest dramatic actors in recent years, starring in some TV movies that have been equal to the finest theater movies. Holbrook could be another Spencer Tracy, or a first Hal Holbrook. His Mark Twain tours have been brilliant. He has been brilliant in one TV movie after another, including *The Minnesota Strip* in 1980. Weaver emerged from his "Gunsmoke" origins to give one super performance after another in a wide array of TV dramas, but has not had a decent

Al Pacino comforts John Cazale in The Godfather Part II.

chance on the big screen. These are two of our great acting talents, neglected by movies.

Another direct descendant of John Garfield's acting style, James Caan, came to prominence as the ill-fated Brian Piccolo in TV's lauded *Brian's Song* and as a supporting actor nominee for his role as Sonny Corleone in *The Godfather* in 1972. Born in The Bronx and reared in Queens, he was the son of a kosher meat dealer. An all-around athlete and daring rodeo competitor, he was also a convincing performer in *Cinderella Liberty* in 1973, *The Gambler* and *Godfather Part II* in 1974, *Comes a Horseman* in 1978, and *Chapter Two* in 1979. His portrayal of the title role in *The Gambler* was for a time considered a dark-horse candidate for Oscar, but it didn't even win a nomination.

More direct descendants of Garfield's acting technique, perhaps more sensitive actors, perfectionists driven to excess to capture the spirit of their portrayals and sometimes difficult to deal with, are Al Pacino, Robert DeNiro, and Richard Gere.

Like Caan, Pacino won a nomination as a supporting actor in *The Godfather* in 1972, for his role as Michael Corleone. He was also nominated as a starring actor in the same role in *The Godfather Part II* in 1974. In addition, he won nominations as a starring actor in *Serpico* in 1973, and *Dog Day Afternoon* in 1975, but was denied Oscar four years straight. He gave other outstanding performances in *Panic in Needle Park* in 1971 and *Scarecrow* in 1975, but was denied nominations. Like Caan, he is from The Bronx, but Italian. He was educated at the Actors Studio and has remained loyal to the stage, winning awards for his performances on Broadway. He remains neglected as far as Hollywood and its Oscars are concerned.

Another New Yorker, Robert DeNiro, did win an Oscar for his supporting part as the young Vito Corleone (the original Brando role) in *The Godfather Part II*, but it was, in fact, a starring role. He was also sensational in *Bang the Drum Slowly* and *Mean Streets* in 1973, *The Last Tycoon* in 1976, and *New York, New York* in 1977, and won other Oscar nominations for *Taxi Driver* in 1976 and *The Deer Hunter* in 1978. His performances as a steelworker who volunteers for service in Vietnam and returns deeply disturbed in *The Deer Hunter* was so powerful that people were shocked when he lost, even to Jon Voight's paralyzed veteran of Vietnam in *Coming Home*.

Although trained for the stage by Stella Adler and Lee Strasberg, DeNiro has made the movies his medium. He actually worked many months as a taxi driver in New York and as a steelworker in Pennsylvania to prepare for his roles in those occupations. He was willing to put on fifty pounds to play the part of faded fighter Jake LaMotta for *The Bronx Bull*. He does what he has to do to become the person he is playing, and he becomes that person with remarkable realism. "He has many persons in him," Elia Kazan says, and critic Paul Gardner remarked, "He undergoes a chilling metamorphosis with each part." He is considered by many critics to be our finest modern actor. One Oscar does not seem enough for him.

Of his acting, DeNiro says, "The more you become a star, the more the temptation to prepare less for your performances. But a star has more responsibility to his performance than another actor. I want to be an actor, not a star. I am not concerned with any awards I receive, only the performance I give. If I don't satisfy myself, then it doesn't matter if I satisfy others. And I am very hard to satisfy. In fact, I haven't been satisfied yet. But I do prepare and I do try to bring something special to each part."

Blooming late, Bruce Dern has developed over twenty years into an actor of intelligence and instinct. Originally typecast in maniacal parts, he has contributed striking characterizations to *The King of Marvin Gardens* in 1972, *The Great Gatsby* in 1974, and *Smile* in 1975. His sole reward has been a nomination for his superb performance in *Coming Home* in 1978, but he lost.

Robert DeNiro is ready to let the enemy have it in The Deer Hunter.

Newcomer Richard Gere, out of Syracuse, has a smouldering sensuality and serious purpose that may pay off in prominence. He has yet to be nominated, but gave impressive performances in *Looking for Mr. Goodbar* in 1977, *Days of Heaven* and *Bloodbrothers* in 1978, and *Yanks* and *American Gigolo* in 1979.

Some critics consider Jack Nicholson to be our finest modern actor. He has won one Oscar, for *One Flew over the Cuckoo's Nest* in 1975. It was a stunning, staggering performance he gave. Yet it is not clear that it was superior to his performances in *Easy Rider* in 1969, *Five Easy Pieces* in 1970, *The Last Detail* in 1973, and *Chinatown* in 1974, for which he won nominations, or *Carnal Knowledge* in 1971 or *The Passenger* in 1975, for which he did not win nominations.

Like DeNiro, Nicholson has not given less than an outstanding performance in each part he's played. Nicholson actually started his career in motorcycle quickies and is one of the few stars to rise from the "B" ranks of films. Although he has a more identifiable personality, Nicholson, too, takes on the coloration of each role and is a remarkable actor.

An actor of top quality, Dustin Hoffman has won only one Oscar, despite nominations for *The Graduate* in 1967, *Midnight Cowboy* in 1969, and *Lenny* in 1974, and performances worthy of nomination in *Little Big Man* in 1970 and *Straight Time* in 1978. *Kramer vs. Kramer* in 1979 finally brought him his Oscar. He also won the New York and Los Angeles Film Critics Award for it.

A Californian, trained at the Pasadena Playhouse but developed on Broadway, Hoffman is a typical modern anti-hero hero, an unlikely star, but an actor of enormous range and depth who brings superb personal touches to each part.

Hoffman says, "It's very hard being an actor. At least, it's hard for me. Maybe because I want to do something special with each part, but each part isn't special. It was only a little easier with *Midnight Cowboy* because the script was so special. I've had good parts since then, but nothing that good. I don't worry about winning awards. I don't know how you judge those things. I sure didn't want to feel I was in competition with Jon Voight in *Cowboy*. I wanted to work with him, not against him."

That Hoffman's incomparable bum, Ratso Rizzo, in *Midnight Cowboy* lost to John Wayne's typical cowboy in *True Grit* is a triumph only of Hollywood's sentimentality. Wayne was a larger-than-life legend whose image will endure long after Hoffman is all but forgotten. Wayne was a personality. Hoffman is an actor, and it has to be hoped that Hoffman's Ratso

Dustin Hoffman in Lenny *is frisked by cops.*

Rizzo is the characterization that will be remembered. It may well have been the most complex and complete characterization of the late 1960s.

Jon Voight won a nomination for his title role in *Midnight Cowboy*, and his stunning performance in that Award-winner perhaps split the vote and made Dustin a loser. Here we celebrate losers who deserve to be remembered, and Dustin Hoffman as Ratso Rizzo is one of the classic cases in kind. The character's desperate scuffling for survival was made painfully real by Hoffman's performance. Ratso will live with Laughton's Captain Bligh, Gable's Rhett Butler, Brando's Stanley Kowalski, Bogart's Rick, and so many other memorable portrayals that didn't win the Oscar.

Laughton, Gable, and Bogart are gone. Garfield, Dean, and Clift are gone. Aging, Stewart and Fonda go on, but rarely in roles worthy of them. Brando and Newman carry on, but rarely in stellar roles. Nicholson and Hoffman select their roles so sparingly that each made only two movies in the last three years of the 1970s. Brando is in his late fifties now and his successors, such as Hoffman, Nicholson, and Pacino, are forty or older as the 1980s begin. Only DeNiro is still in his mid-thirties. The acting tigers of the 1970s may begin to give way to young lions in the 1980s. However, like Muni and Tracy in the 1930s, they have given us roles to remember, whether or not properly rewarded for them.

F I V E

The Actresses

HOLLYWOOD long has favored actors over actresses. It is not clear if this is because more women are faithful fans of films than men. In general, the meatier roles have gone to actors. More actors have been superstars.

In the history of Hollywood, three actresses have stood out—Katharine Hepburn, Bette Davis, and Ingrid Bergman. Hepburn has had the most Oscar nominations, eleven, and the most victories, three. Bergman also has had three victories—in seven nominations—but one was in the supporting category. Davis has had ten nominations and two victories. Typically, Hepburn and Davis did not win for the films for which they are most famous.

Hepburn won for *Morning Glory* in 1933, *Guess Who's Coming to Dinner* in 1967, and *The Lion in Winter* in 1968. She was nominated for *The African Queen* in 1951, but did not win. In our polls, the critics considered this the finest female performance in film history. The fans rated it sixth best. The fans rated her performance in *The Philadelphia Story* ninth best, the critics set it twelfth best. She was nominated for this in 1940, but did not win.

She topped both the fans' and critics' lists of actresses. She was nominated for the most different films by the fans, eighteen, and the critics, eight. She received the most votes for all films from both.

Clearly, Kate is special. She was born in November of 1907 in Hartford, Connecticut, to a prominent family. Her father was a famous surgeon, her mother a

noted suffragette who early crusaded for birth control. As one biography notes, she was brought up "in an atmosphere of complete spiritual freedom and spartan physical discipline." Educated at Bryn Mawr, she went on to reflect this upbringing as an adult. She was the first to wear slacks in Hollywood. (Marlene Dietrich also wore them.)

She began acting as an amateur at age twelve. She was on Broadway by the time she was twenty-one. Opinionated and temperamental, she was frequently fired from casts for the trouble she caused. But there was no doubt that she could act.

She entered movies with *A Bill of Divorcement*, opposite John Barrymore, in 1932, when she was twenty-four. She won her first Oscar for her third film, *Morning Glory*. She did not win another for more than twenty years, but had many hits.

In 1934, she made an unsuccessful return to Broadway in *The Lake*. She was stung by critic Dorothy Parker's famous comment that she "ran the gamut of emotions from A to B."

Hepburn provided delightful performances in 1938 in the films *Bringing Up Baby* and *Holiday* and in 1940 in *The Philadelphia Story*, all with Cary Grant. She made a successful return to Broadway in *The Philadelphia Story* before making the movie.

The film version of *The Philadelphia Story* also starred James Stewart. It won the Academy Award for him and the New York Critics Award for Hepburn. It is best remembered for her delightful Tracy Lord. In this madcap comedy of high society manners and morals,

Katharine Hepburn with Humphrey Bogart in The African Queen.

One of many Katharine Hepburn-Spencer Tracy comedy classics, Woman of the Year.

she set the style for all the poor little rich girl roles to follow.

She was married once, early in her life, from 1928 to 1934, to Ludlow Ogden Smith. Although she has protected her privacy fiercely, she is known to have had romances with sculptor Robert McKnight, billionaire Howard Hughes, agent Leland Hayward, and actor Spencer Tracy.

Her romance with Tracy endured twenty-five years, from their first film together, *Woman of the Year* in 1942, to their last, *Guess Who's Coming to Dinner* in 1967, after which he died. Their romance was protected by the Hollywood press and accepted by all concerned. At one point during his final illness, she alternated with his wife, Louise, spending her time at his bedside.

Yet, she seemed to some the epitome of the spinster and is best remembered for her role as the spinster Rose Sayer, opposite Humphrey Bogart's Charlie All-

Bette Davis with George Brent in Dark Victory.

Bette Davis with Leslie Howard in Of Human Bondage.

nutt, in *The African Queen*. He won the Academy Award for it, she didn't. His was a great performance, but hers may have been greater, full of a flint which gave off sparks.

One critic recalls,"It is the morning after. The prim and virginal Katharine has at last surrendered in the cabin of Bogart's boat. How do we know—with no lovemaking scene, no explicit dialogue? Miss Hepburn simply emerges from the cabin, takes a breath of air, looks out at the world in a new way, and we know. Her greatest moment!"

Katharine Hepburn has made more than forty movies in nearly forty years through the end of the 1970s. She has won more Best Actress Academy Awards than any other actress, but ironically she is best remembered for a role for which she did not win. She stamped each character with her peculiar personality, and once said, "Show me an actress who isn't a personality and I'll show you a woman who isn't a star."

Bette Davis is a great star who said, "I was the first star who ever came out of the water looking wet." She was pretty, but never a "pretty girl." She, too, was a personality.

Davis won Oscars for *Dangerous* in 1935 and *Jezebel* in 1938, but is better remembered by far for *Of Human Bondage* in 1934, *Dark Victory* in 1939, and *All About Eve* in 1950. She was not even nominated for her role as the bitchy Mildred in the film version of W. Somerset Maugham's *Bondage*, but the oversight was so outrageous that hundreds of members of the Academy wrote her name on their ballots anyway.

She was born Ruth Davis in April of 1908 in Lowell, Massachussetts and wanted to be an actress early on. Not an immediate hit, however, she was rejected as a student by Eva Le Gallienne and fired from her first role in summer stock by George Cukor. In 1930, she failed a screen test at Goldwyn Studios, but tested for and was signed by Universal despite studio head Carl Laemmle's comment when he first saw her, "She has as much sex appeal as Slim Summerville."

George Arliss brought her to Warners to play opposite him in *The Man Who Played God* in 1932. She made many mediocre movies there before she convinced Jack Warner to let her do *Bondage* on loan to RKO. "Go hang yourself," he'd said.

Of Human Bondage was her twenty-second film. "I only got the part because no other star wanted to play

Bette Davis slaps crippled Joan Crawford in What Ever Happened to Baby Jane?

such a despicable woman," says Davis.

Director John Cromwell tried to glamorize her, but Bette insisted on playing the slut her character was. For instance, when she awoke in bed in the morning, she was a mess. Costar Leslie Howard didn't like the idea of an American playing a British part with a British cast, but she quickly mastered a Cockney accent.

"Yew cad, yew dirty swine," she says to the crippled hero. "I never cared for yew—not once. I was always making a fool of yuh. Yuh bored me stiff. I hated yuh. It made me sick when I had to let yuh kiss me. I only did it because yuh begged me. Yuh hounded me, yuh drove me crazy, and after yuh kissed me, I always used to wipe my mouth. Wipe me mouth."

It is believed by many that the film community was so furious that Davis did not get even a nomination for *Bondage* that it voted her the Award for *Dangerous* the next year, even though it was a mediocre movie.

She was so good, Frank Capra tried to get her for *It Happened One Night* but Warners refused a second straight loan-out. So the part and an Academy Award went to Claudette Colbert. Davis later got even when Colbert had to drop out of *All About Eve* with a bad back. Davis got the part, if not the Oscar. Later she

went to Claudette and told her, "I owe you my life." Claudette sighed and said, "You killed me."

Davis was put in so many mediocre movies at Warners that she walked out one day, forfeiting the part of Scarlett O'Hara in *Gone With the Wind* in the process. She would not have wanted to play it opposite Errol Flynn, but it would have been her only chance to play opposite Clark Gable, the other great star of the 1930s.

She went to England and sued to get out of her contract. She lost, but won greater respect from Warners, who even paid her court costs. Returning, she played a *Gone With the Wind*-type role in *Jezebel* in 1938 and won her second Oscar. The following year she played an even greater role in *Dark Victory.*

Frank Nugent wrote in the *New York Times,* "Bette Davis won an Academy Award last year for her performance in *Jezebel,* a spottily effective film. Now, it is more than ever apparent that the award was premature. It should have been deferred until her *Dark Victory* came along. Miss Davis is superb. More than that, she is enchanted and enchanting.

"Admittedly it is a great role—rangy, full-bodied, and designed for a virtuosa, almost sure to invite the faint damning of 'tour de force.' But that must not detract from the eloquence, the tenderness, the heartbreaking sincerity with which she has played it."

Her performance as the doomed Judith Traherne, opposite George Brent and Humphrey Bogart, lost to Vivien Leigh's Scarlett O'Hara, which is the all-time favorite of the fans in our poll and fourth finest in the critics' portion. So one can not complain. Her Judith however was a better performance than Bette had given in either of her Oscar winning roles.

It may be the most controlled performance she ever gave. "Marry?" she says to Brent. "Oh, wouldn't it be marvelous if we could...have a real wedding...and be given away...church bells and champagne...and a white frock and orange blossoms and a wedding cake. That's one thing I won't have missed, and you're giving it to me. I can never love you enough."

She says, "When I made *Dark Victory,* Jack Warner said, 'Who wants to see some dame go blind and die?' But he let me do it because I wanted it so much." She adds, "I approved of my performance in *Dark Victory* more than I did the one I gave in *Of Human Bondage,* but I was not as disappointed in not winning the Award. Everyone said I would win for *Of Human Bondage,* so I took it for granted I would. I was heartbroken when I lost. But I learned you can never take an Oscar for granted. It was easy to accept losing for *Dark Victory* because Vivien Leigh did such a good job in *Gone With the Wind.*"

Her career continued to rise in the early 1940s, but began to decline toward the end of the decade. *All About Eve* in 1951 was about a fading star, Margo Channing, supposedly modelled on Tallulah Bankhead. The part was supposed to go to Marlene Dietrich, then Claudette Colbert, but Bette got it. She considers it her all-time favorite. "My part was exactly right for me. I didn't have to worry about my looks. If you have to be concerned about your appearance, acting goes out the window. Margo Channing was past forty. So was I. I was supposed to look the way I did."

Time Magazine wrote, "Actress Davis, who submits herself to harsh lighting, unflattering camera angles, and messy makeup, gives the picture's showiest role, which may be the best performance of her career." It said she played "a thoroughly convincing theatrical first lady given to spats, rage, and drunken maunderings. She commands sympathy and even admiration for a character whom the audience is prepared to hate."

The New York Critics voted it the finest female performance of the year. Both Bette, as the falling star, and costar Anne Baxter, as the shooting star, were nominated by the Academy and may have divided votes. The Oscar went to Judy Holliday for *Born Yesterday*. In our poll, both fans and critics rated it above Holliday's performance. They, in fact, termed Bette's the second best performance ever by an actress.

In the film, Margo says, "Funny business, a woman's career. The things you drop on your way up the ladder—so you can move faster—you forget you'll need them again when you go back to being a woman. That's one career all females have in common, whether we like it or not—being a woman. Sooner or later, we've got to work at it, no matter what other careers we've had or wanted. And in the last analysis, nothing is any good unless you can look up just before dinner, or turn around in bed, and there he is. Without that, you're not a woman. You're something with a French provincial office, or a book full of clippings. But you're not a woman."

Davis has been married and divorced four times. She always said whatever she won for Eve, she lost when she met and married her costar in it, Gary Merrill. She has three children, two of them adopted, and has continued her career through many ups and downs. She even took out an ad in a trade paper to advertise her availability as an actress in the late 1950s. She scored a success in the early 1960s with another faded star, Joan Crawford, in *What Ever Happened to Baby Jane?* Altogether, she has made more than eighty movies in almost fifty years and as the 1970s ended was still active in her seventies.

Ingrid Bergman's career was less controversial, though her personal life was more controversial. Born in Stockholm in August of 1915, she became Sweden's leading actress. Her performance in the Swedish film *Intermezzo* in 1936 led David O. Selznick to bring her here for an American version in 1939, opposite Leslie Howard. She enjoyed one success after another, including *Casablanca* in 1943 and *Gaslight*, for which she won an Oscar, in 1944.

She and Dr. Peter Lindstrom had been married since 1937 and had a daughter, Pia, now a TV commentator in New York. When Ingrid left him in 1948 for the famed director Roberto Rossellini, there was surprising agitation against her. She was called "Hollywood's apostle of degradation" on the floor of the U.S. Senate. Presumably, attitudes would be different today. Although she married Rossellini in 1950 and had three children with him, she was kept from Hollywood for seven years at the height of her acting talent. Her films with him were failures.

She returned triumphantly to win an Oscar for *Anastasia* in 1956. Ironically, Bergman was cast in *Anastasia* only after Jennifer Jones turned it down and, earlier, she got *Gaslight* and *Casablanca* after Hedy Lamarr turned them down.

Her marriage to Rossellini was, curiously, annulled in 1957. She then married Swedish theatrical producer Lars Schmidt the next year. Bergman has acted infrequently since, but she won her third Oscar for a supporting part in *Murder on the Orient Express* in 1974 and received another nomination for *Autumn Sonata* in 1978, by which time she was in her sixties. She won another New York Critics Award for this film.

Aside from Bette Davis, Ingrid Bergman, and Vivien Leigh, four others have won Best Actress Awards twice—Olivia De Havilland, Jane Fonda, Elizabeth Taylor, and Glenda Jackson. De Havilland and Fonda have been nominated five times each, Taylor and Jackson four times.

De Havilland won with *To Each His Own* in 1946 and *The Heiress* in 1949. Both were superb performances, comparable to those she gave in *Hold Back the Dawn* in 1941 and *The Snake Pit* in 1948, but it is the latter for which she is best remembered.

Her performance as Virginia, the housewife who lands in a lunatic asylum, was a powerful part of a motion picture that was daring for its time. "I think of it as my best," she has said. Bosley Crowther in the *New York Times* wrote that she did "a brilliant, heart-rending job" and called the film "true" and "illuminating."

The New York Film Critics voted her performance the best of the year, as it did her role in *The Heiress* the following year, but her *Snake Pit* lost out to Jane Wyman's *Johnny Belinda* in the Oscar race.

De Havilland also was nominated as Best Supporting Actress for *Gone With the Wind*, but lost out to teammate Hattie McDaniel. Olivia says, "I was deeply disappointed until I realized I really wasn't a supporting actress."

Elizabeth Taylor had to be helped into the auditorium in 1960 after surviving a serious, well-publicized bout with pneumonia. Her Oscar for *Butterfield 8* that year was strictly due to sentiment. In retrospect, it is difficult to believe that Deborah Kerr was denied for *The Sundowners* that year.

Liz's Academy Award for *Who's Afraid of Virginia Woolf?* in 1966 was something else, a well-earned reward for her finest performance. The New York Critics agreed, as did the critics and fans in our poll. The critics put it in the top ten of all time, the fans rated it third best ever.

Glenda Jackson's triumph for *Women in Love* in 1970 was surprising, but there was a scarcity of celebrated opposition that year, although Jane Alexander's deeply moving performance in *The Great White Hope* was superior. The gifted Jackson's triumph for *A Touch of Class* over Joanne Woodward in *Summer Wishes, Winter Dreams* in 1973 was even more surprising.

Jane Fonda's victory for *Klute* in 1971 was no surprise, but that the critics in our poll rated it the third best performance ever among actresses and the fans voted it fourth best was. Jane was again honored with the Oscar for her sensitive portrayal in *Coming Home* in 1978. She might well have won for *They Shoot Horses, Don't They?* in 1969, which the critics in our poll rated in the top ten of all time.

Henry Fonda's daughter, Jane, has had a lot better luck than he's had in the Oscar races. The political activist, born in 1937, has been making films since 1960, but she did not get any outstanding opportunities until the late 1960s. She then came into her own in the 1970s.

In our poll, the critics nominated Katharine Hepburn for eight performances, Bette Davis for seven, and Judy Garland and Jane Fonda for six. Only Hepburn, Davis, and Leigh drew more votes from the critics than Fonda. Only those three, and Taylor, lured more votes from the fans. Clearly, she has climbed high in the ranks of great actresses.

One of the greatest of American actresses, Helen Hayes, is a two-time Oscar winner, once in a starring part in *The Sin of Madelon Claudet* in 1931–32 and again in a supporting part in *Airport* in 1970. In the

Jane Alexander with James Earl Jones in The Great White Hope.

almost fifty years in between she worked primarily on the stage.

Another great actress of the American stage, Tallulah Bankhead, made only fifteen films in a career that covered nearly fifty years. Only one was memorable, *Lifeboat* in 1944. She won the New York Critics Award for this and was nominated for an Oscar, but did not win it.

Lynn Fontanne and her husband Alfred Lunt were both nominated for *The Guardsman* in 1931–32, but both lost and returned to the stage. Over the years, many actresses have used the stage as a stepping stone to films, but few great stage actresses have repeated their success in films.

Among one-time winners, the most nominated has been Greer Garson, who was up for Oscar seven times. Her winning part, in *Mrs. Miniver* in 1942, was the second of five straight nominations and was her most memorable portrayal. She got the part only after Norma Shearer decided that at thirty-eight she was too old to play a middle-aged mother.

Swanson was nominated for *Sadie Thompson* in the first Oscar ceremonies, covering 1927–28. Janet Gaynor won for *Seventh Heaven, Street Angel,* and *Sunrise.* Swanson was nominated again for *The Trespasser,* 1929–30. The winner was Norma Shearer for *The Divorcee.* Ruth Chatterton was nominated for *Madame X* in 1928–29 and *Sarah and Son* in 1929–30, but lost in both years.

Greta Garbo was nominated for *Anna Christie* and *Romance* in 1929–30, *Camille* in 1937, and *Ninotchka* in 1939. She gave another notable performance, in *Anna Karenina* in 1935, but was not nominated. Her reputation as a recluse and glamorous lady appears to have clouded her artistry as an actress, but she was an artist and she won the New York Critics Awards for *Anna Karenina* and *Camille.* She never won an Academy Award and it is one of Oscar's notable omissions.

Garbo was born in Stockholm in 1905. She was the daughter of an unskilled laborer who took work where he could get it. She was thirteen when he died and she had to go to work. In her first job she lathered men's faces for shaves in a barber shop. Then, she worked as a saleslady in a department store. Chosen to represent the store in a publicity film, she began her film career and then made films for other firms. When accepted by the Royal Dramatic Theater, she truly commenced her career as an actress.

She was discovered by and became the protégée of Mauritz Stiller, who revolutionized the Swedish cinema. In Europe to sign Stiller to an MGM contract in 1924, Louis B. Mayer reluctantly agreed to sign the "fat actress," too, since Stiller refused to sign without her. Stiller failed in America, while Garbo succeeded. Garbo reluctantly did not accompany Stiller when he returned to Europe. A broken man, he died in 1927.

Although she was awkward, became known for big feet, and lacked a fine figure, Garbo had great facial beauty. Known as "The Mystery Woman" even in her early years here, she protected her privacy with a passion that only stirred added interest in her.

She lives now in New York, France, and Switzerland and to this day photographers stalk her but have been unable to get a close-up view of how she looks in her seventies.

She was known to have had romances with silent-screen star John Gilbert, directors Stiller and Rouben Mamoulian, artist Cecil Beaton, conductor Leopold Stokowski, financier George Schlee, millionaire Aristotle Onassis, and nutritionist Gaylord Hauser, but she never married, which added to her reputation of being unattainable. Today Garbo is a wealthy woman who owns priceless property on some of Beverly Hills'

swankiest streets. She remains one of the great stars of all time, known by name to many who have never seen even one of her films.

She began making movies in Europe in 1922 and made only twenty-four films in America between 1926 and 1941 before retiring. When she made the transition from silents to talkies, MGM movie ads proclaimed, "Garbo Talks!" The film was *Anna Christie* in 1930 and her first words were, "Git me a viskey, ginger ale on the side—and don't be stingy, baby."

She was famous for the phrase, "I vant to be alone." She said it in *Grand Hotel* in 1932, but insisted that in real life she said, "I vant to be *left* alone."

Her top performance came in *Camille* and it is a well-remembered film for which she should have been honored. As Marguerite—a lady with a love for camellias as well as wealthy men—she ensnares Armand Duval, portrayed by the young Robert Taylor, in 19th-century Paris in this depiction of the Alexander Dumas novel. Romantic and poetic, *Camille* is a beautiful film.

Taylor said later that Garbo was so aggressive during the love scenes that she scared him. He admitted almost dropping her during the deathbed scene, the most famous in the film. But what showed on the screen was magic. In the scene Garbo says, "Armand has taught me that all love is not selfish, nor goodness dull, nor men faithless. Let me love you. Let me live for you. Don't let's ask more from heaven than that—God might get angry."

Armand has returned to her to be with her at her deathbed. She tells him, "Perhaps it is better if I live in your heart where the world can't see me." Her voice stills. Her face stills. Her face goes lifeless as Armand cries, "Marguerite, don't leave me."

The famous woman's director George Cukor has said, "This was one of those cases where an actress was born to play a part. It usually is a sort of sobbing, victim part as played by others, but Garbo played it boldly, as if she knew she was the author of her own misery and accepted it. She says in it, 'Look here, I'm just a girl like all the rest. I'm a tart like all the rest.' She was enormously erotic in it. But very intelligent, very disciplined. She did the big scene so delicately—she had only to clear her throat and you knew she was dying.

"Although she was not big at the box office and her career was starting to decline when she did *Camille,* she was a star who demanded her large salary in advance and the biggest budgets and best crews for her films, and it showed in them.

"I hope I helped her in *Camille,* but it was her work and it was wonderful. When I saw it for the first time in

Greta Garbo in Camille.

many years, I was staggered by what I saw on the large screen. I am proud of the film and feel hers was one of the great underrated performances in the history of films."

Camille lost to Luise Rainer's performance in *The Good Earth.* Luise Rainer's performance in *The Great Ziegfeld* had won the previous year. Ironically, Rainer was regarded as "another Garbo" when she arrived from Austria in 1935. After two straight triumphs, Rainer's career careened downhill and the Oscar came to be considered "a jinx," but in reality more performers have benefited from it than have been hurt by it. Rainer had landed two great roles and perhaps could not live up to them later. She experienced a stormy marriage to playwright Clifford Odets, created trouble at MGM, and made a few failures before being banished.

Aside from Garbo, some fine actresses who never won Oscars are Deborah Kerr, Geraldine Page, Irene Dunne, Barbara Stanwyck, Rosalind Russell, and Shirley MacLaine. Also, in the supporting actress category, are Thelma Ritter, Ethel Barrymore, and Agnes Moorehead. Kerr and Ritter were nominated six times, Page and Dunne five times, Russell, Stanwyck, MacLaine, Barrymore and Moorehead four times each. Notably neglected have been Judy Garland and Marsha Mason, who collected two nominations each; Carole Lombard, Jean Arthur, Miriam Hopkins, Dorothy McGuire, Margaret Sullavan, Mary Astor, Marlene Dietrich, Julie Harris, Lee Remick, and Gena Rowlands, who collected only one nomination each; and Ida Lupino, Myrna Loy, Marilyn Monroe, Lauren Bacall and Betty Field, who were never nominated.

Deborah Kerr may be the most outstanding omission

Agnes Moorehead, long neglected by Oscar, in How the West Was Won.

of Oscar. She was born in 1921 in Scotland and studied ballet at the Sadler Wells ballet school in England. She then turned to drama and developed as an actress in Shakespearean productions. Her first film found her playing a Salvation Army volunteer in George Bernard Shaw's *Major Barbara* in 1941.

She made eight films in England, most of them fine, before coming to the United States to play opposite Clark Gable in *The Hucksters* in 1947. She has made more than thirty-five films here, but retired in 1969 and now lives in Switzerland with her husband, writer Peter Viertel.

Kerr was nominated for *Edward My Son* in 1949, *From Here to Eternity* in 1953, *The King and I* in 1956, *Heaven Knows Mr. Allison* in 1957, *Separate Tables* in 1958, and *The Sundowners* in 1960. At one point, she was nominated in three straight years and four out of five. She won the New York Critics Award for *The Adventurers*, *Heaven Knows Mr. Allison*, and *The Sundowners*. The critics in our poll rated her performance in *From Here to Eternity* one of the top ten of all time. Yet, not one Oscar was ever given her.

Bette Davis was offered the role of Anna in *The King and I* but, to her great disappointment, Warners refused to loan her to 20th Century-Fox for it. Kerr got the part and played it to perfection, opposite Yul Brynner.

She always played a perfect lady—even in *Tea and*

Ethel Barrymore and Jeanne Crain in Pinky.

Sympathy in 1956, for which she deserved another nomination. In this, she recreated her 1953 Broadway stage triumph opposite John Kerr.

As the wife of the headmaster at a boys' school, when she gives herself to the youth suspected of being less than a man, she says, "When you speak of this in future years—and you will—be kind." She says it so well your heart aches for her.

Joan Crawford originally was offered the role of Karen Holmes in *From Here to Eternity* but turned it down because she considered it unladylike. It was the first unladylike role Kerr received and she fought to get it. She played Karen Holmes, the wife of the commandant of a military base at Pearl Harbor in the days prior to Dec. 7, 1941. She played a woman who was willing to give herself to anyone until she is taken by Sgt. Warden, as played by Burt Lancaster. Their love scene as they lay on the beach with the waves washing over them was sensual and daring in its day, and is considered to be the most memorable scene in the movie.

My personal favorite Deborah Kerr role is the part she played in *The Sundowners*—Ida, the wife of Paddy, played by Robert Mitchum, an itinerant worker in the sheep sheds of Australia. Life is hard. She has little. She goes on gamely, seldom complaining. But there is a scene at a train station in which she mutely but magnificently expresses the injustice of life.

She sees and envies a well-dressed lady who has much more and for whom life obviously is much easier. Kerr does not have to say a word. Her expression tells all. You can read her eyes as easily as if she has spoken. She says, there, but for the grace of God, go I.

It is a small piece of acting, but there has been no greater in screen history. Here we had a magic mating of the camera and the performer's expressive face in an incomparable close-up. With that one scene, Deborah Kerr established herself as an actress of unsurpassed sensitivity.

It was not a big picture, hardly remembered by most filmgoers. Kerr made few big pictures and had few roles so large as to be unforgettable. Hers seldom were the key roles in the major movies she made. Perhaps this is why she was overlooked so often by Oscar, if not by the nominators. In *The King and I* she was overshadowed by the flamboyant part of the King, as played by Yul Brynner. In *From Here to Eternity* she was overshadowed by meatier roles played by Montgomery Clift and Burt Lancaster.

Kerr's performance in *The Sundowners* in 1960 was daunted by "the return from death" of Elizabeth Taylor and her showier role in *Butterfield 8*. That Taylor received the gift of Oscar that year out of sentimental kindness was cruel to Kerr. It was, frankly, unforgivable. Compare the two performances sometime.

Deborah Kerr and Burt Lancaster in the famous beach scene in From Here to Eternity.

The Actresses, Part II

L IKE MANY ACTORS, many actresses who specialized in light comedies have been neglected by Oscar. Academy voters seem disinclined to reward light-comedy players with heavy Awards, though it takes skills similar to those of heavy-drama artists to carry off such parts with real style.

Marie Dressler in *Min and Bill* in 1930–31, Claudette Colbert in *It Happened One Night* in 1935, Loretta Young in *The Farmer's Daughter* in 1947, Judy Holliday in *Born Yesterday* in 1951, Audrey Hepburn in *Roman Holiday* in 1954, Katharine Hepburn in *Guess Who's Coming to Dinner* in 1968, and Diane Keaton in *Annie Hall* in 1977 are the only light-comedy winners in more than fifty years of Hollywood's Best Actress Awards.

Among those who performed memorably in many light-comedy classics without Oscar's nod have been Irene Dunne, Rosalind Russell, Carole Lombard, Jean Arthur, and Myrna Loy.

Irene Dunne originally played the part of Anna in *Anna and the King of Siam* in 1946, before it was made into *The King and I*, the Broadway musical and Hollywood movie starring Deborah Kerr and Yul Brynner. Dunne might well have been nominated for her performance, but she was not. She was nominated earlier for *Cimarron* in 1931, *Theodora Goes Wild* in 1936, *The Awful Truth* in 1937, and *Love Affair* in 1939, and later for *I Remember Mama* in 1948, but without winning Oscar.

Dunne was born in Louisville and trained as a singer at Chicago Musical College. She failed an audition at New York's Metropolitan Opera, but became a musical star on Broadway and played Magnolia in Ziegfeld's national company of *Show Boat* in 1929.

Signed by RKO, she made her first movie the following year and made more than forty films in less than fifteen years before retiring to Republican politics, campaigning for Eisenhower in the 1950s, and serving as alternate delegate to the United Nations. As an actress, she had delicate beauty and played dignified ladies, not only in tearjerkers, but in madcap comedies.

She was effective dramatically in *Penny Serenade* opposite Cary Grant in 1941 and *A Guy Named Joe* opposite Spencer Tracy and Van Johnson in 1943. But, she was especially effective in light comedies and perhaps hit her peak in *The Awful Truth* opposite Grant in 1937. Longtime *New York Times* critic Howard Thompson termed it, "The funniest, slyest comedy-playing of her career."

She was sly. She made it look easy. So it was easy to pass her over. The same was true of Rosalind Russell.

Rosalind Russell, born in Connecticut in 1908, trained at the American Academy of Dramatic Arts and was an exceptionally stylish lady who made more than fifty films between 1934 and her death in 1976. She was nominated for comedies such as *My Sister Eileen* in 1942 and *Auntie Mame* in 1958 and for dramas such as *Mourning Becomes Electra* in 1947 and *Sister Kenny* in 1946. She should have been nominated for *His Girl Friday* in 1940, *Picnic* in 1956, and *Gypsy* in 1962.

Irene Dunne with Rex Harrison in Anna and the King of Siam, forerunner of the musical The King and I.

Rosalind Russell, right, and Janet Blair shoot a scene for My Sister Eileen as director Al Hall and cameraman Joseph Walker watch.

Rosalind Russell was expected to win for Mourning Becomes Electra but did not.

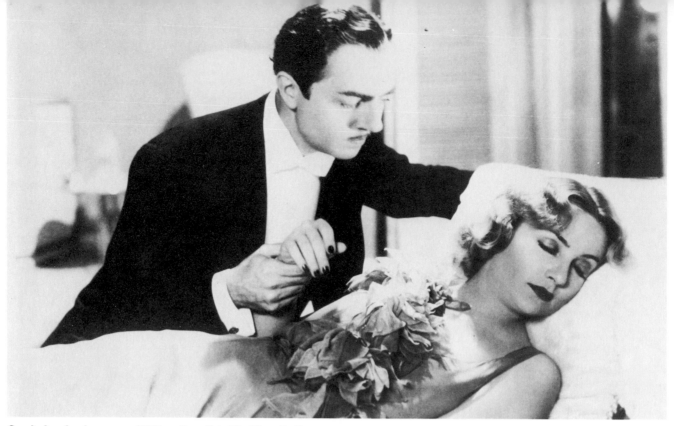

Carole Lombard concerns William Powell in My Man Godfrey.

While light comedy was her forte and *His Girl Friday* made her a star, she may have been most effective as the rather desperate spinster in *Picnic*—a deeply moving portrait. One of the leading ladies of Hollywood society, she was heavily favored to win for *Mourning Becomes Electra* in 1947 but was beaten by her best friend and the longest shot in the field, Loretta Young, another lovely lady of light comedy, for *The Farmer's Daughter*. The audience gasped when the Award was announced. On her way to Russell's "victory party," Young asked, "What about Roz? What'll I say to Roz?" She said she was sorry and they embraced.

Before she was given the part of Hildy Johnson in *His Girl Friday*, it was turned down by Carole Lombard, Jean Arthur, Ginger Rogers, Janet Gaynor, and Claudette Colbert. It made Russell a star.

Lombard was already a star. She was born in Indiana but reared in California, and broke into movies at age twelve in *A Perfect Crime* in 1921. She appeared in some fifty films prior to her death in a plane crash while on a War Bond-selling tour in 1942.

Carole appeared in Mack Sennett's slapstick comedies and had made more than thirty movies before she hit with Howard Hawks' *Twentieth Century* in 1934. Critic Howard Thompson called it, "a screamingly funny and biting farce, brilliantly teaming the lady with John Barrymore as two former lovers and show-biz personalities playing cat-and-mouse on a train."

Lombard was an earthy, lively lady, originally wed to William Powell but perfectly cast later as Clark Gable's real-life wife. She was nominated only once, for her rousing portrayal opposite Powell in *My Man Godfrey* in 1936. She might well have won for it or for any one of several other animated and inventive madcap portrayals.

Jean Arthur was also nominated only once, for *The More the Merrier* in 1943, but she should have been nominated for *Mr. Deeds Goes to Town* in 1936, *You Can't Take It with You* in 1938, *Mr. Smith Goes to Washington* in 1939, and *The Talk of the Town* in 1942. One of the most underrated performers in the history of Hollywood, she gave character to comedies of class, wisecracking in her throaty voice. Her directors adored her. Frank Capra called her "my favorite actress." George Stevens called her "one of the greatest comediennes the screen has seen"—a greatness never truly rewarded.

She was born in 1905 in New York City and quit school in her teens to become an actress. She made more than eighty movies between 1923 and 1953. Later, she taught drama at Vassar and other colleges.

Capra said of her, "She doesn't do very well in crowds, and she doesn't do very well with people, and she doesn't do very well with life, but she does very well as an actress.

"She was afraid. She'd drum up all sorts of excuses for not being ready. Turn the camera on and she'd

116

blossom out into something wonderful. And she could do anything, could express love or hate or anything. And when the scene was over she'd go back into that dressing room and cry." She once said, "It's a strenuous job every day of your life to live up to the way you look on that screen."

Never even nominated, Myrna Loy was another who was excellent in light comedies. She was born in Montana in 1905, but reared largely in Los Angeles. She supposedly was the model for a plaster statue which adorns Hollywood High.

Myrna Loy started in show business as a chorus girl in the live show which preceded the feature films at Grauman's Chinese Theater. Because of her exotic looks, she was typecast in movies as a vamp, often Oriental, for about ten years beginning in 1925. Then she broke into light comedy opposite Bill Powell in 1934 in the first of numerous *Thin Man* movies in which they played Nick and Nora Charles. The public loved them. One year she was voted America's favorite actress.

She made more than eighty-five films in all and was successful in dramatic parts, such as *The Best Years of Our Lives* in 1946, before she retired in 1969. She was inactive in films during World War II, working for the Red Cross and later as a U.S. representative with UNESCO.

Many of Hollywood's so-called "glamour girls" played light comedy effectively. Marlene Dietrich is a classic case.

She was born in 1901 in Berlin. She has masked her early life in mystery but it is known that she turned up in the chorus line of a touring musical revue in 1921 and trained as an actress at Max Reinhart's School of Drama. In the late 1920s she was discovered by Josef von Sternberg who became her mentor and cast her opposite Emil Jannings in the classic *The Blue Angel* in 1930, for which she became famous and in which she made famous "Falling in Love Again."

She left a husband and daughter behind when von Sternberg took her to Hollywood in 1930. After she had made a series of films with him, Dietrich brought her family to Hollywood. When later sued for alienation of affection by von Sternberg's wife, Dietrich won. She saw little of her husband or von Sternberg after that, but had romances with such notables as John Gilbert, Gary Cooper, Douglas Fairbanks, Jr., Noel Coward, and Erich Maria Remarque.

Gilbert had two great romances in his life—Garbo, with whom he made a series of passionate silent films, and Dietrich, who tried to revive his career early in the talkies. Dietrich went from Gilbert to Cooper. She tried to get Gilbert into her first film in this country, *Morocco*, in 1930, but Cooper was cast instead. They say Gilbert didn't stop drinking until the day he died a few years later.

Dietrich was a siren with haunting eyes, long legs, and a smoky voice, capable of the sort of sultry singing which gave her a cabaret and concert career in her later years. A friend, Hemingway, said, "If she had

Alan Ladd, Jean Arthur, and Van Heflin played the leads in Shane. *Neither Ladd nor Arthur won Oscars. Nor did* Shane.

Marlene Dietrich with Clive Brook in Shanghai Express.

directed everyone—in a sexy way so she got her way. She is the quintessential sex goddess. She is mother as sex, sex as it was intended. God, she was beautiful!"

Few glamorous ladies of the silver screen ever received or really deserved nominations for Oscars. Elizabeth Taylor has been an exception. Even so, it is not clear that her rewards came as much for her performances as her prominence. Married to hotel heir Nicky Hilton, actor Michael Wilding, producer Mike Todd, and singer Eddie Fisher, married and remarried to actor Richard Burton, married now to politician John Warner, the beautiful Liz has had a controversial life. She was nominated for *Raintree County* in 1957, *Cat on a Hot Tin Roof* in 1958, and *Suddenly Last Summer* in 1959 before she broke through with Oscars for *Butterfield 8* in 1960 and *Who's Afraid of Virginia Woolf?* in 1966.

Ava Gardner also achieved more fame for her romances than for her performances. She was married to Mickey Rooney, bandleader Artie Shaw, and superstar Frank Sinatra, and had celebrated romances with billionaire Howard Hughes and racketeer Johnny Stompinato, who were also two of Lana Turner's playmates.

A Southern beauty from North Carolina, Ava became a major star in the 1940s and is still active, despite time out to live the sort of role she played in Hemingway's *The Sun Also Rises*, an international lady with a home in Madrid and a passion for Spanish matadors. The role she played in *The Barefoot Contessa* supposedly was modelled after her real life. She might have merited a nomination for one or two performances and did receive one for *Mogambo* in 1953.

Lana Turner, another of the beauties of films in the 1940s, might have merited a nomination for *The Postman Always Rings Twice* in 1946 and did receive one for *Peyton Place* in 1957.

Turner was married to bandleader Artie Shaw, actor Lex Barker, restaurateur Stephen Crane, millionaire Bob Topping, and three others. She had celebrated romances with actor Fernando Lamas, singer Tony Martin, the reclusive Hughes, and the ill-fated Stompinato. Off-screen drama came to her life when teenage daughter Cheryl Crane stabbed Stompinato to death and was found innocent on the grounds that she feared for her mother's life. The situation was fictionalized by Harold Robbins in the novel *By Love Possessed* and, curiously, Turner took the lead when it was made into a movie in 1961. Here, art imitated life, but took no Awards for it.

Another beauty of films in the 1940s, Rita Hayworth never won an Oscar nomination, though she

nothing but her voice, she could break your heart with it. But she also had that beautiful body and the timeless loveliness of her face."

Her ability as an actress was always in dispute. She made about twenty films in Germany between 1923 and 1930 and more than thirty in the United States through 1958. She could easily have been given nominations for *Destry Rides Again* in 1939, *The Spoilers* in 1942, *Witness for the Prosecution* in 1958, or *Judgment at Nuremberg* in 1961, but she wasn't and she never won an Oscar.

Of her real skill, Edward G. Robinson said, "I am not sure I would call it talent; it is something beyond that—mystery, unavailability, feminine mystique. Before I worked with her I thought she was arrogant, temperamental, demanding, perhaps synthetic. Playing with her, I learned we shared a common passion, work. Be on time, know the lines, toe the marks, say the words, be ready for anything.

"She discovered the trick of putting on her makeup under the same lighting with which she would be filmed. She knew everything technical—lighting, cameras. She

might have deserved one or two, notably for her well-remembered titled role in *Gilda* in 1946, in which she stripped while singing "Put the Blame on Mame, Boys."

She was born Margarita Carmen Casino of Spanish parents in New York in 1918 and became a Latin dancer in her early days. She wed five men, including Orson Welles, singer Dick Haymes, and Prince Aly Kahn, spiritual leader of many Moselms. She had celebrated romances with studio head Harry Cohn and glamour guy Victor Mature.

Rita gave clever light-comedy performances in *The Strawberry Blonde* with James Cagney in 1941 and *My Gal Sal* with Mature in 1942 and danced effectively in *You'll Never Get Rich* in 1941 and *You Were Never Lovelier* in 1942 with Fred Astaire and *Cover Girl* in 1944 with Gene Kelly. She also gave good dramatic performances in *Blood and Sand* in 1941, *Separate Tables* in 1958, and *The Story on Page One* in 1960.

Hayworth was a cousin of Ginger Rogers, with whom she made the celebrated *Flying Down to Rio* in 1933, *The Gay Divorcee* in 1934, *Roberta* and *Top Hat* in 1935, and others. Rogers too was effective in light comedy, especially in *Tom, Dick and Harry* in

1941 and *The Major and the Minor* in 1942. She won an Oscar for dramatics in *Kitty Foyle* in 1940.

As Fred Astaire and Gene Kelly learned, dancers do not often win Oscars, no matter how skilled their artistry, no matter how brilliant, entertaining, and enduring their films. Nor do singers, although Julie Andrews won for *Mary Poppins* in 1964 and perhaps should have won for *The Sound of Music* in 1965.

It's hard to believe, but Doris Day was offered the lecherous role of Mrs. Robinson played by Anne Bancroft in *The Graduate* in 1967, but turned it down because her advisors regarded it as unsuitable for her. She did win a nomination for an Oscar for the light comedy *Pillow Talk* in 1959.

Although enormously popular, neither Alice Faye nor Betty Grable, top musical comedy stars of 1930s and 1940s films, ever won or even rated award nominations. Both were glamour gals more than they were artists of song and dance.

Lauren Bacall was more than a glamour gal, more than merely the wife of Humphrey Bogart and Jason Robards. She was effective with Bogie in *To Have and Have Not* in 1944, *The Big Sleep* in 1946, *Dark Passage* in 1947, and *Key Largo* in 1948, but she never really got to display her musical comedy skill as

Natalie Wood and Rosalind Russell, non-Oscar-winners, sing along with Karl Malden in Gypsy.

Rita Hayworth in her famed pin-up picture of the 1940s.

119

she later did on Broadway in *Cactus Flower* in 1968 and *Applause* in 1970, for which she took a Tony. She is famous for her "If you want anything, just whistle" line directed at Bogie in *To Have and Have Not*, but she is an actress of quality even though she was completely overlooked by Oscar.

Natalie Wood may be thought of as a pretty face, but she was nominated as Best Actress for *Rebel Without a Cause* in 1955, *Splendor in the Grass* in 1961, and *Love with the Proper Stranger* in 1963. Originally a child star, she debuted in *Tomorrow Is Forever* in 1946. She also gave good performances in *West Side Story* in 1961 and *Gypsy* in 1962, but these were diluted because she did not do her own singing. Married for a second time to actor Robert ("R.J.") Wagner, she continues her career, but largely in lightweight parts.

Marilyn Monroe was another glamour gal who never received a nomination for an Academy Award, but she may have deserved one or two. Many say she was strictly a sex symbol who didn't deserve awards for acting. Certainly she didn't early in her career. But, she gave better performances than many admit.

Billy Wilder, who directed her in *Some Like It Hot* in 1959, said, "Anyone can remember lines, but it takes a real artist to come on the set and not know your lines and give the performances she did."

More generously, Josh Logan, who directed her in *Bus Stop* in 1956, said, "She came as near genius as any actress I ever knew." Of her performance in this film, Bosley Crowther wrote in the *New York Times*, "You'll find her a dilly." He said, "Logan has got her to be the beat-up B-girl of Mr. Inge's play, even down to the Ozark accent and the look of pellagra about her skin. He has got her to be the tinseled floozie, the semi-moronic doll . . . he has got her to light the small flame of dignity that sputters pathetically in this chippie and to make a rather moving sort of her." This was, in fact, an extraordinarily moving performance which years later leaves viewers affected. It deserved a nomination, maybe even an Oscar.

Another for which she deserved a nomination and maybe an Award was *The Misfits*. This was her final film, as it was Clark Gable's. It was one of Montgomery Clift's last. It was written by Marilyn's husband, the playwright Arthur Miller. It was a powerful film, underrated in its time, marked by superb performances by Gable, Clift, and Monroe, who were, indeed, misfits. In it, Monroe revealed depths beneath the showy surface that few suspected of her.

Born Norma Jean Mortenson in 1926 to an unmarried mother with a history of suicidal psychiatric problems, Marilyn was reared in orphanages and foster homes after her mother was placed in an institution. At sixteen, she went to work to escape a bad early marriage. Discovered by a photographer, she became a model and won a movie contract. Publicized into popularity through a series of increasing roles, she was already one of Hollywood's biggest box office stars and a sex symbol by the time she married baseball's Joe DiMaggio.

She was famous for her dumb blonde beauty, her wiggling figure, and her breathless speaking voice, but she was sensitive and insecure throughout her career. She could not go anywhere without attracting attention and it scared her. She once said, "A sex symbol becomes a thing. I hate being a thing."

She wanted more than anything to be accepted as an actress. She proved herself an artist in *The Misfits*, but by then drink and drugs had all but done her in. A week before the premiere of the picture, she divorced Miller. A month later, she entered a hospital to be treated by another in a series of psychiatrists she sought out. About eighteen months later, she was found dead on her bed from an overdose of sleeping pills.

Thelma Ritter could not be confused with a sex symbol. But she was a lively lady and an actress of excellence. She was nominated not just once, but six times for Academy Awards in the supporting actress category, all within the span of twelve years—for *All About Eve* in 1950, *The Mating Season* in 1951, *With a Song in My Heart* in 1952, *Pickup on South Street* in 1953, *Pillow Talk* in 1959, and *Birdman of Alcatraz* in 1962. She never won.

Thelma Ritter was born in Brooklyn in 1905. She worked without great reward on the stage for many years. As a wisecracking character actress, she received steady work and general recognition, but no real rewards in films between her debut in *Miracle on 34th Street* in 1947 and her death in 1969. She laughed off Oscar, but he might have made her happy. She deserved him. She was strictly a spear-carrier. She never had a starring part. She never had to face the fame of a Marilyn Monroe.

Walter Brennan won Oscar three times as a supporting actor, but no supporting actress has won the golden statuette more than twice—a success scored by only one—Shelley Winters, for *Diary of Anne Frank* in 1959 and *A Patch of Blue* in 1965. Helen Hayes won for *The Sin of Madelon Claudet* in 1931–32 and *Airport* in 1970 and Ingrid Bergman for *Gaslight* in 1944 and *Murder on the Orient Express* in 1974, but in both cases the first Oscar was for a starring part, the second for a supporting part.

Marilyn Monroe shows her hand, and other things, at paddle ball in The Misfits. *It's not the rubber ball that Clark Gable, left, Eli Wallach, center, and Montgomery Clift, right, are so happy about. That's the neglected Thelma Ritter, center, too.*

Thelma Ritter never shook hands with Oscar.

Aside from Thelma Ritter's six, the most nominations for a supporting actress are four by Ethel Barrymore, Agnes Moorehead, and Lee Grant.

Barrymore was nominated for *None But the Lonely Heart* in 1944, *The Spiral Staircase* in 1946, *The Paradine Case* in 1947, and *Pinky* in 1949. She won for the first. Moorehead was nominated for *The Magnificent Ambersons* in 1942, *Mrs. Parkington* in 1944, *Johnny Belinda* in 1948, and *Hush, Hush Sweet Charlotte* in 1964. She won the New York Critics Award for *Ambersons* but never won an Oscar. It is sad.

Lee Grant was nominated for *Detective Story* in 1951, *The Landlord* in 1970, *Shampoo* in 1975, and *Voyage of the Damned* in 1976. She won for *Shampoo*.

Anne Revere was nominated for *Song of Bernadette* in 1943, *National Velvet* in 1945, and *Gentleman's Agreement* in 1947 before being blacklisted during the Communist hunt. She did win for *National Velvet*.

Claire Trevor was nominated for *Dead End* in 1937, *Key Largo* in 1948, and *The High and the Mighty* in 1954. She won for *Key Largo*.

Celeste Holm was nominated for *Gentleman's Agreement* in 1947, *Come to the Stables* in 1949, and *All About Eve* in 1950. She won for the first.

Geraldine Page is made up to be matronly in Pete 'n' Tillie.

Teresa Wright was nominated as a supporting actress for *The Little Foxes* in 1941 and *Mrs. Miniver* in 1942 and as a leading actress in *The Pride of the Yankees* in 1942. She captured the supporting part of her dual nominations in 1942. Although she played many leads effectively, she never again was nominated for a lead.

Angela Lansbury and Maureen Stapleton have been three-time losers in the supporting actress category, Lansbury was nominated for *Gaslight* in 1944, *The Picture of Dorian Grey* in 1945, and *The Manchurian Candidate* in 1962. Stapleton was nominated for *Lonelyhearts* in 1958, *Airport* in 1970, and *Interiors* in 1978. Both artful actresses, it is regrettable they have been neglected.

It is difficult to believe that Fay Bainter, Ruth Gordon, Eileen Heckart, Elsa Lanchester, and Mildred Dunnock were nominated only twice each, but at least Bainter, Gordon, and Heckart each won once. Bainter won for *Jezebel* in 1938, but lost for *The Children's Hour* in 1961. Gordon won for *Rosemary's Baby* in 1967 and lost for *Inside Daisy Clover* in 1965. Heckart won for *Butterflies Are Free* in 1972 and lost for *The Bad Seed* in 1956.

Lanchester was nominated for *Come to the Stables* in 1949 and *Witness for the Prosecution* in 1957; Dunnock for *Death of a Salesman* in 1951 and *Baby Doll* in 1956. Both have been notably neglected.

Dunnock's performance in *Salesman*, especially, was a classic.

An excellent actress, Gloria Grahame, was nominated for *Crossfire* in 1947 and for *The Bad and the Beautiful* in 1952, scoring in the latter. Anne Baxter won as Best Supporting Actress in *The Razor's Edge* in 1946, but lost as a lead in *All About Eve* in 1950.

It is especially difficult to believe that Jane Darwell, Mary Astor, Jo Van Fleet, Geraldine Fitzgerald, Mildred Natwick, Sylvia Sidney, and Estelle Parsons have been nominated only once each, although Darwell, Astor, and Van Fleet did at least win their one. All have long lists of superior performances.

Darwell won for *Grapes of Wrath* in 1940, Astor for *The Great Lie* in 1941, Van Fleet for *East of Eden* in 1955. Fitzgerald lost for *Wuthering Heights* in 1939, Natwick for *Barefoot in the Park* in 1967, Parsons for *Rachel, Rachel* in 1968, and Sidney for *Summer Wishes, Winter Dreams* in 1973.

Sidney, born in 1910, started making movies in 1927. She was memorable as Drina in *Dead End* in 1937, but got few meaty roles after that until *Summer Wishes* when she was in her sixties. A talented lady, she has been neglected as much by the fates as by Oscar.

Madeline Kahn is a gifted comedienne who lost nominations for supporting parts in *Paper Moon* in 1973 and *Blazing Saddles* in 1974, but leads for lady comics come few and far between.

Ranking with Deborah Kerr and Thelma Ritter as actresses neglected by Oscar are Geraldine Page, nominated six times, and Barbara Stanwyck and Shirley MacLaine, nominated four times each.

Geraldine Page was nominated as supporting actress in *Hondo* in 1953, *You're a Big Boy Now* in 1967, and *Pete 'n' Tillie* in 1972 and as starring actress in *Summer and Smoke* in 1961, *Sweet Bird of Youth* in 1962, and *Interiors* in 1978. She won New York Drama Critics Awards for her roles in the Broadway productions of *Summer and Smoke* and *Sweet Bird of Youth*, but has won no film honors, despite deserving them. Possibly because she does not seem to be a "star type." She is a splendid actress of passion and sensitivity who has been given less then twenty films in more than thirty years of occasional opportunities in Hollywood.

The daughter of a doctor, she was born in Missouri in 1924. She began acting in the early 1940s and reached stardom on the stage in the early 1950s. She married an underrated actor, Rip Torn, who may have been neglected because of the name he adopted as an actor. (He was born Elmore Rual Torn.)

Barbara Stanwyck was nominated for *Stella Dallas*

Barbara Stanwyck weds Burt Lancaster, to her regret, in Sorry Wrong Number.

in 1937, *Ball of Fire* in 1942, *Double Indemnity* in 1944, and *Sorry, Wrong Number* in 1948. She won the New York Critics Award for *Stella Dallas*. She won an Emmy for "Big Valley" on television. She was a lead actress in successful dramas on Broadway.

Born Ruby Stevens in Brooklyn in 1907, Stanwyck was orphaned early and reared by relatives and friends. She quit school at the age of thirteen to work in a department store, but took some talent as a dancer to the chorus of the Ziegfeld Follies at the age of fifteen.

Stanwyck made more than eighty movies between 1927 and 1965 and at one time in the middle 1940s was the highest paid woman in the country. She married twice—first vaudevillian Frank Fay and later, movie star Robert Taylor. She is known as a hardworking professional without temperament who used her range to its widest potential.

She gave especially effective performances in *Golden Boy* in 1939 and *Meet John Doe* in 1940, but it was *Stella Dallas* that made her a star and it is as Stella Dallas that she is best remembered. As a low-life lady who marries into high society, then falls out and eventually gives up her beloved daughter to the better life, she was superb. Standing in the rain, watching through a mansion window as her daughter is married, then walking off into the night triumphantly, Stanwyck wordlessly delivered the classic scene of her career.

Shirley MacLaine was nominated for *Some Came Running* in 1958, *The Apartment* in 1960, *Irma LaDouce* in 1963, and *The Turning Point* in 1977 and deserved nomination for *Being There* in 1979. Her performance as a lay-around lady in *The Apartment* was deeply touching. Her performance with Anne Bancroft and their exchanges in *The Turning Point* crackled with electricity.

She was born Shirley MacLean Beatty in 1934 in Richmond, Virginia. It is ironic that both she and her brother, Warren Beatty, have been denied Oscars despite many superlative performances.

Dancing from the age of four, she made it on Broadway in *Pajama Game* when lead Carol Haney broke her leg and Shirley replaced her. Since then MacLaine has made many movie musicals and starred in night clubs and television specials. Her dramatic talent is equal to her musical comedy skills. For a while, her career careened downhill but she returned to prominence in the late 1970s.

Debbie Reynolds is another night club and musical movie star of note who has made a number of enormously entertaining films. They include the celebrated *Singin' in the Rain* in 1952 and *The Unsinkable Molly Brown* in 1964, for which she won an Academy Award nomination. She was also successful in the light comedy *Divorce American Style* in 1967.

A most neglected performer has been Judy Garland. She is remembered best as a child star, an adult neurotic, and a great, stylish singer, but she also was a good dramatic actress and awesome all-around per-

Shirley MacLaine has had it with Anne Bancroft in The Turning Point.

Shirley Temple is flanked by Jack Haley and Alice Faye in Poor Little Rich Girl.

former. She was nominated for her leading role in *A Star Is Born* in 1954 and supporting part in *Judgment at Nuremberg* in 1961, but lost both times. She deserved to be nominated for *The Wizard of Oz* in 1939, *Meet Me in St. Louis* in 1944, *Easter Parade* in 1948, and *A Child Is Waiting* in 1968, but was not.

She was awarded a special Oscar for *Oz*, but merited more. Surprisingly, perhaps, the critics rated her performance as wide-eyed Dorothy fifth and fans rated it eighth in our polls of most memorable performances. Fans also ranked her role in *A Star Is Born* in the first fifteen. Fans and critics alike nominated her for six different performances and placed her sixth of all-time among actresses in total votes for these performances.

Garland was born Frances Gumm in Grand Rapids, Minnesota, in 1922, daughter of vaudevillians. She debuted on stage at three and in her early years was part of a sister singing act. Her mother pushed her into a career as a performer.

Judy was signed by MGM after an audition with Louis B. Mayer. He liked her singing, but not her looks. He called her "my little hunchback," which hurt terribly. Although long-legged, she had poor posture, was given to being overweight, and was always self-conscious of her figure. When Mayer could not get Shirley Temple on loan, he agreed to let Garland do *Oz*, and her charming performance and unforgettable rendition of "Somewhere over the Rainbow" made her a star. She was sixteen.

Stardom was too much for her. She turned to pills and drink. She had unsuccessful marriages with David Rose, Vincente Minnelli, Sid Luft, and Mark Herrin before her final marriage to Mickey Deems. She had three children, including Liza Minelli, who won an Oscar for *Cabaret* in 1977. Garland never won one, nor did her frequent costar, Mickey Rooney.

In the last fifteen years of her life, she seemed afraid to perform, often was unable to perform, and frequently was sued or fired. Yet she provided some memorable performances and concerts. After several suicide attempts, she died of an overdose of sleeping pills in 1969 at the age of forty-seven.

On the night of the Academy Award ceremonies in 1954, Judy was the favorite to win for her role as Vicki Lester in *A Star Is Born*, a role played years earlier by Janet Gaynor and years later by Barbra Streisand. But Judy was in the hospital, following the difficult delivery of her son.

Cables were laid along the corridors. A scaffold carrying a portable television camera was set outside the window of her room. She was wired for sound and dressed in her fanciest bedwear. Technicians scurried about. All was set for her to accept her Award by remote pickup.

Many assembled in the room. All watched the long telecast. Finally, came the Best Actress Award. The winner was Grace Kelly for *A Country Girl*. The technicians set about dismantling the set and unwiring

Judy. She laughed a little and asked that they not electrocute her.

Sid Luft hugged her and cursed the Academy. She said, "They shouldn't give it to me, although I deserved it." They opened a bottle of champagne, anyway, and drank.

Most never come that close, even though they may deserve it.

Ida Lupino was outstanding in many of her more than fifty films between 1933 and 1976, but never won a nomination for an Academy Award. She was most memorable in *The Light That Failed* and *They Drive by Night* in 1940, *High Sierra* and *The Sea Wolf* in 1941, *Moontide* in 1942, *The Hard Way* in 1943, *In Our Time* in 1945, and *Devotion* in 1946. She won the New York Critics Award for *The Hard Way* in 1943, but was ignored by Hollywood. Sarcastically, she called herself "the poor man's Bette Davis" and put down her lack of recognition as an actress. She was truly, however, a sensitive, versatile actress and she became one of the first successful women writer-producer-directors of films and television dramas from the early 1950s on.

Betty Field made fewer films, but was another actress who was outstanding in many movies and never won a nomination. She was most memorable in *Of Mice and Men* in 1940, *Kings Row* in 1942, *Tomorrow the World* in 1944, and *The Southerner* in 1945. She was a powerful performer who deserved greater recognition.

Margaret Sullavan was nominated only once, for *Three Comrades* in 1938, for which she won the New York Critics Award but not the Academy Award. She made only sixteen films, but might well have been nominated for *The Shop Around the Corner* and *The Mortal Storm* in 1940 and *Back Street* and *So Ends Our Night* in 1941. Her subtle talent and engaging personality left an immense impact on the screen, for all her lack of credits.

She went from summer stock to Broadway with pals Henry Fonda and Jimmy Stewart, and Fonda was the first of her four husbands. She won the New York Dramatic Critics Award for Broadway's *Voice of the Turtle* in 1943. Dissatisfied with her life, she took an overdose of sleeping pills in 1960 and was recently the subject of a moving biography by her daughter Brooke, with Leland Hayward, titled *Haywire*.

Merle Oberon was a classic beauty who did something more than decorate over fifty films in England and the United States between 1930 and 1973. She may not have been a great actress, but she was effective in many fine films and will be remembered forever for her classic Cathy opposite Laurence Olivier's

Ida Lupino with Humphrey Bogart in High Sierra.

Betty Field looks happy enough with Lon Chaney, Jr. and Burgess Meredith in a light moment in Of Mice and Men.

Heathcliff in *Wuthering Heights* in 1939, for which she won a nomination but not an Award.

Martha Scott also was a one-time nominee, for recreating her Broadway role as Emily in *Our Town* in 1940. She was a skillful dramatic actress too and is well-remembered for *One Foot in Heaven* in 1941. She deserved greater opportunities. She continues as a character actress in films and television, and gave a fine performance in *The Turning Point* in 1977.

Dorothy McGuire with Gregory Peck in Gentlemen's Agreement.

Dorothy McGuire was nominated only for *Gentleman's Agreement* in 1947, but did not win. She also gave skilled and sensitive performances in *Claudia* in 1943, *A Tree Grows in Brooklyn* and *The Enchanted Cottage* in 1945, *The Spiral Staircase* and *Till the End of Time* in 1946, *Trial* in 1955, *Friendly Persuasion* in 1956, and *The Dark at the Top of the Stairs* in 1960, for which she was not nominated.

She was another to come out of that nursery of dramatic talent, Omaha. She was a teenager when she made her stage debut opposite Henry Fonda, and she made her Broadway debut as understudy to Martha Scott in *Our Town*. Long married to the famous photographer John Swope, she frequently accompanies him on assignments around the world. Now retired from acting, she has left behind a brilliant array of underappreciated performances.

Jean Simmons was nominated as a supporting actress for her role as Ophelia in Olivier's *Hamlet* in 1948 and as a starring actress in *The Happy Ending* in 1969, but she was worthy of nominations for *The Actress* in 1953, *Elmer Gantry* in 1960, *All the Way Home* in 1963, and one or two other roles she played superbly. She is another notable actress who never won Oscar.

Eleanor Parker is an excellent actress, still active, who was at her peak in the 1950s. She was nominated for leading parts in *Caged* in 1950, *Detective Story* in 1951, and *Interrupted Melody* in 1955, but never won. Earlier, she was effective in *Pride of the Marines* in

1945 and *Of Human Bondage* in 1946. Her considerable career has now spanned more than thirty years.

Many have been neglected in recent years. Anne Bancroft did win for her first nomination, as Annie Sullivan in *The Miracle Worker*, in 1962, but she lost when nominated for *The Pumpkin Eater* in 1964, *The Graduate* in 1967, and *The Turning Point* in 1977.

Bancroft may be as fine an actress as we have had on the screen or stage. She was born Anna Maria Louise Italiano in The Bronx. She studied dancing and acting, broke into the business in the infant days of television, and endured minor roles in "B" movies in the early 1950s before she returned to New York to take a Tony for her part opposite Henry Fonda in *Two for the Seesaw* in 1958.

The next year she won another Tony as well as the New York Drama Critics Award for *The Miracle Worker*, then took the Oscar when she repeated her role in films. She made fifteen mediocre films, including *Treasure of the Golden Condor* and *Gorilla at Large*. She then became more selective and has made only ten more films, including 1979's *Fatso*, which she also wrote and directed. A funny lady off screen, she is married to funny-man Mel Brooks.

Both the critics and fans in our poll placed her Annie Sullivan in *The Miracle Worker* in the top ten of most memorable performances by actresses. Both placed her Emma in *The Turning Point* in the top twenty-five. The critics also placed her Mrs. Robinson in *The Graduate* in the top twenty-five. It is difficult to guess which she will best be remembered for. One can hope that other roles of similar stature lie ahead of her.

Lee Remick is another actress, also originally a dancer, who has had to go to a different medium—in her case, television—for recognition denied her in films. She was born in 1935 in Quincy, Massachusetts, trained on TV, and made a spectacular debut in movies as the sexy young drum majorette in *A Face in the Crowd* in 1957. She then scored heavily as the sexy wife in *The Long Hot Summer* in 1959 and established herself as a star as a rape victim in *Anatomy of a Murder* in 1959. This role was turned down by Lana Turner.

Remick won nomination for an Oscar as a drunk in *Days of Wine and Roses* in 1962, but the big prize has escaped her and she has since then had few parts worthy of her tremendous talent, at least not in films. She has proven her rare talent in a series of TV leads.

The gifted Tuesday Weld is another in a long list of one-time starlets whose ability as an actress long went unnoticed. She was born Susan Ker Weld in New York in August of 1943, supported her widowed mother and family as a child model and actress, reportedly had a nervous breakdown before she was ten, and was drinking and attempted suicide at twelve.

She made her first movie at thirteen. She made many mediocre movies thereafter and attracted attention for her free life-style. She finally began to achieve respect as an actress in the middle 1960s. She made a mistake in turning down the Faye Dunaway role in *Bonnie and Clyde* in 1967, but was impressive in the less successful *Pretty Poison* in 1968. She won nomination as supporting actress in *Looking for Mr. Goodbar* in 1977 and was superb in the television drama *Mothers and Daughters* in 1979, but her talent has mostly been neglected.

Another of today's strongest actresses, Piper Laurie, was denied opportunities because she started as a starlet. She was strictly window dressing in such films as *Francis Goes to the Races* and *Son of Ali Baba* in the early 1950s. She finally proved deep dramatic talent as Paul Newman's crippled girlfriend in *The Hustler* in 1961, but she retired from the screen after that.

She was born Rosetta Jacobs in 1932 in Detroit, and was the wife of critic Joseph Morgenstern before returning to Hollywood to win an Academy Award nomination as a supporting actress for her mother role in *Carrie* in 1976. She has been accepting occasional roles since. Recently she earned rave reviews as Karl Malden's wife and the mother of their restless brood in *Skag* on television in 1980.

It is hard to believe that Gena Rowlands broke onto Broadway as understudy to the lead in *The Seven Year Itch* in 1952, in the mindless, sexy part portrayed later on film by Marilyn Monroe. Rowlands established herself as a dramatic actress of ability as the young girlfriend of Edward G. Robinson in Broadway's *Middle of the Night* in 1956.

She married actor-writer-director John Cassavetes in 1954 and entered movies in 1958. Although she scored in *Lonely Are the Brave* in 1962, she may have afterward limited her opportunities by performing primarily in her husband's avante-garde films. She was stunning, however, in *Faces* in 1968, *Minnie and Moskowitz* in 1971, *A Woman Under the Influence* in 1972, for which she was nominated for an Oscar, and *Opening Night* in 1978, for which she should have been nominated.

Despite her lack of recognition, there may be no more talented actress performing today. She matched the immortal Bette Davis, point for point, in an acclaimed television pairing in *Strangers* in 1979.

Rowlands and Cassavetes have three children between the ages of ten and twenty. Their relationship has been tempestuous but enduring. Their arguments on sets are legendary. She says, "I admire him and would rather work with him than with anyone else. I would rather live with him than with anyone else. And sometimes I would just like to throw him right out the window."

Gena Rowlands in A Woman Under the Influence.

Karen Black with Jack Nicholson in Five Easy Pieces.

Valerie Perrine in Lenny.

A troubled Diana Ross in The Lady Sings the Blues.

A stunning talent newly arrived on the scene is that of Meryl Streep. Possessed of an angular beauty and thoughtful sensitivity, she won a nomination as a supporting actress for her stunning performance in *The Deer Hunter* in 1978 and honors for *The Seduction of Joe Tynan* and *Manhattan* in 1979. She won the New York and Los Angeles Critics Awards and an Oscar for her supporting role in *Kramer vs. Kramer* in 1979.

Karen Black in *Five Easy Pieces* and Valerie Perrine in *Lenny* made explosive debuts in 1970 and 1974, respectively, and won nominations as supporting actresses. Both might well have won. Neither has had outstanding opportunities since.

Kathleen Quinlan was superb as the unsettled young lady in *I Never Promised You a Rose Garden* in 1978, but somehow was overlooked in nominations.

Diana Ross was sensational singing and acting as Billie Holliday in *Lady Sings the Blues* in 1972. She was nominated, but did not win. Since then she has had only mediocre opportunities.

Similarly, Diahann Carroll, despite a nomination for *Claudine* in 1974, has had few chances to express her rare talent.

Cicely Tyson has had few big screen opportunities since *Sounder* in 1972. She has, however, proven herself to be one of the great actresses on TV.

The late 1970s suggests that the early 1980s may mark not only equality for women in everyday life, but in films as well. An increasing number of stellar roles for ladies are appearing. An increasing number of artistic actresses are appearing as well.

Jane Fonda, born in December of 1937, has been nominated for Oscars five times and has taken two. She is at the peak of her enormous power and already ranks with the immortals.

Faye Dunaway, born in January of 1941, has been nominated for Oscars three times—for *Bonnie and Clyde* in 1967, *Chinatown* in 1974, and *Network* in 1976, and won for the last. She is also at her peak.

Ellen Burstyn, born Edna Rae Gilooly in December of 1932, the daughter of a plumber, has been nominated for *The Last Picture Show* in 1971, *The Exorcist* in 1973, *Alice Doesn't Live Here Anymore* in 1974, for which she won, and *Same Time Next Year* in 1978. A former night-club chorine and actress in TV soap operas, she discovered the script for *Alice*, put together the package from rewriting to casting, and sold it to Warners for ten percent of the profits. Clearly, she is in command of her career.

Louise Fletcher was born to deaf parents in Alabama in July of 1934. Her father was a minister. Louise acted in summer stock and graduated to television in the late 1950s. Hampered by her height—at 5'10" she was too tall for some leading men—she married a producer and retired from acting in the early 1960s. She returned to her profession when offered a part in her first film, Robert Altman's *Thieves Like Us* in 1974, and then won an Oscar for her role as hardhearted nurse Ratched in *One Flew over the Cuckoo's Nest* in 1975. Her acceptance speech, given in part in sign language for her parents, was eloquent. She did not get many good opportunities in the late 1970s but has superb skills that should not be neglected.

The ladylike but lethal Jane Alexander was born in Boston in October of 1939, the daughter of a wealthy orthopedic surgeon, and schooled at Sarah Lawrence and the University of Edinburgh. She won a Best Actress nomination for repeating her role on Broadway in Hollywood's *The Great White Hope* in 1970 and Supporting Actress nominations for *All the President's Men* in 1976 and *Kramer vs. Kramer* in 1979. Her performance in *Hope* was overpowering, but she lost to Glenda Jackson for *Women in Love*. Alexander's performance as Eleanor Roosevelt in a recent television drama was remarkable, also. She is an actress of rare sensitivity. She may not be a "star type," but may yet get good chances to display her power.

Born in April of 1944 to wealthy member of high society and educated at Sarah Lawrence, Jill Clayburgh developed her acting talent in summer stock. She played leads in such musicals as *The Rothschilds* and *Pippin* on Broadway, made it big in movies in *An Unmarried Woman* in 1978 and *Starting Over* in 1979, for which she won Academy Award nominations, and she won the best actress award at the Cannes Film Festival for *An Unmarried Woman*. She may need only the right chances to make it as a major star.

Actresses such as Clayburgh, Sally Field, Diane Keaton, and Marsha Mason are impressively versatile, equally at home in comedic and dramatic parts.

Sally Field, born in November of 1946 in Pasadena, found fame and fortune in foolish roles, primarily as "The Flying Nun" on TV, and as a girlfriend to glamour guy Burt Reynolds. She established herself as an actress of great talent in television drama and, later, in films. In the title role in *Norma Rae* in 1979, she won both the New York and Los Angeles Critics Awards and the Oscar for Best Actress.

Sissy Spacek, a blue-eyed blonde from Texas, has specialized in neurotic teenage parts, which is quite a specialty. But the lady has talent. Born Mary Elizabeth Spacek on Christmas Day in 1949, she was twenty-four when she played a fifteen-year-old killer effectively in *Badlands* in 1973. She won an Oscar nomination as the lead in *Carrie* in 1976. Following that she was terrific in *Welcome to L.A.* in 1977 and as Loretta Lynn in *Coal Miner's Daughter* in 1980.

Diane Keaton won an Oscar for her first nomination, as the cutie-pie in Woody Allen's *Annie Hall* in 1977. In the film, she played a kooky lady. It was the sort of part she often plays in Allen's films. Offscreen, she had a romance with Allen, as well as with Warren Beatty and ballet star Mikhail Baryshnikoff.

Although she won for *Annie Hall*, Keaton may have given a greater performance in 1977 in the purely dramatic, nerve-shattering *Looking for Mr. Goodbar*. This skilled lady may need only a few roles outside her Allen ones to establish herself as a performer of great range.

Marsha Mason's marriage to writer Neil Simon does not appear to have limited her. It provided her with a powerful part in the largely autobiographical *Chapter Two* in 1979. Mason, born in April of 1942 in St. Louis, developed as an actress on and off Broadway. She arrived as a star in Hollywood with nominations for Oscars for her roles as the floozy in *Cinderella Liberty* in 1973 and a lonely lady in *The Goodbye Girl* in 1977. She lost both but was good enough to have won in either.

She scored heavily again in 1979 as a writer's second wife in *Chapter Two* and as the doctor to a dying girl in *Promises in the Dark*. Although she was Oscar nominated for only *Chapter Two*, again, she was good enough to win in either. As we have learned, justice does not always triumph in the honoring of outstanding film performers and performances, but one can always hope that as long as they remain in the race, the good will get their reward eventually.

Psycho *with Janet Leigh, John Gavin, and Anthony Perkins.*

Cecil B. DeMille, *here at his desk, was denied by Oscar.*

community of movies and even the most artistic of these was not worthy of Awards.

Of course, Alfred Hitchcock is not the only neglected director, only the best known. One other well-known director who never won an Oscar is Cecil B. DeMille. He was a master of the spectacle, his films were enormously popular, and he was a prominent public personality, partly due to a popular radio show, "Lux Radio Theater," which ran from 1936 through 1945.

His family had ties to the theater and DeMille studied acting in New York and broke onto Broadway in 1900. With Samuel Goldwyn and Jesse Lasky, he formed a motion picture partnership in the early days of the silents. *The Squaw Man* in 1914, their first film, was an enormous success. With it, they more or less founded Hollywood as the movie capital. DeMille produced, directed, and wrote many great hits of the 1920s including *The Ten Commandments* in 1923 and *The King of Kings* in 1927.

With the coming of the talkies he turned out such great hits as *The Sign of the Cross* in 1932, *Cleopatra* in 1934, *The Crusades* in 1935, *The Plainsman* in 1937, *Union Pacific* in 1939, *North-West Mounted Police* in 1940, *Reap the Wild Wind* in 1942, *Unconquered* in 1947, *Samson and Delilah* in 1949, *The Greatest Show on Earth* in 1952, and *The Ten Commandments* in 1956. Only *The Greatest Show on Earth* and *The Ten Commandments* were nominated for Best Picture honors, however. *Show* won. DeMille received his only directorial nomination for it, but he did not win. *Commandments* was nominated, but lost. DeMille was not nominated.

Two others besides Hitchcock were nominated as many as five times without winning. One was King Vidor, the other, Clarence Brown.

An early great, Vidor ranks with the most neglected in Oscar ranks. Vidor was nominated for *The Crowd* in 1927–28, *Hallelujah* in 1929–30, *The Champ* in 1931–32, *The Citadel* in 1938 and, after years in retirement, *War and Peace* in 1956—without winning. He could well have been nominated for *Street Scene* in 1932, *Our Daily Bread* in 1934, *Stella Dallas* in 1937, *Northwest Passage* in 1940, or *Duel in the Sun* in 1947.

As a schoolboy in Texas, he developed a passion for movies and went to work at a local nickelodeon. He bought a camera and shot local news events to sell to theaters. He and his wife, Florence, went to Hollywood to seek their fortune and she became a star actress. He became a leading director, making his mark with the silent *The Big Parade* in 1925.

In the early days of sound, the "talkies" were just that, almost all talk and no action. Vidor was one of the pioneers in effectively using sound to provide atmosphere. In his first talkie, the all-black musical *Hallelujah!* in 1929, he worked on location in silent form and then added the sound track. Arthur Knight points out in *The Liveliest Art*, that Vidor evoked mood with "the rhythmic swell of Negro spirituals, a woman's scream, a barking dog heard in the distance, the sounds of the swamp."

Vidor had a feeling for his fellow men, which, while pessimistic, produced some of the most moving individual scenes and full films in Hollywood history. His *The*

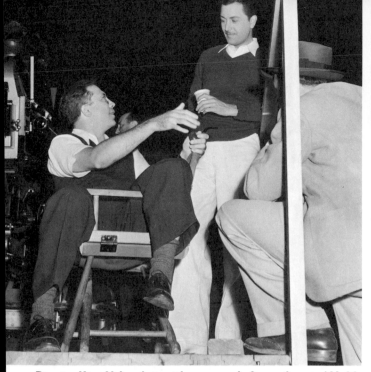

Director King Vidor chats with—guess who?—on the set of H. M. Pulman, Esq. That's the young Robert Young.

The Crowd, the King Vidor classic, which should have won Oscars.

Crowd is considered to be one of the great silent films of all time, a remarkably realistic and pessimistic view of the individual lost in the complexity of modern life. It lost to *Wings* in 1928, the first year of the Academy Awards. Vidor lost to Frank Borzage, who directed *Seventh Heaven* that year. Today, *The Crowd* is considered far superior.

Clarence Brown was nominated for *Anna Christie* in 1929–30, *A Free Soul* in 1930–31, *The Human Comedy* in 1943, *National Velvet* in 1945, and *The Yearling* in 1946 without winning. He was sentimental and romantic, a gentle man who had a reputation for dealing well with difficult stars. He directed Garbo in two silents—*Flesh and the Devil* and *A Woman of Affairs*—and five talkies—*Anna Christie, Romance, Inspiration, Anna Karenina,* and *Conquest*. He also directed *Ah, Wilderness* in 1935, *Idiot's Delight* and *The Rains Came* in 1939, *The White Cliffs of Dover* in 1942, and *Intruder in the Dust* in 1950.

Brown studied under the great European Maurice Tourneur, established himself with *The Eagle* with Rudolph Valentino and Vilma Banky in 1925, and had a noteworthy career of nearly thirty-five years without winning one Oscar.

Stanley Kubrick has been nominated four times—for *Dr. Strangelove* in 1964, *2001: A Space Odyssey* in 1968, *A Clockwork Orange* in 1971, and *Barry Lyndon* in 1975. He deserved nominations for *The Killing* in 1956 and *Paths of Glory* in 1957. He has not won an Oscar, but he has been one of the most inventive filmmakers. He makes few films and devotes a great deal of time to each.

Ernst Lubitsch, Sam Wood, and William Wellman have each been nominated three times without winning. Lubitsch was nominated for *The Patriot* in 1928–29, *The Love Parade* in 1929–30, and *Heaven Can Wait* in 1943. He was not nominated for *Monte Carlo* in 1930, *The Smiling Lieutenant* in 1931, *Broken Lullaby* in 1932, *Ninotchka* in 1939, *The Shop Around the Corner* in 1940, or *To Be or Not to Be* in 1942, although all were hailed as worthy. *Ninotchka* was nominated, but Lubitsch was not. He was a master of sophisticated comedy, which has been considered largely unworthy of Awards.

Lubitsch was another pioneer in the effective use of sound. In the early days, the cameras were locked in a sound-proof box. Lubitsch took them out of the box, shot silent, and dubbed in dialogue and other sound later. He was spectacular in the use of the camera. For example, in *Broken Lullaby* in 1932, an Armistice Day parade was shot through the crutches of a one-legged soldier. Generally, he had a touch so light, yet so clear it came to be known as the "Lubitsch Touch."

Sam Wood was nominated for *Goodbye, Mr. Chips* in 1939, *Kitty Foyle* in 1940, and *Kings Row* in 1942. He was not nominated for *A Night at the Opera* in 1935, *Our Town* or *Kitty Foyle* in 1940, *The Pride of the Yankees* in 1942, *For Whom the Bell Tolls* in 1943, or *Command Decision* or *The Stratton Story* in 1949. *Our Town, Kitty Foyle, The Pride,* and *For Whom* were nominated, but he was not. He was an unusually versatile director who did well with slapstick comedy, romantic drama, and spectacles, but he never received Awards.

Wellman was nominated for *A Star Is Born* in 1937, *Battleground* in 1949, and *The High and the Mighty* in 1954. He should have been nominated for *Wings* in 1927–28, *The Public Enemy* in 1931, *Nothing Sacred* in 1937, *Beau Geste* in 1939, *The Ox-Bow Incident* in 1943, or *The Story of GI Joe* in 1945. He could have been nominated for *The Light That Failed* in 1939 and *Roxie Hart* in 1942. *Wings* won the first Oscar, but Wellman was not even nominated. *The Ox-Bow Incident* was nominated, but Wellman was not.

Wellman was a troubled youth who was put on probation for car theft. He quit school to travel with a hockey team. When World War I broke out, he joined the French Foreign Legion as an ambulance driver, then became an ace pilot with the Lafayette Escadrille. He was awarded the Croix de Guerre after his plane was shot down.

After the war, he was a wing-walker with a barnstorming air troupe. He met Douglas Fairbanks, landed a plane on his estate, and asked him for work. From messenger boy, he became a bit actor, then director of cowboy films. He was directing Buck Jones films while John Ford was directing Tom Mix movies, and they used to exchange ideas.

Wellman made his mark with *Wings* and its classic air sequences. He went on to do a lot of lusty films. A heavy drinker and hard talker, he was a tough taskmaster on sets and had fights with Spencer Tracy and John Wayne, among others, but he got their best performances out of them.

He once said, "We went to San Antonio to shoot *Wings*. They wanted me to do the dogfight, but I wouldn't because there weren't any clouds. To do the dogfight against blue skies would have been like photographing a lot of flies. I waited thirty-three days.

The studio sent someone to threaten me, but I threw him out.

"Finally, I got the clouds and we got a dogfight that still stands. I had sixty-five planes in the air. I had over a thousand men. Some got hurt but not seriously. The whole thing took exactly five minutes and it still stands up fifty years later. It made the movie. They didn't invite me to the preview. They thought they had a bust. They had a hit. I'm proudest of that picture.

"Zanuck didn't want to do *Public Enemy*. He'd just done *Little Caesar*. I told him I'd make it the toughest gangster film of all. I did it. I wrote *A Star Is Born*. They didn't like it. I thought it was a hell of a story. I did it and it worked. Since then, it's been done and done.

"I bought *The Ox-Bow Incident* with my own money—the only time I did that. For $6,500. A beautiful story, but the guy who wrote it couldn't sell it. No one would let me do it until I took it to Zanuck. We'd had a beef and hadn't spoken for years. But I was desperate and took it to him. He knew it wouldn't make money, but let me do it. I loved it.

"I loved a few I did. The director makes the movie whatever it is, but he isn't the guy who sells tickets. Hitchcock, maybe. Not many. I don't care about awards. I just care about the movies I make." Maybe, but he was a master of movies who deserved rewards he never received.

A notable three-time nominee who never won was Busby Berkeley. He was, however, primarily a dance director. A category was created for him—dance direction. It lasted three years and he was nominated each year—for *Lullaby of Broadway* in 1935, *Gold Diggers of 1937* in 1936, and *Varsity Show* in 1937, but he did not win.

The elaborate musicals of Busby Berkeley featured countless girls in spectacular settings, but he never gained an Academy Award.

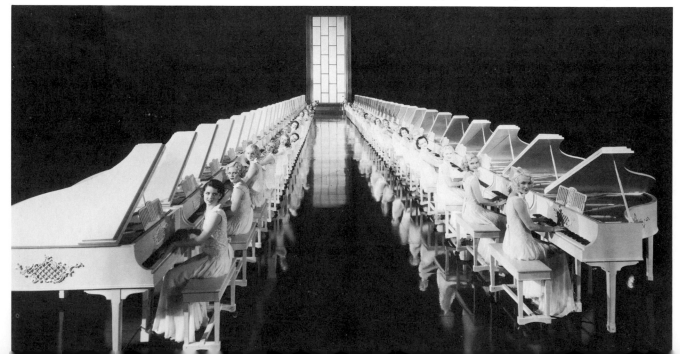

Berkeley also is well-remembered for *Whoopee* in 1930, *Gold Diggers of 1933*, and *Gold Diggers of 1935*, *Footlight Parade* in 1933, *Roman Scandals* in 1933, *Babes in Arms* in 1939, *Strike Up the Band* in 1940, *Ziegfeld Girl* in 1941, *For Me and My Gal* in 1942, *Girl Crazy* in 1943, *Call Me Mister* in 1951, and *Rose Marie* in 1954.

The son of a director and actress, he was on the Broadway stage at age three. In the 1920s he turned to the stage as a career and developed as a dance director. In the 1930s he shifted to movies in Hollywood. He codirected almost all of his films with others who handled the straight material.

Berkeley bored holes in the floors and ceilings so that he could shoot up or down on stages filled with hundreds of scantily clad ladies dancing intricate routines on ornate sets. He developed the overhead boom and shot from unusual angles. His work was spectacular, wildly inventive, and widely imitated.

Some of his dance numbers seem more like nonsense than art today, but he has become a cult figure admired by many for his influence on the early musicals.

More recently, three other directors batting 0-for-3 have been Arthur Penn, Stanley Kramer, and Richard Brooks.

Penn, an eminent television and stage director, was nominated for *The Miracle Worker* in 1962, *Bonnie and Clyde* in 1967, and *Alice's Restaurant* in 1969. The first two, especially, were extraordinary pieces of work and worthy of Awards.

Kramer was nominated for *The Defiant Ones* in 1958, *Judgment at Nuremberg* in 1961, and *Guess Who's Coming to Dinner* in 1967. He might have been nominated for *Champion* or *Home of the Brave* in 1949, *Death of a Salesman* in 1951, *The Wild One* or *The Caine Mutiny* in 1954, *On the Beach* in 1959, *Inherit the Wind* in 1960, or *Ship of Fools* in 1965. An independent director-producer before it became fashionable, Kramer bucked the establishment to turn out meaningful "message" films and deserved an award somewhere along the way, other than the Irving Thalberg Award he received in 1961 for the consistent high quality of his filmmaking.

Brooks was nominated for *The Professionals* in 1966, *In Cold Blood* in 1967, and *Looking for Mr. Goodbar* in 1977. It is interesting that he was nominated as director of these films, but that the films were not nominated for Best Picture. *In Cold Blood* deserved a Best Picture nomination. *Goodbar* hit with as much impact as any movie of recent years.

Originally a sportswriter and radio writer, Brooks also wrote books that were turned into films (including *Crossfire* in 1947, which dealt with anti-homosexuality

in its book form, but with anti-semitism as a movie). Brooks might well have been nominated as director of *The Blackboard Jungle* in 1955, *The Catered Affair* in 1956, *Cat on a Hot Tin Roof* in 1958, *Elmer Gantry* in 1960, *Sweet Bird of Youth* in 1962, or *The Happy Ending*, which this skilled craftsman wrote, produced, and directed for his wife, Jean Simmons, in 1969.

Non-winners nominated twice include directors Ernst Lubitsch, W. S. Van Dyke, Henry King, Mark Robson, Robert Rossen, and Otto Preminger.

The Berlin-born Lubitsch was a master of sophisticated comedy who was successful in both the silent and sound eras. He was nominated for *The Love Parade* in 1929–30 and *Heaven Can Wait* in 1943, but was as well known for *Ninotchka* in 1939, *To Be or Not To Be* in 1942, and many other fine films in a thirty-year string of hits. He received a special Oscar, but not as a reward for a film.

Woody Van Dyke was a versatile director nominated for *The Thin Man* in 1934 and *San Francisco* in 1946, but also well known for many musicals, westerns, and outdoor epics.

Henry King was a durable director whose career covered fifty years. He was nominated for *Song of Bernadette* in 1943 and *Wilson* in 1944, but also did well with *In Old Chicago* in 1938, *Jesse James* in 1939, *Stanley and Livingstone* in 1939, *Twelve O'Clock High* in 1949, and *The Gunfighter* in 1950.

Montreal-born Mark Robson worked with Robert Wise on the editing of the Orson Welles masterpieces *Citizen Kane* and *The Magnificent Ambersons* and won nominations for *Peyton Place* in 1957 and *The Inn of the Sixth Happiness* in 1958, but, unfortunately, not for *Champion* or *Home of the Brave* in 1949, or *Bright Victory* in 1951.

Robert Rossen was smeared during the Communist hunt in the 1950s, but he won nominations for *All the Kings Men* in 1949 and *The Hustler* in 1961. He should have won nominations for *The Roaring Twenties* in 1939, *The Sea Wolf* in 1941, *A Walk in the Sun* in 1946, *Johnny O'Clock* and *Body and Soul* in 1947, and *The Brave Bulls* in 1951.

The bald, outspoken Otto Preminger has become almost as much a public personality as Hitchcock and DeMille due to his frequent talk-show appearances. The Viennese-born former assistant to famed Max Reinhardt in Austria won nominations for *Laura* in 1944 and *The Cardinal* in 1963 and might have won for *The Moon Is Blue* in 1953, *The Man with the Golden Arm* in 1955, or *Anatomy of a Murder* in 1959.

Aside from DeMille, notable non-winners nominated only once include Henry Hathaway, William Dieterle,

Mervyn LeRoy, foreground, directs Robert Taylor in a scene from Johnny Eager. *Cameraman Hal Rosson is behind LeRoy.*

Mervyn LeRoy, John Farrow, Robert Siodmak, Jean Negulesco, Edward Dmytryk, John Sturges, and Howard Hawks.

Hathaway was nominated for *Lives of a Bengal Lancer* in 1935, Dieterle for *The Life of Emile Zola* in 1937, LeRoy for *Random Harvest* in 1942, Farrow for *Wake Island* in 1942, Siodmak for *The Killers* in 1946, Negulesco for *Johnny Belinda* in 1948, Dmytryk for *Crossfire* in 1947, Sturges for *Bad Day at Black Rock* in 1955, and Hawks for *Sergeant York* in 1941.

Superior with suspense, Hathaway also directed *The House on 92nd Street* in 1945, *Kiss of Death* in 1947, and *Call Northside 777* in 1948, as well as *The Desert Fox* in 1951. Dmytryk also directed *Murder My Sweet* in 1944, *The Caine Mutiny* in 1954, and *A Walk on the Wild Side* in 1962.

Dieterle, brilliant at biography, directed *The Story of Louis Pasteur* in 1935, *Juarez* in 1939, *The Hunchback of Notre Dame* in 1939, and *Dr. Ehrlich's Magic Bullet* in 1940. Siodmak also did *The Spiral Staircase* in 1946, and Negulesco also directed *Humoresque* in 1946.

Farrow was married to Maureen O'Sullivan at one time and they had a daughter, Mia, now an actress. His directorial credits include *Two Years Before the Mast* in 1946 and *The Big Clock* in 1948. Sturges was superior with westerns, including *Gunfight at the OK Corral* in 1957 and *Last Train from Gun Hill* in 1959. He also filmed *The Old Man and the Sea* in 1958.

Hollywood does neglect its own. A leader in the film community, the versatile Mervyn LeRoy did wonders with *Little Caesar* in 1930, *I Am a Fugitive from a Chain Gang* in 1932, Anthony Adverse in 1936, *Blossoms in the Dust* in 1941, *Johnny Eager* in 1941, *Madame Curie* in 1943, *Thirty Seconds over Tokyo* in 1944, and *Mister Roberts* in 1955, without winning an Academy Award.

Hawks is regarded as one of the great directors and the fact that he has not won even one Oscar must be regarded as a great oversight. He was nominated only for *Sergeant York* in 1941, not for *The Dawn Patrol* in 1930, *The Crowd Roars* in 1932, *Scarface* in 1933, *Twentieth Century* in 1934, *Bringing Up Baby* in 1938, *Only Angels Have Wings* and *His Girl Friday* in 1939, *Ball of Fire* in 1941, *To Have and Have Not* in 1944, *The Big Sleep* in 1946, *Red River* in 1948, and *Rio Bravo* in 1959.

Born in Indiana but reared in California, he broke into films as a young man working with props at the studios. He was a professional automobile racer on the side and became one of the most versatile directors. He could handle everything from light comedy to heavy drama, from war films to westerns. A cult has sprung up around him, celebrating his neglected works. He may have been neglected because he was not an innovator—he had a simple style that hid his technical excellence.

A bit of a loner, shy of writers, stern on his sets, Hawks once said "the greatest director was John Ford. I think he is a lot better than I am, but I like it when people say I'm somewhere near as good as he is. I enjoyed it when he said I made the best westerns. But

Neglected director Howard Hawks with Loretta Young.

he did. I did my best. I'm not ashamed to admit I emulate anything that anybody has done that is any good. I don't do it the same way, but I learn from it.

"I think that motion is far more interesting than just talking. It is a motion picture, after all. On the stage, what you hear may be most important. On the screen, what you see may be most important. Which is why good stage plays don't always make it on the screen.

"I've tried to make my dialogue go fast, faster than most in movies. Sometimes we'll put a few unnecessary words on the front of a sentence and a few on the end and we let the actors' talking overlap. You still hear everything you have to hear and it works well. This is realistic.

"I believe in realism. I put truth in my pictures. Things I've seen and heard. They say I repeat myself, but that's because when you find something that's real and works you want to stay with it. A fighter with a good left hook doesn't just throw one good one and then not throw another one the rest of the fight.

"I can kill three people and get them off to the morgue before that guy that made *The Wild Bunch* can get one of them on the ground. I don't use slow motion effects because we don't see life in slow motion and I want you to see my story on the screen the way you'd see it in life.

"I shoot as plain as I can shoot. I don't go in for all these special effects. I don't go for crazy camera angles. You don't see things from way up high or way down low, you know. There's nothing new, anyway. They've been making movies a long time and they've tried everything. You've seen it all. I say, keep it simple."

This brings us to Orson Welles, another non-winning director, nominated only once—for *Citizen Kane* in 1941. He should also have been nominated for *The Magnificent Ambersons* in 1942, *Journey into Fear* in 1943, *The Lady from Shanghai* in 1948, and *Touch of Evil* in 1958. It is argued that what he did had been done before, but no one ever put together camera angles and lighting to show the subjects and story in such revealing ways or used lighting and sound systems as effectively in portraying the human condition. He, however, did not keep it simple.

Welles was born in Kenosha, Wisconsin, in May of 1915. His parents were wealthy. His father was an inventor, his mother a concert pianist. A child prodigy, he was painting, writing poetry, and reciting Shakespeare before most children talk. He was eight when his mother died and his father took him on a world tour. He was twelve when his father died and he went to live with a Chicago doctor. Graduating from private school, Orson turned down college scholarships to go to

Orson Welles wrote, directed, and starred in *Citizen Kane*, but all lost the Oscar race. Everett Sloane and Joseph Cotten were not winners either.

Ireland and study at Dublin's Gate Theater.

He went back and forth between Broadway and Europe before he broke onto the Broadway stage as an actor. John Houseman took him to Phoenix to work in his theater there, then formed The Mercury Theater with him. They went on radio with it in 1938 with a stock company doing drama, much of it experimental. Their adaption of H. G. Wells' *The War of the Worlds* on Sunday night, the 30th of October, 1938, as a Halloween prank depicting the invasion from outer space of a small town in New Jersey, actually sent many into the streets in panic, created a sensation, and made Welles a star.

As Houseman faded into the background, though long a major force in films and theater, Welles went to Hollywood. Several screenplays were junked—one an adaptation of Joseph Conrad's *Heart of Darkness*, on which the recent *Apocalypse Now* was based. Then "The Boy Wonder"—aged twenty-six—hit the heights with the controversial *Citizen Kane*, which told a story in documentary fashion as film never had before.

It endures as one of the world's great cinema masterpieces. Either it or *Gone With the Wind* is generally voted the greatest American motion picture of all time. As good as *How Green Was My Valley* and its direction by John Ford were, the fact that they beat out *Citizen Kane* and Welles is Oscar's most massive mistake. Contributing to its defeat was the campaign by William Randolph Hearst, the publisher on whom Kane was based, to discredit the film. In addition, the film was not a commercial success.

Welles' studio, RKO, stepped in and took over partial control of his future films. The studio cut *The Magnificent Ambersons* ruthlessly, yet it has remained a marvelous picture of the American past and a film which has grown in stature over the years. The film was nominated for an Oscar, but Welles was not.

Lacking complete control of his films, Welles' career began to slump. He bounced back with the bizarre, breathtaking thriller *The Lady from Shanghai* for Columbia in 1948. Neither he nor his film was nominated for an Academy Award, but *The Lady from Shanghai* holds up better than many that were. When the film was finished, he was divorced by his star, Rita Hayworth. The film did poorly at the box office, all but finishing Welles as a major force in Hollywood. The public simply was not ready for his staggering originality.

He made *Macbeth* for Republic, but lacked the money to make it right. Moving to Europe, he later made *Othello* more effectively. In Europe he mostly made movies that were not successful, were not finished, or were not released. All along he survived by working well as an actor in various films. Returning to the United States, he wrote and directed *Touch of Evil* in 1958. It did not do well here and was not nominated for any awards. It did wonderfully well in Europe, winning film festival prizes, and today is considered a masterwork almost in a class with *Kane*.

Returning to Europe he turned out a film version of Kafka's *The Trial* that lacked that budget to be the movie it might have been. He did *Chimes at Midnight*, a collection of Shakespearean scenes, in 1966, and while it did not do well, some consider it one of his finest films. Returning again to America, he since has worked irregularly as an actor and a director. The once slim, handsome Welles has become something of a jolly fat man who tells intriguing stories while guesting on television talk shows. His was a genius which never was rewarded as it deserved.

Many outstanding directors never have been nominated for even one Oscar. These include Rouben Mamoulian, Edmund Goulding, John Cromwell, Mitchell Leisen, Fritz Lang, Lloyd Bacon, Nick Ray, and Raoul Walsh.

The Russian-born Mamoulian studied at the Moscow Art Theater and later in London where he first directed for the stage. He came to the U.S. in the early 1920s and made his mark on Broadway with *Porgy*, before Gershwin transformed it into an operetta. He went into films with other stage directors when movie moguls thought they best knew how to handle sound on the new "talkies." But he was one of those who re-liberated the camera by shooting, and then dubbing.

In his first film, *Applause* in 1929, he opens with a closeup of the great star Helen Morgan's aging face as she reminisces about her youth, then he pans to a picture of her youthful face. In one long shot we see only her feet as she leaves the theater and the feet of the men she encounters on her way, and hear only snatches of the dialogue. In *Love Me Tonight* hunted deer bound across the screen in waltz time. Later in the film, characters carouse across a nobleman's chateau chanting, "The son of a gun is nothing but a tailor," as if it was a Christmas carol.

Mamoulian handled an early Technicolor epic, 1935's *Becky Sharp*, beautifully and imaginatively. His finest film may have been *Dr. Jekyll and Mr. Hyde* in 1932 or *Queen Christina* in 1933, in which he brought out the greatest in Garbo. He also did 1939's *Golden Boy* and 1941's *Blood and Sand*. He had not done a film in almost ten years when he directed *Silk Stockings* in 1957. He was sadly neglected.

Goulding's many fine films include *Grand Hotel* in 1932, *The Dawn Patrol* in 1938, *Dark Victory* in 1939, *The Old Maid* in 1939, *The Razor's Edge* in 1946, and *Nightmare Alley* in 1947.

Cromwell's splendid work includes *Of Human Bondage* in 1934, *The Prisoner of Zenda* in 1937, *Algiers* in 1938, *Made for Each Other* and *In Name Only* in 1939, *Abe Lincoln in Illinois* in 1940, *So Ends Our Night* in 1941, *Since You Went Away* in 1944, *The Enchanted Cottage* in 1945, and *Anna and the King of Siam* in 1946.

Leisen was a romantic and his best work may have been *Hold Back the Dawn* in 1941, *Lady in the Dark* in 1944, and *To Each His Own* in 1946.

Bacon did many of the memorable Busby Berkeley musicals and also such barn-burners as *The Oklahoma Kid* in 1939, *Brother Orchid* and *Knute Rockne—All American* in 1940, and *Action in the North Atlantic* in 1943.

Lang did brooding, dark works of *film noir* such as *Man Hunt* in 1941, *The Ministry of Fear* and *The Woman in the Window* in 1944, *Scarlet Street* in 1945, and *The Blue Gardenia* in 1953. Lang has a cult following, as does Ray.

Ray studied under Elia Kazan and John Houseman. He turned out such stylized films that he has been favored by French devotees of the *auteur theory*, who feel that the great director truly is the author of his film. His socially rebellious work included *They Live by Night* in 1949, *Knock on Any Door* in 1949, *In a Lonely Place* in 1950, *The Lusty Men* in 1952,

Neglected director Raoul Walsh lets 'em know what he wants on location for High Sierra.

Johnny Guitar in 1954, *Rebel Without a Cause* in 1955, and *Bigger Than Life* in 1956.

He was once married to actress Gloria Grahame, but had problems with sex, drink, drugs, and gambling, according to an old writer-friend, Myron Meisel. Meisel says, "His hurt and toughness permeate his best films, expressed with the most acute ability in film history.... He could make films so intense, so visually expressive and so thematically compelling that for all the brevity of his directing career he was undeniably one of the greatest artists ever to work in film." French critic Jean-Luc Goddard regarded Ray as a man who created art, and a giant. Yet, Ray was not nominated one time for an Oscar.

Nor was Raoul Walsh ever nominated. A rugged gent and hardworking professional, he turned out *High Sierra, Manpower, They Died with Their Boots On,* and *The Strawberry Blonde* in one year, 1941. His hard-hitting directorial achievements also included *The Roaring Twenties* in 1939, *They Drive by Night* in 1940, and *White Heat* in 1949.

Walsh was the son of a clothing designer in New York. He ran away to sea, then returned to work as a cowboy in the Southwest. He started to act and landed in Hollywood in 1912 as an actor for and assistant to the great D. W. Griffith. Walsh directed the tremendously successful silent *What Price Glory* in 1926.

He pioneered outdoor sound with the use of a mobile newsreel truck on *In Old Arizona* in 1929. A jackrabbit jumped through the windshield and the glass cut one of Walsh's eyes badly. He had it taken out and he wore a patch thereafter. He had been playing the lead but turned it over to Warner Baxter, who won the second Best Actor Oscar with it.

Walsh once said, "The loss of one eye never mattered much. All I ever needed was one. It was one of those things that happens to you in life. I think we early directors lived life more fully than some of those since. And our way of life showed in the kind of films we did.

"I always worked fast. I believed it was a motion picture, so I moved it. A lot of actors didn't like to work with me because of this, but the good ones liked it. I discovered John Wayne and he was a great star and a great American. He was working on a set and I liked his looks and gave him a part. Also his name.

"I worked with Jimmy Cagney and Humphrey Bogart, great guys. Cagney just did his job, but Bogie grumbled about it. I got along with him because I was as tough as he was and he couldn't bluff me. I got along with Errol Flynn because I could drink as good as he could and didn't give a damn about his sex life.

"Directing? You get a good story, throw the script away, get good actors, and let them tell the story as simply as possible."

Walsh was the one who borrowed John Barrymore's body from the funeral home the day he died and propped him up on drinking buddy Flynn's couch as a surprise for the saddened Flynn. Walsh was one of a kind that goes back to the early days of Oscar and one of those skilled directors whose neglect by Oscar is total and almost tragic.

It is an old story, which continues to this day. Sydney Pollack, Sidney Lumet, Peter Bogdanovich, John Frankenheimer, John Cassavetes, Martin Scorsese, Alan J. Pakula, Sam Peckinpah, Roman Polanski, George Lucas, and Robert Altman are modern directors of awesome accomplishments who have not won Oscars.

Pollack was nominated only for *They Shoot Horses, Don't They?* in 1969, not for *Jeremia Johnson* in 1972 or *The Way We Were* in 1973. Polanski, the little giant of Polish film, was nominated for *Chinatown* in 1974, but not for *Rosemary's Baby* in 1968.

Lumet was nominated for *12 Angry Men* in 1957, *Dog Day Afternoon* in 1975, and *Network* in 1976, but not for *Long Day's Journey into Night* in 1962, *The Pawnbroker* in 1965, *Serpico* in 1973, or *Murder on the Orient Express* in 1974. Frankenheimer was not nominated once for *All Fall Down, The Manchurian Candidate* or *The Birdman of Alcatraz* in 1962, *Grand Prix* in 1966, *The Gypsy Moths* in 1969, or *The Iceman Cometh* in 1973.

often led him into thorny territory and he has not always emerged unscraped, but that instinct has sometimes paid off with incredibly high rolls."

Critic Martin Knelman has said, "Clearly, he still has what only a handful of Hollywood directors have ever had—the talent and will to make great pictures after a string of failures."

Huston says, "I don't know what a great director is, so I can't tell you if I'm one of them. If you get the right people together you've, got a chance to do a picture right, but sometimes you do good work but the finished product doesn't come out right. I can't even tell you what was my best work. Or worst. Asking a director to name his favorite picture is like asking a father to name his favorite son. He may name the one with the harelip. You may love the imperfect one."

Although some of his films, such as *Beat the Devil, Moby Dick, The Misfits,* and *Reflections in a Golden Eye* are not generally regarded as great pictures, there are cults that consider them among the greatest ever made. Almost certainly you have to consider John Huston, along with Alfred Hitchcock, Howard Hawks, Stanley Kubrick, Stanley Kramer, William Wellman, Orson Welles, and one or two others of the neglected as among the great directors, although, as the movie community has voted it, I suppose you would have to distinguish the two-time Award-winners as the class of the clan.

These include Lewis Milestone, Frank Lloyd, Leo McCarey, Joseph Mankiewicz, Robert Wise, Elia Kazan, George Stevens, Fred Zinnemann, and Billy Wilder.

Milestone, McCarey, Lloyd and Wise were nominated only three times each. Milestone won for *Two Arabian Nights* in 1927-28 and *All Quiet on the Western Front* in 1929-30, but lost for *The Front Page* in 1931. The Award for *Arabian* was the only time it was given for comedy direction. Other outstanding films he directed include *The General Died at Dawn* in 1936, *Of Mice and Men* in 1939, *A Walk in the Sun* in 1945, and *Les Miserables* in 1952.

Lloyd won for three films—*The Divine Lady, Weary River* and *Drag*—in 1928-29 and for *Cavalcade* in 1932-33, but not for *Mutiny on the Bounty* in 1935. Other outstanding films he directed include *A Tale of Two Cities* in 1935 and *If I Were King* in 1938.

Wise did not win for *I Want to Live* in 1958, but did for *West Side Story* in 1961 and *Sound of Music* in 1965. His other outstanding directorial achievements include *The Set-Up* in 1949, *Executive Suite* in 1954, *Somebody Up There Likes Me* in 1956, and *The Sand Pebbles* in 1966.

McCarey, a master of human comedy, won for *The Awful Truth* in 1937 and *Going My Way* in 1944, but not for *The Bells of St. Mary's* in 1945. Other achievements include *Duck Soup* in 1933, *Ruggles of Red Gap* in 1935, and *Good Sam* in 1948.

Mankiewicz was nominated four times. He won for *A Letter to Three Wives* in 1949 and *All About Eve* in 1950, but not for *Five Fingers* in 1952, and *Sleuth* in 1972. Originally an outstanding screenwriter, his other directorial triumphs include *People Will Talk* in 1951, *Julius Caesar* in 1953, *The Barefoot Contessa* in 1954, and *The Quiet American* in 1958.

Kazan and Stevens were nominated five times each.

Kazan, the genius from the stage, won for *Gentleman's Agreement* in 1958 and *On the Waterfront* in 1954, but notably not for *A Streetcar Named Desire* in 1951, *East of Eden* in 1955, or *America, America* in 1963. He was cofounder of the Actors Studio and "The Method" style of acting, which produced Brando, Dean, Newman, and so many more. Kazan also directed such powerful films as *A Tree Grows in Brooklyn* in 1945, *Boomerang* in 1947, *Pinky* in 1949, *Panic in the Streets* in 1950, *Viva Zapata* in 1955, *A Face in the Crowd* in 1957, and *Splendor in the Grass* in 1961.

Stevens, a movie pioneer who originally directed shorts and worked with Hal Roach on early Laurel and Hardy comedies, won for *A Place in the Sun* in 1951 and *Giant* in 1956, but not for *The More the Merrier* in 1943, *Shane* in 1953, or *The Diary of Anne Frank* in 1959. Extremely selective, his slim list of less than fifteen films in less than thirty-five years included, at his peak, *Gunga Din* in 1939, *Penny Serenade* in 1941, *The Talk of the Town* in 1942, and *I Remember Mama* in 1948.

Zinnemann was nominated seven times, Wilder eight times.

Fred Zinnemann, born in Vienna and holder of a master's degree in law from the University of Vienna, was a film fan who found work as an assistant with movie companies in Paris and Berlin. He then came to California and assisted Berthold Viertel, Robert Flaherty, and Busby Berkeley before getting his break. He won for *From Here to Eternity* in 1953 and *A Man for All Seasons* in 1960, but not for *The Search* in 1948, *High Noon* in 1952, *The Nun's Story* in 1959, *The Sundowners* in 1960, and *Julia* in 1970. He was not nominated for *Act of Violence* in 1949, *The Men* in 1950, *Oklahoma* in 1955, *A Hatful of Rain* in 1957.

Billy Wilder also was born in Vienna and studied law at the University of Vienna, but he did not graduate. He worked as a newspaper reporter in Vienna and Berlin, supporting himself on the side as a taxi-dancer.

"I was a gigolo," he has said. Also a film fan, he found some work as a screenwriter in the German movie industry, but, a Jew, he fled to California when the Nazis came into power.

He lived with Peter Lorre while learning English and commenced a collaboration with Charles Brackett which produced scripts for such successful comedies as *Ninotchka* in 1939 and *Ball of Fire* in 1942 and such successful dramas as *Double Indemnity* in 1944, *The Lost Weekend* in 1945, and *Sunset Boulevard* in 1950. He and Brackett won Oscars for the writing of the last two. Wilder and I. A. L. Diamond won Oscars for the writing of *The Apartment* in 1960.

Wilder won other Oscars for his direction of *The Lost Weekend* in 1945 and *The Apartment* in 1960, but not for *Double Indemnity* in 1944, *Sunset Boulevard* in 1950, *Stalag 17* in 1953, *Sabrina* in 1954, *Witness for the Prosecution* in 1957, or *Some Like It Hot* in 1959.

Only three men have won three or more Academy Awards for direction. Presumably, this puts them at the peak of the mountain. Frank Capra captured three in six nominations, William Wyler three in a record twelve nominations, John Ford a record four in only five nominations.

Capra, Sicilian-born son of an immigrant California orange-picker, was a college graduate in chemical engineering who drifted into film work simply while looking for work. Originally, he created comedy scenes for Mack Sennett and Harry Langdon in silent times. He had a flair for comedy with a social message and it was his movies which made crusty Harry Cohn's Columbia Studios successful.

Capra won for *It Happened One Night* in 1934, *Mr. Deeds Goes to Town* in 1936, and *You Can't Take It With You* in 1938, but not for *Lady for a Day* in 1932–33, *Mr. Smith Goes to Washington* in 1939, or *It's a Wonderful Life* in 1946. He was not nominated for *Lost Horizon* in 1939 or *Meet John Doe* in 1941 and has been considered out-of-date and given few opportunities since the middle 1940s.

His autobiography was entitled *The Name Above the Title* and he claimed to be the first to attain that honor among directors, preceding Hitchcock and DeMille. He subscribed to the "auteur theory" and his motto was "one man, one film." His theme was the little man bucking a corrupt society and his movies were almost all of a pattern. They may be considered corny today, but they were heartwarming, good movies.

He told me once, "My movies got people into the theater, they entertained them, and they made them think, which I think is a pretty good combination. I identify with the common man and I think he is capable of uncommon deeds. They say I'm old-fashioned, but I think the old values—love, honesty, wanting to do for others as you would want to have them do for you—will endure. Today's movie business is cynical and mercenary and so I want no part of it. I'm happy lecturing to those who will listen."

On the basis of nominations, Wyler would be the dean of directors. He won for *Mrs. Miniver* in 1942, *The Best Years of Our Lives* in 1946, and *Ben-Hur* in 1959, but not for *Dodsworth* in 1936, *Wuthering Heights* in 1939, *The Letter* in 1940, *The Little Foxes* in 1941, *The Heiress* in 1949, *Detective Story* in 1951, *Roman Holiday* in 1953, *Friendly Persuasion* in 1956, or *The Collector* in 1965. He was not nominated for *Dead End* in 1937, *Jezebel* in 1938, *Roman Holiday* in 1953, or *The Desperate Hours* in 1955.

Born in Germany, a business student in Switzerland and a violin student in Paris, Wyler was brought to this country and placed in films by a cousin of his mother's, Carl Laemmle, then head of Universal. Wyler started as a publicist and worked his way into the industry. He debuted as an assistant producer and director on the silents *The Hunchback of Notre Dame* in 1923 and, ironically, the original *Ben-Hur* in 1927. Working with a favored cameraman, Gregg Toland, Wyler developed a style in which key scenes were shot in single, long takes, instead of a succession of short cuts, and so he sustained intensity and interest.

Wyler demanded discipline and dedication from his actors. Each take might be filmed twenty, forty, eighty, or a hundred times before he was satisfied with it. Many hated him for this. But they loved him for their rewards. More starring and supporting performers won Oscars under his direction—fourteen—than under any other director. Nine won under Kazan. Wyler once said, "Nothing worthwhile comes without hard work and sacrifice. I was not a fancy director, but I sought perfection. It is not attainable, but it is worth shooting for."

John Ford once told me, "We work hard making my films, but we have one hell of a lot of fun." He was born Sean O'Feeney, the youngest of thirteen children of Irish immigrants who operated a saloon in Portland, Maine. He joined his brother, Francis Ford, in Hollywood where Francis, a former stage actor, had become a writer and director. John worked as a stuntman and an extra, appearing in D. W. Griffith's *The Birth of a Nation* in 1915. He directed Harry Carey westerns, changed his name in 1923, and directed two significant silents, *The Iron Horse* in 1924 and *Four Sons* in 1928.

John Ford won four Oscars, but never for one of his westerns. Neither Henry Fonda nor Alice Faye, a visitor to the set of The Grapes of Wrath, won. Nor did that film.

Ford won Oscar for *The Informer* in 1935, *The Grapes of Wrath* in 1940, *How Green Was My Valley* in 1941, and *The Quiet Man* in 1952, but not for *Stagecoach* in 1939. He was somehow not nominated for *The Lost Patrol* in 1934, *The Hurricane* in 1938, *The Long Voyage Home* in 1940, *My Darling Clementine* in 1946, *The Fugitive* in 1947, *Fort Apache* in 1948, *Three Godfathers* or *She Wore a Yellow Ribbon* in 1949, *Rio Grande* in 1950, *The Searchers* in 1956, or *The Man Who Shot Liberty Valance* in 1962.

A rough-cut, but soft-hearted man, a man's man but a sentimentalist, Ford formed close friendships with John Wayne, Ward Bond, Jimmy Stewart, Henry Fonda, and Victor McLaglen, who frequently starred in his films. His directorial technique was simple, but eloquent. Although generally considered the greatest of all Hollywood directors, he did not care about Awards, but wondered why none of his had come for his beloved westerns. In my interview, he asked me, "Where would Hollywood be without the western? Why is it so unappreciated as an art form?"

He shot most of his westerns in Monument Valley, where California, Arizona, and Utah meet, and other directors did not dare trespass on this site. "It has everything—desert, rivers, mountains," Ford said. "Just as the old West had everything that is a part of the American spirit. Motion pictures are pictures. They are pictorial. Few ever remarked on the pictorial beauty of my western films, but if pictorial beauty can't be a part of the greatness of a film I don't know what can be."

If the voters did not, the critics did. Much as this book does not want to criticize winners of Oscar so much as it wants to celebrate the most memorable of losers, likewise the devoted cult of Ford fanciers does not want to criticize the splendid films for which he won so much as it wants to celebrate those, especially westerns, which lost. Ford fans may be divided among which are the best, but united in feeling that the best do not always win.

EIGHT

The Classic Losers

MOVIES ARE MADE as well today as any day in the history of films. There just aren't as many of them. There was a time in the late 1930s and early 1940s when ten motion pictures were nominated for Academy Awards annually, a time when movies of enduring merit were denied Oscars simply because only one winner is selected each year.

In 1936, when *The Great Ziegfeld* won, *Anthony Adverse, Dodsworth, Libeled Lady, Mr. Deeds Goes to Town, Romeo and Juliet, San Francisco, The Story of Louis Pasteur,* and *A Tale of Two Cities* did not win.

In 1937, when *The Life of Emile Zola* won, *The Awful Truth, Captains Courageous, Dead End, The Good Earth, In Old Chicago, Lost Horizon, 100 Men and a Girl, Stage Door,* and *A Star Is Born* did not win.

In 1938, when *You Can't Take It With You* won, *The Adventures of Robin Hood, Alexander's Ragtime Band, Boys Town, The Citadel, Four Daughters, Grand Illusion, Jezebel, Pygmalion,* and *Test Pilot* did not win.

Hollywood may have hit its peak in 1939 when *Gone With the Wind* won. *Dark Victory, Goodbye, Mr. Chips, Love Affair, Mr. Smith Goes to Washington, Ninotchka, Of Mice and Men, Stagecoach, The Wizard of Oz,* and *Wuthering Heights* did not win. *Beau Geste, Golden Boy,* and *The Hunchback of Notre Dame* were not even nominated.

In 1940, when *Rebecca* won, *All This and Heaven Too, Foreign Correspondent, The Grapes of Wrath, The Great Dictator, Kitty Foyle, The Letter, The Long Voyage Home, Our Town,* and *The Philadelphia Story* did not win. *The Great Dictator* was not nominated.

When *How Green Was My Valley* won in 1941, *Blossoms in the Dust, Citizen Kane, Here Comes Mr. Jordan, The Little Foxes, The Maltese Falcon, One Foot in Heaven, Sergeant York,* and *Suspicion* did not win. *Ball of Fire, Penny Serenade, The Sea Wolf,* and *Blood and Sand* were among the missing.

In 1942, *Mrs. Miniver* won, but *The Invaders, Kings Row, The Magnificent Ambersons, The Pied Piper, The Pride of the Yankees, Random Harvest, The Talk of the Town, Wake Island,* and *Yankee Doodle Dandy* did not, while *Now Voyager, My Sister Eileen,* and *This Above All* did not even make the list.

We could go on and on.

In 1935 when *Mutiny on the Bounty* won, *The Informer, Les Miserables, The Lives of a Bengal Lancer,* and *Top Hat* were among those that did not. In 1948 when *Hamlet* won, *The Treasure of the Sierra Madre, The Snake Pit,* and *Johnny Belinda* were losers. *The African Queen, The Naked City, Red River,* and *The Search* were not nominated.

In 1952 when *The Greatest Show on Earth* somehow won, *High Noon, Moulin Rouge,* and *The Quiet Man* lost, while *Singin' in the Rain, The Bad and the Beautiful, Come Back, Little Sheba,* and *Viva Zapata* were not nominated. In 1967, when *In the Heat of the Night* won, *The Graduate, Bonnie and Clyde,* and *Guess Who's Coming to Dinner* were losers, while *In Cold Blood, Cool Hand Luke, The Dirty Dozen,* and *Divorce American Style* were not nominated.

In 1968 when *Oliver* won, *2001: A Space Odyssey* was not even nominated. In 1970 when *Patton* won, *Five Easy Pieces* and *M*A*S*H* lost and *The Great White Hope* and *I Never Sang for My Father* were not nominated. In 1972 when *The Godfather* won, *Cabaret*, *Sounder*, and *Deliverance* lost and *Fat City* and *Lady Sings the Blues* were not nominated.

When *The Sting* won in 1973, *American Graffiti* and *The Exorcist* lost, and *The Last Detail*, *Cinderella Liberty*, *The Paper Chase*, *Save the Tiger*, *Bang the Drum Slowly*, and *Serpico* were not nominated. When *Annie Hall* won in 1977, *The Turning Point*, *Star Wars*, *Julia*, and *The Goodbye Girls* lost and *Close Encounters of the Third Kind* was not nominated.

As with the acting Oscars, where there is just one winner every year, the others are going to look like losers. As suggested earlier, maybe there should be more than one winner some years when there is more than one outstanding film, and maybe none when there are none. Or perhaps there should be other categories so seriously neglected areas of the art could be honored.

Any selections are certain to be subjective and, so, controversial. If a film merits an honor in its time, then it should not be criticized because it does not wear well with time. On the other hand, it is clear that some movies age better, are better remembered, and endure as classics more than many that took higher honors in some years.

It is, frankly, hard to figure out how some movies won while others lost and still others were not even nominated. *How Green Was My Valley* endures as a great film, but *Citizen Kane* places 1-2-3 in every poll of the finest films ever made in America. *Rebecca* is good Hitchcock, but *The Grapes of Wrath* is great cinema and lands in the top ten of just about every poll of all-time favorite American movies.

A large *Los Angeles Times* poll of fans found *The Wizard of Oz* fourth and *The African Queen* fifth among all-time movie favorites, yet *The Wizard of Oz* was not a winner and *The African Queen* was not even a nominee. The American Film Institute poll placed both in its all time top ten, along with *2001: A Space Odyssey* and *Singin' in the Rain*, which were not even nominated in their years.

Among the most influential films of all time as selected by a University of Southern California Performing Arts poll of producers and critics were *Citizen Kane*, *Grapes of Wrath*, *2001*, *Stagecoach*, *The Treasure of the Sierra Madre*, *Star Wars*, and *The Informer*, all Oscar losers.

The noted historian Arthur Schlesinger, Jr. once wrote, "I venture to suggest that a list of ten movies denied the Best Picture Award would be quite as impressive as the ten best Oscar pictures." His list: 1. *Citizen Kane*, 2. *Modern Times*, 3. *2001: A Space Odyssey*, 4. *High Noon*, 5. *Nashville*, 6. *The Grapes of Wrath*, 7. *The Wizard of Oz*, 8. *The Front Page*, 9. *King Kong*, 10. *To Be or Not To Be*.

The front jacket of David Zinman's *50 Classic Motion Pictures* portrays ten classics. Not one of them won an Oscar as Best Picture.

The most honored films of all time include more movies that were not honored than it does those that were. At the head of this list has to be *Citizen Kane*. It is generally regarded as the finest film. Critic Cecilia Ager wrote, "It's as though you never had seen a movie before." Critic William Bayer wrote, "It has been said many times, but let it be said again, Orson Welles' *Citizen Kane* is the greatest film ever made. That is a fact there is no way around."

It is, as he admits, imperfect, but so ambitious it was bound to be flawed. It tried for more and reached farther than any other film yet made. It told a story as no motion picture had before or has since, with an absolutely astonishing and arresting power.

It was simply, said Welles, "a portrait of a public man's private life." It was a fictionalized account of powerful, wealthy publisher William Randolph Hearst's life· and career. Many like Bayer are amused that Welles treated Hearst's life the way Hearst treated the truth in his newspapers—lightly—and many are convinced it was cunning.

Welles was twenty-six when he made the movie. He filmed it in four months in secrecy for a mere $800,000. He feared his studio, RKO, would want to interfere if it found out that he was taking a dark look at the bright lives of the wealthy, a dim view of the sad side of success, a caustic look at the corruption of power. He worried that RKO would not like the way he did it.

Welles produced and directed the film. He claimed to have written it, but the Writers Guild intervened to get Herman J. Mankiewicz credit as coauthor of the screenplay. Welles wanted every credit, but insiders believe Mankiewicz deserves most of the credit for writing. Welles also starred in the movie.

His picture was nominated for an Academy Award and he was nominated as director, actor, and coauthor of the original screenplay, an unsurpassed sweep, though he won only the latter. Gregg Toland was nominated for the cinematography, John Aalberg for the sound recording, Robert Wise for his film editing, others for art direction. It is incredible that all lost.

The staging, the use of sound, the use of photography all were inventive, imaginative, ingenious, focusing

Citizen Kane *with Orson Welles, Joseph Cotten, and Everett Sloane.*

the eyes and ears, all the senses of the viewers on the subjects and the story they had to tell in a way that had not been done before and has not been done since.

It was not the first film to use deep focus photography, nor the first to shoot from above and below, but it did so more effectively than others had. It zoomed in and out to give us the close look or the long long that made each scene most meaningful. We were made aware of the smallest detail in the largest way.

It was not the first film to use overlapping dialogue or wide variations of sounds from whispers to screams, but the very hearing of it stimulates us. It was a veritable circus of sight and sound. Some say you can see it ten times, fifty times, and see something new in it every time and be stirred by it every time. This may not be true of any other movie.

The film starts with the death of Charles Foster Kane and tells his story in a series of flashbacks. The camera pans along a misty landscape up to a castle on a hill. A single light is on. Suddenly, snowflakes swirl. Suddenly, we see we are within that lit room and the snow is within a glass ball held by an old man. He is Kane and he is dying. He says one word, "Rosebud." He says it softly. The word comes at us as if from afar. Perhaps from deep within his heart. He dies. His hand opens and the glass ball smashes on the floor.

A newsman seeks out the secret of that last word and the secret of the great man's life through interviews with his associates, played by Joseph Cotten, Everett Sloane, George Coulouris, Paul Stewart. We see Kane's mother, Agnes Moorehead, coming into a fortune and turning her son over to a financier for rearing. We see the boy hurl his sled at the man as he realizes his childhood is being stolen from him. At twenty-five, he inherits his holdings, defies his guardian, and takes control of a New York newspaper.

His love of the good life surpasses his love of good deeds. There is a party at the office of *The Enquirer* that is a riot of colors, though the film is in black and white. Welles marries socially prominent Ruth Warwick, who is the President's niece and wants to be a President's wife. Welles, too, wants to be President, but he soon wearies of his wife. We see their marriage deteriorate in a single stunning scene composed of short takes at the breakfast table over the years. Welles takes a mistress, pretty, but common.

He runs for governor, but revelation of his love nest ruins him. When his wife and son die in an accident, he marries his mistress. He tries to make her a great singer, much as Hearst tried to make Marion Davies a great actress. Kane builds her a lavish opera house, but her debut is a disaster. The scene, shot partly from behind the singer into the bright lights for the first time, is dazzling, His critic, Cotten, starts to write a critical review, but drinks himself unconscious and is fired. Welles, himself, finishes the review, ripping her.

147

He builds a mansion, Xanadu, much as Hearst built his San Simeon castle. Scenes where the mansion is being stocked with treasures from all over the world are staggering. When this museum of a mansion is not filled with freeloaders, the great man and his alcoholic lady are lost there and the vision of loneliness is almost unbearable.

The last years limp away. He dies. Newsreel cameras invade his sanctuary. They pile personal objects together for one shot. Later, some junk is burnt in a bonfire. The camera closes in on a sled on which the word, "Rosebud" appears, fading into the fire, a symbol of lost youth, of a life that was not what it might have been. The camera fades back to the beginning, focusing on the fog-shrouded mansion. The single lighted window now is dark.

The cast, many of them members of Welles' Mercury Theater, performs perfectly as an ensemble. To this day, critics discuss the psychological riddles of the film. It may be the most discussed movie of all time. Countless articles and books have been written about it.

Hearst threatened to sue if the film was released and offered to repay the studio its costs if the negative could be bought. Scheduled to open in February of 1941, the film was delayed but finally brought out. Hearst banned all ads and mentions of Welles in his many newspapers. Perhaps this helped publicize the picture, but it was a critical success, not a commercial one.

Only its low cost saved it from being a financial disaster. And the Academy denied it at Awards time,

as if to damn this affront to the establishment, and in so doing put the integrity of Oscar forever in doubt. Forty years later, the film's stature surpasses all but one or two that won one of those statuettes.

When John Steinbeck wrote *The Grapes of Wrath*, few thought of it as a movie. It was a depressing story of desperate people driven from the dustbowl during the Depression. Darryl Zanuck bought it for 20th Century-Fox for $75,000, the highest price paid for rights to a book in the 1930s. He found great opposition to filming it. Many in the movie industry felt films were for fun, not social messages. Trade papers campaigned against it.

A daring and dedicated man, Darryl Zanuck assigned it to Nunnally Johnson to adapt and John Ford to direct without interference. They turned out a movie that was a milestone in honesty in Hollywood and set the stage for films of social significance to follow.

This was in 1940, on the eve of World War II. When it came out it was called Communistic and an assault on America. But at its world premiere in New York, the audience stood and cheered at the end. Mark Murphy of the *New York Times* wrote, "They all seemed to think it a great movie, something strong, something about the common and poor people living and working together." Archer Winsten of the *New York Post* wrote, "As long as motion pictures confine themselves to a pure amusement function, they remain a shining palace built on sand. When, as in *The Grapes of Wrath*, they join the battle of living issues, they anchor themselves in an enduring rock."

The Grapes of Wrath *burial scene with Henry Fonda.*

The story concerned the Joad family of Oklahoma. Jane Darwell played Ma Joad and Russell Simpson played Pa Joad. Henry Fonda played son Tom. There were other children. Charles Grapewin and Zeffie Tilbury played Grampa and Granma. John Carradine played Casy, an itinerant preacher.

As the film opens, Tom is walking along a highway, returning home after four years served in prison for killing a man in a dance-hall brawl. He finds the family farm dead of dust and the family of twelve about to load its life onto an old pickup truck and leave for The Promised Land, California, and its good life in the fruit orchards. Tom is looking for a better life, anyway. Gregg Toland's camera focuses on Ma parting with her pitiful keepsakes, burning old letters. "I'm ready," she says, simply, poignantly, at dawn.

It is a joy ride for the young, a death ride for the old. The overloaded car rides roughly over the road. Grampa dies and is buried alongside the road with a note left in a fruitjar to explain it to any authorities who might worry about it. Tom writes, "This here is William James Joad, dyed of a stroke, old, old man. His fokes buried him because they got no money to pay for funerals. Nobody kilt him. Jus a stroke and he dyed."

Granma dies, but Ma holds her in her arms, pretending she is sick, so authorities will not stop them as they cross into California. They find ten thousand migrants seeking less than a thousand jobs. They are herded like criminals into a detention camp where conditions are worse than those they left behind. Here, children cry from hunger and beg for food, Here, friends fight one another for the few jobs the labor recruiters offer. Guards fence them in, seeking to keep order.

A riot breaks out and the camp is burnt down. A woman is shot, a deputy injured, and Casy is taken away by the police. The Joads move on to another camp, where Tom finds work in the fields. One night he encounters Casy, who now is leading the laborers' fight to get living wages. Vigilantes raid the strikers. One kills Casy, crushing his skull. Tom kills him. Tom must run, rather than return to be sent to prison, though he regrets leaving his family.

Tom says of Casy, "He was like a lantern... He helped me see things." He says he has been thinking about some people having so much and others so little. He says, "I been wondering if all our folks got together and yelled...?" Ma says, "They'd cut you down just like they done to Casy." Tom says he must try. Ma wonders how she'll know where he is, how he is. Tom says he'll be "wherever there's a fight so hungry people can eat."

Ma's spirit should be sapped, but it is not. She says,

"Rich fellers come up. They die. Their kids ain't no good. And they die out. But we keep a-coming. We're the people that live. Can't wipe us out. Can't lick us. We'll go on forever. Cause we're the people."

Jane Darwell was in her sixties, well into a fifty-year career of more than 200 films, and with this superb performance this great lady won her only Oscar. John Ford won his second for his sensitive direction.

At thirty-five, that fine actor, Fonda, received what was to be his only Oscar nomination. Unforgivably, he lost. And the picture lost to a routine thriller, *Rebecca*. Screenwriter Nunnally Johnson lost to Donald Ogden Stewart for *The Philadelphia Story*.

The black-and-white cinematography of Gregg Toland, who was so much a part of *Citizen Kane's* impact, too, was not even nominated. Nor was the art direction of Day and Mark Lee Kirk. The sets and photography were realistic, a critical part of the film's truth. Later, *Life Magazine* published a series of real-life scenes of the Okies side by side with those in the film and the similarities were remarkable.

One of the great films of all time was denied the Oscar it so richly deserved and the denial grows more poignant with the passing years.

It is ranked in the top ten or twelve, often near the top, on many polls of great or most significant American films. It won the New York Critics Award, as did *Citizen Kane*, *The Informer*, *The Treasure of the Sierra Madre*, and many more which did not win Academy Awards.

The Informer in 1935 brought John Ford his first Oscar, but the film failed to win the prize. It brought other Oscars to Victor McLaglen as Best Actor, Dudley Nichols for his screenplay, and Max Steiner for his score, but the photography of Joseph August and the sets of Van Nest Polglase and Charles Kirk were overlooked and the film itself was outvoted by *Mutiny on the Bounty*.

Cliff Reid produced *The Informer* for RKO. Ford had wanted to make it for five or six years. The Irishman was moved by Liam O'Flaherty's tale of life in revolt-torn Ireland, but others thought it too dark, its hero too unheroic. Ford got the go-ahead to do it only if he could do it quickly and cheaply. He finished it in four weeks for $200,000. He did not take a salary, accepting a percentage of the profits, which were small.

As far back as the 1920s the Irish were rebelling against British rule. In the film a guerrilla band huddles in their homes, hides in dark corners, hits and runs. For some, the hunger of their lives moves them more than their hatred of the oppressors. So it is for Gypo, as played by the bear-like McLaglen. Too cowardly to carry off a killing, he is exiled from his friends.

In The Informer, *Victor McLaglen accuses Donald Meek of a crime McLaglen committed as Preston Foster takes it all in.*

As the film opens, Gypo is looking at a poster offering a twenty-pound reward for information on his fugitive friend, Frankie, played by Wallace Ford. Gypo tears down the poster, but it is caught by the wind and pursues him as he lumbers along the dark street. It lands at the feet of a street-walker, his girlfriend, Kate, played by Margot Grahame. She calls his attention to it with the first word spoken: "Gypo!"

They pass another poster offering passage to America for just ten pounds. Kate says, "Twenty pounds and the world is ours." Gypo is neither bright, nor brave. He goes to the police, informs on his friend, and claims his reward. Frankie is found and killed. Instantly, Gypo's life turns into one of terror. He thinks he has been spotted. He believes he is being followed. He flees down dark streets.

He spends some of his ill-gotten gains on drink and is drunk when he attends Frankie's wake. Gypo pretends sympathy, but is suspected when coins spill from his pocket. He wanders Dublin's slums, spending his loot on drink, on a whore, on treats for the lads at a fish-and-chips joint. But he is brought before a court of his fellows. He tries to blame another, but is not believed.

Under pressure, he confesses. Sentenced to die, he escapes. He hides in Kate's flat, falling asleep like a child. She goes to the guerrilla leader, played by Preston Foster, to plead for his life. In so doing, she gives away his whereabouts. Gypo's former pals gun him down. Dying, he staggers into a church, where Frankie's mother, Una O'Connor, prays for her lost son.

Part of Nichols' superb scene:

The vestibule of the church: Gypo comes in with a slow, stiff walk, his arms limp at his sides. Dazedly, he sees the font and reverently he dips his hand in and tries to cross himself, but that hand weighs a ton and he cannot do it. Stiffly, he turns and staggers through the narrow door. We next see him inside the church, swaying in the dim, mysterious light. Then he sees a kneeling figure in a black dress, alone in the church. He staggers on with that stiff, slow walk, finally reaching the kneeling figure. Gypo swallows the blood in his mouth and stands there weaving before her, and his voice is a thick whisper.

"'Twas I informed on your son...forgive me," pleads the bleeding Gypo.

"I forgive you. You didn't know what you were doing," Frankie's mother says, tears streaming down her face.

Rising gratefully, Gypo looks up and calls, "Frankie ...Frankie. Your mother forgives me."

He staggers to a statue of Christ and falls dead at His feet.

It was simply stunning from start to finish, this tale of greed, deceit, terror, courage, and cowardice spanning a few hours in the lives of a few people, so powerfully set in the shadows of the Dublin of the day, so realistically portrayed by the principals, so simply and dramatically told by Ford and his fellows.

Richard Watts of the *New York Herald-Tribune* called it, "as stark and impressive a tragedy as the screen has ever produced." Many consider it today one of the milestone masterpieces of the movies and are regretful that it did not reap the rewards it so richly deserved.

Another of Ford's masterworks that did not reap its deserved rewards was *The Long Voyage Home*. It came out in 1940, the same year as *The Grapes of Wrath*. It, too, was nominated, but it, too, lost to *Rebecca*. Ford was not nominated as director of *The Long Voyage Home* as he was for *The Grapes of Wrath*.

Walter Wanger's United Artists and Argosy production, Gregg Toland's cinematography, and Dudley Nichols' screenplay were nominated, but did not win. Toland's foggy waterfront, sea, and saloon photography were marvels of mood. Nichols' script was especially important as it was an adaptation of four one-act plays by Eugene O'Neill, only one of which contained the title *The Long Voyage Home*.

Not one of the actors was nominated though the movie was superbly played by John Wayne as Ole Olsen, Thomas Mitchell as Driscoll, Ian Hunter as Smitty, John Qualen as Axel, Ward Bond as Yank, and Barry Fitzgerald as Cocky. Wayne was thirty-three and this was his second important film. He was not as important as the film. He played a simple person and played him simply. He never again was as good.

The story was of men at sea and in port and their yearning for home. Most have given up the ghost of this dream, but it stays alive in them through their hopes that the youngest of them, Ole, will make it back to Sweden. Somehow, they know he will not, as they did not. Somehow they know their home is the sea.

They are merchantmen on a tramp steamer, which rides roughly over the oceans of the world. In this case, their cargo is explosive and dangerous—ammunition for wars they want no part of. They have come from America to London and they spend their brief leave in the saloons of the foggy waterfront, drinking their loneliness away.

In the *New York Times*, Bosley Crowther wrote, "*The Long Voyage Home* is a story of men, of eternal suffering in a perilous trade, of life and tragic death in the dirty, heroic little cargo boats that sail the wet seas." He says Ford "has fashioned a stark and tough-fibered motion picture which tells with lean economy the never-ending story of man's wanderings over the waters of the world in search of peace for his soul.

"It is harsh and relentless and only briefly compassionate in its revelations of man's pathetic shortcomings. But it is one of the most honest pictures ever placed upon the screen. It gives a penetrating glimpse into the hearts of little men. And because it shows that out of human weakness there proceeds some nobility, it is far more gratifying than the fanciest hero-worshipping fare."

It is an almost unflawed film, compact and powerful. It ends sadly, but inevitably. It merits remembering as one of the classics of cinema.

Another arduous journey over water was told by John Huston in *The African Queen* with Humphrey Bogart and Katharine Hepburn. Huston wrote it with the late James Agee. This one was written with good humor, a winking at the world, yet it tells the truth about its people and contains as many moments of high drama as it does low comedy.

Produced by S. P. Eagle and adapted from a novel

The Long Voyage Home with Ward Bond, John Wayne, Joe Sawyer, and John Qualen.

by C. S. Forster, it tells the tale of two people marooned in a war-torn African town who flee for safety over treacherous jungle rivers on an old and decrepit boat. A prim missionary, Rose Sayer, as played by Hepburn, talks a river rat, Charlie Allnut, as played by Bogart, into taking her along in this primarily two-character tale.

Their social contrast could not run deeper, yet romance develops incongruously between these unlikely but lonely shipmates as they bond together to endure the treachery of nature. It is a beautiful film, full of the heroism that beats beneath the breasts of the least of us, full of the humor that makes life endurable.

It was perfectly cast and perfectly played by Bogart and Hepburn. Both were nominated for Oscars. Bogart won, but Hepburn did not. She is better remembered for it than for any of the three films she won for.

Huston and Agee were nominated for the adaptation, but did not win. Huston was nominated as director, but lost to George Stevens for *A Place in the Sun*. The latter lost the Best Picture Award to *An American in Paris*.

It is difficult to believe *The African Queen* was not even nominated as Best Picture. It is remembered by many as one of the five or six finest films of all time.

Huston told another tale of high adventure in *The Treasure of the Sierra Madre* in 1948. It was nominated as Best Picture, but lost to *Hamlet*. Huston won as Best Director, while his father won as Best Supporting Actor, the only time a father and son have won in the same year. Huston won as writer, for his adaptation of B. Traven's book. It is difficult to believe the star, Bogart, was not even nominated. It was his first role out of a trenchcoat, so to speak, and he is as well remembered for this role as any he ever did.

The story of this Warner Bros. film, produced by Henry Blanke, was of the traditional search for treasure. The setting was Mexico. A sorry lot—Bogart, Huston, Tim Holt—set out on their adventure. Early on, Curt (Huston) tells Dobbs (Bogart) that once man has a taste of gold, he is never satisfied until he gets more. Dobbs says, "No, that wouldn't happen to me—not to Fred C. Dobbs."

"Thus the theme of the movie is laid bare," writes critic William Bayer. "Despite fair warning of what is to come, Dobbs is corrupted and then devoured by greed. His gold destroys him and, at the end, insane with fear and thirst, he is cornered and slaughtered by ruthless bandits, and his treasure is scattered to the winds.

"*The Treasure of the Sierra Madre* is a picture about the breakdown of the adventurer's code. Under pressure, the principal character becomes cowardly and selfish, the adventure fails, the treasure is lost, the

camaraderie dissolves. As an action film, it works extremely well. But there is more to it than that. It is a psychological thriller with a moral bias, always human and never allegorical."

It is superb, unforgettable, even haunting. It was a costly film to do, the first to be shot on location following World War II. Jack Warner gave the go-ahead to Huston, then fretted throughout the long shooting. Conditions of filming were primitive, but the cast endured as the adventurers they portrayed did not. Warner did not want the Bogart character to die in the end, but Huston stuck to his guns and die Dobbs did as he had to if the inevitable was to be met head on.

Bayer considers the film correct in every case, pure, perhaps perfect, containing classic moments: the glint in Bogart's eyes as Huston weighs out the gold; the look of them the night they decide each will take care of his own share; the trust on Huston's face as he is taken off by apparently peaceful Indians; the shadow of the bandit as he appears behind Bogart; the way his band toys with the terrified prospector before finishing him off; the way the band is caught as they go to town to sell the adventurers' burros; their execution—a long scene played in Spanish, without a word of English, yet told visually as well as a movie can tell a tale.

Many agree with the critic. It has landed in the top twenty of the finest films ever made, yet is only one of thirty-five selected for this chapter as classics which never captured Oscar in the more than fifty years of the Academy Awards.

Essentially an adventure story, it is to a great extent also a western, a classic one.

Although *Cimarron* won one of the first Oscars, the first great western probably was John Ford's *Stagecoach* in 1939. Prior to this, westerns were mostly shoot-'em-ups, many of them shorts and serials. Ford dwelt on the character of the people who lived in the old West. In somewhat traditional form, he confined a varied group in close contact with one another for a period of time so their personalities could work against one another in keeping with the social standards of that place and that time.

The types he portrayed became common in westerns to follow. There were John Wayne as the good guy, The Ringo Kid; Thomas Mitchell as Dr. Josiah Boone, the drunkard doctor; Donald Meek as Peacock, the whiskey salesman; John Carradine as Hatfield, the gambler; Louise Platt as Lucy, the high-flown lady; Claire Trevor as Dallas, the fallen lady; Andy Devine as Buck, the stagecoach driver; and George Bancroft as Curley, the sheriff.

This western made Wayne a star. He became a part of Ford's "stock company." Yakima Canutt did most of

Stagecoach *with John Wayne and Claire Trevor.*

the stunts, as he was to in many of Ford's westerns, and there even was a character in the film called "Yakeema," played by Elvira Rios. Yakima himself played the part of a cavalry scout. Jack Holt had played in many of Ford's early westerns and his son, Tim, played Lt. Blanchard.

Although most of the scenes were shot on studio stages, the outdoor locale was Monument Valley, Arizona, which was to become Ford's favorite site. He told me, "It has everything the old West had, except the people." Ford took his characters on a stagecoach ride through the wild West and through adventures westerners have been having ever since.

In the film, telegraph lines are cut, the Indians attack, the cavalry rides to the rescue behind the blasting of a bugle. There is a poker game, a chase on horseback and a gunfight in which the hero single-handedly blows away the three Plummer brothers. Ford liked life scenes like births, weddings, and funerals. Here, there is the birth of a baby. Unexpectedly, the good guy rides away at the end with the prostitute with the heart of gold.

If all this sounds standard, it is well to remember that this film was a trailblazer which set the standards. Here, the theme song, "Bury Me Not on the Lone Prairie," sounds right. The script by Walter Wanger, an adaptation of Ernest Haycox's *Stage to Lourdsburg* is just right. It was all so well done, Orson Welles said he watched the film forty times while preparing *Citizen Kane*, though there is no similarity in the finished products.

Walter Wanger's United Artists production was

nominated for the Academy Award but lost to *Gone With the Wind*. Ford was nominated as director, but lost to Victor Fleming, the last of three directors who worked on *Gone With the Wind*. The editors were nominated, but lost. The cinematographer was nominated, but lost. Those who scored the film were nominated and won. The only actor nominated, Thomas Mitchell, won as supporting player.

It was a wonderfully well done movie and only one of four or five all-time classics which lost that year, including *Mr. Smith Goes to Washington*, *Wuthering Heights*, *The Wizard of Oz*, *Of Mice and Men*, *Ninotchka*, *Love Affair*, and *Dark Victory*.

Maybe the most underrated western, maybe the most underrated of movies, producer Lamar Trotti's *The Ox-Bow Incident* was nominated for an Oscar in 1943, but Trotti was not nominated for his adaptation of Walter Van Tilburg Clark's novel. William Wellman was not nominated as director. None of the actors were nominated, and it is not as well remembered as it should be. For those of us who remember it, it remains one of the most shattering experiences in moviegoing.

There had been a few films about lynching, but none that hit with this impact. There were no howling mobs, no histrionics. There was not a lot of law in the old West and men were inclined to take justice into their own hands, whipped by some of the passions that stirred Southern whites who feared the erasure of their society by blacks.

This is a western. It is a story of life in the old West, of cowboys on horseback, and of the cattle that represent life to them. The men carry guns. But there is

The Ox-Bow Incident *with Anthony Quinn and Dana Andrews about to be lynched.*

no hero to stop an injustice from taking place. The story is told simply, moving steadily to its inevitable climax.

Two weary cowboys, Henry Fonda and Henry Morgan, ride into a desolate town. The only sign of life is an old dog that trots across their path. Morgan remarks on how dead the town is. In search of life, they head for the saloon and drink straight whiskey to wet their parched throats.

A cowboy bursts in to tell those there that cattle rustlers have killed a local rancher. The men led by Harry Davenport, a former major in the Confederate forces, form a posse to catch the killers. Only a few oppose them. The authority in the town does not stop them. Even the boardinghouse lady, Jane Darwell, goes with them to "do her duty." The visiting cowboys go, too, as if to be a part of something. A few go in hopes of maintaining order.

After a cold, dark, lonely search they find three men by a campfire, a homesteader, Dana Andrews, and his helpers, a Mexican, Anthony Quinn, and a senile old man, Francis Ford (John Ford's older brother and a beloved character actor). They have some of the rancher's cattle. They are presumed guilty.

Andrews pleads that he purchased the cattle, but he has no bill of sale. Quinn accepts persecution. Ford does not know what is happening to him. The posse votes to lynch the three. A few, including Fonda, vote

against it, but do not act against it. Andrews asks time to write a letter to his wife and children. In a gesture of justice, the major gives him until dawn.

He writes the letter and gives it to a sympathetic member of the mob, but refuses to let him read it to the rest. At dawn in Ox-Bow Valley, the men pray, then are put upon their horses, and nooses, strung around an old tree limb, are set around their necks. When the major's son refuses to whip a horse, the major drops him with a blow from his pistol butt. The horses are whipped out from under the men and they hang.

On the way back to town, they encounter the sheriff, who tells them the rancher is not dead and the rustlers who shot him are in jail. He says, "The Lord better have mercy on you, because you won't get it from me."

The others, seeking to ease their consciences, turn on their leader: "If you ask me, it's the major we ought to lynch." Disgraced, the major goes home and shoots himself. The others gather in the saloon and listen to Martin's letter: "A man just naturally can't take the law into his own hands ... because he's not just breaking one law, but all laws ... If people touch God anywhere, where is it but through their conscience?" They raise some money for the victim's family and the two visiting cowboys ride off to take it and the money to them. As they ride out, the town is quiet again. The old dog goes back across their path the other way. Nothing has changed. Life here remains as it was.

In the *New York Times*, Bosley Crowther praised the moviemakers for making a movie with so little commercial promise. He considered the film uncompromising and true. He said Wellman directed it "with a realism that is as sharp and cold as a knife," that for sheer, stark drama it is "hard to beat." It is as strong and rings as true today as yesterday.

Another of the most powerful films of injustice which was sadly neglected was *Paths of Glory*, Stanley Kubrick's 1957 masterpiece of life in the military in World War I. It won no nominations, yet endures like *The Ox-Bow Incident*, as a small movie in size and scope but a large film in its lingering impact.

As William Bayer writes, the film is based on the theory that soldiers are merely pawns in the hands of generals who play at war as if it were a game of chess. The foot soldier lives under traditional military tyranny. The officers corrupt themselves in their quest for position and power and their men pay for their mistakes.

The scenes of men at war are overwhelming. A French company is sent on a suicide mission. Three men who are seen to have acted cowardly are brought back, court-martialled, and sentenced to be executed as an example to the others. A sympathetic colonel, Kirk Douglas, seeks to intervene in their behalf, but he is not bold enough to state his case strongly. An unforgiving general, Adolphe Menjou, ridicules his weakness.

The men are not brave. They whimper. They are executed. There is a moving postscript in which a German girl is forced to sing for French troops, but forces them to see the inhumanity of war. Kubrick, Douglas, and Menjou all are notable non-winners in Oscar races.

Kubrick worked without salary on the film. He was to be paid a percentage of the profits, but there were none. The movie was not a commercial success. Somehow it was made for less than one million dollars, yet it did not turn a profit. The military hated it. For awhile it was banned on United States bases and it is still banned in France. For those who saw it, it was unforgettable.

Another classic film concerning a case of injustice is *I Am a Fugitive from a Chain Gang*, which received nominations as Best Picture and for Paul Muni as Best Actor in 1932–33, but did not win either. Mervyn LeRoy was not nominated as Best Director, though he should have been, and he never won an Oscar.

An American soldier returns from World War I and quits his old job in a factory to pursue his ambition to be an architect and build bridges. He drifts into the South in search of work, is innocently involved in a robbery, is caught, and is sentenced to ten years at hard labor on a chain gang. Here, life is, as it was, merciless.

He escapes, goes north, and makes a respectable life for himself as president of a construction firm. A lady in love with him finds out his secret and forces him to marry her on the threat of revealing his past. He falls in love with another lady and his wife betrays him. He gives up his fight not to be extradited on the promise that he now will shortly be paroled because of his new place in life.

Going back, he finds himself bound into the old misery, the promises made to him that he would be freed, broken. He escapes again, but this time feels he cannot try to make a decent life for himself and accepts life on the run, on the outside of society. He goes back to bid a last goodbye to his girlfriend. Late at night, he emerges from the bushes to face her. She is horrified by his haunted look. She says, "It's been almost a year since you escaped."

He says, "I haven't escaped. They're still after me. They'll always be after me. I hide in rooms all day and travel by night. No friends. No rest. No peace. Forget me, Helen. I had to see you tonight. Just to say goodbye."

Despairing, she says, "It was all going to be so different."

Bitterly he replies, "It is different. They've made it different." He hears a sound. Desperately, he says, "I've got to go."

"Can't you tell me where you're going?" she asks. He shakes his head. "Will you write?" she asks. He shakes his head. "How do you live?" she asks.

As he disappears into the darkness, he hisses, "I steal."

It is an ending I never have forgotten. The noted critic Pauline Kael called it "one of the great closing scenes in the history of film." Critic David Zinman said, "As a grim, stark document of social injustice, the film had no peers."

The movie was based on a book about Robert Burns, a World War I veteran who was sentenced to a Georgia chain gang after a five-dollar holdup, escaped, made a good life for himself, was turned in by his wife, returned to prison, escaped again, made another good life for himself, was recaptured, returned, finally was paroled, but refused a pardon.

Broadway playwright Sheridan Gibney was assigned to do the script and worked in secrecy with Burns, who at the time feared recapture. By the time he was done, Gibney believed Burns to be guilty and later refused to do rewrites for fear of him. Nevertheless, his script portrayed Burns as an innocent victim of circumstances.

The Maltese Falcon *with Peter Lorre and pal Humphrey Bogart.*

In any event, the chain gangs were ghastly and Governor Ellis Arnall of Georgia acted as attorney for Burns in his last criminal case and later led the battle that abolished chain gangs in his state. The power of films in the early years was such that they led to many wrongs being righted, and this was one of the most significant movies ever made.

In a sense, the first great crime film, the one that established the private detective type of film, was John Huston's suspenseful *The Maltese Falcon*, based on the novel by Dashiell Hammett.

It established Bogart as a star and the cream of the trenchcoat crowd. It was nominated for an Oscar, as was supporting star Sidney Greenstreet. Both lost. Huston and Bogart, Peter Lorre and Mary Astor were not nominated. All were magnificent in this superbly crafted thriller.

It set the style for many movies to follow. It opens in Sam Spade's dingy office. A mysterious lady tells a tale of being followed by a hood, but she does not know why. Shortly, Spade's partner and the hood are dead. In exchange for a kiss and cash, the lady hires Spade to protect her.

The trail takes him to an unlikely team—fat Kasper Gutman, played by Greenstreet, making his screen debut at sixty-one, and little Joel Cairo, played by Peter Lorre. They are a sinister pair. When Spade slaps

Lorre, he tells him, "When you're slapped, you'll take it and like it." Greenstreet gurgles, "Oh, gad, sir, you are a character."

He admits he is searching for a statuette or jewels, the falcon. He offers to pay Spade for his help. Spade follows a trail of death and finally finds the bird. He delivers it to the nasty two, joined by the beautiful lady, who, it turns out, was interested in the prize for herself. It turns out to be a fake. "You bloated idiot," the furious little man screams at the fat man. Greenstreet rumbles a belly laugh. Such is life.

Spade squeals on them to the cops, then tells them to pick up the lady at his apartment. She pleads for his favor: "From the very first instant I saw you I knew I loved you." Hard as it is, he is tough enough to resist her. "I hope they don't hang you, precious, by that sweet neck," he says. She is taken away. A friend picks up the statue and asks Spade what it is. As the movie ends, he says, "The stuff that dreams are made of."

Hal Wallis' Warner Bros. production is perfection of its kind. This film was to be done many times, but never better. It had, in fact, been done twice before, once in 1931 with Ricardo Cortez, again in 1936, as *Satan Met a Lady*, with Warren William, and Bette Davis in the Mary Astor role. At the time of this version, Astor was in headlines because of a scandalous romance with George S. Kaufman. George Raft turned the male lead down, so Bogart got it. The cast worked as a team. Young Huston made his mark.

Huston was a thirty-five-year-old screenwriter who wrote the script as well as directed the movie. Bosley Crowther called him "an American match for Alfred Hitchcock," but Huston went other ways, while Hitchcock, the transplanted Briton, continued with his suspenseful mysteries.

Many films can be considered classic losers in the Oscar races, but *Psycho* seems to be the one that had the greatest impact and has endured the longest in the minds of most moviegoers. It may be the most successful fright film ever made. Hitchcock made it in 1960 with his own money for less than one million dollars. It made more than fifteen million.

Hitchcock never had made a horror film, per se, but he noted horror films were doing well at the box office at that time and determined to make this one. He felt he could make one better than others had, without spending a lot of money. He interviewed and hired an unknown, Joseph Stefano, to adapt a pulp novel by Robert Bloch. Hitchcock and Stefano worked together on it. As always, Hitchcock had his way as the adaptation progressed.

Hitchcock admits he likes to tease the audience, play tricks on it, manipulate it. He never did it better. A beautiful young lady enters the film. She is desperate for money and is tempted to steal from a dishonest old man. She takes the money, but blunders and is almost caught. Stopping at a motel, she confesses to a sympathetic young man and decides to return the money. We are relieved for the heroine. She takes a shower as though to cleanse herself.

While in the shower, a woman stabs her to death. This scene may be Hitchcock's best, one of the best a movie has had. It is so unexpected and horrifying many people stopped taking showers; some cannot take one to this day without thinking of this scene.

Now, we are only forty-five minutes into the movie and the heroine is dead and the audience is stunned. We come to think that the young man's mother, who manages the motel, is the murderer. We seem to see her murder a detective. Our sympathy shifts to the unfortunate young man. Of course, he is the killer. His mother is dead and he is dressed as his dead mother. But it comes to us as a shock, only one in a series of shocks.

Superbly crafted, the movie moves with cunning. Hitchcock was able to get Anthony Perkins cheaply to play the clean-cut young man because he owed Paramount, the parent studio, a film. The clean-cut Perkins forever after would be remembered best as the mother-lover maniac-killer. Hitchcock wanted a prominent

actress for the heroine to increase the shock of her death at mid-movie. He settled on Janet Leigh as affordable. She is best remembered today for her death scene in the shower.

There was an element of horror to *Sunset Boulevard*. This 1950 film may be the best movie ever made about movies. A fading, aged silent-movie queen lives in grotesque elegance in a mansion served by a butler who once was her husband and director. When a cynical screenwriter wanders in, it is as if he has fallen into a world of nightmares haunted by a maniacal madwoman. There are rats in the empty swimming pool. There is in the film a neurotic burial by candle-light of a pet monkey. At the finish, we see the aged queen's fingers twisted into claws.

Billy Wilder wanted to open the film with a camera panning over a row of corpses. The last one would be the screenwriter's and when the camera got to him he was to sit up and start his narration. Wilder was dissuaded from this, but he put together a motion picture that cut to the heart of Hollywood.

Cynically seeing it in its worst sense, he shows it as a world of egotistical tyrants who fan the flames of hot properties while burying the old before their bodies are cold. Norma Desmond believes the world is waiting for her return. Life plays a cruel trick on her, making her think the time has, at last, come. In the end we know that time never will come. She is the only one who does not know this.

Charles Brackett's Paramount film, director Wilder, and stars Gloria Swanson, William Holden, and Erich von Stroheim all were nominated for Academy Awards, but all lost. Another film about an actress, *All About Eve*, and its director, Joseph Mankiewicz, were winners. Wilder and Brackett did win for their story and screenplay.

Life in other societies was depicted poignantly in *A Place in the Sun* and *A Streetcar Named Desire* the following year, losers to *An American in Paris*.

In *Streetcar* another lady of faded elegance lives another life of illusions. Blanche DuBois (Vivien Leigh) invades the home of Stanley and Stella Kowalski (Marlon Brando and Kim Hunter) in New Orleans and destroys their acceptance of their lot with her pretensions. She leads on a hopeful gent (Karl Malden), but there is no hope for her. Vengefully, the animal with the soiled T-shirt (Brando) brings her briefly to earth by raping her.

Eliza Kazan did a masterful job of adapting and directing Tennessee Williams' powerful play. The actors did a remarkable job of depicting the personalities. Three of the four leads won Oscars, the only case of its kind. Incredibly, Brando did not. Like the play,

A Streetcar Named Desire *with Marlon Brando and Vivien Leigh.*

A Place in the Sun *with Montgomery Clift and Shelley Winters.*

East of Eden *with James Dean.*

this Charles Feldman film for Warner Bros. is unforgettable, bringing to light the growling of the animal that is in all of us. *Streetcar* did win New York Critics honors.

George Stevens won directional honors over Kazan for *A Place in the Sun,* but the film did not win. Lead actor Montgomery Clift did not win. Lead actress Elizabeth Taylor and supporting actress Shelley Winters were not even nominated. Still, producer Stevens' Paramount version of Theodore Dreiser's famed novel, *An American Tragedy,* was one of the most emotionally moving motion pictures ever made.

A young man on the make (Clift) falls in with a fellow factory worker (Winters), but then falls for the beautiful daughter of the factory owner (Taylor) and cannot resist the temptation to shoot for "a place in the sun." The common girl grows restless. Pregnant, she demands her young man marry her. Instead, he murders her so he can be free to go for romance and riches at the top. Caught, his dreams crash around him.

A near-perfect film and near-perfect performances came along in the wrong year, but endure remarkably well and remain among that select group of losers who deserve to be celebrated as classics.

Less perfect, but in many ways as emotionally moving, was *East of Eden.* It was not nominated in 1955, but director Elia Kazan, actor James Dean, and supporting actress Jo Van Fleet were. Van Fleet won. Actor Raymond Massey and actress Julie Harris were not nominated. The acting throughout was sensitive, terrific.

This ageless story of the generation gap between fathers and sons, between a harsh father, Massey, and his uncertain son, Dean, on a California farm as World War I nears, is poignant. Nothing the son does is right. Nothing he tries pleases his father. His girl, Harris, cannot console him. Needing love, he seeks his mother and finds her to be the madame of a whorehouse, Van Fleet.

Kazan produced and directed this film for Warner Bros. Paul Osborne adapted the book by John Steinbeck. The art direction of James Basevi and Malcolm Bert depicted the place and period effectively. The score by Leonard Rosenman helped provide power to the picture. The acting was stunning. Dean and Massey did not like each other. They were from different worlds. So their conflict set off sparks which suited this story.

The critics were mixed on this picture from the first. A few make it a masterpiece. As author of this book I assume I am entitled to pick a few personal favorites and this is one of them.

N I N E

The Classic Losers,
Part II

ONE OF THE FIRST great films to be overlooked by Oscar was King Vidor's *The Crowd*. Released in 1928, it was the last and one of the finest of the silent films, but it could not compete with the excitement over the talkies in the first Academy Awards ceremonies, covering the 1927-28 season. It was not nominated for an Oscar, though Vidor was. He lost. Yet, it was his masterpiece.

A milestone among movies of social realism, it told the story of an office worker, James Murray, lost in an office full of workers, an individual almost alone in the anonymity of the crowded city. Without words, it told a poignant tale of loneliness in the then modern society of the big city as well as stories told with words. It was deeply pessimistic, but remarkably realistic. It used the camera to tell a touching story.

Vidor was interested in the individual. Asked by Irving Thalberg what he might do next for MGM, he said, "Life." Thalberg liked that idea and asked why Vidor hadn't mentioned it before. Vidor said he hadn't thought of it before. He says, "I approached that film with the thought that I would just see what happened to a man as he went through an ordinary life. He was born and then had to bear responsibility for his family when his father died. He had to approach a city, look for a job, meet a girl, fall in love, sleep with the girl and marry her, have children with her.

"Along the way I became aware how the average man is lost in the big city, how meaningless the average job is. I wanted to show a tall building and pick out one window, one floor, one office, one desk, one man. In

those days you couldn't go up to shoot through the twenty-second floor of a building. So we built a 15-foot scale-model of a building lying on its side and shot down on it.

"On a big, empty stage we had 200 men working at 200 desks. We shot a still of them as well as action shots of them, dissolving from exterior to interior shots.

"I thought a star face would destroy the anonymity of the lead, so I looked for an unknown and found James Murray. He was an extra I spotted and asked to come see me. He never showed up so I had to hunt him down. He was just right."

The film worked wonderfully well and still looks special today. Vidor thought Murray might be a tremendous star so he signed him to do *Show People* with Marion Davies, but he didn't show up for the shooting. He did do a few other roles. Vidor found him drunk in the gutter one day and tried to help him. Some time later on Vine Street a bum approached Vidor and asked for a buck. Vidor saw it was Murray and took him to the bar at Musso's on Hollywood Boulevard, bought him a drink and offered him a job. Murray said, "Screw you."

Murray drifted to New York and was working as an extra on an MGM film shooting on location on a bridge over the Hudson River. He was bragging how he'd been a star at the studio earlier. Nobody believed him. They were all drunk. Murray climbed on the railing and either jumped or fell into the river. Later, they found him floating face down, drowned. That was in 1936.

In 1979, Vidor, hungry for a comeback, was circu-

The General *with Buster Keaton.*

lating at the studios a script he'd written, *The Actor*, about Murray. Vidor said, "I think it'd make a very good film. About an actor who can't take success. Too much of an average common man, you know."

Charles Chaplin did win a special Award "for versatility in writing, acting, directing, and producing *The Circus* at the first ceremony, but the movie was not nominated as Best Picture. He was nominated as Actor and Director, but did not win. It was silent, so that was that.

He was stubbornly sticking to silents. In 1931 he made *City Lights*, and in 1936, he made *Modern Times*. These did not win nominations. Later, he made talkies *Monsieur Verdoux*, *Limelight*, and *The Great Dictator*, but they did not win either.

Hollywood lost its opportunity to honor Chaplin with a real Oscar for the finest of his post special Oscar productions, *City Lights*. Chaplin spent more than a year shooting it because, as he put it, he had "worked himself into a neurotic state of wanting perfection." He came as close to it here as man can come. Each scene is exquisite. As producer, director, and actor, he was a genius.

The little tramp braves the big city and encounters a beautiful flower girl, but finds her to be blind. The scene lasts little more than a minute, but took five days to shoot. What looks easy is only made to look easy by hard work. He wants to help her. He is willing to fight

for her. He agrees to throw a fight for money, but his accomplice vanishes and he is left to battle a brute. He does, with awesome acrobatics. It is more than mere comedy—we care.

He succumbs to the promises of help from a fellow drunk, a millionaire who is snobbish when sober and destroys his hope. Desperate, the Tramp commits a crime and goes to jail. Finally, he returns to his flower girl, but he has failed her. He has been beaten by the big city.

He has suffered for her. Does he still love her, or does he hate her for this? Bill Bayer writes, "Suddenly one is in the realm of poetry. The expressions on Chaplin's face and on the face of the girl say so much on so many levels that they defy analysis."

There is slapstick here, such as when Chaplin swallows a whistle and cannot silence it. It is as effective done silently as it would be with sound. There also is drama, as deep as it would be with words, and poetry, as pure as it would be spoken. It did not deserve to be overlooked by Oscar merely because it was silent. It spoke to us in a thousand tongues.

Similarly, Buster Keaton's *The General* came along in 1927, just in time to be considered for an Academy Award, but was dismissed without nomination because it was silent. Many consider this the classic comedy of the silent period. Historian Ephraim Katz writes, "It is a brilliantly conceived and executed story in which the comic situations and gags complement one another in perfect harmony. The authentic look of the background and the Matthew Brady-like quality of the photography added a dimension of beauty to the production which remains authentic to this day."

Critic Steven Earley writes, it is "a radical departure from the 1920s and is Keaton's best film. It is dramatic comedy and some consider it superior even to Chaplin's 1925 *The Gold Rush*." Keaton himself considered it his best work. He was a genius comparable to Chaplin, but where Chaplin's Little Tramp always was defeated by life, Keaton's unsmiling common man always succeeded in overcoming overwhelming odds.

The story of *The General* is that of a Southern engineer, Keaton, who loves his locomotive, The General, more than even his girlfriend, Annabelle. The Civil War is raging and The General is hijacked by Union soldiers with Annabelle aboard. Keaton sets out to bring both back from the North to Southern soil. He succeeds, despite dreadful problems. The athletic Keaton performs fantastic feats of acrobatics. There is a cast of thousands and the action is of epic proportions. The sight gags are so good that less than fifty subtitles are needed to tell the story.

This suspenseful film, exciting as well as funny, actually was based on a true incident which gives a sense of reality to the film. There is a series of magnificent scenes. One shows Keaton desperately feeding a dwindling supply of wood to the furnace of his locomotive as it flees its pursuers. He turns to find his girlfriend neatly sweeping scraps out of the cab because they displease her. He mocks her, makes as if to strangle her, then kisses her. Bayer writes, "No one can fail to be moved by so gracefully executed a sequence of gestures illustrating that special combination of fury and love which men sometimes feel toward the women they adore."

With the coming of sound, comedians such as W. C. Fields and the Marx Brothers came to the fore, whose spoken words were as funny as their physical postures. Many of their movies can be considered classics.

My favorite of several by the Marx Brothers is *A Night at the Opera*, which received no nominations in 1935 but has made people laugh for forty-five years, and laugh as hard today as they did yesterday. There was Groucho with his leering eyes, painted mustache, cigar, stooped walk, and irreverent wit. There was Chico with his ill-fitting clothes and improbable Italian accents, and there was Harpo with his silent tongue, shrill whistles, beeping horns, and maniacal manner.

Swindler Otis B. Driftwood (Groucho) persuades wealthy Mrs. Claypool (Margaret Dumont) to sponsor an opera company to assure her place in high society. The director (Sig Rumann) signs up singers Rodolfo

A Night at the Opera with, standing, Sig Rumann, and Marx Brothers Harpo, Chico, and, seated right, Groucho.

(Walter King) and Rosa (Kitty Carlisle). Not knowing this, Groucho has signed Rosa's sweetheart, Ricardo (Alan Jones). When the company sails from Milan to New York, Ricardo, his friend Fiorello (Chico), and Rodolfo's former servant Tomasso (Harpo) stow away.

Groucho asks a steward if he has any stewed prunes. The steward says he does. Groucho says, "Well, give them some hot coffee. That'll sober them up." Given a dinner check, Groucho says, "Nine-forty, this is outrageous." Handing it to the woman with whom he is dining, he says, "If I were you, I wouldn't pay it."

The cabin scene may be the most famous bit of funniness in films. Everyone winds up in this small room at once. A manicurist squeezes in. She asks Groucho if he wants his nails long or short. He says, "Better make 'em short, it's getting crowded in here." A cleaning lady squeezes in and announces she's there to mop up. Groucho says, "You'll have to start on the ceiling. It's the only place that isn't being occupied." A girl comes to the door and asks if her aunt is in the cabin. Groucho says, "If she isn't you can probably find somebody just as good." She asks to use the phone. "Use the phone?" asks Groucho. "I'll lay you even money you can't even get into the room." Finally, one too many is in the room. Margaret Dumont makes her grand entrance, opens the door, and is engulfed by a sea of humanity that floods out.

Nonsense? Of course. But what is high art? Is the ability to make people laugh less important than the ability to make them cry? The Marx Brothers made audiences laugh until they cried and they were as essential to movies as anyone.

They hit their height with A Night at the Opera. In the climax in New York they disrupt the opera with inspired nonsense. Harpo and Chico slip the music to "Take Me Out to the Ball Game" into the orchestra stands. Groucho hawks popcorn and peanuts down the aisle. Harpo and Chico kidnap Lassparri so Ricardo can get his chance. The lovers are reunited. The matron is happy. Groucho and Chico are arguing about the singer's contract. At one point, Chico has pointed out a sanity clause. Groucho says, "You can't fool me. There ain't no Sanity Claus."

Irving Thalberg produced the film for MGM. Sam Wood directed it. George S. Kaufman and Morrie Ryskind adapted it. But it was Groucho and his gang that made it a classic of madcap comedy.

Similarly, The Bank Dick must be considered classic comedy, although it is supposedly too low-life to be elevated to contention for Oscars. Yet if there is no place for honors for such fountains of fun, what worth have the honors? The film is as funny today as the day it opened in 1940. Fields is long gone, but he still makes people laugh.

The original story and screenplay were written by Mahatma Kane Jeeves. That was Fields, of course. He wrote the screenplay on scraps of paper between bouts of drunkenness, then threw away the scraps and played it as it went. There was no producer listed for this Universal epic because Fields ran the entire show. Edward Cline directed, but Fields predominated.

Egbert Souse (pronounced Soo-say) is a worthless rascal who hangs out at the Black Pussy Cat Cafe to escape the henpecking of his petty wife Agatha (Cora Witherspoon) and her mean mother Hermisillo Brunch (Jessie Ralph). He hates his only child Elsie Mae (Evelyn Del Rio). He is resting on a park bench when two bank robbers pause to squabble over their loot. One knocks the other out, then trips over the bench as he tries to escape the cops. When they arrive, Egbert is sitting on him.

Hailed as a hero, he is made a guard by the bank president. That night at the Black Pussy Cat Cafe he is talked into investing his "reward" in the Beefsteak Mine by a con man, J. Frothingham Waterbury (Russell Hicks). Envisioning a life of splendor, Souse concludes his only work will be writing receipts. "By then I'll have a fountain pen," he notes. Feeling he deserves a reward, he talks his son-in-law, Og Oggilby (Grady Sutton), a teller, into stealing it.

His work at the bank does not go well. Egbert jumps a kid in a cowboy suit carrying a gun. "Is that gun loaded?" he asks. The boy's mother says, "Certainly not. But I think you are." Marching indignantly from the scene, she asks her son if he wouldn't like to have a nose like that stuffed with nickels.

The bank examiner, J. Pinkerton Snoopington (Franklin Pangborn) arrives to inspect the books, but Egbert gets him drunk and nearly kills him. By the next morning, the mine has come through, but the first bank robber returns to re-rob the bank, taking not only money but the mine stock. He also takes Egbert to drive the getaway car.

Fields does not drive well. "Give me the wheel," howls the horrified robber. "Here it is," says Souse, pulling it off and handing it to him. A tree limb kayos the criminal and Egbert screeches to a stop on the edge of a cliff.

Hailed as a hero again, he gets his reward this time. He even sells his story to a movie company. He can live any way he wants now. So he goes back to the good old Black Pussy Cat Cafe.

Eventually, more sophisticated comedy came into favor, as funny as but no funnier than the madcap antics of the Marx Brothers or the irreverent wit of W. C. Fields. Maybe the best of the unrewarded ones was Frank Capra's Meet John Doe in 1941.

Meet John Doe *with Barbara Stanwyck and Gary Cooper.*

Fired from her job on a newspaper, Barbara Stanwyck invents a letter from a John Doe threatening to jump off City Hall on Christmas Eve to protest injustices against the little man in her farewell column. Public reaction is so strong that the editor, James Gleason, offers to hire her back.

He is horrified to find out that the letter is a phony. However, rather than risk being exposed by a suspicious rival newspaper, he reluctantly agrees to her idea to hire someone to play the part. She picks a bum, former baseball pitcher Long John Willoughby, as played by Gary Cooper. All he wants is the money for an operation on his sore arm.

Although warned by his buddy Walter Brennan to beware of being corrupted by cash and luxury, Long John rather likes the life in the hotel suite he hides out in while the columnist invents a story for him. He becomes a sort of folk hero and she persuades the publisher, Edward G. Arnold, to put him on national radio. She writes a speech preaching brotherhood and he reads it.

When John Doe clubs spring up across the country, Long John becomes scared and flees. However, finding his message is making people live a better life, he becomes the leader of a national John Doe movement. The publisher promises to form a third political party to elect John Doe as President and give him the opportunity to do good.

The editor reveals that the publisher will break his promises and use John Doe as a pawn in a corrupt administration. Doe threatens to tell the truth at a rally, but when he mounts the podium at the rain-soaked outdoor affair, the publisher's men pull him down. The publisher takes the microphone and condemns Doe as a phony, who has pocketed club dues and never had any intention of jumping off City Hall.

Discredited, Doe decides the only way he can keep his movement alive is to really jump. On Christmas Eve, in the snow, he is pulled back by Barbara. "If it's worth dying for, it's worth living for," she pleads. The little people turn up. Regis Toomey says, "We're with you." Ann Doran says, "We need you." Cooper turns to Arnold and says to him, "There you are—the people. Try and lick that."

Corny, yes—but, terrifically well done and extremely moving. There is in most of Capra's finest films a combination of light humor and heavy drama that struck at universal truths we were not so sophisticated as to reject in those days.

Immodestly, Capra says, "I think for seven-eighths of the film it's a great, great film with great power, great emotion. But the ending was always weak. And we tried different endings as we previewed the picture around the country, but none was satisfactory to me or to the audiences.

"Then we got a letter from someone who'd heard about our problem and suggested the only satisfactory ending would be to have the John Does themselves ask him to stay with them. I'm surprised we didn't think of it. So we brought the cast back and filmed that and used it. It was the fifth ending.

"It was the best ending we could come up with, but it still wasn't good enough," he concludes. Still, it worked.

The film was not nominated that year, nor was Capra who wrote the original screenplay and produced the picture with Robert Riskin. Cooper was nominated, but for *Sergeant York.* He won. Stanwyck was nominated, but for *Ball of Fire.* She never won. Brennan and Gleason were nominated, but for other films. It was Gleason's only nomination. Arnold was not nominated. He never was for any film. Neither Gleason nor Arnold ever won Oscars.

Capra's most successful film was *Mr. Smith Goes to Washington.* Country boy Jefferson Smith (James Stewart) is sent to Congress to fill an unexpired term. His state's party boss (Edward Arnold), senator (Claude Rains), and governor (Guy Kibbee) see him as a dodo who will do their bidding. A shrewd secretary (Jean Arthur) is assigned to shepherd him.

He sees Washington with wonder. He is brought back to earth when the cynical press corps call him a clown. He wants to resign, but the senator persuades

Three great character actors, Edward Arnold, Eugene Pallette, and Guy Kibbee, left to right, in Mr. Smith Goes to Washington.

him to stay with the promise to sponsor a boys' camp on a site in their state. His secretary helps him draft a bill and falls for him.

She tells him the senator owns the land and will sell it for fat profits when a highway bill claims the land planned for his camp. Smith confronts the senator, who tells him the facts of life. "You leave your ideals at the door," he says. Smith threatens to expose him, but the senator beats him to the punch by claiming in a speech before the Senate that Smith stands to profit from the deal.

Smith stands up for his ideals. He tells the truth to the Senate in a fillibuster designed to block the senator's bill. He stands up and fights until he falls to the floor in exhaustion. He has turned the tide. Confessing, Rains runs. Stewart is hailed as a hero.

Corny? Yes. But bravely done and strongly told. At the premiere at the National Press Club in Washington, most politicians walked out. Alben Barkley, the majority leader of the Senate, condemned the movie because he felt it made senators "look like a bunch of crooks." The Senate voted to condemn it, 96–0. Other studios were so fearful of the wrath of Congress they offered Columbia $2 million to shelve the $1.5 million film. Columbia refused and newspaper reviewers came to the rescue with acclaim for the film, which became a big box-office hit.

The film, producer-director Capra, star Stewart, supporting star Rains, the writer of the original story, and the writer of the screenplay all were among nominees for Oscars. Only story-writer Lewis Foster

won. Arthur and Arnold were not nominated and never won an Oscar.

It was a tough year, 1939, to win. *Gone With the Wind* got the Oscar. *Stagecoach, Wuthering Heights,* and *The Wizard of Oz* also lost—but it is ridiculous to consider these classics losers.

Wuthering Heights may be the finest romantic film the screen has seen. The film, director William Wyler, star Laurence Olivier, supporting star Geraldine Fitzgerald, and screenwriters Ben Hecht and Charles MacArthur all were nominated. Only cinematographer Gregg Toland won, for his black-and-white photography.

It was just the wrong year. There were too many great films deserving to be honored.

But there was a lot right with Samuel Goldwyn's screen version of Emily Bronte's novel. It is set in the foggy moors of Yorkshire, and tells the story of a fiery stable boy, Heathcliff, played by Laurence Olivier, who falls in love with Cathy, played by Merle Oberon. She is of a higher social estate than he, but in their youth they walk the moors together and dream their dreams.

Overhearing Cathy tell a servant that she dare not degrade herself by marrying Heathcliff, Heathcliff leaves to seek his fortune. Regretfully, Cathy marries a man of position, Edgar, played by David Niven. Heathcliff returns rich, still with the old fire in him, and vengefully buys Wuthering Heights from Cathy's dissolute brother, paying off his debts. He cannot talk Cathy into leaving Edgar, so he marries Edgar's sister, Isabella, played by Geraldine Fitzgerald.

Laurence Olivier and Merle Oberon were memorable as Heathcliff and Cathy in Wuthering Heights.

Cathy is brokenhearted. Pride has caused her to let her one love escape. She grows ill. As she is dying, Heathcliff carries her to the window for a last look at their beloved moors. She says she will wait for him in the next world and there they will be, at last, together. She dies. For the next twenty years, he mourns her death and waits to die. He scorns his wife, his life is a waste. Finally, at the finish Heathcliff rejoins his Cathy.

The film was pure romance, so beautifully staged, played, and realized as to be considered the classic of its kind.

Hecht and MacArthur (husband of Helen Hayes and father of actor James MacArthur) wrote the screenplay on speculation. They took it to Goldwyn, but he didn't want to do it. He didn't like period pieces, disliked gloomy stories, disliked the death of a hero or heroine.

They took it to Walter Wanger, who bought it for $50,000. Wanger took it to Goldwyn who told him to do it without him. Wanger took it to Bette Davis, who took it to Jack Warner and asked him to buy it for her. Wanger then told Goldwyn that Warner was about to buy it for Bette, so Goldwyn bought it for Merle Oberon.

Goldwyn hired William Wyler as director and hired Wyler and John Huston to "improve" the script. Wyler wanted an all British cast. Goldwyn had Oberon, Niven, and Fitzgerald, but no one to play Heathcliff.

MacArthur had met Olivier and recommended him. He had come to Hollywood to test for the male lead in Queen Christina, but been rejected by Garbo. He and Vivien Leigh were married to others, but having an affair. Goldwyn liked him, but was insulted when Olivier said he would do the movie only with Leigh.

Olivier returned to England and Wyler followed him to try to talk him into making the movie. Finally, he succeeded. He offered Leigh the second female lead, but she refused and it went to Fitzgerald. Goldwyn wired her she'd never get a better part. Following Olivier to Hollywood, she landed the part of Scarlett O'Hara.

While Leigh was making love to Clark Gable, Olivier was making love to Oberon. Olivier and Oberon hated each other. She said he spit when he spoke close to her face before kissing her. He complained it was hard to get close to such a pock-marked face, an affliction from childhood that the otherwise beautiful lady concealed with makeup. Yet their romantic scenes were believable.

Goldwyn still didn't like the idea of his two leads dying at the end. It was he who dreamed up the final scene of the two lovers walking off together on white clouds on their way to heaven. Wyler hated it and

refused to shoot it. He was suspended and it was shot. Goldwyn loved it and later called the film his favorite of all time, although he made many marvelous ones.

As Leigh will be forever remembered as Scarlett O'Hara, so will Olivier be remembered as Heathcliff, even more so than as Hamlet. As Stewart is remembered best as Mr. Smith, so Judy Garland forever will be remembered as Dorothy.

Sam Goldwyn wanted a big musical that would attract adults and children alike. His story editor thought of L. Frank Baum's classic The Wizard of Oz, bought a copy at Pickwick Bookstore on Hollywood Boulevard and gave it to Goldwyn along with a synopsis. Goldwyn liked the synopsis and had his lawyers purchase rights to the book from the Baum estate for $15,000.

He then started to read the book. He was not a fast reader. Although it was a children's edition, it took him a week. He did not like the book. Jock Whitney and his sister, Dorothy Payson, later owner of the Mets, who had an interest in the new Technicolor process, tried to buy the rights from him, but he sold them to Louis B. Mayer.

Mayer had hired songwriter Arthur Freed to make musicals for MGM. Freed would make MGM the musical center of cinema with such films as Singin' in the Rain, Meet Me in St. Louis, and many more, but this was to be his first project. He had read the Oz books as a boy and begged Mayer to buy The Wizard from Goldwyn for his first project. Mayer did, for $75,000, but because the fantasy was such a complex project, he got Arthur to agree to be associate producer under Mervyn LeRoy, newly hired by his studio. However, Mayer had LeRoy so busy on other projects, he really acted only as advisor.

Freed had cast the characters in his mind—Judy Garland as Dorothy, May Robson as Aunt Em, Charley Grapewin as Uncle Henry, W. C. Fields as the Wizard, Fanny Brice as the good witch, Edna Mae Oliver as the bad witch, and vaudevillians Buddy Ebsen, Ray Bolger, and Bert Lahr as the Scarecrow, Tin Woodsman, and Cowardly Lion.

Fields turned his part down because he wasn't offered enough money. Ed Wynn turned it down. Frank Morgan got it. Fanny Brice turned her part down and Billie Burke, the widow of the great showman Flo Ziegfeld and a one-time Broadway beauty, took the part. Oliver turned down her role. It was offered to Gale Sondergaard, a recent Oscar winner, but she thought it beneath her. Margaret Hamilton got it and became Judy's best friend on the set. Sara Blandish replaced Robson.

Bolger wasn't happy with his part and got Ebsen to trade roles. Then Ebsen got sick and was replaced by Jack Haley. The Tin Woodsman was encased in an aluminum suit and aluminum dust was sprayed on his face to match the suit. Ebsen developed a skin reaction and cough from it and had to be hospitalized. A paint was sprayed on Haley and it worked better, but he was miserable throughout. He said later, "None of us had any idea we were creating a classic. It was just a job." To cut costs, the supporting players were each paid only $1000 to $2500 a week. The dog who played Toto—a female cairn terror—and her trainer were paid $650 a week.

Arthur Schenck, head of MGM's Loew's office in New York, said he couldn't sell the film without someone like Shirley Temple in the lead. Garland was not a star and too old anyway, while Temple was still a big box-office star and at ten the right age. Garland had been promised the film and was brokenhearted when it was taken from her. Mayer arranged a deal to borrow Temple from 20th Century-Fox in exchange for the loan of Clark Gable and Jean Harlow, then filming *Saratoga*. When Harlow suddenly died, the deal was cancelled and Garland got the part.

Garland was seventeen, however, and having an affair with Artie Shaw, the bandleader. She had to play an innocent farm girl who was at the most thirteen or fourteen. Her body was bound in a specially constructed corset, her breasts painfully strapped down.

Freed hired Harold Arlen to do the music and E. Y. "Yip" Harburg to do the lyrics. They turned out a superb score. "Somewhere over the Rainbow" wasn't in it originally, but Freed needed a song to bridge her flight from the farm in Kansas to the emerald city of Oz. Arlen couldn't come up with anything for weeks. One day he was inspired during a car ride down Sunset Boulevard at the point where it starts to be the Strip. He had his wife pull over—right in front of Schwab's drugstore and he wrote the music on the spot.

They returned home and he telephoned Harburg to come over to hear it. Harburg thought it too grand, too operatic. They sent for Ira Gershwin for advice. Ira heard the song and suggested that Arlen slow it down to simplify it. He did and Harburg dreamed up the rainbow angle in a few days and did the lyrics.

Then at the initial screening, the film ran too long. Some experts didn't like the song, and it was ordered cut. Freed threatened to quit if it was. Mayer liked him and appeased him by ordering it left in. The song won the Oscar and became symbolic of the picture. Without it, the film would not be what it is.

Baum, the author of *The Wizard of Oz*, was a New York editor. He had four sons, but had always wanted a daughter. He devised Dorothy as the daughter he wished he had. He wrote *The Wizard of Oz* in 1899 and other Oz stories in a series of following books. They were among the three best-selling children's series of all time, but his efforts to produce successful Broadway plays or Hollywood films based on them failed before his death. It took ten writers to turn *Oz* into the movie it became.

The story was simple. Knocked unconscious during a tornado, a young girl dreams her way into a fantasyland. Once there, she finds it hard to return to reality. A good witch helps her, a bad witch hinders her. Along the way, she encounters a straw man who needs a brain, a tin man who needs a heart, a lion who needs courage. They go "down the yellow brick road" to seek the wonderful wizard who can help them. He turns out to be a phony, of course. He can barely help himself.

At the beginning of her dream, she lands in the land of the munchkins. Midgets had to be brought in from all over the world to play the parts. They were so small that helpers had to be stationed in the bathrooms to help them on and off the toilets. They were so small they were sometimes treated as children by others, who were often cursed. The midgets were rowdy, almost uncontrollable. Housed in a Culver City hotel, they were bussed to and from the nearby studio. Once they shocked passers by "mooning" the world with their rears pressed against the bus windows.

George Cukor was originally hired to direct the film, but he left almost immediately. Richard Whorf was brought in, but he was fired almost immediately. Finally, Victor Fleming was set. King Vidor finished the film when Fleming left to be the last of those to direct *Gone With the Wind*. Fleming was a patient man who could deal with problem pictures.

It was a difficult film to make, with many special effects required. A lot that was shot never showed up on the screen. It took five weeks and cost $80,000 to film a sequence in which the four are attacked by "jitterbugs," and the whole sequence was scrapped.

The film was in preparation for eighteen months and took twenty-two weeks to film. Budgeted at $2 million, it cost just under $2.8 million to complete. In the first three years of its release it earned only a third of its cost. It took twenty years for the film to break even.

The Wizard of Oz received mixed reviews originally. One critic wrote "the fantasy is as heavy as a wet fruitcake and has no sense of humor." Russell Maloney in the *New Yorker* wrote that the picture had not a trace of good taste, imagination, or ingenuity. But

Frank Nugent in the *New York Times* wrote that not since *Snow White* had any fantasy succeeded so well. It was popular, but no blockbuster until television took it years later. It was so popular with this new audience that it has become an annual hit on the home screens. Money from television made it a profit-maker.

As seen now, it is a beautiful film, full of fascinating characters and performances, full of marvelous music, and dripping with theatrical energy and charm. In its time it was nominated as Best Picture, but its director and stars did not receive nominations. Judy did receive a special Oscar for her outstanding performance as a screen juvenile that year but it was a miniature statuette, not the full-sized or even over-sized one she deserved. *The Wizard of Oz* was nominated for its special effects and art direction, but somehow did not win. The movie's real recognition came after its time.

Similarly *Snow White and the Seven Dwarfs* was considered a cartoon when it came out in 1938—a long cartoon, but a cartoon, nevertheless. It won one Oscar, a special one, for being "a significant screen innovation which has charmed millions and pioneered a great new entertainment field for the motion picture cartoon."

From conception to finished film it took five years. The Walt Disney Studios grew from 125 employees to 750 during that time and all of them worked on *Snow White* at one time or another. The finest artists, graduates of the finest art schools in the country, came to work, many of them as apprentices. The drawing was simple but true, and took hundreds of thousands of frames. Yet it was not nominated for art direction.

The Grimms' fairy tale was as frightening as most fairy tales. To lighten it, Disney's story editors and writers emphasized the roles of the dwarfs. They are not even named in the original story. Can you name them now? They were charming. There still were sequences involving the wicked stepmother that some said frightened more children than Frankenstein's monster.

The score was marvelous. With music by Frank Churchill and lyrics by Larry Morey, "High-Ho," "Whistle While You Work," and "Some Day My Prince Will Come" all became hits. Yet not even one was nominated. The Prince does come, Prince Charming of course, awakening Snow White from her sad sleep.

A young lady named Margery Belcher, later to become Marge Champion of the Gower and Champion dance team, modelled for the drawing of Snow White. A long-forgotten lady named Adrienne Castillotti was her voice. The names of the dwarfs, by the way, are Dopey, Grumpy, Sneezy, Happy, Sleepy, Bashful, and Doc.

Disney's original estimate of the cost was $250,000. It kept increasing until the final cost of the one-hour-and-twenty-two-minute movie ran to ten times that. Disney had to borrow from the banks. He risked his studio on this first full-length animated feature. No one knew if adults would take their children to see it, much less go to see it themselves. He got a break when New York's famed Radio City Music Hall agreed to take it sight unseen for its big Christmas show. The reviews were wonderful and the movie caught on. To date it has earned ten times its cost.

The *New York Herald-Tribune* reviewer said, "It ranks with the greatest motion pictures of all time." It does. It was unique and delightful and it blazed a trail over which many delights have followed. Disney was only thirty-six when it was finished.

Many feel that he made better full-length animated features later, notably the fantastic *Fantasia*, but *Snow White* was the one that started it all and the best-remembered of all. It was not his biggest money-maker. Live-action features are easier and cheaper to make. *Mary Poppins* made him $30 million. *Snow White*, however, was his hit of hits. It deserved more recognition from Oscar than it received.

Special effects had become an advanced art in films by 1968 when *2001: A Space Odyssey* was released. Although this film was made primarily in London, it was produced and directed by American Stanley Kubrick, starred Americans Kier Dullea and Gary Lockwood, was put together primarily by American technicians, and was financed by an American movie company, MGM. It is one of those fringe films which qualifies for this book on American movies.

Arthur Clarke wrote the original story and collaborated with Kubrick on the screenplay. It is based on a science-fiction fantasy of life as it may be lived in a future time, but well-laced with reality. Kubrick got many corporations, government and private research institutions, and scientists to contribute to the believability of the life envisioned. As a result, the technology looks more authentic than that in *Star Wars* and the several other spectacular but sensationalistic films of this sort that have followed.

This was Kubrick's baby. He convinced MGM to spend more than $10 million on it at a time it was in financial trouble. It has not returned any great profit. Many disliked it when it came out. They were not ready for such a primarily visual experience. But from the awesome opening thirty minutes, when dancers portray the apes that first inhabited earth, with not a word spoken, to the magical close in which a "star-child" image appears, which some consider a religious experience, the film is full of stunning sequences. We are moved as much by the machines as the people. We are moved.

William Bayer says, "By now the controversy has passed and *2001* has been more or less accepted as one of the very few great films of our time. As a science-fiction fantasy it remains unexcelled. No other picture in the genre even comes close. As a horror story, too, it is a towering achievement, not on the same scream-inducing level as Hitchcock's *Psycho*, but in a subtler and far more haunting way." Yet, in 1968, it was not even nominated for an Academy Award. Kubrick was, both as director and co-scripter, but he has never won. It was nominated for art direction, but did not win. It won only for special visual effects. It merited much more.

Films used to be simpler. Life was simpler. There was extravagance in many early musicals, especially the Busby Berkeley creations, but the Fred Astaire-Ginger Rogers musicals were really simple affairs spotlighting the dancing of its star and his partner. David Zinman writes, "Simplicity in filming was an Astaire innovation." Bill Bayer writes, "*Top Hat* may be the best of the Astaire-Rogers musicals because, in addition to the songs of Irving Berlin and the excellence of the dances, it is the simplest and most pure."

Astaire and Rogers made ten movies together for RKO. Five were directed by Mark Sandrich, who, for the most part, simply let them dance. Their first, *Flying Down to Rio* in 1933, made them stars when their "Carioca" stole the show from the stars, Gene Raymond and Dolores Del Rio. They became the stars of Pandro Berman's productions of *The Gay Divorcee*, in which they danced "The Continental," in 1934, and *Top Hat*, in which he danced his most famous solo—"Puttin' on My Top Hat"—in 1935. Both movies were nominated for Oscars, but lost. Inconceivably, neither Astaire nor Rogers were even nominated, as if their musical marvels were unworthy.

Astaire was thirty-six at the time of *Top Hat*. A Broadway star, he was suspect after a screen test which brought the conclusion, "Slightly bald. Can't act. Can dance a little." He was short, skinny, and unattractive. He had a high forehead, a long face, and big ears. He could, however, dance more than a little. He was the best tap dancer the screen has seen. Despite a husky voice, he could sing a song like Berlin's *Cheek to Cheek* with charismatic charm. He had an elegance and grace in everything he did. He was effective in light comedy, speaking with sly humor. He was sophisticated and came to be considered a model of charm.

Ginger Rogers was twenty-four when *Top Hat* was made. She was lovely. Astaire and Rogers actually disliked each other. He kept tearing the frills off her costumes, while she regarded him as rude. Yet there was a chemistry between them that comes along only once in a good while. It made for a perfect pairing of unlikely partners. He made her seem desirable. She made him seem sexy.

Most of their movies had like story lines. He falls for her and chases her until she catches him. They did not kiss until the end of their eighth film, *Carefree*, after their fans demanded it.

In *Top Hat*, he tap dances after her across Europe. They come together to dance, fall apart, eventually get together through a series of misadventures. The story is silly, but it is a classic worthy of honors if only because of his dancing, alone and with her. They hit their heights in this one and became the most popular pair of all time.

Top Hat *with Fred Astaire and Ginger Rogers.*

Astaire never won a nomination for an Oscar as a dancer and lost his only nomination as an actor late in his career. Two years after leaving Astaire, Rogers won her one Oscar as an actress. Astaire continued with a variety of partners after Rogers left him, but never with the success he'd had with her. Nor did he regain that success when they later reunited for a couple of films. He retired after World War II when Gene Kelly, more of an athletic, acrobatic type, was coming into his own as Astaire's successor. In 1948 he made a highly successful comeback as a replacement for the ailing Gene opposite Garland in *Easter Parade*.

Gene Kelly's *An American in Paris* won an Oscar in 1951 but with the sort of snobbery Academy voters so often showed he was not even nominated. He was nominated as a performer only once, for *Anchors Aweigh* in 1945, but lost. He is best remembered, however, for *Singin' in the Rain* in 1952. It finishes in the first ten of favored movies of all time in numerous polls.

Singin' in the Rain is unpretentious, simple, light, yet its musical numbers are marvelous. It is funny, and its satire cuts to the bone. It is the story of Hollywood in the time of the transition to the talkies in the late 1920s. Jean Hagen plays a sex goddess who cannot talk without making people laugh and she succeeds in talkies only with the dubbed-in voice of Debbie Reynolds. Hagen loves her costar, Kelly, who loves Debbie. Donald O'Connor plays his sidekick and Cyd Charisse plays one of his dancing partners. None of the principals ever won an Oscar.

This Arthur Freed MGM production, directed and choreographed by Stanley Donen and Kelly, scripted by Betty Comden and Adolph Green, with songs by Freed and Nacio Herb Brown, was simply dazzling. Maybe it is the best musical in Hollywood history. Four top production numbers stood out. One was the title number, an ingenious solo by Kelly that is considered to be a classic among dance sequences. Another was a lovely duet by Kelly and Reynolds, sung and danced on an empty sound stage to the love song, "You Were Meant for Me." Another was a deft "Make 'em Laugh" by the delightful Donald O'Connor, who never really had the chance to make the most of his considerable skills in movies. The last was the "Broadway Ballet," danced by Kelly and Cyd Charisse and a cast of thousands in a thrilling parody of Busby Berkeley's spectacular closing numbers.

A different, darker type of musical was 1972's *Cabaret*. Christopher Isherwood wrote short stories which were turned into the Broadway play *I Am a Camera* by John Van Druten. Years later, Joe Masteroff turned it into the play *Cabaret* and producer Cy

Gene Kelly in Singin' in the Rain.

Feuer, director-choreographer Bob Fosse, and screenwriter Jay Alleb made it a movie with Liza Minnelli, Joel Grey, Michael York, and an excellent supporting cast. Songs were by John Kander and Fred Ebb and the score by Ralph Burns. Geoffrey Unsworth's photography was stunning.

The setting is Berlin, the time just before World War II when the Nazis were coming to power with a cruelty that could not yet be accepted by the people. Joel Grey, as the emcee at the Kit-Kat Club, is symbolic of the evil that is developing and of the pre-war decadence of the day. He is superb and his hypnotic character ties the picture together. A great talent, he is the son of Mickey Katz, famed Yiddish comedian.

Minnelli, daughter of the great musical star Judy Garland and the great musical director Vincente Minnelli, inherited an arresting talent as singer, dancer, actress, and all-around showwoman. She is perfect as Sally Bowles, who works at the club and lives at the boarding house where so much of the drama is played out. She would have York as her lover, but he will not have her. He will have her only as a friend. He will

Cabaret *chorus line fronted by Joel Grey.*

have his own life. He is Isherwood, the young homosexual and writer who tells the tale.

This film is forbidding, frightening, electric, explosive, a distinct departure from the escapist entertainment and sweet triumph of good over evil in most musicals which preceded it. The songs as sung by Grey ("Willkommen" and "Money") and Minnelli ("If You Could See Her Now" and "Cabaret") and by the chorus of future Nazis ("Tomorrow Belongs to Me") are powerful, meaningful, and marvelously well done.

The movie was nominated for an Oscar but lost to *The Godfather.* However, the director, Fosse, and his stars, Minnelli and Grey, as well as the photographer, art director, film editor, sound editor, and musical scorer all won Oscars. One wonders what was left to be wrong with the film that it did not win. Nothing was wrong with it. Almost everything was right with it. It was just another classic loser.

A marvelous musical in which the story mattered as much as the music was 1977's *The Turning Point.* It may be the best movie ever made about ballet. It is similar to 1979's awesome *All That Jazz* in showing the sweat, sacrifice, and energy that enters into the exhausting preparation of dancers and their dances.

The ballet comes to town. Its aging star, Anne Bancroft, visits her rival from years gone by, Shirley MacLaine, who gave up her career to have a home and family. MacLaine's daughter, Leslie Browne, has the ability to be a great ballerina, and Bancroft takes her to New York. MacLaine follows over the summer vacation, leaving behind her husband, also an ex-ballet dancer. MacLaine has an affair. Her daughter has an affair with the star of the company, Mikhail Baryshnikov. MacLaine and Bancroft duel for the affections of MacLaine's daughter, the daughter Bancroft never had. They also try to decide between them who made the better, wiser choice.

These superb actresses gave off sparks in their confrontations. Both were nominated as Best Actress, but they lost to Diane Keaton for *Annie Hall.* It was unfortunate, especially for the neglected MacLaine, who has never won an Oscar. Browne and Baryshnikov were nominated, but lost. Their dancing was superb, especially Baryshnikov's. He is the ranking male dancer in the world today.

Herbert Ross and Arthur Laurents produced the picture for 20th Century-Fox and their Hera Productions. Ross directed it and Laurents wrote it. Robert Surtees photographed it. Albert Brenner and Marvin March designed it. William Reynolds edited it. All won nominations; none won.

This was a superb blend of dance and drama, beauty and reality. On dramatic content alone it qualified as a contender for honors. The poetry of its dance simply lifted it up and put it on a higher plane than most movies can ever hope to attain. If the movies were not mainly a visual medium it would be easier to understand how this poetry could be put aside in evaluating *The Turning Point.*

Much the same applies for *All That Jazz,* which won eight nominations for Oscars in 1979. Bob Fosse's autobiographical film dealing with his drive for perfection, with the death wish, with the dance, was dazzling. Directed and choreographed by Fosse, written by Fosse and Robert Alan Arthur, superbly photographed by Giuseppe Rotunno, it is an overpowering pictorial experience. It plumbs the depths of the human experience, primarily through Roy Scheider's virtuoso performance.

Some of the dance numbers are dynamic, others charming; all are charismatic. The performances in support of Scheider are superb. His heart operation near the end is presented so vividly it horrifies some viewers. In the end, unlike the real-life result, Scheider is zipped up in a plastic bag, his death wish realized.

If time is the measure for films, it is not yet possible to dub *All That Jazz* as a classic loser, but it is my guess this one will endure as a classic. But only time will tell if, for example, Ben Vereen's incredible dancing talents as displayed in this film will be put to use on the

All That Jazz *with Roy Scheider center.*

screen as were Fred Astaire's and Gene Kelly's. Vereen is black, as was Bill Robinson, and Robinson's talents, displayed in Shirley Temple movies, never were really featured in films. Had they been, more might agree with the many that feel "Bojangles" was even more brilliant than Astaire.

In the late 1960s, a series of films were made that changed the face of film. Two of these came along in 1967, *The Graduate* and *Bonnie and Clyde,* but they lost the Oscar to *In the Heat of the Night.* In 1969, *Butch Cassidy and the Sundance Kid* offered a different sort of western. In 1970, *Five Easy Pieces* presented a penetrating look at modern society which has been copied repeatedly since.

The brilliant Warren Beatty, neglected in Oscar races, maybe because of his reputation as a lover off the screen, conceived and produced *Bonnie and Clyde* for Warner Bros. and Seven Arts. He starred in it opposite Faye Dunaway as Clyde Barrow and Bonnie Parker, real-life criminals of the 1930s. Gene Hackman, Michael Pollard, and Estelle Parsons were superb in supporting performances. All were nominated. Parsons won. David Newman and Robert Benton—the latter the 1979 Oscar-winning director of *Kramer vs. Kramer*—wrote it. Burnett Guffey photographed it superbly and deservedly won an Oscar. The others lost, including Robert Penn, who directed it in dazzling style.

The film starts with photographs of those two in their time. We get a feeling for them and their time. The terrible things they do are fun for them. They want fun and fame. In front of the music of banjos, Rudy Vallee, and "We're in the Money," we follow them on their flight across the Midwest in Depression days. Clyde is impotent, but love develops between them.

They are romanticized in the film, but come to a bloody end in what has been called "a ballet of death." Shot in slow motion as bullets riddle and jerk their bodies about, this spectacular finish does not look as striking today because it has been copied so often, but it was the first of its sort and stunning at the time. Penn says it was done this way to make them look like they were disappearing into an old photograph.

This is dark comedy, deadly romance. Because it romanticized these criminals and crime and because it was so violent, it was at first condemned by many critics. It became a *cause celebre* of the cinema. It brought youth into the theaters and eventually earned more than $20 million. It excited so many that the critics took a second look and many found it fascinating. As time goes on, it is taking on the look of a classic, a departure and a triumph.

Butch Cassidy and the Sundance Kid similarly romanticized crime and criminals, but with a lighter tone. Paul Newman and Robert Redford were captivating as the colorful cowboy duo. This account of their adventures and misadventures in the old West was told with enormous enthusiasm and charm. Katharine Ross was attractive as the girl in a man's world. Again, the duo came to a spectacularly bloody death.

The Graduate *with Anne Bancroft and Dustin Hoffman.*

Five Easy Pieces *with Jack Nicholson and William Challee.*

John Foreman produced the film for 20th Century-Fox and George Roy Hill directed it with great humor. William Goldman wrote it and Conrad Hall photographed it. All were nominated, and Hall and Goldman took home Oscars. But neither Redford nor Newman was nominated and neither has yet won one of those statuettes. Nor has Hill.

The film may have looked like lightweight fare at first, but it has gained in popularity with the years and now ranks high in polls of fans, which should not be sneered at as insignificant. Its popularity inspired the pairing of the two stars a few years later in the Academy Award-winning The Sting.

The Graduate, produced by Lawrence Turman, represented a breakthrough in the way today's bored society is depicted. It is dark comedy, but not too dark. It is a light-hearted but sophisticated look at the manners and morals of the country club cocktail crowd. It was nominated as Best Picture, but did not win. Its director, Mike Nichols, did win. Buck Henry and Calder Willingham wrote it with a deft touch.

Dustin Hoffman as the young man uncertain which way to pursue his life following his discharge from the service and Anne Bancroft as the bored housewife who lures the young man into an awkward affair do wonderfully well with their roles. Both were nominated for Oscars but both lost. The film won the New York Critics Award. Robert Redford was offered the title

role, but against the advice of his management, turned it down. Dustin Hoffman became a star in it.

It led in its way to a harsher view of contemporary society in Five Easy Pieces. The comedy is here, but darker. The hero, Jack Nicholson, is older, though equally uncertain. Born to wealth and culture, he returns from a role as a roughneck in the oil fields to take a last look at the life that was laid out for him and finally to reject success as one's only goal in life.

Nicholson is overpowering in his performance. His travelling companion as he moves across country, Karen Black, could not have better played the role of the cheap dame with a rich heart. Both were nominated for an Oscar, but both lost. Their scenes together are excellent. Her acting in the scene in which he dumps her is stunning. His scene in which he strives to communicate with his stroke-silent father for the first time is a *tour de force* of the highest magnitude.

Five Easy Pieces is a remarkable bit of moviemaking, giving such an intimate look into the human heart as to be deeply disturbing. Robert Rafelson and Richard Wechsler produced it for Columbia with considerable skill. Rafelson directed it dynamically, but did not gain even a nomination. The film remains masterful, revealing, enduring, disturbing.

So, here are thirty-five classic films that Oscar overlooked. They are far from the only ones of consequence to be neglected.

T E N

Western and Adventure Films

I T IS ALMOST impossible to believe that only one western has won an Oscar and that one, *Cimarron*, came way back in the 1930–31 period, fifty years ago.

In the meantime, such nominated classics as *Stagecoach, High Noon, Shane, The Ox-Bow Incident, Of Mice and Men*, and *Butch Cassidy and the Sundance Kid* were losers. Such classics as *Red River, Bad Day at Black Rock, The Misfits*, and *The Searchers* were not even nominated. To say nothing of *The Treasure of the Sierra Madre* which, even more than most westerns, was a cross between western and adventure films. It was nominated, but lost.

Adventure films, a broad category including war movies, have done better with seven winners. If we include a sports film like *Rocky* or spectacles such as *Around the World in 80 Days* and *The Greatest Show on Earth*, this number swells to ten.

Even so, such classics as *Les Miserable, Lives of a Bengal Lancer, Gunga Din, Viva Villa, Captain Blood, The Adventures of Robin Hood, San Francisco, The Long Voyage Home, Twelve O'Clock High, Mr. Roberts, The Caine Mutiny, The Guns of Navarone, A Walk in the Sun, Jaws*, and *Apocalypse Now* were nominated losers. Such classics as *The African Queen, A Tale of Two Cities, Captains Courageous, The Sea Wolf, Beau Geste, Paths of Glory*, and *Stalag 17* were not even nominated.

As important as the western has been to Hollywood, it seems by far to be the most neglected category of films in Oscar races.

Earlier I listed *Stagecoach, The Ox-Bow Incident*, and *Butch Cassidy and the Sundance Kid* among classic losers. I was charmed by the last. Many might think it of lesser stature. But most agree that *High Noon, Shane*, and *Red River* belong with the finest films ever made.

Stanley Kramer made *High Noon* with United Artists backing, but made it on the Columbia lot for the heavy-handed Harry Cohn. When the picture was being prepared for release, Cohn asked Kramer for a print. Kramer refused. Cohn signed Kramer's name to a request for a print from United Artists and screened it. When Kramer angrily confronted Cohn to complain about interference, Cohn snapped, "It doesn't matter, it's a piece of crap, anyway." Some thought otherwise.

High Noon, written by Carl Foreman and directed by Fred Zinnemann, won the New York Critics Award as best picture of 1952. Bosley Crowther of the *New York Times* said that every five years or so someone with an appreciation for legend and poetry scoops up cliches from the westerns and turns them into a thrilling and inspiring work, and that such a rare and exciting achievement was *High Noon*. It was called a work of art, fit to challenge *Stagecoach* as the all-time best of its breed.

It was a simple tale of courage as a reluctant sheriff, Gary Cooper, is left alone to face a desperado while the townspeople wait, but will not help. Ready to retire, he goes against the wishes of his bride, Grace Kelly, to do his duty.

Lesser roles are played superbly by Lloyd Bridges,

High Noon *with Gary Cooper, blasting away.*

Shane *with Alan Ladd, Jean Arthur, and Van Heflin.*

The Wild Bunch *with William Holden, spilling his guts, and Ernest Borgnine.*

Thomas Mitchell, Otto Kruger, and Katy Jurado. It is a beautiful film with the feeling of an old cowboy ballad and it was as well done as a western can be.

The next year, *Shane* came along. Produced and directed by George Stevens, adapted from a Jack Schaefer novel by A. B. Guthrie, Jr., it tells a classic tale of good versus evil. It was possible in the old West to be a gunfighter and do good, but even there, evil spills into it.

A handsome man of mystery, Alan Ladd, moves in on a family: Van Heflin, Jean Arthur, and Brandon De Wilde. The contrast between the man of action, Ladd,

and the pacifist, Heflin, is drawn strongly. Reluctantly, Heflin's wife, Arthur, is drawn to Ladd. Their love is unspoken but poignantly depicted. She hates him for teaching her son to handle a gun, however. Eventually the blond god must take on the dark knight, Jack Palance.

Scored by Dimitri Tiomkin—who is credited with much of *High Noon*'s success—beautifully photographed by Loyal Griggs against Wyoming's Grand Teton mountains, studded with stunning depictions of a fistfight and a gunfight, marked by perhaps the finest funeral scene movies have had, the film presents the legends of the old West more powerfully and yet more subtly than any other film has ever done. Crowther was startled to find another classic western arriving within a year and called it "a rich and dramatic painting of the American frontier scene."

Red River was a rousing good adventure yarn, produced and directed by Howard Hawks. A contemporary of John Ford and often compared to Ford, Hawks was less a poet and more a man of action. While Ford was well honored, Hawks never received rewards. But in *Rio Bravo, The Big Sky,* and especially *Red River,* he did overwhelmingly fine work.

Red River centers around a cattle drive and the conflict between a man of action, John Wayne, and a poet, his adopted son, Montgomery Clift. John Ireland plays a thorn between them and Joanne Dru, who was to marry Ireland, plays the love interest. Walter Brennan, Noah Beery, Jr., and Harry Carey, Sr. and Jr. support the leads. The acting is superb.

Wayne plays a ruthless leader who despairs that his son is not manly. As the drive rocks ruggedly along the Chisholm Trail, Clift is driven to prove his manliness and replace his father as leader. There is violence and brutality. These were not soft men and life was not easy. A stampede is pictured in stunning fashion. The black-and-white photography by Russell Harlan is as well done as any in film history.

Controversy remains over the ending. Borden Chase, who wrote the story and screenplay, wanted Wayne, badly wounded in a shootout with Ireland, to die during a following shootout with Clift. Hawks did not want Wayne to die and has Clift refuse to shoot Wayne at the finish. If this weakens the film, so be it. The 1948 film remains tremendously strong.

Many others regard *The Wild Bunch, McCabe and Mrs. Miller,* and *One-Eyed Jacks* as unrecognized classics. They did not win Oscar nominations, but cults have sprung up around them.

For his own company, Marlon Brando hired Stanley Kubrick to direct and rewrite a Sam Peckinpah script. It wound up with Brando directing his own version. He'd spend an entire day shooting a scene that lasted three minutes on screen. He'd shoot 10,000 feet of film for 300 that was used. In the end, he'd prepared six months and shot six months and had 1,000,000 feet of film.

He cut to four hours and forty-two minutes and 80,000 feet. Someone else had to cut to two hours and twenty-one minutes and 40,000 feet. A year after it was finished, Brando called the actors back to shoot a new ending. The total cost was $6 million. But after *One-Eyed Jacks* was released in 1961, it returned twice that amount and *Newsweek* called it, "one of the most intriguing westerns ever made."

Yet, *One-Eyed Jacks,* like *Rio Bravo, The Wagonmaster, The Searchers, My Darling Clementine, The Misfits, Major Dundee,* and *Junior Bonner* were among excellent westerns which did not receive a single nomination for an Academy Award in any category.

One-Eyed Jacks came out in 1961. Almost ten years later, Peckinpah's *The Wild Bunch* came out in 1969. This movie has been condemned for its violence. It is violent. We have a couple of hundred violent deaths. When the men are shot, they bleed. We see, head-on, a man's throat cut. Peckinpah believes violence was a part of the old West. He shows it to us in slow motion to make it more vivid.

But Peckinpah's vision of the old West was that of a violent place in which there was not the traditional duel between good and evil because the distinctions became blurred during the difficulty of that life. He does not romanticize his outlaws. He depicts the railroaders as ruthless businessmen, the cavalry as reluctant bunglers. He presents a picture of the old West which may be more accurate than the others. William Holden, Robert Ryan, Ernest Borgnine, Warren Oates, and others of the outlaws gave vivid portraits of that breed.

McCabe and Mrs. Miller (1971) was an offbeat view of life on the frontier deftly directed by Robert Aldrich and acted with great animation by Warren Beatty and Julie Christie. Another was *Welcome to Hard Times* (1966), Burt Kennedy's outstanding but overlooked screenwork starring Henry Fonda.

One of the first great westerns was the first outdoor talkie, *In Old Arizona,* Raoul Walsh's 1929 movie starring Warner Baxter as The Cisco Kid. Baxter won an Oscar for his role. One of the great traditional westerns was William Wyler's *The Westerner* in 1940, starring Gary Cooper and winning for Walter Brennan a third Best Supporting Actor Academy Award.

It was in 1930's *The Virginian* that Cooper spoke the immortal words, "When you call me that . . . smile." Cooper fit the part of the tight-lipped hero from the Owen Wister novel, the first western to rise above dime-novel, pulp-fiction status.

Throughout the 1940s and 1950s, John Ford dominated the western. It is as good a reason for this book as any that he won more Oscars than any other director but did not win one for his favored westerns. In an interview years ago, he told me, "I preferred my westerns to my other films because I like the way life was lived in the old West better than in any other period of our life. I loved the pioneer spirit and the simplicity of the people. I dislike the fact that the beauty of the West

In Old Arizona *with Warner Baxter and Dorothy Burgess.*

In the almost twenty years between *Stagecoach* and *The Searchers*, Ford moved toward a more visual style with less spoken language. Ford's dearest friend, John Wayne, gave one of his finest performances in *The Searchers* as a strong, silent man—a man apart from his fellow men who lives by his own law and does what he feels he must. When his family is slaughtered by Comanche Indians he goes on a five-year rampage of revenge and searches for his kidnapped niece, Natalie Wood. Finding her changed by her captives, he wants to kill her but cannot. His ordeal finished, he finds himself a man without a mission and thus without a reason for living.

Ford's weakness, if he had one, may have been that until his later films he regarded the Indians as lowly and did not treat them with the sympathy history indicates they deserve. They were victims who victimized their victimizers. He took the side of the cowboy and then the military in a one-sided fight. In *The Searchers* however he makes his hero as cruel and cunning as the villains and in so doing gives us a balanced view of the West that was. He uses the color photography of Winton Hock handsomely. The adventure is turned into art.

John Steinbeck's striking short story, *Of Mice and Men*, was turned into a marvelous movie by Lewis Milestone in 1939. Burgess Meredith as George and Lon Chaney, Jr., as his retarded sidekick Lenny are superb. George dreams aloud about a life for them on a farm when they save enough money to buy one. "Tell me again about the rabbits, George," says Lenny. As the sailors in *The Long Voyage Home* never will go home again, so too will the cowboys in *Of Mice and Men* never find their farm. You know it is not to be and you hate it.

as captured by the camera is so seldom even noticed by critics. Movies, after all, are a visual experience, and the less said in them the better. I don't think a lot about honors, but I think it is demeaning to the western that I received honors for other films and none for my westerns."

Although *Stagecoach* (1939) is generally regarded as his masterpiece, many prefer *The Searchers* (1956), and there are holdouts for *My Darling Clementine* (1946), *Fort Apache* (1948), *She Wore a Yellow Ribbon* (1949), *The Man Who Shot Liberty Valance* (1961), and *Cheyenne Autumn* (1964).

Of Mice and Men *with Lon Chaney, Jr., Burgess Meredith, and Roman Bohnen.*

An old man, marvelously played by Granville Bates, would go with them if he could, but they will not go. The heavy, a cruel cowboy played by Bob Steele, and a harlot, a thoughtless lady played by Betty Field, get in their way and there is nothing the boss, Slim, as played by Charles Bickford, can do. There is nothing anyone can do. The ending is inevitable and tragic. This is true tragedy, a western as well acted and emotionally moving as any the movies have produced.

Humor made its mark in westerns with *Destry Rides Again*, the 1939 film produced by Joe Pasternak and directed by George Marshall from the novel by Max Brand. Four men played *Destry* in films, from Tom Mix to Audie Murphy, but Jimmy Stewart was best. Joel McCrea was the other. As the mild-mannered cowboy who can handle a gun when he has to, Stewart fit perfectly.

However, the film really belongs to Marlene Dietrich, playing Frenchy, the saloon girl who displays her legs and sings "See What the Boys in the Back Room Will Have." Her catfight with Una Merkel, an angry wife whose husband has lost his trousers in a poker game, is the classic ladies fight in films. It took five days to film the two minutes on screen and the actresses refused doubles.

When Marlene drops earrings into her plunging cleavage, Allen Jenkins comments, "Thar's gold in them thar hills," a classic line that wowed the critics in the early release, but was ordered out by the Hays office before long. Such charm and humor weren't frequently found in westerns, but turned up in *Cat Ballou* in 1955 and *Butch Cassidy and the Sundance Kid* in 1969.

Cat Ballou won an Oscar for Lee Marvin as a drunken cowboy who moves about on a drunken horse, but *Ballou* was not nominated as Best Picture, nor was its inventive director Elliott Silverstein nominated as Best Director. Still this saga of the sloppy gunslinger with the tin nose was splendidly played by Marvin. Jane Fonda, by the way, was Cat, not Marvin, and marvelously good-humored.

Robert Aldrich made some wonderful westerns, notably *Apache* and *Vera Cruz* in 1954 and *The Last Sunset* in 1961. Budd Boetticher made many, including *Ride Lonesome* in 1959. Delmar Davies made several, specifically *Broken Arrow* in 1950, *3:10 to Yuma* in 1957, and *Cowboy* in 1958. William Fraker's *Monty Walsh* in 1970 was excellent. Henry Hathaway did a number, including *True Grit* in 1969, which had a lot of humor in it and won for John Wayne his one Oscar.

Henry King's 1939 *Jesse James*, with Tyrone Power as Jesse and Henry Fonda as brother Frank, was notable, as was his 1950 *The Gunfighter* with Gregory Peck. Anthony Mann's *Winchester '73* in 1950, with Jimmy Stewart, was one of many excellent westerns he did. Arthur Penn's *The Left-Handed Gun* in 1958 with Paul Newman and *Little Big Man* in 1970 with Dustin Hoffman were exceptional. So was Sydney Pollack's *Jeremiah Johnson* in 1972 with Robert Redford.

William Wellman's *The Ox-Bow Incident* in 1942 was, of course, a classic. Many consider *Giant* in 1956 a giant, but I thought Jimmy Dean miscast in a role Alan Ladd turned down. Dean was too young and Ladd too old for the role. Director George Stevens did well with this modern-day tale of the old West starring Rock Hudson and Elizabeth Taylor.

Richard Brooks made two wonderful westerns, *The Last Hunt* in 1955 and *The Professionals* in 1966. Neither was nominated for an Oscar, although Brooks won a nomination as director of the latter.

Bad Day at Black Rock in 1955 was not nominated, but John Sturges was for his strong direction and Spencer Tracy was for his splendid performance as a modern detective in an old West town.

John Huston's 1960 *The Misfits* may be one of the most underrated movies of all time. It told a touching tale of modern-day cowboys Clark Gable, Montgomery Clift, and Eli Wallach. They are made to see how misplaced they are in the new West by a lonely lady, Marilyn Monroe. She has hysterics as they rope proud, wild stallions for dogfood. Gable says, "I'm doing the same thing I always did. They just changed things around." The neglected Thelma Ritter provides a splendid performance as Marilyn's friend.

Arthur Miller's poetic script deals with life and death. Wallach says, "Maybe all there is is the next thing. Maybe we shouldn't listen to people. People dyin' all the time—husbands and wives not teachin' each other what they need to know." Gable says, "Dyin's natural as livin'. People afraid to die are afraid to live." Near the end, Gable says wistfully to Monroe, "I bless you, girl. If there could be one person..." She asks, "How do you find your way back in the dark?"

It was Gable's last film and close to Monroe's last. It came as Clift's career was starting its deadly downward slide. The physical effort of the roping scenes may have claimed Clark's life. He left behind a classic.

Lonely Are the Brave, a 1962 film directed by David Miller and starring Kirk Douglas, was a little-noticed but brilliant depiction of an old-fashioned cowboy lost in a modern-day West. *Hud*, a 1963 film directed by Martin Ritt and starring Paul Newman, Melvyn Douglas, and Patricia Neal, was another wonderfully well done Western. It won dnomination as Best Picture, but lost. It won nominations for all three principles, and Douglas and Neal won. Her performance may be among the most moving in the history of films. The ever-underrated Newman lost. There have not been two better movies made in Hollywood, to say nothing of two better westerns.

If you separate westerns from other adventure films, war films have dominated the genre. Oscars were won by *Wings* in 1927–28, *All Quiet on the Western Front* in 1929–30, *Bridge on the River Kwai* in 1957, *Lawrence of Arabia* in 1962, *Patton* in 1970, and *The Deer Hunter* in 1978. Epics like *Mutiny on the Bounty* in 1935 and *Ben-Hur* in 1959 won. Spectacles such as *The Greatest Show on Earth* in 1952 and *Around the World in 80 Days* in 1956 won. One sports film, *Rocky,* won in 1976.

On the other hand, I already have listed many notable nominated losers. These include *The Caine Mutiny,* which received seven nominations, *The Long Voyage Home,* which received six, and *The Sea Hawk* and *The Story of GI Joe,* which received four each—all failed to win even one Oscar in any category. Classics like *Gunga Din* in 1937, *The Set-Up* in 1949, *The Red Badge of Courage* in 1951, and *Paths of Glory* in 1957 did not receive even one nomination.

Adventure films in their purest form were so well done in the 1930s that they seemingly exhausted the supply of stories and only an occasional epic like John Huston's *The Man Who Would Be King* in 1975 has come along lately. Henry Hathaway's *The Lives of a Bengal Lancer* in 1935, starring Gary Cooper, Franchot Tone, Richard Cromwell, and C. Aubrey Smith, was an exciting case in kind. In this one, Douglas Dumbrille as Mohammad Khan says to his captive, "We have ways of making men talk."

In director George Stevens' *Gunga Din* in 1939, Sam Jaffe, later the kindly doctor in the Ben Casey television series, played the half-breed bugler. Cary Grant, Douglas Fairbanks, Jr., and Victor McLaglen played the adventurers. Based on Rudyard Kipling's poem, the story and screenplay were written by no less than Ben Hecht, Charles MacArthur, William Faulkner, and Joel Sayre, among others. Maybe a classic, maybe not, but as exciting as a movie could be.

William Wellman's story of French Foreign Legion life, *Beau Geste,* was brought to the screen in 1939 by Gary Cooper, Ray Milland, Robert Preston, Brian Donlevy, J. Carroll Naish, and Susan Hayward. *The Charge of the Light Brigade* in 1936 was well enacted by Errol Flynn, David Niven, and Olivia De Havilland.

Flynn was an important figure in adventure films of the 1930s. He may or may not have been an artist as

Gunga Din with Douglas Fairbanks Jr., Victor McLaglen, and Cary Grant holding an enemy hostage.

Captain Blood with Errol Flynn and his pirate band. That's Guy Kibbee leaning on the rail, taking in some salt air.

The Adventures of Robin Hood—Errol Flynn is pointed out to Olivia De Havilland.

an actor, but he was a wonderfully flamboyant fellow who fit his heroic roles almost as well in the early talkies as Douglas Fairbanks, Sr., had in the silents.

Flynn's first was *Captain Blood* in 1935. It was nominated, but its director, Michael Curtiz, and its star, Flynn, were not. However, this was the last year write-ins were permitted and one of the last years where results were revealed, and write-in Curtiz finished second to John Ford for *The Informer* in the directorial race.

Rafael Sabatini's novel was brought to the screen with thrilling grandeur. As Dr. Peter Blood, a falsely imprisoned escapee turned pirate who duels Basil Rathbone and wins the hand of fair maiden Arabella (Olivia De Havilland), Flynn was spectacular.

I was but a boy of seven or eight when *Captain Blood* came out. I was thrilled by it. I clearly recall one Saturday trying to decide whether to see this movie again or a movie I had not seen. There was really no contest. I have seen it countless times since then.

I have no illusions about its being high art. I suppose you could consider it my particular kind of camp. I have seldom seen even the best of films more than two or three times through, but when the rare chance comes to see this one again, I do, and it brings back warm memories of my boyhood.

I suppose all fans have those films which for one reason or another—often not for good reasons, often not for great films—turned them on to movies, and I think this was the one for me. It even turned me on to books, for the novel was one of the first I ever read in my youth—that, too, because of the movie.

Flynn's films excited the adventurous spirit in many of us. *The Sea Hawk* in 1940 was another of his spectaculars.

Flynn, De Havilland, and Curtiz came together again for *The Adventures of Robin Hood* in 1938, which probably can be considered a classic—tongue in cheek, of course. Flynn's crew of cutthroats, including Alan Hale, became his merry band. Rathbone again was a villain, along with Claude Rains.

The advertising blurb read, "Only the rainbow itself can duplicate its brilliance." It was, indeed, a tremendous step forward in the use of Technicolor. It was a beautiful, light-hearted tale told as well as Hollywood has told such tales.

It was not easy to bring such classics to the screen effectively, but Hollywood did many well in those days. Standouts included *Les Miserables* in 1935 with Fredric March and Charles Laughton; *A Tale of Two Cities* in 1935 with Colman; Mervyn LeRoy's *Anthony Adverse* in 1936 with March and De Havilland; and John Cromwell and W. S. Van Dyke's *The Prisoner of*

Zenda in 1937 with Colman, Douglas Fairbanks, Jr., David Niven, Raymond Massey, Madeleine Carroll, and Mary Astor.

Among the outstanding historical epics overlooked by Oscar were Woody Van Dyke's *San Francisco* in 1936 with Clark Gable, Spencer Tracy, and Jeanette MacDonald, and Henry King's *In Old Chicago* in 1938 with Tyrone Power, Don Ameche, and Alice Faye. *San Francisco* told the story of the 1906 earthquake; *In Old Chicago* portrayed the 1871 fire.

The earthquake was so vividly depicted that some critics called it a climax without comparison in the history of films. Perhaps it raised an otherwise routine

In Old Chicago *with Alice Brady, an Oscar winner for this film, and* Tyrone Power, never one.

The Sea Wolf *with John Garfield backing up Edward G. Robinson.*

film into the rank of classics. The earthquake took twenty minutes on screen and ten days on the sound stage with outdoor shots used for background. James Basevi, MGM's special effects genius, was the man behind it, as he was also for the hurricane in *The Hurricane*, John Ford's 1937 marvel starring Dorothy Lamour, Jon Hall, Thomas Mitchell, and Raymond Massey.

Ford's *The Long Voyage Home* may have been the most moving story of the sea. Victor Fleming's 1937 *Captains Courageous*, another adventure yarn based on a book by Rudyard Kipling, starring Spencer Tracy, Lionel Barrymore, Melvyn Douglas, Freddie Bartholomew, and Mickey Rooney was simply marvelous. It took Tracy to his first Oscar, but all in it were remarkably good.

The Sea Wolf, based on the novel by Jack London, written by Robert Rossen, and directed by Michael Curtiz, starred Edward G. Robinson, John Garfield, and Ida Lupino. It was a well-played, wildly exciting tale of violence on the high seas with a hint of the Laughton Captain Bligh in the Robinson Wolf Larson.

Of all the outdoor, heroic, or biblical epics produced and directed by Cecil B. DeMille, none worked as well as *Reap the Wild Wind* in 1942 with John Wayne, Ray Milland, Robert Preston, Raymond Massey, Charles Bickford, and Paulette Goddard. Curling his hair for his role, Milland suffered burns that made him bald for life. The sea scenes were sensational.

King Vidor's *Northwest Passage* in 1940, starring Spencer Tracy, Robert Young, and Walter Brennan, was a notably rugged depiction of man's pioneer spirit. Henry King's *Stanley and Livingstone* in 1939 starred Tracy and Brennan in the famous story of the search through darkest Africa for Dr. Livingstone, who turned out to be Sir Cedrick Hardwicke. Asks Stanley, "Dr. Livingstone, I presume?"

Stretch as we will, we cannot elevate the *Tarzan* films, even those starring Johnny Weissmuller and Maureen O'Sullivan, to classic levels, but they were fun and they were popular. An African film which worked well was *King Solomon's Mines* in 1950 with Stewart Granger and Deborah Kerr. Another was *Roots of Heaven* with Errol Flynn, Trevor Howard, Eddie Albert, and Orson Welles, and, of course, there was *The African Queen*.

Maybe the best story of hunters was John Boorman's *Deliverance* in 1972, acted with animal eroticism by Burt Reynolds, Jon Voight, and others. This was a greatly underrated movie, maybe because it was in its way horrifying. This showed hunters deteriorating in the wild. It may have influenced strongly the 1978 Award winner *The Deer Hunter*.

Rocky in 1976 was the first sports film to take an Oscar. The script by Sylvester Stallone and the acting of Stallone, Talia Shire, and Burgess Meredith were excellent, but all lost out in the Oscar race. The audience grew involved with the characters and rooted at the finish as if the climactic championship fight were real.

Mark Robson's *Champion* in 1949 with Kirk Douglas, Robert Rossen's *Body and Soul* in 1947 with John Garfield, Robert Wise's *The Set-Up* in 1949 with Robert Ryan, and John Huston's *Fat City* in 1972 with Stacy Keach were remarkable ring films with powerful performances by their leads.

Deliverance with Burt Reynolds and Ronny Cox as hunters.

Bang the Drums Slowly *with Robert DeNiro, Michael Moriarity, and Vincent Gardenia in the famous bathtub scene.*

Sam Wood's *The Pride of the Yankees* in 1942, with Lou Gehrig played effectively by Gary Cooper, was probably the first baseball film of artistic note. Babe Ruth played himself in this one, by the way. By far the best baseball film made is John Hancock's *Bang the Drum Slowly* with splendid performances by Robert DeNiro, who has yet to win an Oscar, and the enormously skilled Michael Moriarity, who hasn't even been getting much chance on the big screen.

There hasn't been an outstanding football film unless you count *Knute Rockne—All-American* with its unforgettable portrait of the great coach by Pat O'Brien and a charming rendition of George Gipp by Ronald Reagan. Basketball? Forget it, although *One on One* in 1977 with the multi-talented Robby Benson came close. Hockey? Again, forget it. *Slap Shot* in 1977 with Paul Newman was funny, but a farce.

The odd sports have done better. Robert Rossen's 1961 tale of pool sharks, *The Hustler*, with smashing acting by Paul Newman, George C. Scott, Jackie Gleason, and Piper Laurie, was a wonderful film worthy of an Oscar. Norman Jewison's 1965 story of card sharks, *The Cincinnati Kid*, with strong performances by Edward G. Robinson, Steve McQueen, Karl Malden, Rip Torn, Ann-Margret, Tuesday Weld, and Joan Blondell, did not attract the attention it merited.

Rouben Mamoulian's 1941 *Blood and Sand*, with Tyrone Power, Anthony Quinn, Laird Cregar, Linda Darnell, and Rita Hayworth, won an Oscar for the color photography of Ernest Palmer and Ray Rennahan. It deserves remembering for its Goya-like beauty and sensitive treatment of the controversial art of bullfighting. *Downhill Racer* in 1969 was a skiing film, starring Robert Redford, which dug deep into the psyche of the athletic competitor.

Peacetime adventure has been well covered in recent years with a series of spectacular and successful disaster epics, but it would be difficult to classify such films as *The Poseidon Adventure*, *The Towering Inferno*, *Airport*, or *Jaws* as anything but fun, although the last three won nominations for Oscars.

The 1975 *Jaws*, with stunning performances by Roy Scheider, Richard Dreyfuss, and Robert Shaw, was a blockbuster which did at least approach art at times. It has earned more than $120 million, which places it second only to *Star Wars* among all-time moneymakers. *Jaws II* has earned another $50 million. *The Towering Inferno* has earned $55 million. Both are in the top twenty all-time favorites.

Historical adventures which endure as outstanding include Jack Conway's *Viva Villa* in 1934 with Wallace Beery, Leo Carrillo, and Fay Wray; Elia Kazan's *Viva Zapata* in 1952 with Marlon Brando, Anthony Quinn, and Jean Peters; and William Dieterle's *Juarez* in 1939 with Paul Muni and Bette Davis. All dealt with wars in Mexico.

The first Oscar winner, *Wings*, was a war movie. It was followed by several fine films on flying, especially in wartime. Among these were Howard Hughes' *Hell's Angels* in 1929–30 with Ben Lyon, James Hall, and Jean Harlow; Howard Hawks' *Dawn Patrol* in 1930–31 with Richard Barthelmess; and Hawks' *Only Angels Have Wings* in 1939 with Barthelmess, Cary Grant, Thomas Mitchell, Jean Arthur, and Rita Hayworth.

Billionaire Hughes was not a recluse in those days, was a pioneer aviator, and did produce and direct the exciting *Hell's Angels*. In it, Jean Harlow uttered the classic line to Ben Lyon, "Excuse me while I slip into something more comfortable." *Dawn Patrol* was Hawks' first talkie, but there was more action than talk in it.

Jaws starred a mechanical shark and assorted swimmers.

Many consider *Only Angels Have Wings* to be Hawks' top picture. Director and historian Peter Bogdanovich once listed it in his all-time top ten along with another Hawks' film, *Rio Bravo*; two Orson Welles' films, *The Magnificent Ambersons* and *Touch of Evil*; two Alfred Hitchcock films, *Vertigo* and *North by Northwest*; and two John Ford films, *The Searchers* and *She Wore a Yellow Ribbon*.

Bill Bayer calls *Angels* "the basic adventure film of the American cinema." This was not a war film. It was about civilians who flew the mail in mountainous South America. Outcasts, they nevertheless performed with pride. There is a lot in it about bravery and honor. It is a masculine film. Much of the film is set in a saloon but there is great action in the air as the men dare the elements. It has become a cult favorite.

Sam Wood's *Sergeant York* in 1941 is one of the better-remembered war stories. It did not win the Best Picture Oscar that year, but it did win the Best Actor Award for Gary Cooper. Playing the true story of a hillbilly in the alien world of the armed forces who wins the highest honors for bravery under fire in World War I, Cooper beat out the millionaire newspaper publisher played by Orson Welles that year in *Citizen Kane*.

Perhaps the most underrated of the war films was Lewis Milestone's *A Walk in the Sun* in 1945. It starred Dana Andrews, Richard Conte, John Ireland, and Lloyd Bridges, and they were not major stars. Perhaps because it did not have major stars, it did not attract a lot of attention. It was, however, a penetrating look at life in the trenches, or, in this case, the jungle.

Wake Island and its director, John Farrow, won nominations in 1942 but did not win Oscars. Farrow did win the New York Critics Award for this surprisingly effective effort in which the stars were supporting players Brian Donlevy, Robert Preston, MacDonald Carey, Bill Bendix, Albert Dekker, and Walter Abel.

Henry King's 1949 *Twelve O'Clock High* was a powerful film of the responsibilities of leadership when men at war are sent into the air to fight and die. Gregory Peck and Dean Jagger were especially effective. Peck won the New York Critics Award. Sam Wood's 1948 *Command Decision* was similarly strong with Clark Gable, Walter Pidgeon, John Hodiak, Brian Donlevy, and Van Johnson.

Edward Dmytryk's version of Herman Wouk's *The Caine Mutiny* did not enjoy the success of Fred Zinnemann's version of James Jones' *From Here to Eternity*, but the Stanley Kramer production of *Mutiny* was a powerful sea saga of men at war. It produced excellent performances from Humphrey Bogart as Capt. Queeg, Jose Ferrer, Fred MacMurray, and Van Johnson.

John Huston's 1951 *The Red Badge of Courage*, starring Audie Murphy and Bill Mauldin, was a controversial version of the famous Stephen Crane novel, but it holds up powerfully. William Wellman's 1945 *The Story of G I Joe*, based on the Ernie Pyle columns, starring Robert Mitchum and Burgess Meredith, was an underrated film.

A sleeper of wartime espionage was *Orders to Kill*, a 1957 thriller with one of Eddie Albert's many overlooked outstanding performances. Another superior portrait of espionage was presented in *Five Fingers* with James Mason in 1952. The movie did not win nomination, but director Joseph Mankiewicz did.

J. Lee Thompson's *The Guns of Navarone*, starring Gregory Peck, David Niven, and Anthony Quinn, was a taut thriller of wartime daring which won Oscar nomination in 1961. The Peck role was turned down by Bill Holden. While it did not win nomination, it gained acclaim for Peck.

Another one of those sleepers that comes along once in a while was *War Hunt* in 1962. This story of a soldier who considers killing a game was a shattering piece of work. John Saxon played the soldier with a young Robert Redford in a supporting role.

The Deer Hunter, which went from men hunting animals to men hunting men, to men being hunted like animals, to men becoming much like animals, won the Best Picture Oscar in 1978. Robert DeNiro and Meryl Streep, though nominated for their overpowering performances, were denied.

Apocalypse Now, which showed the savagery and insanity of the same jungle war in Vietnam, was nominated but denied the Oscar in 1979. Two of its key characters, the hunter, Martin Sheen, and the hunted, Marlon Brando, were denied even nominations.

Francis Ford Coppola's incredibly expensive epic adventure is a classic loser of its kind. But if *Stagecoach, High Noon, Red River, The Ox-Bow Incident, Gunga Din, The Long Voyage Home, The African Queen, Paths of Glory*, and *The Treasure of Sierra Madre* could be passed over, why not *Apocalypse Now*?

Apocalypse Now *with Marlon Brando and Martin Sheen.*

ELEVEN

Crime and Suspense Films

THERE HAVE BEEN only five winners from the fields of crime and suspense in the annual Oscar races.

There was not a winner among crime movies until 1967 when *In the Heat of the Night* won, followed by *The French Connection* in 1971, *The Godfather* in 1972, and *The Godfather Part II* in 1974. The latter two are the only original and sequel to gain the Best Picture Awards. Incredibly, only one suspense film has won—1940's *Rebecca*.

Nominated losers among crime films have included *I Am a Fugitive from a Chain Gang*, *The Informer*, *The Maltese Falcon*, *Double Indemnity*, *Bonnie and Clyde*, *Chinatown*, *Taxi Driver*, and *Dog Day Afternoon*. Not even nominated were *Little Caesar*, *Public Enemy*, *Scarface*, *The Petrified Forest*, *High Sierra*, *This Gun for Hire*, *The Asphalt Jungle*, *I Want to Live*, *The Postman Always Rings Twice*, *Psycho*, and *In Cold Blood*.

Nominated losers among suspense films have included *Foreign Correspondent*, *Spellbound*, *Suspicion*, *Gaslight*, *Witness for the Prosecution*, and *Anatomy of a Murder*. Not even nominated were *Laura*, *The Manchurian Candidate*, *Murder on the Orient Express*, and such Hitchcock classics as *Rear Window*, *Vertigo*, *Shadow of a Doubt*, *Notorious*, *The Paradine Case*, *Strangers on a Train*, *To Catch a Thief*, *The Wrong Man*, and *North by Northwest*. Hitchcock's nominated losers were *Foreign Correspondent*, *Suspicion*, and *Spellbound*. His *Rebecca* won.

Suspicion succeeded in spite of a feud between stars Cary Grant and Joan Fontaine. Joan was not the easiest woman to get along with, but it didn't show on the screen. The original ending had him dying, but audiences demanded and received a new ending with them together at the finish. Grant later remarked, "Anyone who knows her and knows me knows that I would have strangled her in the first reel."

Many regard *Vertigo*, 1957, as Hitchcock's best. The hero, James Stewart, who suffers from a fear of heights, is a detective who follows the wife, Kim Novak, of a client. He falls in love with her, saves her from one suicide effort but, because of his vertigo, fails to save her from a second. Later he meets a girl who looks much like the first and tries to make her over into the first girl. He discovers she is, indeed, the first girl and that he has been the dupe in a murder plot. In the climax, Stewart must mount a dizzying church steeple. Other Hitchcock climaxes have taken place on the face of Mount Rushmore *(North by Northwest)*, the Statue of Liberty *(Saboteur)*, and a carousel run amok *(Strangers on a Train)*. Many of Hitchcock's characters have psychological problems.

Spellbound was the first film to feature psychologists and psychoanalysis, although George Kukor's great *Gaslight* in 1944, with Charles Boyer and Ingrid Bergman, was a pioneer psycho-thriller. *Spellbound* featured Gregory Peck and Bergman. *Strangers on a Train* had an ingenious plot in which one man, Robert Walker, offers to swap murders with another, Farley Granger, while each establishes an alibi. It was all in keeping with Hitchcock, who once startled strangers on

Suspicion *with Cary Grant and Joan Fontaine.*   Double Indemnity *with Fred MacMurray and Edward G. Robinson.*

an elevator by remarking to a companion, "I didn't think the old man would bleed so much."

The Paradine Case was comparable to Billy Wilder's 1957 *Witness for the Prosecution* and Sidney Lumet's 1974 *Murder on the Orient Express* as a complex, captivating whodunit with an all-star cast.

Otto Preminger's imaginative *Laura* in 1944 with Dana Andrews, Clifton Webb, and Gene Tierney was suspense at its best, and Joseph Mankiewicz's confounding *Sleuth* in 1972 with Laurence Olivier and Michael Caine challenged watchers fiercely.

John Frankenheimr's 1962 *The Manchurian Candidate* was pure suspense at its most masterful, starring Frank Sinatra, Laurence Harvey, Angela Lansbury, and Janet Leigh in a triumph of terror.

Such films were worthy of Awards.

There are those who think Orson Welles' 1958 *Touch of Evil* and 1948 *Lady from Shanghai* equal, in their way, to *Citizen Kane*. From the first scene when Welles, gone to fat and a figure of evil, suddenly appears on the scene of a crime, *Touch of Evil* is a stunning film. It is full of fascinating scenes that lead us on a crooked trail of crime. Charlton Heston and Janet Leigh support Welles wonderfully well. Peter Bogdanovich calls *Touch of Evil* "possibly the greatest thriller ever made." *The Lady from Shanghai* concludes with a pursuit through an amusement park house of mirrors, one of the most startling sequences in cinema history.

Richard Thorpe's *Night Must Fall* in 1937, in which Robert Montgomery slyly portrayed a psychotic killer who walked around with his victim's head in a hatbox, was one of the most memorable of suspense pictures. Charles Laughton's *Night of the Hunter* in 1955, in which Robert Mitchum played a crazed killer, was one of the most overlooked of the great thrillers.

Overhearing a murder in the making when the telephone lines get switched, and unable to convince anyone it was not her imagination, the neglected Barbara Stanwyck gave a *tour de force* in the shattering *Sorry, Wrong Number* in 1948. *Wait Until Dark* in 1967 was a gripping portrait of a blind girl, Audrey Hepburn, held captive.

Two James M. Cain novels were turned into splendid dramas of suspense. These were *Double Indemnity* in 1944 with Edward G. Robinson, Fred MacMurray, and Barbara Stanwyck—none of whom ever won an Oscar—and *The Postman Always Rings Twice* with John Garfield and Lana Turner—neither of whom ever won. The plotting was ingenious, the action stunning in both.

Otto Preminger's *Anatomy of a Murder* in 1959, with James Stewart, Ben Gazzara, Arthur O'Connell, and Lee Remick, was a clever, classic case of crime. Stewart won the New York Critics Award. *Anatomy of a Murder* and *Double Indemnity* each received seven different Academy Award nominations without winning one. Only two movies have gotten more without winning.

Foreign Correspondent in 1940, *The Killers* in 1946, *The Asphalt Jungle* in 1950, Detective Story in 1951, and *In Cold Blood* in 1967 each won four different nominations without winning one. Only *Foreign Correspondent* was nominated as Best Picture, however.

The earliest masterpieces of crime movies which blazed the trails over which the others followed—Mervyn LeRoy's *Little Caesar* with Edward G. Robin-

I Am a Fugitive from a Chain Gang *with Paul Muni, foreground.*

Key Largo *with Claire Trevor and Edward G. Robinson.*

son in 1930, William Wellman's *The Public Enemy* with Jimmy Cagney in 1931, and Howard Hawks' *Scarface* with Paul Muni in 1932—did not gain nominations as Best Pictures, but no movies are better remembered.

LeRoy's *I Am a Fugitive from a Chain Gang* with Muni in 1932 did gain nomination, but not the Oscar it so richly deserved. Cagney starred in *The Roaring Twenties* in 1939, *White Heat* in 1949, and *Kiss Tomorrow Goodbye* in 1950, which some cults consider classics of crime cinema. Robinson starred in John Huston's compelling *Key Largo* in 1948.

There was a series of powerful prison melodramas in the 1930s, including *Two Seconds* with Robinson in 1932, *20,000 Years in Sing Sing*, the only pairing of Spencer Tracy and Bette Davis, in 1933, *San Quentin* with Bogart in 1937, and *Each Dawn I Die* with Cagney in 1939. *Two Seconds* is the least well known but may have been the best. In the two seconds between being seated in the electric chair and being electrocuted, Robinson relives his depressing Depression-era life. A homely man, he is conned into marrying a dime-a-dance girl and driven to kill her.

In 1958 came the classic *I Want to Live*, which was not nominated for an Academy Award but won one for Susan Hayward. In the film, she fought for her life and lost, concluding it in the gas chamber. The story was true, based on newspaper accounts of the case of Barbara Graham. It was directed by Robert Wise and its mood was enhanced by the jazz playing of Gerry Mulligan, Art Farmer, Bud Shank, Shelly Manne, and others.

A true but offbeat look at prison life was presented in *Bird Man of Alcatraz*, John Frankenheimer's touching tale of a lifer who finds solace in the study of bird life. The 1962 movie did not gain a nomination as Best Picture, but did gain one for Burt Lancaster as Best Actor, though he lost.

Bogart starred in a series of outstanding detective and criminal films. It included the unforgettable *The Petrified Forest* with Leslie Howard and Bette Davis in 1936, *Dead End* in 1937, *The Roaring Twenties* in 1939, *High Sierra* and the magnificent *Maltese Falcon* in 1941, *Key Largo* in 1948, *Beat the Devil* in 1954, and *The Desperate Hours* in 1955. As Duke Mantee, he held a group captive in a desert diner in *The Petrified Forest*. It was the forerunner of many such films to follow.

Huston's 1954 *Beat the Devil*, cowritten with Truman Capote, costarring Peter Lorre, Robert Morley, Jennifer Jones, and Gina Lollobrigida, has a cult following that considers it the classic of satirical crime. His earlier *The Asphalt Jungle*, 1954, was a low-budget blockbuster starring Sterling Hayden, Louis Calhern, James Whitmore, and Jean Hagen, with Marilyn Monroe in a bit that attracted attention.

As well-built as she was, Marilyn went to audition for Huston with falsies provided by agent Johnny Hyde. Spotting her, columnist James Bacon, considering this the ultimate in insecurity, suggested that she take them out. She couldn't bring herself to do so, saying "Johnny says they are looking for a sexpot with big bosoms." Asked about the falsies, Huston said, "I reached in and took them out. And told her she had the part." It launched her career.

Jules Dassin's 1958 *The Naked City* with Barry Fitzgerald and Howard Duff was an underrated movie that spawned one of the great television series. Robert

The Lodger, *Laird Cregar*.

Siodmak's 1946 *The Killers* with Edmond O'Brien and Ava Gardner was a strong adaptation of an Ernest Hemingway story. Both *The Naked City* and *The Killers* were produced by Mark Hellinger, one of the literary balladeers of Broadway.

He may not have had top billing, but the burly, brilliant, short-lived Laird Cregar was the star of three of the finest crime films—*I Wake Up Screaming* with Victor Mature, Betty Grable, and Carole Landis in 1941; *This Gun for Hire* with Alan Ladd, Robert Preston, and Veronica Lake in 1942; and *The Lodger* in 1944. He played Jack the Ripper in *The Lodger*. Ladd was made a star with his cold-eyed performance in *This Gun for Hire*, a Whit Burnett and Albert Maltz adaptation of a Graham Greene novel, well directed by Frank Tuttle.

Richard Widmark was made a star with his maniacal laugh as he pushed old ladies in wheelchairs downstairs—sort of fast—in the surprisingly powerful *Kiss of Death* in 1947. The film may offer Victor Mature's only outstanding performance. Richard Fleischer's *Compulsion* in 1959, with Bradford Dillman and Dean Stockwell as the true-life fun-killers Loeb and Leopold, and with Orson Welles, was a stunning study of insanity.

William Wyler's 1951 *Detective Story*, starring Kirk Douglas, Bill Bendix, and Eleanor Parker, was an outstanding adaptation of a Sidney Kingsley stageplay.

Stanley Kubrick's *The Killing* with Sterling Hayden in 1956 is considered a classic by some. Jim Fulton is one of several screen experts who considers *Orders to Kill* with Eddie Albert in 1957 an undiscovered masterpiece.

Raymond Chandler's Philip Marlowe private eye books, so brilliantly done as to be regarded as art, spawned a few marvelous movies, notably *Murder My Sweet* with Dick Powell in 1945, *The Big Sleep* with Bogart and Bacall in 1946, and *Farewell, My Lovely* with Robert Mitchum in 1975.

Stanley Kramer's *The Defiant Ones* with Tony Curtis and Sidney Poitier in 1958 was, while a tale of two jail escapees, a deeper story of racial prejudice between white and black men bound together. It was sensitive, strong, stirring. It was nominated as Best Picture. Both actors were nominated, too. Neither the film nor the actors won an Oscar but the film did win the New York Critics Award that year.

While the brilliant *Bonnie and Clyde* was a nominated loser in 1967 to *In the Heat of the Night*, the chilling true account of a senseless farmlands massacre, *In Cold Blood*, adapted from Truman Capote's book and directed by Richard Brooks, was overlooked. Brooks was nominated for both his writing and directing, but lost. The powerful film, starring Robert Blake and Scott Wilson, was not even nominated.

More recently, Terence Malick's 1973 *Badlands*, about a young couple who go on a senseless spree of killing and based on a true story, deserved far more

This Gun for Hire with Alan Ladd and Veronica Lake.

Chinatown *with Jack Nicholson.*

Bonnie and Clyde *with Faye Dunaway and Warren Beatty.*

recognition than it received. Likewise, Martin Scorsese's 1976 *Taxi Driver*, about a restless, rootless fellow, Robert DeNiro, who suddenly erupts, is an underrated masterpiece of mood.

Chinatown in 1974, directed by Roman Polanski and starring Jack Nicholson and Faye Dunaway, gained nominations for all, but won none. Yet, it was a classic detective story in the Raymond Chandler tradition of old L.A. with John Huston contributing a minor role of major quality.

The same year, *The Conversation* won a Best Picture nomination and star Gene Hackman a Best Actor nomination, but neither won. Director Francis Ford Coppola was nominated for *The Godfather Part II*, not for *Conversation* even though it was an excellent depiction of electronic snooping.

Sidney Lumet's *Dog Day Afternoon* in 1975, with strong performances by Al Pacino and Chris Saradon, won nominations for all, but no Oscars. John Casale was also outstanding in this thriller of crazed gunmen who bungle a bank robbery and hole up in the bank with hostages while the city goes crazy around them.

Finally, Richard Brooks' 1977 *Looking for Mr. Goodbar*, a fictionalized account of a true case of a lonely lady who winds up being stabbed to death by one of several strangers she brings to her room from a bar, may have been one of the most explosive movies ever made, but it was not nominated. Starring Diane Keaton and Richard Gere, as well as Richard Kiley and Tuesday Weld, in overpowering performances, the picture itself was astounding. At the showing I attended, several left in horror during the final terrifying minute or two. Others who stayed actually moaned and groaned. Many hated it. So, how could it win honors, even if it was fantastic film-making?

The film was strong stuff, as strong as anything pictures have produced. Frankly, I do not know if it was good or bad. Perhaps it was too strong, perhaps it was shock for shock's sake. Yet what was being depicted was true, if almost too real to endure. I cannot get it out of my mind. An exceptional movie does not leave us. It is with us forever, and this was an exceptional movie which will be remembered long after others are forgotten.

Finn. The girl they want, Mary, is his kitchen slavey, but he passes off his wife, Lola, as the one they want. She asks, "Is dear Daddy really dead?" Oliver replies, "I hope he is. They buried him."

Running into the real daughter, they realize their mistake. Laurel says, "That's the first mistake we made since that guy sold us the Brooklyn Bridge." Returning to the saloon, they try to take back the deed. It goes back and forth. Laurel sticks it down his shirt. Lola chases him into a bedroom, onto a bed, and searches him for it while he almost evaporates in ecstasy. Finally, she tickles him until he helplessly surrenders the deed.

Lola and her husband lock it up in the saloon safe. That night the boys seek to steal it back. Stan tries to hoist Ollie into an upstairs room by a pulley. Stan lets go of the rope to spit on his hands and Ollie comes crashing to earth. Mickey Finn, roused, rushes out and chases them. They hide in a piano. He decides to play the piano. It comes apart in pieces. They grab his gun, force him to open the safe, chain him to a chandelier, and, with Mary, ride off into the sunset to go for the gold.

Both suffered strokes in the 1950s, but Laurel lingered on until 1965, bedridden. One day he told his nurse, "I'd much rather be skiing than doing this." She asked, "Oh, Mr. Laurel, do you ski?" Laurel said, "No, but I'd much sooner be skiing than doing what I'm doing." A few minutes later, he died.

W. C. Fields was from Philadelphia and hated it, but before he died he left instructions to have inscribed on his tombstone, "On the whole, I'd rather be in Philadelphia." He hated most things, but the famous line, "Any man who hates small dogs and children can't be all bad," was not said by him but about him by humorist Leo Rosten.

Fields hated and mistrusted most people. The former vaudevillian and juggler scattered his money in many of the towns he played as he travelled across country so he would never wind up anywhere without funds. After his death, few of these bank accounts were uncovered.

Of Chaplin, he said, "The son of a bitch is a ballet dancer."

He made up names for his bank accounts and movie parts, including Charles Beagle, Primrose Magoo, Otis Criblecoblis, Ampico J. Steinway, Felton J. Satchelstern, and Mahatma Kane Jeeves. His names for others included, A. Pismo Clam, Filthy McNasty, Cuthbert J. Twillie, and Larson E. Whipsnade.

He wrote the plots of his movies on scraps of paper, the backs of matchbook covers, and so forth, then threw these away and made them up as he went along.

He usually played a pitchman, petty chiseler, pool hustler, card shark, snake-oil salesman, or so forth.

I picked *The Bank Dick* as his best, but others are partial to *Poppy* (1936), *You Can't Cheat an Honest Man* (1939), or *Never Give a Sucker an Even Break* (1941) which was his personal philosophy of life.

He also said, "I must have a drink for breakfast," and, "I exercise extreme self-control. I never drink anything stronger than gin before breakfast." He once complained, "Somebody left the cork out of my lunch." Asked why he didn't drink water, he pointed out, "Fish f- -- -- - in it."

He also believed, "If at first you don't succeed, try, try again. Then quit. No use being a damn fool about it." He also said, "I never vote for anyone. I always vote against."

He once spiked Baby Leroy's milk with gin on the set. The youngster's mother was outraged. Fields told her, "Walk him around. Let the little bastard walk it off." When the boy had to be helped home, finished for the day, Fields snorted, "The kid's no trouper."

Mae West's particular brand of busty, bawdy humor broke out all over *She Done Him Wrong* in 1933, in which she costarred with the young Cary Grant. This was an adaptation of her stage hit *Diamond Lil*, which she herself wrote. She played Lady Lou, a Bowery entertainer who goes for the gems from her gents until Grant, as a Salvation Army officer, of all things, comes into her life.

She struts on, announcing, "When I'm good, I'm very good. When I'm bad, I'm better." Winking, she adds, "It's not the men in my life, it's the life in my men." She says, "It's not what I do, but how I do it. It isn't what I say, but how I say it. And it's how I look when I do it and say it." She wrote most of these memorable lines.

She may not have been a great actress, but she was a great personality. When someone gasped at her gems, "My goodness!," she said, "Goodness had nothing to do with it." It became the title of her autobiography. In *She Done Him Wrong*, she tells Grant, "Why don't you come sometime and see me. I'm home every evening." This evolved into her classic invitation, "Come up and see me sometime." When Grant starts to sweat, she grins and notes, "Ah, you can be had."

She made ten movies and wrote eight of them. One of her best was the one with W. C. Fields, *My Little Chickadee*, in 1940. Kissing her hand, he asks, "Ah, me, may I partake of another morsel?" He continues kissing and nibbling up her entire arm. His cunning character brought out the best in her.

W. C. Fields in sexy bathtub scene with Eddie "Rochester" Anderson in You Can't Cheat an Honest Man.

She had a mirror above her bed. "I like to see how I'm doing," she said. But she was married only briefly and seldom seen with men. Of her, Fields said, "All bosom and behind and nothing in between," but there was more than met the eye.

In *Poppy*, Fields sells a "talking dog," having made him seem to speak through ventriloquism. As Fields walks away from his beloved pet, counting his money, the dog says, "Just for that, I'm not going to talk any more." Fields got out of there fast.

After his death, it turned out that he willed his money to establish a "W. C. Fields College For Orphaned White Boys And Girls, Where No Religion Of Any Sort Is To Be Preached." His heirs contested it and won. It was one of the few times he ever lost—except at Oscar time.

With his bulbous nose, the straw hat that kept popping off his head, his frisky cane, his chewed-down cigar, and such other props as crooked pool cues or golf clubs, Fields made magic. He was a unique comic and his films were funny. Apparently that is not enough for Awards.

The same can be said about the Marx Brothers—Groucho, Chico, Harpo, and, for a little while, Zeppo. I named *A Night at the Opera* (1935) as their funniest film, but others prefer *The Cocoanuts* (1929), *Animal Crackers* (1930), *Monkey Business* (1931), *Horse Feathers* (1932), *Duck Soup* (1933), or *A Day at the Races* (1937).

George S. Kaufman, S. J. Perelman, Morrie Ryskind, and many others wrote many of Groucho's lines, but he helped, and he delivered them with immaculate timing. In *The Cocoanuts*, he says, "One for all and all

for me. Me for you and three for five." In *Animal Crackers*, he said, "I shot an elephant in my pajamas. How he got into my pajamas I'll never know."

Told in *Horse Feathers* that there's a man outside with a big black mustache, Groucho says, "Tell him I've already got one." Told, "The Dean is furious. He's waxing wroth," Groucho says, "Tell Roth to wax the dean for awhile."

Courting various ladies, usually Margaret Dumont, he would say, "You're the most beautiful woman I've ever seen, which doesn't say much for you.... Your eyes shine like the pants of my blue serge suit." A woman pleads with him, "Hold me closer." He replies, "If I hold you any closer, I'll be behind you."

Groucho says, "Remember, men, we're fighting for this woman's honor. Which is probably more than she ever did." A lady says, "I've never been so insulted in all my life." Groucho says, "Well, it's early yet."

A lady announces to him, "I'm Beatrice Ryner. I stop at this hotel." Groucho leers, "I'm Ronald Kornblow. I stop at nothing." A hotel cop hollers through a door, "Do you have a woman in there?" Groucho replies, "If not, I'm wasting my time."

In *Duck Soup*, Groucho shows a document to his counsel and says, "It's so simple a child of ten could understand it." Aside to Chico, he says, "Run out and find me a child of ten. I can't make heads or tails of this."

In *Animal Crackers*, Groucho says, "We'll search every room in the house." Chico asks, "What if it ain't in the house?" Groucho says, "Then we'll search the house next door." Chico asks, "What if there ain't no

One of Woody Allen's many marvelous comedies, Play It Again Sam, *with Diane Keaton.*

house next door?" Groucho says, "Then we'll build one."

In *Duck Soup*, Groucho shows a document to his council and says, "It's so simple a child of ten could understand it." Aside to Chico, he says, "Run out and find me a child of ten. I can't make heads or tails of this."

The Marx Brothers romped through one madcap comedy after another, committing mayhem on madness, slapsticking sanity to death. They were as important to movies as the greatest actors and actresses, and their films made you laugh as hard as the most touching tragedies made you cry.

They enjoyed great rewards, but never one of those statuettes.

Bing Crosby and Bob Hope, with their Road pictures, and Abbott and Costello, with their nonstop nonsense, were among the biggest box-office stars of the 1940s. It's doubtful that their comedies could be ranked with the classics, but they made a lot of people laugh.

There has been a revival of outrageous comedy in films, mainly by Mel Brooks. Presumably no one would have thought of nominating *The Producers* (1968), *The Twelve Chairs* (1970), *Blazing Saddles* (1974), *Young Frankenstein* (1974), *Silent Movie* (1976), and *High Anxiety* (1977).

Brooks developed a stock company of comedy talent, including Dom DeLuise, Gene Wilder, Marty Feldman, and Madeline Kahn, some of whom have gone on to do their own outrageous satires. He also used Zero Mostel effectively in *The Producers*, Cleavon Little in *Blazing Saddles*, and Cloris Leachman and Joe Boyle in *Young Frankenstein*, to cite a few.

Although the films were all nuttiness, there is inspired nonsense nonstop in each. In *The Producers* the lead is trying to get on with the production of a play called "Springtime for Hitler," which has an unbelievable production number of the same name. A highlight of *High Anxiety*, a spoof of Hitchcock films, is Brooks' Sinatra-like crooning of a love song in a saloon. Blacks ordered to do a spiritual by bigots in *Blazing Saddles* respond with Cole Porter's "I Get a Kick out of You."

Bad taste abounds. In *Twelve Chairs*, Frank Langella and Ron Moody do epileptic bits to beg money from crowds in the city streets. The invention is irresistible. In *Silent Movie* the only speaking is by mime Marcel Marceau.

My favorite is *Young Frankenstein*. Arriving at Transylvania Station ("Track 29"), Dr. Frahnk-ensteen is greeted by the hunchback, Igor. He offers to cure him of his hump. "What hump?" asks Igor. From then, the classic is clouted left and right, which is about the way the hump moves around on the hunchback's back.

The monster tries to be a good guy, but it's hard. Breaking into a man's house, he is offered hot tea. The man turns out to be blind and pours the steaming tea into the monster's pants, but the monster holds his silence. He rapes the doctor's frigid fiancée and she loves it. In the end, he is sitting in a warm bed in a lavish mansion in Westchester County, reading *The Wall Street Journal*.

In *Take the Money and Run* (1969), Woody Allen's attempt to rob a bank is bungled because the teller and her superiors cannot read his handwriting on his holdup note. In *Bananas* (1971), *Play It Again Sam* (1972),

Sleeper (1973), and *Love and Death* (1975), Allen offered other hilarious satires on the life we've led and movies we've known.

Brooks and Allen are both Jewish and their humor springs from minority slants and slurs. Reminiscing about his childhood in a ghetto, Allen remembers, "We lived in a basement. My father had to jump up to commit suicide." Another time, he waxes nostalgic about when he almost drowned in a pond—his life flashed before his eyes. Reminiscing about fishing in the pond, milking cows in the barn, loving ladies in the hay, he suddenly realizes, "This is someone else's life flashing before my eyes."

Allen also has something of a stock company, notably Diane Keaton and his ex-wife Louise Lasser ("Mary Hartman, Mary Hartman"). But his humor is less basic and more realistic than Brooks', if not necessarily better.

With *Annie Hall* in 1977, Allen showed more of the serious side of a funny man's life (largely his own) and became the first person since Orson Welles to win Oscar nominations for picture, direction, and acting. Welles didn't win, but Woody won for his picture. Since it was strictly his, it is hard to understand why he didn't win for direction, too.

Also, few can understand why his *Manhattan* with a marvelous performance by Mariel Hemingway, the niece of Ernest, was not even nominated in 1979.

The Brooks and Allen films are a far cry from the comedies of the early days of the talkies.

Ernst Lubitsch bridged the gap between Chaplin and Keaton and W. C. Fields and Groucho Marx as he made the transition from silents to talkies with a sophisticated touch dubbed the "Lubitsch Touch." He went from musical comedies to the romantic comedies of the 1930s and 1940s.

Lubitsch's early hits were *The Love Parade* in 1929, *Monte Carlo* in 1930, *The Smiling Lieutenant* in 1931, and *Trouble in Paradise* in 1932. All had class. In *The Love Parade*, there is a running gag where Maurice Chevalier tells a risque joke repeatedly to different people. Each time he gets to the punchline, his voice sinks to a whisper and the camera moves away to view the scene from afar.

The sophisticated comedies of the 1930s were lightweight, frivolous on the surface, yet amusing and entertaining, well-acted and directed by masters of this sort of thing. A few were worthy of Awards. Fewer received any. Most were, at least, memorable.

Cary Grant and William Powell were wonderful light comedians who never received Academy Awards. Spencer Tracy received a couple of Oscars, but not for the light comedy roles he played so well.

Grant starred in *Topper* and *The Awful Truth* in 1937, *Bringing Up Baby* and *Holiday* in 1938, *His Girl Friday* in 1940, *My Favorite Wife* in 1940, *The Philadelphia Story* in 1941, *The Talk of the Town* in 1942, *Arsenic and Old Lace* in 1944, and *People Will Talk* in 1944. He costarred with Irene Dunne in *The Awful Truth* and *My Favorite Wife*, Rosalind Russell in *His Girl Friday*, Jean Arthur in *The Talk of the Town*, and Katharine Hepburn in *Bringing Up Baby*, *Holiday*, and *The Philadelphia Story*. Ronald Colman shared the lead in *Talk of the Town* and Jimmy Stewart in *The Philadelphia Story*.

Spencer Tracy, a great dramatic actor with a flair for comedy, costarred with friend and lover Katharine Hepburn in *State of the Union* in 1948, *Adam's Rib* in 1949, *Pat and Mike* in 1951, *The Desk Set* in 1957, and *Guess Who's Coming to Dinner* in 1958. He costarred with Joan Bennett as parents of Elizabeth Taylor in *Father of the Bride* in 1950.

Bill Powell costarred with Myrna Loy in *The Thin Man* in 1934 and its sequels in 1936, 1939, 1945, and 1947. He costarred with Carole Lombard in *My Man Godfrey* in 1936 and Irene Dunne in *Life with Father* in 1947. Dunne costarred with Charles Boyer in the delicious *Love Affair* in 1939.

Lombard costarred with John Barrymore in *Twentieth Century*, which made her a star. She went on to shine in *Nothing Sacred* in 1937 and *Made for Each Other* in 1939. Claudette Colbert costarred with Clark Gable in the triple-Oscar winner *It Happened One Night*.

The plots of most of these screwball comedies are not worth reporting, but they all had style. Howard Hawks' *Twentieth Century*, Frank Capra's *It Happened One Night*, George Cukor's *The Philadelphia Story*, and Leo McCarey's *The Awful Truth* probably were the best, although there is a cult following for Hawks' *Bringing Up Baby*. Others revere *His Girl Friday*, a remake of the Ben Hecht-Charles MacArthur frenzy, *Front Page*.

Cukor did most of the Tracy-Hepburn pictures and most of them were marvelous. They were a perfect pairing and they read witty lines with relish. My favorite is *Adam's Rib*. At the conclusion, Tracy threatens a startled Hepburn with a gun. The grin on his face as he starts to eat the gun is as delicious as the chocolate of which the gun was made.

Capra's *Mr. Deeds Goes to Town* in 1936, *Mr. Smith Goes to Washington* in 1939, *Meet John Doe* in 1941, and *It's a Wonderful Life* in 1947 were dramatic comedies with considerable depth to them. They preached messages that were as American as apple pie, cherry trees, and log cabins, but with a light touch. All were worthy of Academy Awards, but none won.

Ernst Lubitsch's most notable success was *Ninotchka* in 1939, which many critics consider one of the classic comedies. Three Russians seek to raise money to buy tractors by selling jewels confiscated from the Grand Duchess. She turns her boyfriend, Melvyn Douglas, on to them and he leads them astray. The Soviets send Ninotchka, Greta Garbo, to straighten out the situation, and Douglas leads her astray.

The Grand Duchess gives her jewels to Garbo in exchange for Douglas, but he pursues Garbo to Russia and on to Constantinople, as she follows the Three Fools on their fools' errands. Eventually, they open a Russian restaurant, where Douglas greets Garbo, ready for dessert. Silly as it sounds, Frank Nugent reported in the *New York Times* that the audience laughed so loudly he had to see the movie twice to hear all the lines.

Classic comedies of the early 1940s were Preston Sturges' *The Lady Eve* with Henry Fonda and Barbara Stanwyck in 1941, Howard Hawks' *Ball of Fire* with Gary Cooper and Stanwyck in 1942, and Elliott Nugent's *The Male Animal* with Fonda and Olivia De Havilland in 1942. They were imaginative, witty, and wonderfully well done. A charmingly wacky story of how three people meet the housing shortage by sharing an apartment in wartime Washington was George Stevens' *The More the Merrier* with Jean Arthur, Joel McCrea, and Charles Coburn in 1943.

The Man Who Came to Dinner in 1941 featured Monty Woolley as a crotchety old man, much like Alexander Woollcott. In a typical exchange, a nurse says to Woollcott, "You shouldn't eat chocolates in your condition, Mr. Whiteside. It's very bad for you." He replies, "I had an aunt who ate a box of chocolates every day of her life. She lived to be a hundred and two. And when she had been dead three days she looked healthier than you."

In *Sitting Pretty* in 1948, another crotchety old gent, Clifton Webb, makes ends meet by babysitting and teaches a misbehaving boy a lesson in manners by dumping a bowl of cereal over his head. This led to a series of Mr. Belvedere sequels.

Sam Wood's *Good Sam* in 1948 was a Capra-like study of a man, Gary Cooper, who is too good for his own good. In one hilarious scene, Good Sam holds up a bus so a fat lady, running from afar, can catch it. He pauses with one foot on the street and the other inside the door, tying a shoelace, while the driver steams. The fat lady comes and runs right on by.

Preston Sturges brought back slapstick comedy in a somewhat sophisticated way with *The Great McGinty*

in 1940, *Sullivan's Travels* in 1941, *The Palm Beach Story* in 1942, and *The Miracle of Morgan's Creek* and *Hail the Conquering Hero* in 1944. Using secondary stars such as Joel McCrea, Eddie Bracken, and Brian Donlevy, Sturges made marvelous satires that are considered classics by critics, but which won no Awards.

The ultimate dumb blonde role won an Oscar for Judy Holliday. She played the mistress of tycoon junk-dealer Broderick Crawford in George Cukor's brilliant *Born Yesterday* in 1950. William Holden costarred.

The 1950s brought comedies with meat on their bones, including John Ford's tough and tender *The Quiet Man* with John Wayne, Maureen O'Hara, Victor McLaglen, and Barry Fitzgerald in 1952, and William Wyler's stylish *Roman Holiday* with Gregory Peck, Audrey Hepburn, and Eddie Albert in 1953.

Otto Preminger's *The Moon Is Blue* with William Holden, David Niven, and Maggie McNamara in 1953 broke barriers in the matter of sophisticated sexual conversation. Billy Wilder's *Some Like It Hot* with Marilyn Monroe, and with Jack Lemmon and Tony Curtis masquerading as ladies in 1959 restored slapstick to an art form.

Rosalind Russell contributed stylish comedy from *His Girl Friday* in 1940 and *My Sister Eileen* in 1942 to *Auntie Mame* in 1958. Jack Lemmon performed stylish comedy throughout the 1960s, starting with the Oscar-winning *The Apartment* in 1960. He has starred in such witty Neil Simon delights as *The Odd Couple* in 1968, *The Out-of-Towners* in 1970, and *The Prisoner of Second Avenue* in 1975.

Lemmon costarred with Walter Matthau in *The Fortune Cookie* in 1966 and *The Odd Couple* in 1968. Matthau starred in such Simon delights as *Plaza Suite* in 1971, *The Sunshine Boys* with George Burns in 1975, and *California Suite* in 1978, as well as *Pete 'n' Tillie* with Carol Burnett in 1972, *The Bad News Bears* with Tatum O'Neal in 1976, and *House Calls* with Glenda Jackson in 1978.

Lemmon and Matthau have been two of the most skilled comic actors of all time. Yet neither has an Oscar to show for comedy, although Lemmon's part in *Mr. Roberts* had comic overtones.

George Segal was outstanding in the wonderfully wacky *Where's Poppa?* in 1970 and *A Touch of Class* with Glenda Jackson in 1973. He needs only more opportunities to rise to the top of the class. Richard Benjamin, ditto. He was splendid in *Goodbye, Columbus* with Ali McGraw in 1969, *Catch 22* in 1970, and *The Sunshine Boys* in 1975.

Where's Poppa? was almost as outrageous as *Harold and Maude* and almost as much a favorite of

Born Yesterday *with Broderick Crawford and Judy Holliday.*

Paper Moon *featured Ryan O'Neal and real-life daughter Tatum, debuting as an actress.*

In A Thousand Clowns, *Martin Balsam tries to explain life to Jason Robards.*

the particular cult that goes strongly for this sort of comedy. Wacky, wonderful Ruth Gordon starred in both. Bud Cort starred as suicidal Harold and Vivian Pickles played his nutty mother in *Harold and Maude*. Gordon was the nutty mother in *Where's Poppa?*

Ryan O'Neal costarred with daughter Tatum in her screen debut in *Paper Moon* in 1973. Peter Bogdanovich directed this lively story of a con man who picks up a kid as his partner as they work their way through the West during the Depression. Madeline Kahn and Tatum both gained nominations as supporting actresses and Tatum at ten became the youngest Award-winner ever.

A Thousand Clowns in 1965 featured a father, Jason Robards, who was something of a con man, wanting to keep his son while living a life style that is unsuitable for a son. Herb Gardner wrote it and it was wonderful. It was nominated for an Oscar, but its director, Fred Coe, was not. Robards gave an inspired performance, but was not nominated. Martin Balsam, as his respectable brother, was, and won.

Catch 22 was black comedy about the madness of the military. The classic military black comedy was Stanley Kubrick's *Dr. Strangelove, or How I Learned to Stop Worrying and Love the Bomb* in 1963. It qualifies for this book, though listed as a British film, because it was made for an American company with American money by an American director and mostly with American actors.

In the film, General Jack D. Ripper, commanding Burpleson Air Base, is a madman who believes fluoridation is a communist plot which is weakening us and has rendered him impotent. A plane carrying a nuclear bomb is sent toward Russia for revenge. The pilot is Major T. J. "King" Kong. The doomsday device was developed by a crippled Nazi expatriate, Dr. Strangelove.

In the White House, liberal President Merkin J. Muffey argues with conservative Chairman of the Joint Chiefs General Buck Turgidson over life, love, and what to do about the bomb. Colonel Bat Guano won't shoot off the lock of a Coke machine to get a dime so he can make a call that might save the human race. General Turgidson won't interrupt a bout in bed with his secretary to go to the War Room for the emergency meeting. President Muffey says, "Gentlemen, you can't fight here—this is the War Room!"

Peter Sellers tells Capucine to "stick 'em up" in The Pink Panther.

The action shifts back and forth between the Air Base and the White House with shots of the plane speeding ever nearer its deadly destination in between. This is a satire, yet suspenseful. The comedy crosses over into dark areas the way a sane man moves over the narrow line into insanity.

Kramer, who originally planned the film as a serious study of the potential failure of fail-safe systems, found it changing into black comedy as he went. After all, madmen rule the world. The senseless is the only thing that makes sense.

Strangelove has suggested that the human race can be continued by having the key political and military leaders go to safety underground with a group of beautiful females, one key man to ten healthy ladies. The key men like that idea and delay doing anything about the bomb.

The original ending was a custard pie fight between the Americans and Soviets but, after viewing previews, Kramer realized the movie had an inevitable ending. He has "King" Kong waving his Stetson and riding the bomb down like it was a bronco.

When it is announced it is on its way, Strangelove, who has several times almost given President Muffey the "Heil Hitler" salute with his wooden arm, announces joyously, "Mein Hitler—I can walk!"

The acting is a triumph for all. Peter Sellers plays three roles, including President Muffey and Dr. Strangelove. George C. Scott plays General Turgidson. Sterling Hayden plays General Ripper. Keenan Wynn plays Colonel Guano. Slim Pickens plays Kong.

The film, director, and Sellers were nominated for Oscars, but none won. Maybe the film was too dark, too daring.

Sellers, perhaps our finest comic actor of recent years, also played the bumbling Inspector Clousseau in a hysterical series of slapstick comedies about *The Pink Panther.* He was denied an Oscar for his nominated role in *Being There* in 1979.

Many consider *Mister Roberts* the classic comedy of war. Others prefer *M*A*S*H.* In both cases, the action is in the military but behind the battle lines. *M*A*S*H* comes closer, but neither is as dark as *Dr. Strangelove.*

Thomas Heggen and Joshua Logan wrote *Mister Roberts* for the stage. John Ford started and Mervyn LeRoy finished directing it for the screen. Henry Fonda, James Cagney, Jack Lemmon, and William Powell performed the parts superbly. Lemmon won his first Oscar.

Mister Roberts was funny, but touching. *M*A*S*H* was pure hilarity. A medical unit steps out of the bloodbath periodically to relieve its tensions. Richard Hooker wrote the book, Ring Lardner Jr. the screenplay. Robert Altman directed. Donald Sutherland, Elliott Gould, Robert Duvall, and Sally Kellerman starred.

Mister Roberts was nominated in 1955, but Henry Fonda, who gave one of his greatest performances in the title role, was not nominated. Nor was *M*A*S*H* nominated in 1969. It later became one of the great television series, starring Alan Alda.

A 1969 comedy that effectively parodies modern morality in sexual matters was *Bob & Carol & Ted & Alice* with Robert Culp, Natalie Wood, Elliott Gould, and Dyan Cannon. Witty and well acted, but daring, it was denied a nomination.

Paul Mazursky directed. He also did such marvelous satires of modern life as *A Touch of Class*, which won Glenda Jackson an Oscar in 1973, *Harry and Tonto*, which won Art Carney an Oscar in 1974, and *An Unmarried Woman* in 1978, which brought Jill Clayburg close to one.

A hilarious satire on modern divorce was *Divorce American Style* with Dick Van Dyke, Debbie Reynolds, Jean Simmons, Jason Robards, and Van Johnson in 1967. Television giant Norman Lear scripted it and Bud Yorkin directed. As critic Richard Schickel pointed out, it was far from a meaningless situation comedy. It was rare in that it had something truthful to say about the way we live, and said it with savage humor.

An unforgettable scene was when all the divorced fathers drove up to pick up their kids from their mothers for the weekend. They all drive off, and one poor kid is left behind, forgotten, until a car backs up to get him.

An episodic comedy with a lot of character was *Carnal Knowledge*, which Mike Nichols directed from a Jules Pfeiffer script. Jack Nicholson and Art Garfunkel have had it with sexual struggles with Candice Bergen and Ann-Margret in a well-done, frank feature of 1971.

As a comedy duo, Elaine May and Mike Nichols were the bitterest, most biting of the 1960s. There was genius to their jests. May directed a terrific comedy, *The Heartbreak Kid* in 1972, adapted by Neil Simon from a Bruce Jay Friedman story. Eddie Albert's son Edward and Elaine May's daughter Jeannie Berlin starred, along with Charles Grodin and Cybil Shepherd.

Warren Beatty turned out a marvelously sophisticated comedy of the good life, *Shampoo*, with Beatty starring with Julie Christie, Lee Grant, Goldie Hawn, Jack Warden, and Paul Simon (half of the Simon and Garfunkel singing duo). Grant won an Oscar in this story of sex and your friendly hair stylist. Hal Ashby directed.

Ashby also directed *The Last Detail*, which, with *Cinderella Liberty*, gave 1973 two touching comedies of service life away from the base. Jack Nicholson starred in *The Last Detail*. He was nominated, as was Randy Quaid. James Caan and Marsha Mason starred in *Cinderella Liberty*. He was not nominated, but she was. All were remarkably good. Richard Dreyfuss did win an Oscar for the deservedly nominated *The Goodbye Girl* in 1977, but Marsha Mason was again neglected.

One of those sleepers which comes along occasionally sneaked up in 1979. It was *Breaking Away*, a low-budget film about the rivalry between town kids in Bloomington, Indiana, and the college kids at Indiana University, about ambition and the lack of it, about the gap between generations. It was scripted by Steve Tesich, directed by Peter Yates, and starred Dennis Christopher, Dennis Quaid, Daniel Stern, Jackie Earle Haley, Paul Dooley, and Barbara Barrie. She won nomination as Best Supporting Actress for the year. This film is funny, yet very real.

Wanting to be as great a bicyclist as the Italians, a young man fills his home with Italian food, music, and so forth, to the frustration of his mother and, especially, his father. In a *Rocky*-like climax, he and his city friends invade the campus to win an annual race from the fraternity boys. At the end, he falls for a French student. In a classic closing scene, his father is stunned to hear him singing in French as he pedals by. The audience is amused, moved, and involved throughout.

In the best of comedies, you get something of life as well as laughter—even if most of them didn't win Oscars.

M*A*S*H finds Jo Ann Pflug, Lt. Dish, trying to figure out if Elliot Gould, Trapper John, has a heart.

T H I R T E E N

Musical and Fantasy Films

I T IS CURIOUS that while Hollywood always has been moved by music, a lot more Academy Awards have gone to musical movies than to musical performers.

Oscar winners have included *Broadway Melody* in 1928-29, *The Great Ziegfeld* in 1936, *An American in Paris* in 1951, *Gigi* in 1958, *West Side Story* in 1961, *My Fair Lady* in 1964, *The Sound of Music* in 1965, and *Oliver* in 1968.

Gigi surpassed *Gone With the Wind, From Here to Eternity*, and *On the Waterfront* by winning nine Awards in different categories, yet not a single performer in the film was even nominated. The same was true when *An American in Paris* won without a single performer being nominated.

If *An American in Paris* wasn't Gene Kelly, what was it? Kelly choreographed and danced spectacularly, yet wasn't nominated. He received only one nomination in his entire career, for *Anchors Aweigh* in 1945, but did not win. Undoubtedly, of course, Vincente Minnelli was strongly responsible for *An American in Paris*. He was nominated as director, but did not win. He did win later for *Gigi*.

Gene Kelly and Stanley Donen teamed up to direct two musicals that rank with the best in Hollywood history and were worthy of Oscars in any category— *On the Town* in 1949 and *Singin' in the Rain* in 1952. *Singin' in the Rain* we have discussed. *On the Town* starred Kelly, Frank Sinatra, and Jules Munshin as three American sailors on twenty-four-hour liberty in New York. It costarred Vera Ellen, Betty Garrett, and

Ann Miller (successor to Eleanor Powell as a tap-dancing delight). The film was a delight.

The only other directors aside from Minnelli to have won Oscars for musicals are Robert Wise for *West Side Story* (with choreographer Jerome Robbins) and *The Sound of Music*, George Cukor for *My Fair Lady*, and Carol Reed for *Oliver*. The directors of the other winners—Harry Beaumont for *Broadway Melody* and Robert Z. Leonard for *The Great Ziegfeld* did not win.

Incredibly, Busby Berkeley did not win for any of his spectacular, influential musical efforts. None of the directors of any of the Fred Astaire-Ginger Rogers musicals ever won either. Only two of these memorable musicals were nominated—*The Gay Divorcee* in 1934 and *Top Hat* in 1935. Neither won, nor did the awesome Astaire and Rogers win for their dynamic dancing.

Ginger won for a dramatic performance, as did Frank Sinatra. Frank, considered by many the greatest entertainer of our time, was never even nominated for a musical performance. The great Judy Garland was nominated for only one—*A Star Is Born* in 1954—and that was more dramatic than musical, and she did not win. Astaire, Sinatra, Garland, and Kelly all won honorary Oscars.

So did Shirley Temple, who was not only the greatest child star of all time, but the greatest star of her time. She never won an Oscar for a performance. Garland didn't even win nomination for her performance in *The Wizard of Oz*, yet it is remembered by fans and critics as one of the greatest ever. Mickey Rooney was nominated for only one musical—*Babes in Arms* in 1939—and did not win. Neither costar Garland nor the movie itself was even nominated. Not one of the Rooney-Garland musicals was ever nominated.

The only stars who have won Oscars for musicals are James Cagney for *Yankee Doodle Dandy* in 1943, Bing Crosby for *Going My Way* in 1945, Rex Harrison for *My Fair Lady* in 1964, and Julie Andrews for *Mary Poppins* in 1964. George Chakiris and Rita Moreno won as suppporting performers in *West Side Story* in 1961. Clearly, Andrews should have recreated her stage role as Liza Doolittle in *My Fair Lady,* but the part went to Audrey Hepburn, who did not do her own singing and was not nominated.

Cagney was not a song-and-dance man in movies, but the old hoofer did sing and dance superbly as George M. Cohan in *Yankee Doodle Dandy.* Crosby sang in *Going My Way,* but his role was more dramatic than musical—he never was nominated for a musical performance. Harrison was not a singer, but he recreated his talk-singing stylish stage role in *My Fair Lady* and was rewarded with an Oscar.

Al Jolson was not nominated for the pioneer talkie, *The Jazz Singer,* in 1927-28. This was really a part-talkie. The first words spoken were his, the classic, "You ain't heard nothin' yet." He did sing two songs, notably, "Mammy."

George Jessel originally was offered the role, but turned it down because he was not offered enough money. Georgie has regretted it ever since.

When the movie *The Jolson Story* was made in 1946, Danny Thomas was offered the role but declined it because he refused to have his nose bobbed. Larry Parks won Best Actor nomination playing the part, but Jolson himself sang. It was a splendid, entertaining film. As the 1980s opened, the dynamic Neil Diamond was struggling to pull off a new version of *The Jazz Singer.*

Jolson went on to do sixteen movies after *The Jazz Singer,* but in many of them he made only cameo appearances or just sang, and in none of them was the great entertainer greatly successful.

Jolson's tap dancing wife, Ruby Keeler, starred in a series of Warner Bros.-Busby Berkeley musicals, many of them with Dick Powell. They included *42nd Street, Footlight Parade, Flirtation Walk, Shipmates Forever,* and the *Gold Diggers* series. Only the first of these was nominated for an Oscar.

In many, Powell, as a musical stage star, gives encouragement to an unknown chorus girl, Keeler. In the end, the unknown replaces the female star of the show at the last minute and becomes a star herself. In *42nd Street,* in 1933, faded producer Warner Baxter

The Broadway Melody, *described as "All Talking—All Singing—All Dancing" in 1927.*

A Busby Berkeley sequence with four of four hundred girls.

Yankee Doodle Dandy *with James Cagney, Joan Leslie, Walter Huston, and Rosemary De Camp.*

gets the backing of Guy Kibbee to do a show which will star the sugar-daddy's girlfriend, Bebe Daniels, opposite Powell, who falls for chorine Keeler.

While Baxter drives his chorus line almost beyond their endurance, tough veterans Ginger Rogers and Una Merkel mother the kid, Keeler. Meanwhile, Bebe is carrying on secretly with boyfriend George Brent. When she spots Brent with Keeler, she does not know it is innocent and starts to tear up the joint, breaking a leg.

The show is about to open. Ginger is the understudy, but she's got a heart of gold under her tough skin. She tells Baxter that Ruby can save the day. He says Keeler's just a kid. Ginger says, "I've been waiting years for a chance like this. If I give it up for somebody else, she's got to be good." Baxter sends for Keeler as the audience cheers. He asks, "You think you can play the lead tonight?"

"The lead?" she gasps. Baxter takes her through a desperate rehearsal. He says, "I'll either have a live leading lady or a dead chorus girl." That night, he sends her on stage: "You're going out a youngster, but you've got to come back a star." She goes out and is sensational. The show's a hit and she's a star. At the finish, she's in Powell's arms.

If it did nothing else, that movie provided the plot for a hundred musicals to follow, and a climactic line, as well, with slight variations.

Once Busby Berkeley put 100 girls, tap dancing, on three round stages revolving in different directions. The next time, he put 100 girls at 100 pianos, and so forth. "I have to keep topping myself and it's tough, but I always come through," he commented modestly.

Looking back on them, such musicals seem silly, but, viewed in perspective, they were light, lively, and lavish entertainment that highlighted the first ten or fifteen years of the talkies.

In the early years, *One Hour with You* in 1931–32, *42nd Street* and *State Fair* in 1932–33, *The Gay Divorcee* and *One Night of Love* in 1934, *Broadway Melody of 1936*, *Top Hat* and *Naughty Marietta* in 1935, and *Alexander's Ragtime Band* in 1938 were nominated. Maurice Chevalier was nominated for *The Love Parade* and *The Big Parade* in 1929–30, opera stars Lawrence Tibbett for *The Rogue Song* in 1929–30, and Grace Moore for *One Night of Love* in 1934.

The trend to operettas pushed Jeanette MacDonald and Nelson Eddy to prominence as "America's Sweethearts" in the 1930s as they costarred in *Naughty Marietta* (1935), *Rose Marie* (1936), *Maytime* (1937), *The Girl of the Golden West* (1938), *Sweethearts* (1938), and *New Moon* (1940). MacDonald also did *The Love Parade* (1929), *The Vagabond King* (1930),

One Hour with You (1932), *Love Me Tonight* (1932), *The Merry Widow* (1934), *Broadway Serenade* (1939), *Smilin' Through* (1941), and *I Married an Angel* (1942). Eddy also did *Rosalie* (1937), *The Chocolate Soldier* (1941), and *Knickerbocker Holiday* (1944). Saccharine fare, well remembered, but never rewarded.

"Sweetheart, sweetheart, sweetheart..." MacDonald and Eddy were romantically so believable on the screen that fans assumed they were sweethearts. They were not, though they liked each other. MacDonald married actor Gene Raymond. Eddy married the former wife of producer Sidney Franklin, Anne. MacDonald yearned to sing grand opera, and did, starring with Ezio Pinza in *Romeo and Juliet* in Montreal, and in one or two other things. Critics however considered her voice small by stage standards. Eddy wanted only to get out of singing. He never saw his films, considering them silly. He used to clown around with Edgar Bergen and Charlie McCarthy on their radio show, singing "Shortnin' Bread." Both MacDonald and Eddy died in the middle 1960s.

Deanna Durbin developed at MGM at the same time as Judy Garland. Louis B. Mayer decided to keep only one of these young girls and chose Garland, whose singing seemed to him more apt to be popular. Durbin attracted attention on the Eddie Cantor radio show. She went to troubled Universal and saved the studio from bankruptcy with a surprise hit, *Three Smart Girls*, in 1936. That was followed with a Best Picture nominee for *100 Men and a Girl* in 1937. In 1938, she and Mickey Rooney were given special Oscars for their personification of the spirit of youth. She made twenty movies through the 1940s, and her fine voice and sweet personality made these films enormously popular.

Kathryn Grayson's operetta style of singing made her a star of the 1940s with *Rio Rita* in 1942, *Thousands Cheer* in 1943, *Anchors Aweigh* in 1945, *The Ziegfeld Follies* in 1945, *Till the Clouds Roll By* in 1946, *Show Boat* in 1951, *The Desert Song* in 1953, and *Kiss Me Kate* in 1956. She also costarred with "The New Caruso," Mario Lanza, in *The Midnight Kiss* in 1949 and *The Toast of New Orleans* in 1950. Lanza starred in *The Great Caruso* in 1951, *Because You're Mine* in 1952, and several more. Grayson and Lanza had thrilling voices, which made their movies memorable.

Grayson and Lanza disliked each other. She complained that in their love scenes he tried to French-kiss her. He protested that he was Italian. He never sang opera. His career ran out as he was driven to drink and pills and grew fat. He died of a heart attack at age thirty-eight in 1959.

The King and I *with Yul Brynner.*

Fiddler on the Roof *with Topol.*

Somewhat more sophisticated musicals came along in the 1940s and 1950s, although *Yankee Doodle Dandy* in 1942 was a throwback, especially in its closing scene with seemingly thousands of people on stage waving American flags. As George M. Cohan, James Cagney reverted rousingly to his song-and-dance origins and gave this sparkling show its sparkle. It was a great movie. Many remember it as a winner, but it was not. Other nominated losers of the 1940s were the Kelly-Sinatra-Grayson *Anchors Aweigh* in 1945 and the beautiful British film on ballet, *The Red Shoes*, in 1948.

Sinatra made his mark as a dramatic actor, but he made such musicals as *Anchors Aweigh, On the Town, Guys and Dolls* (with Brando and Jean Simmons) in 1955, *High Society* (with Bing Crosby and Grace Kelly) in 1956, *The Joker Is Wild* (as comic Joe E. Lewis) in 1957, and *Can Can* in 1960, as well as many lesser efforts. Hollywood never really successfully captured his unique talent as a singer.

Crosby scored dramatically, too, but was most popular for his musicals and comedies. He was never honored for these. He is perhaps the only pop singer whose musical gifts transferred successfully to the big screen.

Gordon MacRae sang the leads in the movie versions of such musicals as *The Desert Song* in 1953, *Oklahoma* in 1955, and *Carousel* in 1956. Shirley Jones costarred in the latter two. Mitzi Gaynor and Rossano Brazzi took the Mary Martin and Ezio Pinza roles in *South Pacific* in 1958. Howard Keel starred in *Calamity Jane* with Doris Day (in a role originally intended for Judy Garland) in 1953 and in *Kismet* in 1955. Day starred in *The Pajama Game* as well as many light musical comedies in 1957. Sidney Poitier, Sammy Davis, Jr., Brock Peters, Pearl Bailey, Dorothy Dandridge, and Diahann Carroll starred in *Porgy and Bess* in 1959. For various reasons, frequently because of miscasting, these blockbuster Broadway hits were not big Hollywood hits.

There were some notable exceptions, however. *The King and I* and stars Yul Brynner and Deborah Kerr all won Oscar nominations in 1956 and Brynner walked away with an Oscar. Two years later, *Gigi* grabbed an Oscar, though stars Leslie Caron, Hermione Gingold, Louis Jourdan, and Maurice Chevalier were overlooked. Three years after that, *West Side Story* walked off with the honors. Stars Natalie Wood and Richard Beymer, who did not sing, were passed over but supporting stars Rita Moreno and George Chakiris, who did sing, were winners. Marni Nixon sang for Wood, Jim Bryant for Beymer. That same year, *Fanny* and Charles Boyer were nominated losers. Leslie Caron and Chevalier were passed over again.

Two of the most memorable musicals movies of the 1950s were Hollywood originals—*An American in Paris* in 1951, which won, and *Seven Brides for Seven Brothers* in 1956, which was nominated but lost. Jane Powell, who made many nice but hardly memorable musicals, hit her peak costarring with Howard Keel in *Seven Brides*, but the highlight was the acrobatic dancing of Russ Tamblyn and others. Tamblyn's dynamic dancing was also a feature of *West Side Story*, but his only Oscar nomination was for a dramatic role in *Peyton Place* in 1957.

The Music Man was a losing nominee in 1962 and its long-neglected star, Robert Preston, was not even nominated. Nor was *Gypsy* even nominated that year, nor its long-neglected stars Rosalind Russell and Natalie Wood. The dynamic Debbie Reynolds was nominated, but not *The Unsinkable Molly Brown* in 1964. *My Fair Lady* was a winning nominee in 1964, as was its star, Rex Harrison.

It is interesting to contemplate how Cary Grant or Jimmy Cagney might have done in the role of Professor Higgins, as it was offered to them before Sexy Rexy got to recreate his stage success. Julie Andrews might well have won an Oscar had she been allowed to recreate her role as Liza Doolittle. As it was, Julie did win that year, for the fantasy *Mary Poppins*. She was a nominated loser for the winner, *The Sound of Music*, a year later.

Had Richard Burton and Robert Goulet been allowed to recreate their stage roles, the elegant *Camelot* might have made it in 1967. *Funny Girl* and Barbra Streisand were nominated the next year and Streisand tied Katharine Hepburn for Best Actress. *Hello Dolly* was nominated a year later, but the spectacular Streisand was not. The Israeli Topol and *Fiddler on the Roof* were nominated losers in 1971. The unforgettable *Cabaret* was a nominated loser, but Liza Minnelli and Joel Grey were winners in 1972. That same year the magnificent *Man of La Mancha* was mishandled as badly as Hollywood ever has botched a Broadway giant. Peter O'Toole was dreadfully miscast in a part sung and acted so spectacularly by the underrated Richard Kiley on Broadway.

The new wave of musicals came along in the early 1970s. *Jesus Christ, Superstar* didn't quite make it in 1973, nor did Streisand's *Funny Lady* in 1975, nor the remake of *A Star Is Born* with Kris Kristofferson playing a role originally intended for Elvis Presley in 1976. John Travolta played a disco-dancer in *Saturday Night Fever* in 1977 and won nomination for an Oscar. The picture was not critically loved, yet made the all-time top ten with more than $70 million earned at the box office. The critically condemned *Grease*, with Travolta in 1978, has done more than $80 million which makes it the fourth largest-grossing film of all time. *Hair*, however, flopped in 1979, as did *Sgt. Pepper's Lonely Hearts Band* earlier.

Lady Sings the Blues in 1972 was a dramatic musical of enormous power. Diana Ross won nomination for an Award and perhaps should have won for her compelling performance as the drug-addicted Billie Holliday. Diana Ross could not sing like Billie, but who could? The movies never effectively used the singing of such jazz-oriented black singers as Billie, Bessie Smith, Ethel Waters, Mildred Bailey, and Ella Fitzgerald. Diana is a stylish singer, the music in the movie was marvelous, and the story came close to the truth.

Martin Scorsese's *New York, New York* in 1977 was a powerful, poignant recreation of the Big Band Era of the 1940s with Robert DeNiro as an obsessed bandleader and Liza Minnelli as a strung-out band-singer. The drama was deemed a disappointment when it came out, but it has grown on a lot of people and its powerful performances and haunting music are remembered better now a few years later than anyone would have expected originally.

The Rose in 1979 was a terrific account of the life of a Janis Joplin-like rock star with a surprising and stunning portrayal by Bette Midler in her Award-nominated debut.

The Turning Point in 1977 and *All That Jazz* in 1979 are classic losers among movie musicals. They join *Cabaret*, *The King and I*, *Singin' in the Rain*, *Seven Brides for Seven Brothers*, *Yankee Doodle Dandy*, *Top Hat*, and a few others of earlier years.

Another might be *The Wizard of Oz*, although that has to be classified as a fantasy. Many musicals have a lot of fantasy in them, of course, or at least an air of unreality. The lover seldom sings of romance in real life, nor does the dying man sing while dying. Even a man who likes to dance seldom does so down the street, in or out of the rain, nor does he dance across tabletops in a crowded cafe, nor do the diners suddenly break into song.

Garland stole the show singing "Dear Mr. Gable" in *Broadway Melody of 1938*, then made the show singing "Somewhere Over the Rainbow" in *The Wizard of Oz* in 1939. She, Ray Bolger, Jack Haley, and Bert Lahr sang and danced delightfully in the *Wizard*, which was an unforgettable combination of fantasy, music, and comedy. The same year she made the memorable *Babes in Arms* with Mickey Rooney, and the next year *Strike Up the Band*, again with Mickey. She and Mickey made nine movies together, many of them stories of kids who need money for a good cause and say, "Hey, let's put on a show." Then, with about fifty cents, they put on a show that rivals the best on Broadway.

Judy made many memorable musicals, including *Meet Me in St. Louis* in 1944. It is sad that her remarkable, charismatic talent was not honored by Oscar.

The Wizard of Oz may be the finest fantasy neglected by Oscar, but then, incredibly, no fantasy, from the heart-warming to the heart-stopping, ever has won an Academy Award.

Few have even been nominated. These few include *Lost Horizon* in 1937, *The Wizard of Oz* in 1939, *Our Town* in 1940, *Here Comes Mr. Jordan* in 1941 (and the remake *Heaven Can Wait* in 1978), *It's a Wonderful Life* in 1946, *The Miracle on 34th Street* in 1947, and after a long gap, *The Exorcist* in 1973, and *Star Wars* in 1977. One wonders if *Star Wars'* successor, *The Empire Strikes Back*, will make it.

Notably absent are all the Disney animated features from the fascinating pioneer *Snow White and the Seven Dwarfs* in 1938, through *Pinocchio* in 1940, *Dumbo* in 1941, *Bambi* in 1942, *Cinderella* in 1950, *Sleeping Beauty* in 1959, and others. Many consider the spectacular 1941 *Fantasia*, a blend of beauty in sight and sound, one of the finest films ever made, animated or not. Walt Disney did win a special Oscar in 1938—for *Snow White and the Seven Dwarfs*, a "significant innovation."

Disney's live-action version of Jules Verne's *20,000 Leagues Under the Sea* is a well remembered, well loved fantasy. It starred Kirk Douglas, James Mason, Peter Lorrre, and Paul Lukas. Mason's performance as Captain Nemo is considered outstanding. The film was beautifully photographed and won Oscars for its color art direction and special effects. A battle between the men of the submarine Nautilus and a giant squid was remarkably well done.

Disney's *Mary Poppins* and its star, Julie Andrews, won nominations in 1964. The film did not win, but Julie did. The picture did take three other Oscars—for film editing, music score, and special visual effects. Costar Dick Van Dyke was not nominated, despite a delightful performance. It was a fascinating picture, telling the tale of a 1910 English nanny who travels through the air under an umbrella and who, with liberal use of magic, straightens out a troubled household and its unruly children.

Frank Capra's *Lost Horizon*, 1937, was controversial in its time but endures as a classic loser. The film was nominated, but Capra was not. A supporting actor, H. B. Warner, was nominated, but the star, Ronald Colman, was not. Jane Wyatt, who later played the mother in TV's "Father Knows Best," was the love interest. Sam Jaffe, later wild-haired Dr. Zorba in TV's "Ben Casey," was the high lama. It won for its film editing and art direction but not for its spectacular photography and settings.

The James Hilton novel told the tale of a British diplomat, Colman, who evacuates a group from the wartorn Orient and finds his plane hijacked into the Tibetan mountains. They crash safely and find Shangri-

The Wizard of Oz *stars Bert Lahr, Jack Haley, Judy Garland, Frank Morgan, and Ray Bolger.*

Meet Me in St. Louis *with Marjorie Main and Judy Garland.*

Lost Horizon showed life as tranquil in Shangri-La. Here, Ronald Colman, Thomas Mitchell, Edward Everett Horton, and Isabelle Jewell wonder why John Howard decided to nap.

La, a land hidden from the hatred, death, ugliness, and despair of the outer world. Here Colman finds great beauty, peace, and serenity. Those who come there age slowly and enjoy a long life.

The high lama wants the diplomat to succeed him, but Colman's brother, John Howard, hungers to return to the real world and to take with him the beautiful, young Margo (Eddie Albert's wife) whom he has found here. Against their better judgment, they decide to go with him. As they start down the snowy mountain, Margo falls and in an unforgettable fantasy of photography withers to her true age of 80 and dies. Horrified, Howard jumps to his death.

Colman goes on, narrowly escaping death in his ordeal before he stumbles to safety in a native village. Returned to civilization, he feels a curious alienation from the world he knew, dislikes what he sees, and longs to return to the other world he had found. Determined, he starts back. Against great odds, he survives and finds Shangri-La. Here, he reclaims the love he found here, Wyatt, and succeeds the fallen lama.

Capra bought the book to read on a train, was fascinated by it and talked Harry Cohn into making it at a cost of $2 million, four times what any other Columbia movie had cost to that time. Originally, a ninety-year-old retired stage actor was cast as the high lama. When Capra called to tell him he had the role, his housekeeper said he had just died. Jaffe got the role, a striking contrast to his Gunga Din and his later Dr. Zorba.

The film was sneak-previewed in Santa Barbara. The opening was harsh, realistic—the burning of a town before the flight. Cohn, Capra, and other Columbia executives sneaked into the audience. To their horror, the audience started to laugh at things they saw on the screen. Later, on the preview cards, the viewers made fun of the whole movie. Cohn was furious at Capra and Capra was mystified. It looked as if they had on their hands a loser which would bankrupt the studio.

While Cohn worried that his New York bosses would find out, Capra worried how to fix the film. He thought for three days and nights and finally in desperation decided to junk the first two reels, cutting the opening twenty minutes. He talked Cohn into inviting the New Yorkers to another preview. When the audience loved the film, the New York bosses loved it. Cohn never could figure it out, but was grateful to Capra.

Capra never admitted it, but he never figured it out himself. He had to try something and what he tried worked. Possibly the first part of the picture was not well done. Perhaps its realism was in too stark contrast to the fantasy that followed, and the audience was lost. Possibly by starting with the plane flight into the mysterious land of Tibet, the audience was held. Possibly the first was just a freak audience.

In any event, the picture was a hit and made a lot of money. Capra calls it, "One of my great hits." There are those who consider it one of the greatest films ever and have seen it twenty, thirty, forty times. When we talk of a perfect place, we call it Shangri-La. Many do not know where the term came from, but it passed from *Lost Horizon* into our language.

Capra's favorite film, and James Stewart's, too, was *It's a Wonderful Life*, which was not treated kindly by the critics when it came out but has grown steadily in stature. It told a tale of a fine man in a small town who would like to get out and make good. He is so busy helping others, however, that he never goes. Finding himself a failure, he wishes he'd never been born. A guardian angel materializes to give him his wish and he sees his town and its people as they'd have been if he hadn't been there.

It was written by the writer Philip Van Doren Stern as a Christmas card to give to friends. Charles Koerner bought it for Liberty Productions, a joint venture of John Ford and Frank Capra. Three great writers, Marc Connelly, Clifford Odets, and Dalton Trumbo had tried scripts, but each missed the mark. Capra gave it to Albert and Frances Hackett and they pulled the fragile story together. Donna Reed, Lionel Barrymore, and Thomas Mitchell costarred.

Bosley Crowther in the *New York Times* knocked its "Pollyanna platitudes." The *New Yorker* critic complained of "baby talk." *Life*, however, praised its blend of comedy and sentiment. James Agee likened it to *A Christmas Carol. Time* said, "*It's a Wonderful Life* is a wonderful movie." It said its only rival as the best movie of the year was *Best Years of Our Lives.* That picture, its director William Wyler, and its star, Fredric March beat out *It's a Wonderful Life*, Capra, and Stewart for the Oscars. Nevertheless, Capra says, "I thought it was the greatest film I had ever made. Better yet, I thought it was the greatest film anybody ever made."

Somewhat similarly, *Our Town* told a tale of life in a small town with the dear departed privileged to see how things go on without them. This Thornton Wilder play probably has been done more times on more stages than any other American work. The 1940 movie directed by Sam Wood and starring William Holden, Martha Scott, Thomas Mitchell, Fay Bainter, Beulah Bondi, Guy Kibbee, and Frank Craven was sentimental, touching, simple, and moving.

Miracle on 34th Street was a nominated loser in 1947, but won a supporting actor Oscar for Edmund Gwenn, who played Santa Claus, here to take care of people like the very young Natalie Wood. Is he or is he not really Mr. Claus? He says he is and carries his case to the Supreme Court. John Payne, Maureen O'Hara, and Thelma Ritter also starred in this heart-warming George Seaton film.

One of the early fantasy films dealing with death was *Death Takes a Holiday* in 1934. Death decides to visit earth to find out about mortals firsthand and figure out why they fear him so. He takes the form of a young nobleman, Fredric March. While he is on his short trip, the world turns topsy-turvy. There is no death, mortals make miraculous escapes from accidents, suicides, and so forth. Only one is not terrified of him when she finds out who he is. He decides he can take her with him when he goes. To her family's horror, she goes with him, wrapped in his cloak, finding in death the love she longed for in life. A terrific film.

Outward Bound, a 1930 film starring Leslie Howard,

Miracle on 34th Street stars Edmund Gwenn and Natalie Wood.

The Portrait of Dorian Gray got old while Dorian, Hurd Hatfield, didn't.

made into *Between Two Worlds,* a 1944 film starring John Garfield, dealt dramatically with a group of passengers who find themselves dead and on a journey to heaven...or hell.

Here Comes Mr. Jordan in 1944 featured Robert Montgomery in the story of an athlete accidentally taken too soon by death. He is permitted to return to life in another's body. In the original, Montgomery played a boxer. In Warren Beatty's remake, *Heaven Can Wait* in 1977, Beatty portrayed a football player. Both films and stars were nominated. There were no winners, except in the audiences.

Shades of the aging illusion in *Lost Horizon* were found in *The Portrait of Dorian Gray* in 1945. Based on an Oscar Wilde story, this told the tale of a handsome young sinner, Hurd Hatfield, who stays young while his concealed portrait grows old. The scene where the aged face on canvas is revealed is stunning. Only the cinematographer, Harry Stradling, won an Oscar. Supporting actress Angela Lansbury was the only major nominee—but the film was unforgettable.

Portrait of Jenny in 1949 told Robert Nathan's story of a painter, Joseph Cotten, down on his luck during the Depression, bitter because he cannot capture beauty on canvas. He meets a curiously old-fashioned young girl, Jennifer Jones. From month to month she appears and reappears in his life, rapidly maturing into a young lady. She will tell him nothing of herself, saying only, "Where I come from, nobody knows. Where I am going, everyone goes."

She is beautiful, and he falls in love with her, paints her, and finds he has beauty on his canvas. She disappears and he searches for her. The search reveals clues that the real Jenny was killed in a hurricane years ago. Still, he continues to seek her, and finds her in a storm like the one that took her. She tells him they will be together forever in spirit, then goes.

The most popular fantasy films, however, are the most horrifying. Horror films featuring men who are monsters or monsters who are men always have been big at the box office and are an important part of the motion picture scene, even though ignored by Oscar.

Lon Chaney, the master of makeup, played a legless man in *The Penalty* in 1920, a cripple in *The Hunchback of Notre Dame* in 1923, an armless man in *The Unknown* in 1924, a deformity in *The Phantom of the Opera* in 1925, a one-eyed man in the *Road to Mandalay* in 1926. These were silents, as was *West of Zanzibar,* in which he played a paralytic in 1929, but eligible for an Academy Award. So were his straight roles as a detective in *While the City Sleeps* in 1928 and an aging railroadman in *Thunder* in 1929.

Dr. Jekyll and Mr. Hyde *starred many in the title role, including, here, Spencer Tracy as the man of the night.*

He also made one talkie, *The Unholy Three* in 1930. It was a remake of his 1925 silent film of the same name. In this he played a woman in disguise. He was an artist as an actor, but unrecognized by Oscar.

Charles Laughton was stunning as Quasimodo in *The Hunchback of Notre Dame* in the 1939 remake. Likewise Herbert Lom was strong as *The Phantom of the Opera* in the remake in 1962.

Robert Louis Stevenson's *Dr. Jekyll and Mr. Hyde* was the story of the scientist who goes mad as he discovers a potion that turns him into a split personality. He is a good man by day, a man of evil by night. The film was made with John Barrymore in 1920, Fredric March in 1932, and Spencer Tracy in 1941. Fans saw a man become a monster before their eyes.

Rouben Mamoulian's version with March may have been the best. He created stunning moods with the camera. In the beginning, the camera is Dr. Jekyll. We see everything from his viewpoint; we do not see him. He goes from his home, through the streets of London, to an operating room before the camera sweeps around to his face for the first time. The tricks that alter his face and body into a monster's are magnificent. The scene in which Hyde forces the saloon singer, Miriam Hopkins, to sing her song and then murders her, is stunning. His head drops down to her, out of the range of the camera, and we see only the bedpost carving of "The Goddess of Love" until he rises triumphantly into view again.

March won an Academy Award for his portrayal,

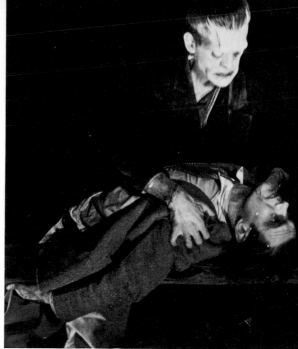

Dracula *starred Bela Lugosi, who sometimes made late visits to ladies in their bedrooms for a drink.*

Frankenstein *featured Boris Karloff as the monster who sometimes offended people.*

the only such victory for a horror film. That was in 1932 and he tied with Wallace Beery's *The Champ*, so each received Oscars. Coincidentally, neither had a child of his own and both had adopted children that year. Accepting his Oscar, March admitted, "I'm wondering how we could have won for 'best male performance of the year.'"

Lon Chaney was scheduled to do *Dracula* when he died. His director, Tod Browning, went ahead with the Broadway star of the play, Bela Lugosi, in the title role of the vampire count, a dead man who lives on by drinking the blood from his victim's necks, preferably beautiful ones.

Lugosi was then asked to do *Frankenstein*, but refused, feeling he would not be known beneath the heavy makeup the part required. Boris Karloff got the part of the monster who was created by Dr. Frankenstein from the pieces taken from dead bodies. James Whale directed the movie.

Both movies came out in 1931. *Dracula* was released on St. Valentine's Day, playfully advertised as "the strangest love story of all." Both were big hits and really started the cycle of horror films that followed. Neither won any Oscar nominations at all, but there are those who believe both deserved Oscars. They have not been topped and are unforgettable.

There is an especially strong feeling by some that Karloff, in particular, gave one of the great underrated performances of all time. Without words, but with his eyes, his body, and his gestures he made the monster

into a bewildered creature to be pitied. There is a scene, cut in some states, in which he strikes up a rapport with a child, then accidentally drowns her.

Hunted down, he dies by burning. Dracula dies with a stake driven through his heart. Both however came back again and again in sequels. Some consider *The Bride of Frankenstein* in 1935, in which Elsa Lanchester costarred opposite Karloff, to be the best of all horror films. Eventually, Lugosi did play Frankenstein's monster.

Lon Chaney, Jr. played Frankenstein's monster, Dracula, and the Wolf Man. His performance in *The Wolf Man* in 1941, as a man driven to wander the world for all eternity as a werewolf, is masterful, yet unfortunately forgotten.

No one who heard him can forget Bela Lugosi in *The Wolf Man* listening to the wolves howl and saying, "Listen to them! Creatures of the night! What music they make!" He was not happy that he was typed forever as the fanged count, however.

Although a classic actor, Karloff did not seem to mind that he was forever after typed as Frankenstein's monster. He once said, "The monster was the best friend I ever had."

Karl Freund, who photographed *Dracula*, directed *The Mummy* in 1932, with Karloff as a man who rises from the dead and returns to the world from his tomb. It was a fine film with a sensitive performance by its star and superb special effects. It had many sequels, too.

Freund directed Colin Clive as Dr. Frankenstein in

Mad Love in 1934. In this, a concert pianist, Clive, loses his hands in an accident. An insane surgeon, Peter Lorre, in his first film in America, grafts onto him the hands of a guillotined murderer. When the pianist finds his hands are those of a murderer, he goes insane for fear of what they may do. They strangle the surgeon.

Freund later returned to his first love and photographed, among others, the sensitive Camille and The Good Earth.

Dracula director Browning directed Freaks in 1932. In this story of a circus sideshow, real "freaks" play most of the parts. A midget loves a trapeze artist. When she finds he is heir to a fortune, she marries him and plans to murder him for his money. His friends, the freaks, find out, chase her through a forest, and take revenge on her. In the end, they have made her a freak like themselves. A shocking picture, few saw it because it was banned in most states.

A sleeper about carnival life admired by many was 1947's Nightmare Alley. It starred Tyrone Power as an ambitious young man who rips off a mentalist, Joan Blondell. He takes his own mind-reading con game off the carnival lot and into swank night clubs. He

becomes a religious cult leader until he is exposed, then becomes a bum.

Memorable in the film was a freak-show attraction called the Geek, a lush who bites off the heads of live chickens in exchange for a daily bottle of booze. At the beginning, Power says, "I can't understand how anybody can get so low." At the end, a boozed-up Power takes a job as a "geek" in the carnival. Someone asks, "How can a guy get so low?" The reply is, "He reached too high."

King Kong in 1933 awed audiences. Captured in the jungle, the giant gorilla is brought to civilization as "an attraction." He escapes, and terrorizes New York. He falls in love with the beautiful Fay Wray, but she, of course, is terrifed of him. He waves her about in one giant paw as he climbs the Empire State Building. There is no escape for the ape. Shot down, he falls to his death. "It was beauty that killed the beast," says Robert Armstrong, the hunter who regrets having captured his prey. This was the forerunner of all the giant animal epics, but none better came along, nor did the sequel of recent years succeed.

Planet of the Apes in 1968 was a fascinating study of a future world in which the apes rule and spacemen,

King Kong took a liking to Fay Wray and did the big town with her.

displaced in time, find themselves regarded as animals. Its ingenious use of makeup transforms men and women not just into mere apes, but apes with personality. It was nominated for its artistic effects, but not for major categories. There were several sequels.

In the 1940s psychological horror films developed in which the fear was less shown than put in our minds. Jacques Tourneur's and Val Lawton's *The Cat People* in 1942 was the first and best of these. These two turned out many others of this kind, including the beloved *The Body Snatchers* in 1945. Don Siegel's 1956 *The Invasion of the Body Snatchers*, starring Kevin McCarthy, became a classic cult favorite. A remake in the late 1970s also found favor with those who think these are the most interesting and misunderstood of films.

A Howard Hawks film in 1951 which starred "Gunsmoke's" James Arness as *The Thing* was a triumph of fright. Alfred Hitchcock's *Psycho* in 1960 is a classic suspense film but can be considered a horror film, too. At least, Hitchcock considered it so. His *The Birds* in 1963 came closer, telling its terrifying tale of birds that get together to attack a town and its citizens due to some curious force of nature. The effects are fascinating and frightening. One ducks for days as birds fly by.

Roger Corman turned out a series of effective and frightening films from Edgar Allen Poe short stories, starting with *The House of Usher* in 1960 and including *The Pit and the Pendulum* in 1961 and *The Raven* in 1963. Vincent Price starred in many of these, as well as the well done *House of Wax* in 1953 and *The Fly* in 1956.

Jack Clayton's *The Innocents* in 1961 was a chiller with a penetrating performance by Deborah Kerr. Robert Wise's *The Haunting* in 1963 starred Julie Harris and Claire Bloom. These led to many haunted-house horror stories, but none were done better. Roman Polanski's *Rosemary's Baby* in 1968 starred Mia Farrow and led to many child-of-the-devil movies. Sissy Spacek as *Carrie* was superbly possessed in 1976 and Piper Laurie was marvelous as her mother.

Maybe the best done of the modern horror stories was William Friedkin's *The Exorcist,* an Oscar nominee in 1973. Linda Blair portrayed a young girl possessed by the devil. Her mother, Ellen Burstyn, in desperation seeks the help of priests to drive the demon from her daughter.

The Planet of the Apes featured marvelous makeup on such as Roddy McDowall, Kim Hunter, and Sal Mineo, left to right.

The Exorcist was called on by Ellen Burstyn when Linda Blair had trouble sleeping nights.

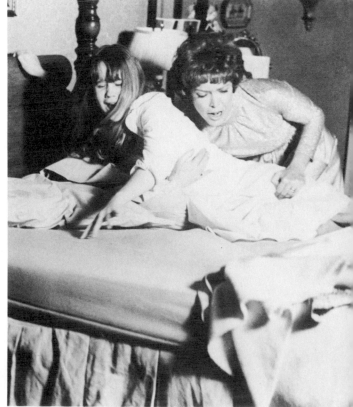

The daughter, Regan, has convulsions, screams at and attacks her mother, and urinates and vomits in front of her—and the camera. A scene where her head turns completely around is startling. Many scenes are startling, shocking, obscene, disgusting, but so well done they grip you. Whatever else it was, it was sensationally well done and deserved more respect and rewards than it received.

The Exorcist has earned almost $85 million, which makes it the fifth biggest box-office film of all time. *Star Wars* has earned $165 million, which makes it the number one box-office blockbuster ever. *Close Encounters of the Third Kind* has earned $77 million, which puts it in the top ten of all-time.

Fritz Lang's *Metropolis* in 1927 was the first science-fiction fantasy denied by Oscar. It took us on a voyage into the future, into a universe in which machines have taken the place of men. It was ingenious. The robots were remarkable. It was copied.

Robert Wise's *The Day the Earth Stood Still* in 1951 was an interesting study of what would happen if an emissary arrived from outer space to warn earthlings of the dangers of nuclear weapons.

On the Beach in 1959 starred Gregory Peck and Ava Gardner in a frightening forecast of lovers doomed with the rest of the world by a nuclear war and radioactive fallout.

George Pal's *Destination Moon* in 1950, *When Worlds Collide* in 1951, and his adaptation of H. G. Wells' *The War of the Worlds* in 1954 were technically excellent and won for him six Oscars for special effects.

Stanley Kubrick's *2001: A Space Odyssey* in 1968, was called by critic Steven Earley, "The most technically advanced and courageous cinema venture of the decade ... easily the most profound and philosophical film of the past several decades." This futuristic look at life as it may be was brilliant and beautiful, a science-fiction fantasy that merited any Award that might be given it, but was not ever nominated for an Oscar.

Its more popular and extremely well-done successor, George Lucas' *Star Wars* in 1977, was far less serious but a lot more entertaining. It won nomination, but no Oscar. Its enormous popularity was deserved. The characters, real and unreal—Luke Skywalker, Princess Leia, Han Solo, Darth Vader, R2D2, C3PO, and so forth—are charismatic. The hardware and special effects are spectacular. Though it is not to be taken seriously, it is great fun. Its 1980 sequel, *The Empire Strikes Back*, introducing the fascinating Yoda, may be better. Creator George Lucas is on a lifelong mission, planning four more—two of the earlier years, two of the later years.

Steven Spielberg's *Close Encounters of the Third Kind*, was another fascinating "space" film, featuring fine performances by Richard Dreyfuss and others on the ground. It was not nominated as a picture or for its performances when it came out in 1977. Reissued in 1980, new sequences had been added, including a dazzling view of the interior of the space ship at the finale. *Alien* in 1979 was another suspenseful shocker in space.

Fantasies are big at the box office, but small at the Oscars window. Realism is rewarded with most Oscars.

Star Wars *featured some interesting types.*

Close Encounters of the Third Kind *included a scene in which Francis Truffaut seems to be leading thousands of Hindus in a rousing chorus of "Closer My God to Thee."*

FOURTEEN

Romance Films

ONLY FIVE ROMANCE FILMS have won Oscars, which is very few if you consider romantic movies to be the heartbeat of Hollywood. These have been *Grand Hotel* in 1931-32, *Cavalcade* in 1932-33, *Gone With the Wind* in 1939, *Mrs. Miniver* in 1942, and *Casablanca* in 1944. As the years go by, we seem to get less romantic. No romance has won an Oscar since the early 1940s, which is a long time.

A separate category has to be considered for classical films such as *Hamlet* in 1948 and *A Man for All Seasons* in 1966—the only two of this type ever to win Academy Awards. Some regard these as romantic in spirit, though they clearly cover different terrains.

Notable nominated losers include *Seventh Heaven* in 1927-28, *Little Women* in 1932-33, *Wuthering Heights* and *Dark Victory* in 1939, *Kings Row* and *Random Harvest* in 1942, *Since You Went Away* in 1944, *Johnny Belinda* in 1948, *The Heiress* in 1949, *A Place in the Sun* in 1951, *Picnic* in 1955, *Separate Tables* in 1958, *The Sundowners* in 1960, and *Ship of Fools* in 1965. Although it crossed several categories, you might also include *The Turning Point* in 1978.

Other nominated losers include *The Divorcee* in 1929-30, *Smilin' Through* and *A Farewell to Arms* in 1932-33, *The Barretts of Wimpole Street* and *Cleopatra* in 1934, *Alice Adams* and *David Copperfield* in 1935, *Romeo and Juliet* in 1936, *The Citadel* and *Four Daughters* in 1938, *All This and Heaven Too*, *Kitty Foyle*, and *The Letter* in 1940, *Blossoms in the Dust* and *Hold Back the Dawn* in 1941, *Heaven Can Wait* and *For Whom the Bell Tolls* in 1943, and *Since You Went Away* in 1944.

Also, *Mildred Pierce* in 1945, *The Razor's Edge* in 1946, *A Letter to Three Wives* in 1949, *Three Coins in the Fountain* in 1954, *Love Is a Many-Splendored Thing* in 1955, *Friendly Persuasion* in 1956, *Peyton Place* and *Sayonara* in 1957, *Cleopatra* in 1963, *Doctor Zhivago* in 1965, *Rachel, Rachel* in 1968, *Love Story* in 1970, *Barry Lyndon* in 1975, and *An Unmarried Woman* in 1978.

Romance may be more than merely man-woman, of course. It can be adult-child. Considered so, *Kramer vs. Kramer* in 1979 qualified as the sixth romantic winner. Certainly, it was romantic in spirit, if realistic in ambition. Here, then, you can include as classic losers *Skippy* in 1930-31 and *The Champ* in 1931-32.

Gone With the Wind may have been the greatest romantic film of all time. It did win the Academy Award. Vivien Leigh as Scarlett O'Hara won too, though Clark Gable as Rhett Butler, maybe the most romantic figure in films, did not.

David O. Selznick could not top it, though he tried a few times, especially with *Since You Went Away* in 1944. Again, we have a lonely lady, Claudette Colbert, coping with life on the home front while her man is away at war. As her daughters, Jennifer Jones and Shirley Temple have to cope, too.

You never see Colbert's husband except in photos, yet you feel love between them so strong even Joseph Cotten cannot comfort her for his absence. This is screen romance at it's subtlest. The farewell scene at

The Heiress *starred Ralph Richardson, Olivia De Havilland, Montgomery Clift, and Miriam Hopkins.*

the train station between Jones and boyfriend Robert Walker is heartbreaking and a dramatic triumph for director John Cromwell.

Wuthering Heights, A Place in the Sun, and *The Turning Point* appear to be the most prominent of the romantic films which were denied Oscars, but others also rank high—notably, *Seventh Heaven, Dark Victory, The Heiress, Kings Row, Random Harvest, Picnic,* and *Since You Went Away.*

Janet Gaynor won the first Best Actress Oscar for *Seventh Heaven* and *Street Angel,* both directed by Frank Borzage, and *Sunrise.* Of these, the best remembered is *Seventh Heaven,* with costar Charles Farrell. It presented a touching portrait of lovers torn apart, and was really a fine film.

In *Dark Victory,* Bette Davis may have given her greatest performance as Judith Traherne, the doomed lady who lives out her last days with George Brent, Humphrey Bogart, and Ronald Reagan. Geraldine Fitzgerald debuted as Judith's confidante.

Tallulah Bankhead had played the Davis part on the stage. David O. Selznick bought the play for Janet Gaynor or Carole Lombard. Davis talked Jack Warner into buying it for her and Edmund Goulding directed. It is remembered as one of Bette's greatest films. Both

Davis and *Dark Victory* were nominated, but lost to Vivien Leigh and *Gone With the Wind.*

Olivia De Havilland and *The Heiress* were nominated in 1949 and De Havilland did win, although *The Heiress* did not. Montgomery Clift, as her suitor, and Sir Ralph Richardson, as her father, also won nominations, but no Oscars. William Wyler was nominated for his direction, but did not win.

This was a superb picture in every sense. It tells of a wealthy but plain lady of the mid-1800s, who displeases her powerful father by falling for a young man who courts her. Her father threatens to disinherit her for he considers the young man a fortune hunter. Her scene when her young man fails to show up to elope with her is extremely moving.

She faces her father and dares him to disinherit her. He is dying and cannot do it. He dies. She inherits her fortune and a life of loneliness. Years later, when her young man returns and asks her to marry him, she agrees. His scene when he shows up only to find the door barred is outstanding.

It is a superlative film, clearly a classic loser.

Random Harvest and its director, Mervyn LeRoy, both were nominated in 1942. Greer Garson was not, but she won for *Mrs. Miniver* that year. Costar Ronald

Colman and supporting star Susan Peters won nominations, but not Oscars. *The Turning Point* is the all-time topper among non-winners with eleven nominations and zero Oscars, but *Random Harvest* and *The Letter* are tied for third with seven nominations and no Oscars.

Random Harvest was written originally by James Hilton, who also wrote *Lost Horizon*. Colman plays a wealthy Englishman who loses his memory during a World War I incident, is hospitalized, and wanders away. A forlorn fellow at this point, he is befriended by a music hall entertainer who helps him back to health and wealth, marries him, and has children by him. He makes a new life with her.

Struck by a taxi, he regains his memory of his former life and returns to his family. Unfortunately, he now has no memory of the three years he spent with Greer. When she discovers this, she goes to work for him as his assistant and yearns for him silently. Eventually, of course, he rediscovers his lost interlude and love for Greer, but many a tear is shed along the way. As unreal as the story may seem, it works.

That same year came *Kings Row*, as well as *Now Voyager*. *Kings Row* and director Sam Wood were nominated losers, but not one member of the splendid cast was nominated. These included Ronald Reagan and Robert Cummings, boyhood friends, and their girlfriends, Ann Sheridan and Betty Field, as well as Charles Coburn and Claude Rains, as doctors.

Sam Wood skillfully directed Henry Bellaman's stunning novel of a 1900s small-town psychology. Dr. Tower (Rains) fearing his daughter Cassandra is insane, keeps her (Field) locked up and denies her the love Parris Mitchell (Cummings) offers. Dr. Tower tutors Parris and he goes off to study medicine.

Meanwhile, the happy-go-lucky ladies' man Drake McHugh (Reagan) goes to the other side of the tracks to be with a railroader's daughter, Randy Monaghan (Sheridan). Working the trains, he has an accident. Believing he has betrayed his daughter Louise (Nancy Coleman), Dr. Gordon unneccessarily amputates Drake's legs.

This gives Reagan the acting opportunity to awaken, discover his loss, and ask his lady, in a hoarse voice, "Where's the rest of me?" a well-remembered line which became the title of his autobiography when he left the movies for politics. This film marked the finest performances of Reagan, Cummings, and Sheridan.

Dr. Tower kills Cassandra and himself. Parris returns to find not only his beloved murdered but his best friend crippled and he strives to mend their broken lives and make new lives for them. As tangled a web as this may seem—and there are elements of mystery and suspense in the story—it works well as period drama.

Small-town life and loves also were effectively depicted in *Alice Adams* in 1935, *Our Town* in 1940, and *Rachel, Rachel* in 1968.

Based on a Booth Tarkington novel, *Alice Adams* is about a poor girl, played by young Katharine Hepburn, seeking the good life through a romance with a rich boy, Fred MacMurray. In the book, she is the true snob and she loses in the end, having to settle for a life of little. In the film, however, she wins the love and life of her dreams. The film and Hepburn were nominated losers.

Rachel, Rachel and its stars, Joanne Woodward and Estelle Parsons, were nominated for Oscars. Unfortunately, director Paul Newman was not, and there were no winners. But this was a splendid, powerful tale of a small-town lady schoolteacher who wants to love a man, is loved by a lady, and finds love hard to find in a town where everyone knows almost everything about your life.

Johnny Belinda, director Jean Negulesco, and stars Jane Wyman, Agnes Moorehead, and Charles Bickford won nominations, but only Wyman won an Oscar. Another star, Lew Ayres, deserved a nomination. Ayres, Bickford, and Moorehead never won an Oscar. All were simply splendid in this story of a deaf-mute farm girl who is encouraged to fight for a life for herself despite her handicap and the lack of faith of others.

Joshua Logan turned William Inge's *Picnic* into a superb play and marvelous movie about lonely people in the midwestern farmlands. A drifter, Bill Holden, disrupts the life of Kim Novak, Rosalind Russell, Arthur O'Connell, Cliff Robertson, and Betty Field. The film and its director were nominated, but did not win. Arthur O'Connell was nominated as supporting actor, but the others did not gain nominations. Others should have been nominated, especially Russell. In her role as a frustrated spinster, she may have given her most touching performance.

Come Back, Little Sheba was not even nominated in 1952, though it won nominations for Shirley Booth and Terry Moore and an Oscar for Booth. Burt Lancaster deserved a nomination for his role as Booth's restless husband, Doc, in this strong, sad story of small-town unrest. Daniel Mann directed this adaptation of another shattering, touching William Inge play.

Separate Tables, David Niven, Deborah Kerr, and Wendy Hiller were nominated in 1958 and Niven and Hiller won Oscars. Director Delbert Mann deserved a nomination. Burt Lancaster and Rita Hayworth also were excellent in this poignant tale of lonely people living in a small hotel.

The most neglected of actresses, Kerr also won

nomination but not an Oscar for *The Sundowners* in 1960. The picture and director Fred Zinnemann and supporting actress Glynis Johns won nominations, but costar Robert Mitchum was overlooked. It was a fine film about the life of migrant sheep families in Australia and had an unforgettable performance by Kerr.

Ship of Fools, director Stanley Kramer, and stars Simone Signoret and Oskar Werner gained nominations but no Oscars in 1965. Costars Lee Marvin, Jose Ferrer, George Segal, Vivien Leigh, and Elizabeth Ashley missed out on nominations in this fascinating study of life on a ship at sea, a throwback to the all-star days of *Grand Hotel* and *Dinner at Eight*.

Grand Hotel won the Oscar in 1931-32, but neither director Edmund Goulding nor any of its stars, Greta Garbo, Joan Crawford, John and Lionel Barrymore, and Wallace Beery, won even nominations in this story of life in a grand hotel in Berlin.

Dinner at Eight came along the next year, directed by George Cukor, adapted from the George S. Kaufman-Edna Ferber stage play. It starred Wallace Beery, John and Lionel Barrymore, Jean Harlow, and Marie Dressler. It did not even gain a single nomination.

In the famous concluding scene of *Dinner at Eight*, Harlow says to Dressler, "You know, I read somewhere that machinery is going to take the place of every profession." And Dressler replies, "Oh, my dear, that's something you'll never have to worry about."

Louisa May Alcott's beloved novel *Little Women* has been acted many times, but never better than in the 1933 movie directed by George Cukor and starring Katharine Hepburn, Joan Bennett, Frances Dee, Jean Parker, Edna May Oliver, and Paul Lukas. Cukor was nominated, but his movie was not. Hepburn won an Oscar that year, but for *Morning Glory*.

Other romantic films which won nominations for Hepburn were *Alice Adams* in 1935 and *Summertime* in 1955, some twenty years apart. She was a young dreamer in the first, a fading spinster in the second. Hepburn also starred with Ginger Rogers in *Stage Door* in 1937, another Kaufman-Ferber stage play brought to the screen. The film and its director, Gregory LaCava, won nominations but not trophies.

It was in the play-within-a-play in *Stage Door* that Hepburn provided scores of imitators with the classic line, "The calla lilies are in bloom again," delivered in her distinctive accent.

The great Garbo won nominations for Eugene O'Neill's *Anna Christie* in 1929-30 and the classic romance *Camille* in 1937. *Camille* costar Robert Taylor said that when George Cukor introduced him to Garbo, she said, "How do you do," and did not say

another word to him other than her lines during the rest of the shooting. However, he also said she was so aggressive in their love scenes that she almost knocked him down a couple of times. It looked a little like that on the screen and worked wonderfully well.

Norma Shearer won nominations for romantic roles in *Their Own Desire* in 1929, *The Divorcee* in 1930, *A Free Soul* in 1931, *The Barretts of Wimpole Street* in 1934, *Romeo and Juliet* in 1936, and *Marie Antoinette* in 1938, and won for *The Divorcee*. But after turning down the Greer Garson role in *Mrs. Miniver*, as too old for her, Shearer's career went into eclipse, while Garson's career rocketed.

Garson received nominations for *Goodbye, Mr. Chips* in 1939, *Blossom in the Dust* in 1941, *Madame Curie* in 1943, *Mrs. Parkington* in 1944, *The Valley of Decision* in 1945, and *Sunrise at Campobello* in 1960, and won for *Mrs. Miniver* in 1942. Most of these were essentially romantic films, and *Random Harvest,* for which she was not nominated, probably was the most romantic. Mervyn LeRoy's *Blossoms in the Dust*, which costarred Garson with Walter Pidgeon, also was a well-portrayed romance.

A great actress, Bette Davis essentially was a romantic actress and some of her greatest hits were romances. She may not have been a great beauty, but she was a great woman and she could depict a woman's feelings extremely well. Aside from *Dark Victory* in 1939, *Jezebel* in 1938, *The Old Maid* in 1939, and *The Private Lives of Elizabeth and Essex* in 1939, *All This and Heaven Too* and *The Letter* in 1940, and *Now, Voyager* in 1942 are remembered with the most affection.

Of Human Bondage was the first Somerset Maugham story Bette Davis did. *The Letter* was the second. It was directed by William Wyler and costarred Gale Sondergaard, Herbert Marshall, and James Stephenson. It gained seven nominations for Oscars, including those for the picture, the director, and the acting of Davis and Stephenson, but won none. Wyler was so tough that Stephenson kept threatening to walk out, but Bette talked him into staying each time.

Still, Davis was best known for her "bitchiness" on screen and off, and in *The Letter* she showed this off to perfection. This is a steamy story set on a rubber plantation in the tropics. In the opening scenes, a gunshot sounds, a man staggers out of a house, and goes down. A woman follows and empties a gun into him.

She then explains to her husband that the man had come to their home and tried to attack her. Nevertheless, the district officer requires her to stand trial. The dead man's Eurasian wife discloses to Bette's attorney that she has a letter written to her husband by Bette asking him to come to her on the fatal night.

The letter would doom Bette and the wife offers to sell it. Bette admits the man was her lover and buys the letter from the wife, who drops it at her feet and forces Bette to kneel before her to retrieve it. Bette is acquitted. When her husband says that they can now go away to start a new life with their savings, she is forced to admit that she spent them to purchase the letter.

It is in this film that she speaks her immortal lines, "Yes, I killed him. And I'm glad, I tell you—glad, glad, glad!" She also says, "With all my heart, I still love the man I killed." Her husband leaves her, which is the end of the Somerset Maugham story. To satisfy the censors, the Hays office, the dead man's wife shoots Bette to death, which is the end of the movie.

Jezebel costarred Henry Fonda. Having walked away from *Gone With the Wind*, Davis tried to catch up with *Jezebel*, an 1800s New Orleans story. It didn't however work as well as a film, but it did win for Bette the Oscar she might have won for the other one. It also won the Best Supporting Actress Oscar for Fay Bainter.

As Julie Marsden, Bette turns down an aristocrat suitor, Buck Cantrell (George Brent), for a business-man, Preston Dillard (Henry Fonda). Pres neglects Julie for business. While unmarried ladies usually wear white to the Mardi Gras ball, Julie wears red, and strapless red at that, and dances the others off the floor.

When Pres chastizes her, Julie wallops him and their engagement is broken. He goes off and brings back a bride from the North, Margaret Lindsay. Julie proceeds revengefully and a duel finally occurs between Buck and Pres, resulting in Buck's death. When yellow fever claims Pres, it is Julie, not his wife, who goes with him to the island colony from which few return.

William Wyler directed. Early in her career, he had embarrassed Bette by asking her, "What do you think of these dames who show their chests and think they can get jobs?" Ready to disapprove him as her director in *Jezebel*, she reminded him of this. He smiled and said, "I'm a much nicer person now." He got the job.

Shooting ran overtime and Henry Fonda had a cutoff clause in his contract. When he went to be with his wife while she gave birth, Bette was left to shoot many of her close-ups with stand-ins. She didn't like it one bit. But Fonda got to be there when his wife had their baby. It was a daughter that they named Jane.

Lawrence J. Quirk, who wrote the book *The Great Romantic Films*, considers *The Old Maid* not only his favorite Bette Davis movie, but his all-time favorite movie: "It is superb romantic drama, with a demonia-cal, bittersweet, love-hate quality and a sweeping dramatic élan that few pictures before or since can match. . . . After *The Old Maid* I considered her the screen's all-time greatest actress."

In it, she runs the range from girlish innocence to womanly vengeance. This is 1861. Charlotte (Davis) loves irresponsible Clem (George Brent). He loves her cousin Delia (Miriam Hopkins). She deserts him to marry responsible Jim (James Stephenson). Charlotte comforts him and when he goes off to the Civil War he leaves her with child. He dies without having married her. She runs an orphanage in which she conceals her illegitimate daughter, Tina. The girl does not know Charlotte is her mother.

Seeing her as an embittered old maid, the widowed Delia brings Charlotte and her child to live with her and arranges a marriage for Charlotte. Charlotte confesses to Delia that the daughter is Clem's. Enraged, Delia tells Charlotte's fiancé she is sick and he runs out on the wedding. Delia then wins away the affections of the child, who hates her rigid old "Aunt Charlotte," and adopts her.

On the daughter's wedding day, Charlotte is tempted to tell Tina the truth, but sadly decides the time to tell her has gone. She says to Delia, "You are the mother she wants and needs tonight. She is not mine. Just as her father was never really mine." After the wedding, Delia has to ask Tina to give her "Aunt Charlotte" a last kiss before going out into the world.

In *Now, Voyager*, Bette again plays an old maid, a dowdy, overweight daughter of a wealthy Boston family dominated by matriarchal Gladys Cooper. As Charlotte, she is rescued by a psychiatrist, Claude Rains, who tears her apart before he can begin making her over. Slimmed down, dressed up, she goes on a cruise where she meets Jerry, as played by Paul Henreid, a lonely man caught in a loveless marriage. They have an affair, but it ends when the cruise ends.

She has, however, regained respect for herself and demands and commands respect when she returns to her family. She soon is engaged to be married to someone she likes but does not love. Paul comes to town on business, however. Seeing him again, she decides she'd rather have the memory of his love than a marriage without love, and breaks her engagement.

After a quarrel with her daughter, the old lady dies and Charlotte breaks down and is hospitalized for psychiatric care. Here she meets Tina, Paul's daughter, a younger version of the woman she had been. She commits herself to making the child the woman she

Penny Serenade *featured Cary Grant, Baby Bibble, Belulah Bondi, and Irene Dunne.*

Now, Voyager *poster.*

could be. For the sake of the child, Paul goes back to his wife.

It is in this movie that there is the famous scene in which Paul lights two cigarettes for Charlotte and gives her one. And it is here that Charlotte says, "Oh, Jerry, we have the stars, let's not ask for the moon."

Max Steiner, maybe the most romantic of the composers, provided magnificent moods with his scores for *Of Human Bondage, Jezebel, Dark Victory, Now, Voyager,* and *The Letter,* as well as *Gone With the Wind, The Treasure of the Sierra Madre, Cimarron, Top Hat, A Star Is Born, Johnny Belinda, Casablanca,* and his Academy Award-winning *The Informer,* and *Since You Went Away.*

Jack Warner never really looked on Bette Davis as a romantic character and wanted Irene Dunne to play the lead in *Now, Voyager,* but Bette fought for it and won. She says, "I had to fight for every role I ever wanted."

Dunne played light comedy especially well, but also was effective in romances, especially *Magnificent Obsession* in 1935, *Love Affair* in 1939, and *Penny Serenade* in 1941. Each was, in its way, touching and memorable.

Charles Boyer was her costar in *Love Affair,* Hedy Lamarr's costar in *Algiers* in 1938, Margaret Sulla-

van's costar in *Back Street* in 1941, and Olivia De Havilland's costar in *Hold Back the Dawn* in 1941.

Looked on as a French kisser, Boyer was sensitive, effective, and underrated. He never says, "Come wiz me to ze Casbah" in *Algiers,* but he says more with his eyes in his scenes with the unbelievably beautiful Lamarr than most men could say with their entire bodies.

Back Street was called by Bosley Crowther, "the quintessence of what is known as a woman's picture." It is the early 1900s. Boyer and Sullavan meet and fall in love. They are to marry on a riverboat. She is delayed, late. The boat and Boyer leave without her.

Years later, they meet again. He has married. She has not. They still love each other and she agrees to see him on the side. They get a back-street apartment. She sacrifices her life for his. He is successful and unwilling to risk his career with a divorce.

He goes to Europe with his wife. They have children. Sullavan waits alone. A brief romance comes and goes. Boyer returns and she tries to break off with him, but cannot. The years go by. He ages better than she, but he will not leave her. In his way, he is as faithful as she is. His children find out and ask him to abandon her, but he will not. He tries to make them understand,

216

but they do not. He says, "Ray, don't ever leave me." She says "I will not."

Stricken by a stroke, he asks his son to place a telephone call to his beloved Ray so he can speak his last words to the woman he loves. His son does, and his beloved hears his last breath. They boy goes to her, but finds her dying. She has her beloved's picture in her hands and dreams of what life with him might have been. She dies with these dreams. Critic Lawrence Quirk calls it "a romantic picture of the first rank... moving and eloquent, with two superb stars... a memorable experience for all who admire durable, well-crafted cinema."

Hold Back the Dawn told a strong story of an opportunist, Boyer, who loves the beautiful Paulette Goddard but romances Olivia De Havilland so that he may marry her, become a citizen, and cross the border to the United States and a new life. When she realizes what he is doing, her heart breaks, her spirit is spent. When he sees what he has done to her, he realizes he loves her. But it is too late.

It is an extremely touching story, wonderfully well-acted by Boyer and De Havilland.

De Havilland also is extremely effective in *To Each His Own*, which won an Oscar for her in 1946. Mitchell Leisen, a master at these stories, directed this, as well as *Hold Back the Dawn*. Olivia is one of those ladies who loves well but not wisely. An airman comes to her small town for a short time. She falls for him, but he goes on his way. She finds she is pregnant. She waits to tell him when he returns, but he is killed in the war and does not return.

She leaves town to have her baby. Returning, the baby is claimed by the wife of her former boyfriend, who believes the baby to be his. Thinking it better for the boy, Olivia leaves him with them and goes to New York. As the years pass, she keeps track of her son through letters and pictures sent by the father. She is successful and he is not. When she is asked for financial help, she returns to buy back her son from them but the boy thinks they are his parents and will not leave with her. So she leaves him.

Years later, there is another war. She is in England and hears her son, a soldier, is coming. He still does not know she is his mother. He accepts her as an old family friend only because he needs her help to arrange a marriage to his girlfriend before he goes off, perhaps to die, as his father did. She is happy just to be a part of his wedding, but a friend lets him know who she really is. He says, "Mother, may I have this dance?" and she has real happiness at last.

Margaret Sullavan, wife of actor Fonda, director Wyler, and agent Leland Hayward, was suicidal in her

Margaret Sullavan and James Stewart, costarring in The Mortal Storm, *celebrate the new year, 1941.*

private life but an appealing, sympathetic character on screen. She made only sixteen movies, which included several romantic classics—*Back Street* and *Three Comrades* in 1938, *The Mortal Storm* in 1940, and *So Ends Our Night* in 1941.

Some consider Barbara Stanwyck's early success, *Stella Dallas*, the classic romantic film. King Vidor directed this superior adaptation of the popular novel by Olive Higgins Prouty. It tells so well a story of mother love that it still seems fresh.

Wealth stripped from him by his father's suicide, John Boles moves to a small town to start a new life. Here he meets and marries Stella, strictly a small-town girl. They have a daughter, but the differences between them soon become apparent to them both. When he gets his chance to go back to the big town, she stays behind with their daughter.

Stella is a devoted mother, but she needs some love in her life and accepts the advances of a good hearted but crude gent, Alan Hale. Her daughter, played by Anne Shirley, does not like him. When her father visits her, he is distressed that she is in such company. When she visits him, she is impressed by the better life.

The father asks for a divorce so he may marry a lady who fits the good life. Stella sees that she is

In the original The Champ, Jackie Cooper rode atop Wallace Beery's shoulders.

The Yearling *starred Jane Wyman, Claude Jarman, Jr., and Gregory Peck.*

spoiling her daughter's chances and agrees to the divorce, provided the father and his new wife will take the daughter and give her a good home. So that the daughter will go with her father, Stella says she wants to go off with Hale and have her own life.

That scene where Stanwyck asks Barbara O'Neil to take her daughter is a tearjerker of the first order. Told how good the girl is, O'Neil sympathetically says, "I know she is—and I know she didn't get it all from her father." But the most memorable scene is the last one. It takes place in the rain, as the shabby Stanwyck stands on a street outside a picture window and watches her daughter wed a wealthy young man in an elegant ceremony, then walks off triumphantly.

For this one, Stanwyck was favored to win the Academy Award she never won. It went to Luise Rainer for *The Good Earth.*

Father-love was wonderfully well-depicted in the original *The Champ,* between Wallace Beery and Jackie Cooper in 1931, and somewhat less realistically in the sequel, between Jon Voight and Ricky Schroeder in 1979. In *Kramer vs. Kramer,* it is portrayed with enormous success, between Dustin Hoffman and Justin Henry in 1979. Cooper was at ten years old the youngest actor ever nominated for an Academy Award (for *Skippy,* directed by his uncle, Norman Taurog, in 1931) until Justin Henry, at eight was nominated for *Kramer* in 1979.

Cooper was the most successful lad in films until Mickey Rooney came along. Rooney made a great romantic film with Spencer Tracy, *Boys Town,* which told of the love of a priest for boys who have gone bad.

The finest films depicting love for animals featured young actors and were romantic in nature—*National Velvet* in 1944 with Rooney and Elizabeth Taylor, *The Yearling* in 1946 with Gregory Peck, Jane Wyman, and Claude Jarman, and *The Black Stallion* in 1979 with Kelly Reno and an aging Rooney. The latter is one of the most pictorially beautiful films ever photographed and deserved nomination as a fine film, but was somehow passed over. Caleb Deschanel's superb photography was overlooked also.

One of the classic films about childhood was George Cukor's adaptation of Charles Dickens' *David Copperfield* in 1935, which starred Freddie Bartholomew as the boy, W. C. Fields as Mr. Micawber, Lionel Barrymore as Dan Peggotty, Basil Rathbone as Clickett, Edna May Oliver as Aunt Betsy, and Maureen O'Sullivan as Agnes.

However, the most truly romantic films remain those that feature the love of man and woman, such as Heathcliff and his Cathy in *Wuthering Heights.* A strong successor was *Jane Eyre* in 1944 with Orson Welles, who was remarkable as Rochester. Another romantic epic was Somerset Maugham's *The Razor's Edge* in 1946 with Tyrone Power, John Payne, Gene Tierney, Anne Baxter, Clifton Webb, and Herbert Marshall.

One of the better-remembered and better-made romantic films was *Intermezzo* in 1940. Ingrid Bergman had starred in a Swedish version a year earlier and was brought to this country by David O. Selznick to do an American version. The Englishman Leslie Howard was brought in to costar with her in this story of a love affair between an aging concert violinist and a young pianist.

In the film, Howard does not want to leave his wife and children, but he goes off on a tour with Bergman. The feeling of love between them is brought to the screen realistically, but they are honorable people and when she realizes how much he misses his daughter she lets him return to his family. A simple story, simply done—tasteful, elegant.

The following year, Ginger Rogers won an Oscar for her romantic role as a shopgirl who wants more, in *Kitty Foyle*. The movie and its director, Sam Wood, also were nominated, but did not win.

The romance between Humphrey Bogart and Lauren Bacall in Hemingway's *To Have and Have Not* overshadowed the adventurous aspects of the story and made the 1944 film memorable. It was in this one that Bacall leaves Bogart with the invitation, "If you want anything, just whistle. You know how to whistle—just pucker up your lips . . . and blow."

Joan Crawford won an Oscar in 1945 for her role as a lady who makes it in business, but finds her daughter (Ann Blyth) with her lover in James M. Cain's *Mildred Pierce*. She followed it in 1946 with a role as a wealthy sponsor for young violinist John Garfield in Fannie Hurst's *Humoresque*.

Letter from an Unknown Woman was a masterpiece of mood and tangled love affairs. It starred Joan Fontaine and Louis Jourdan in 1948.

Deborah Kerr gave one of her great performances in *Tea and Sympathy* in 1956 as the wife of a macho headmaster, Leif Erickson, at a boys' school. She befriends a shy boy, John Kerr, and in the end takes him to her bed to relieve him of his fear that he may be, as accused, a homosexual. All three recreated the roles they had played so well in the stage version of Robert Anderson's poignant play.

The 1950s were not a great period for romance in movies, but 1954's *Three Coins in the Fountain* with Dorothy McGuire, Jean Peters, Maggie McNamara, Louis Jourdan, Rossano Brazzi, and Clifton Webb, and 1955's *Love Is a Many-Splendored Thing* with William Holden and Jennifer Jones, and 1957's *Sayonara* with Marlon Brando, James Garner, Red Buttons, Ricardo Montalban, Miiko Taka, and Miyoshi Umeki were notable nominees. The latter two dealt with romances between American men and Asiatic women. Buttons and Umeki won supporting Oscars. Umeki later played the role of the housekeeper in TV's "The Courtship of Eddie's Father."

After *The Sundowners* in 1960, the 1960s were short on romance. Then came *Love Story* in 1970 with Ryan O'Neal and Ali McGraw in a screen adaptation of Erich Segal's best-seller that some considered soap-opera sentiment, but which was really a rather touching account of an affair between two straight-talking youngsters of today.

Finally, *Coming Home* in 1978 was more a romance than it was a war story. It did deal effectively with the problems of young men who came home crippled physically or mentally by combat, but it is love that leads Jon Voight back to a reason for living—his love affair with Jane Fonda while her husband, Bruce Dern, is himself off fighting that Vietnamese war.

Although Voight plays a paraplegic, there is a nude love scene with Fonda that steams up the screen. Love scenes are a part of romantic movies, of course, but in the early years they were limited to kisses and smouldering looks. A Charles Boyer could say more with a smouldering look at Hedy Lamarr than many men could say with a thousand words.

When Boyer spoke of love in his soft French accents or Ronald Colman spoke of it in his cultured British tones, they spoke poetry. When Clark Gable grinned at a girl there was something of the animal in him, but as playful as a tiger cub. He was saying to her, "Hey, why don't we do it? It's fun." A Marlon Brando is all animal. Full-grown tiger. Hungry.

Conversely, sex might be a part of love, but it was the love that mattered most to a Janet Gaynor or a Katharine Hepburn. Greta Garbo smouldered, but Norma Shearer was regal. Bette Davis and Ingrid Bergman wanted love that would last forever. Today, for a Diane Keaton it's a kick. And Jane Fonda says, "Let's do it. It's healthy."

Love scenes were found to be big box-office in the early days. Adolph Zukor, head of Paramount Pictures, put the "It" Girl, Clara Bow, in the first Academy Award-winner, *Wings*, strictly to get some sex in the story. A Lana Turner or Rita Hayworth became stars simply because the sight of them suggested sex.

Turner says, "I could do more with the quiver of a lip or the shrug of a shoulder than all the nude men and women achieve today by baring it all." Love? "I see people shoving their tongues down each other's throats and thrashing their nude bodies on top of each other (on the screen) and that is not it," she replies.

John Garfield was a great womanizer off the screen and he and Lana gave off sparks on screen in *The Postman Always Rings Twice*. Gable and Turner had great chemistry together in *Honky Tonk*. Hayworth peeled off a glove and you would have thought she went to the buff in the strip-tease in *Gilda*.

You had only to watch Olivier and Oberon in *Wuthering Heights* to know they had a love which would last into eternity. Ironically, they did not then like each other in real life, though they later became friends.

Dead End *starred Billy Halop, Charles Peck, Bernard Punsley, Sylvia Sidney, and Joel McCrea.*

A Streetcar Named Desire *with Kim Hunter, Marlon Brando, and Vivien Leigh.*

Hunter in 1962, *The Cardinal* in 1963, *The Pawnbroker* in 1965, *Easy Rider* and *They Shoot Horses Don't They?* in 1969, *I Never Sang for My Father* and *Joe* in 1970, and *American Graffiti* and *Summer of '42* in 1971.

And: *The Candidate* in 1972, *Save the Tiger, Paper Chase,* and *The Last Detail* in 1973, *Harry and Tonto, Lenny,* and *Alice Doesn't Live Here Any More* in 1974, *The Day of the Locust* in 1975, *I Never Promised You a Rose Garden* in 1977, *Days of Heaven* in 1978, and *The China Syndrome* in 1979.

Among films which won no Oscars although receiving numerous nominations in various categories were *The Little Foxes,* which was given nine nominations; *The Nun's Story,* eight; *A Star Is Born* (1954), *Lenny, The Long Voyage Home,* and *Cat on a Hot Tin Roof,* six each; and *Crossfire* and *Death of a Salesman,* five each.

Among memorable movies which received no nominations at all were *City Streets* in 1931, *Home of the Brave* in 1949, *The Wild One* in 1953, *Sweet Smell of Success* and *The Big Knife* in 1955, *A Face in the Crowd* in 1957, *Wild River* in 1960, and *Home of the Brave* in 1962.

Many of these losers are regarded by critics and fans as among the greatest films of all time and finish in the top ten or top twenty or first fifty or first one hundred of the best, and most important, or most influential, of all time when polls are taken.

Orson Welles' *Citizen Kane* is the classic loser, but many consider his *Magnificent Ambersons* superior. A period picture, it tells the tale of a powerful family in a small town and what happens as the people of the family die and the family loses power and the town dies and a new, big town is born in its place.

It is the only film Welles directed in which he did not act. Where *Citizen Kane* cries out for attention, *Ambersons* sneaks up on you. The subject matter is less spectacular, but more moving. It is lyrical, poetic. Bill Bayer points out that not only is the film nostalgic in nature, but the viewer is nostalgic for the beginning of the film by the time it ends.

Technically, it may be more innovative than and superior to *Kane.* The photography of varied lighting by Stanley Cortez is extremely distinguished. The sound is striking. Dialogue overlaps, and diminishes as characters recede, or is muffled in architecture or environment.

The acting of the Welles stock company—and others—Joseph Cotten, Tim Holt, Ray Collins, Dolores Costello, Anne Baxter, and Agnes Moorehead— especially Agnes Moorehead—is marvelous. It is said that this may be the only autobiographical movie Welles ever made. In any event, he did it with love.

Unfortunately, the financial failure and controversy of *Citizen Kane* caused RKO to strip Welles of much of his power by the time *Ambersons* was finished. He left to start another film in another country and tried to coordinate the cutting of *Ambersons* with Robert Wise in Hollywood. Their finished version ran 148 minutes and RKO wanted only 88 minutes. The studio cut many scenes and reshot a few with another director.

Of the sixty missing minutes, Welles says forty-five were critical to the movie. It is vague in places, jumpy in others. Released as half a twin-bill with a Lupe Velez movie, *The Mexican Spitfire, Ambersons* was sold down the river. If not the masterpiece it might have been, it does remain a masterpiece which has grown in stature with the years.

A poll of British film critics selecting the ten greatest

Elmer Gantry *costarred Burt Lancaster and Shirley Jones.*

The original A Star Is Born *starred Janet Gaynor, Fredric March, and Adolphe Menjou.*

films of all time had Welles' *Kane* and *Ambersons* as the only American movies on the list.

Other fine neglected films of small-town life include *Dodsworth* and *Our Town.* Sidney Howard's stage adaptation of Sinclair Lewis' stinging novel *Dodsworth* was brought to the screen brilliantly by William Wyler with splendid performances by Walter Huston, Mary Astor, and Ruth Chatterton.

Sensationalistic, but stylish, was the romantic *Peyton Place* in 1957, which was nominated for Best Picture and gained nominations for actress Lana Turner, supporting performers Arthur Kennedy, Hope Lange, and Diane Varsi, and director Mark Robson. It led to a celebrated television series which made stars of Ryan O'Neal and Mia Farrow.

Life on the farmland of the Southwest in the days before World War I was splendidly brought to the screen by Terence Malick in *Days of Heaven.* The acting by Richard Gere, Brooke Adams, Linda Manz, and Sam Shepard were first-rate, and the photography by Nestor Almendros was phenomenally poetic, perhaps the finest color photography ever put on a screen.

The Grapes of Wrath captured the plight of the transplanted farm family during the Depression in as gripping a movie as has been made. *The Good Earth* captured the plight of the poor farm family in a starving China.

King Vidor's *The Crowd* captured poetically the plight of the little man and his family in the big city of the early 1900s. Robert Altman's *Nashville* and *Welcome to L.A.* grabbed big chunks of life in modern entertainment capitals and held them up to a harsh light.

Elia Kazan's *Wild River* told a moving tale of changing times down South during the Depression with vivid characterizations by Montgomery Clift and Lee Remick. Kazan's *East of Eden* spoke eloquently through powerful performances by Raymond Massey and James Dean of the generation gap growing in a farm family before World War I.

Sounder and its splendid stars, Cicely Tyson and Paul Winfield, were nominated but did not win in Martin Ritt's moving tale of changing times for a black family down South.

The Pawnbroker spoke of many things—the way an experience like life in a Nazi concentration camp can scar a man for life, the way a man loses courage as he ages, the way life in the big city can be a terrifying experience for a survivor. It was a great movie with one of the great performances of all time by Rod Steiger. But it won no Oscars.

An early 1900s account of life in the big city was strongly done by Rouben Mamoulian in *City Streets.* *Dead End* was a devastating account of Depression life in a ghetto. Samuel Goldwyn's adaption of the Sidney Kingsley stage play was harshly realistic on its single ghetto set, designed by Richard Day. Joel McCrea, Sylvia Sidney, Humphrey Bogart, and Claire Trevor gave strong performances, but only Trevor was nominated and she did not win. The Kids, by the way, were Billy Halop, Huntz Hall, Leo Gorcey, and Bobby Jordan. The picture was nominated, but did not win. The director, William Wyler, was not even nominated. Most memorable was a scene in which the gangster, Bogie, seeks to reunite with his mother, Marjorie Main, and is all but spit upon. It was a memorable movie. More recently, Martin Scorsese's *Mean Streets* powerfully depicted the life of young people in the big city.

The Blackboard Jungle, starring Glenn Ford and Sidney Poitier, was a frightening indictment of life in a ghetto school. Nick Ray's *Rebel Without a Cause* captured through powerful performances by James Dean the alienation of fathers and sons and the alienations of young people at the high school level better than any film of its kind.

Laslo Benedek's *The Wild One*, starring Marlon Brando and Lee Marvin, about a motorcycle gang that terrorizes a small town, started a cycle of motorcycle movies, but really was about the frightening rebellion of many young people in the modern culture. It led to Peter Fonda's influential *Easy Rider* in which rebellious members of the drug culture travel cross-country, seeing the country through the eyes of today's restless youth. This led in a way to *Five Easy Pieces* in which with a persuasive performance Jack Nicholson shows how a young man decides he will not live the way his elders expect him to.

The Summer of '42 was a touching tale of young people growing up in a vacation town. *The Last Picture Show* was Peter Bogdanovich's extremely moving story of young people growing up in a dying town. It had superb performances by two of their elders, Ben Johnson and Cloris Leachman. Francis Ford Coppola's *American Graffiti* was a surprisingly strong account of high school life and young people moving toward maturity.

The script for *American Graffiti* was written by George Lucas, the young genius later behind *Star Wars*. It was rejected by every major studio before it was rescued by another genius, Coppola, fresh from UCLA. Set in the early 1960s, it was the *Rebel Without a Cause* of the 1970s, a varied and significant film wonderfully well done.

Life among the aging was treated with dramatic might in *Death of a Salesman*, with Fredric March, and *Harry and Tonto*, with Art Carney. The same theme was successfully dealt with in *I Never Sang for My Father*, with Melvyn Douglas, which, with the help of Gene Hackman, touched deeply on the alienation of parents and children, the difficulty of keeping a family together today.

The Little Foxes, the Lillian Hellman play with Bette Davis, told a forceful tale of power in a family and the murderous greed of its members. More recently, *Who's Afraid of Virginia Woolf?*, the Edward Albee play with Elizabeth Taylor and Richard Burton, Sandy Dennis and George Segal, spoke powerfully of the hatreds that too often grow between husband and wife.

Cat on a Hot Tin Roof, the Tennessee Williams sizzler, spoke with biting words of the gaps between father and son, husband and wife, the over-sexed and the mis-sexed, with Elizabeth Taylor, Paul Newman, Burl Ives, and Mildred Dunnock coming to life on the big screen.

Dark at the Top of the Stairs, with Robert Preston and Dorothy McGuire, spoke eloquently of family life torn apart by sudden death. *Picnic* spoke of life and loneliness and reaching out.

Come Back, Little Sheba depicted powerfully and poignantly the alienation of a wife, Shirley Booth, and her wandering, drinking husband, Burt Lancaster. Early on, *A Free Soul* spoke strongly of how a drunken father, Lionel Barrymore, turns his daughter into a drunkard, Norma Shearer.

Lost Weekend may have been the finest film about alcoholism, but *The Country Girl*, with Grace Kelly,

(Center) In The Last Picture Show, *Timothy Bottoms and Jeff Bridges ask for suggestions on what tune to play on the juke box. (Right) In* American Graffiti, *Ronny Howard and Cindy Williams have a last dance the night before Ronny goes off to college. On TV, Ronny, of course, was famous as Opie on "The Andy Griffith Show," while Cindy became famous as Shirley on the "Laverne and Shirley" show.*

Easy Rider *took Dennis Hopper, Peter Fonda, and Jack Nicholson on a cross-country spin.*

In I Never Sang for My Father, *dad Melvyn Douglas challenges son Gene Hackman.*

In The Man with the Golden Arm, *junkie Frank Sinatra is hauled off to jail.*

Bing Crosby, and Bill Holden, and *Days of Wine and Roses*, with Lee Remick, Jack Lemmon, and Charles Bickford, were equally gripping and well done tales of the deadliness of drink.

A Hatful of Rain, with Bickford, Don Murray, and a performance by Anthony Franciosa that should not have been overlooked, spoke in two tongues of father-son alienation and the deadliness of drugs. Otto Preminger's *The Man with the Golden Arm*, starring Frank Sinatra in a part originally offered to Marlon Brando, was a daring, damning indictment of drugs.

These Three, starring Joel McCrea, Merle Oberon, and Miriam Hopkins, did not measure up to Lillian Hellman's original stageplay, *The Children's Hour*, but still told a daring story for its day of the way the world looks at homosexuality. A spoiled child is the villain of the piece.

A Separate Peace was a sleeper, discovered by a few, which told a touching tale of youthful homosexuality, called by Rex Reed the finest film on youth yet made. *Boys in the Band* dealt with adult homosexuals frankly and sympathetically.

Bigotry was brought brilliantly under a microscope onto the big screen in *Boomerang, Crossfire, The Defiant One, To Kill a Mockingbird, Home of the Brave, Sounder, Joe*, each a worthy work, and in *Lady Sings the Blues*, which dealt with being black, the nocturnal world of jazz, and the destructive influence of drugs.

Three Faces of Eve with Joanne Woodward and *The Snake Pit* with Olivia De Havilland presented staggering stories of the mentally torn, psychiatrists, and an insane asylum. *David and Lisa* and *I Never Promised You a Rose Garden* were moving accounts of mental problems among teenagers.

Bright Victory with Arthur Kennedy was a compelling account of going blind. *Johnny Belinda* with Jane Wyman and *The Heart Is a Lonely Hunter* with Alan Arkin were moving accounts of being mute.

The Men with Marlon Brando was a brilliant, tough account of what it is like to become a paraplegic. It preceded by many years the stunning version in *Coming Home* with Jon Voight.

Wartime dramas of life behind the fighting front which did not deal directly with fighting but which dealt in deeply moving terms of the waste of war include *The Mortal Storm, Three Comrades*, and *Paths of Glory*, as well as *Watch on the Rhine, The Search, The Diary of Anne Frank*, and *Judgment at Nuremberg*. All were worthy of Awards.

Maybe the most moving was Fred Zinnemann's *The Search*, which dealth touchingly with the friendship of a soldier in post-war Berlin, Montgomery Clift, with a lost youngster, Ivan Jandl, while his mother, Jarmila Novotna, wanders the country seeking him. If you have a dry eye at the end, you have a hard heart.

The loneliness of wanderers are depicted in touching ways in John Ford's *The Long Voyage Home* and Josh Logan's *Bus Stop*. In Logan's *Picnic* the loneliness of a wanderer, William Holden, is matched by those with roots, Kim Novak and Rosalind Russell.

Loneliness, hunger, and desperation during Depression times were driven deep into your senses in *They Shoot Horses, Don't They?*, a taut tale of marathon dance contests with Jane Fonda, Michael Sarrazin, and Gig Young. Young, a gifted actor long neglected by Hollywood, gave an Academy Award-winning performance after which he made only two minor films. A few years after his triumphant night, he shot his wife and himself to death.

In All the President's Men, *Robert Redford portrayed a reporter. Most reporters look like Redford, especially male reviewers of film books.*

In Sweet Smell of Success, *Tony Curtis horns in on Burt Lancaster.*

In A Face in the Crowd, *Pat Neal and Andy Griffith share a laugh. Perhaps the car wouldn't start again.*

Julia *costarred Jane Fonda and Vanessa Redgrave.*

Loneliness in prison was poignantly portrayed by Burt Lancaster as *The Bird Man of Alcatraz*. Loneliness and a yearning for success was poignantly portrayed by Montgomery Clift in *A Place in the Sun*.

The great were portrayed on the screen in such Oscar-neglected films as *Abe Lincoln in Illinois* with Raymond Massey, *Young Lincoln* with Henry Fonda, *Disraeli* with George Arliss, *The Life of Louis Pasteur* with Paul Muni, *Edison the Man* with Spencer Tracy, and *Boys Town* with Tracy as Father Flanagan. Others include *Dr. Ehrlich's Magic Bullet* with Edward G. Robinson, *Madame Curie* with Greer Garson, *The Spirit of St. Louis* with James Stewart as Charles Lindbergh, *The Pride of the Yankees* with Gary Cooper as Lou Gehrig, *Wilson* with Alexander Knox, *Moulin Rouge* with Jose Ferrer as Toulouse Lautrec, and *Bound for Glory* with David Carradine as Woody Guthrie.

Of these, maybe the most notable losers were Muni's magnetic Pasteur and Ferrer's stunning Toulouse-Lautrec. The color photography and dynamic sequences in John Huston's *Moulin Rouge* also are memorable, in fact unforgettable, and this film figures as one of the greatest of those denied the Oscar.

Religion was strongly dramatized in *The Song of Bernadette, The Nun's Story, The Robe, The Cardinal,* and *Elmer Gantry*. Jennifer Jones won an Academy Award for *Bernadette*. Audrey Hepburn could well have for *The Nun's Story*. Burt Lancaster won an Oscar for *Gantry*, and the film could well have won, too.

Big business was given excellent dramatic study in John Houseman's and Robert Wise's *Executive Suite* with William Holden, Fredric March, Walter Pidgeon, Dean Jagger, Barbara Stanwyck, June Allyson, and Shelley Winters—also in Arthur Miller's *All My Sons* with Edward G. Robinson, in *Patterns* with Van Heflin and Ed Begley, and in John Avildsen's *Save the Tiger*, which brought Jack Lemmon an Oscar.

Politics were dealt with powerfully in Frank Capra's *Mr. Smith Goes to Washington* and *Meet John Doe*—also in *The Candidate* with Robert Redford and in *All the President's Men* with Redford and Dustin Hoffman, and Award-winning Jason Robards. The latter story was told in terms of the newspaper investigation of the Watergate scandal.

A Walter Winchell-like gossip columnist and the terror he spreads was strongly portrayed by Burt Lancaster with Tony Curtis in the underrated *Sweet Smell of Success*. The power television can wield was demonstrated dramatically in *Network* with William Holden, Faye Dunaway, and Peter Finch, who won a posthumous Oscar.

One of the most underrated of films was *A Face in the Crowd*, Elia Kazan's explosive story of an Arthur Godfrey sort of television star as portrayed by Andy Griffith. Godfrey may have been true to his plain folks sort of image, but Griffith betrayed his brilliantly and Lee Remick lent sensual support.

The battle between society and satirist Lenny Bruce was presented explosively by Dustin Hoffman in *Lenny*, which had a fascinating portrait of a showgirl by Valerie Perrine.

Hollywood and the movie industry has examined itself in unflattering terms in such films as *A Star Is Born, The Goddess, The Big Knife, The Bad and the Beautiful, Sunset Boulevard,* and *What Ever Happened to Baby Jane?*, and denied itself Oscars for these.

Sunset Boulevard and *What Ever Happened to Baby Jane?* came close to being horror stories. John Cromwell's *The Goddess* offers a searing portrait of an unhappy Marilyn Monroe-like sex-symbol, Kim Stanley. Robert Aldrich's *The Big Knife*, written by Clifford Odets, offers a cruel characterization of a movie mogul by Rod Steiger. Louis B. Mayer wept and Harry Cohn flew into a rage when they saw it. Each believed it to be about him.

Vincente Minnelli, who saw his beloved Judy Garland overwhelmed by fame, insecure with success, driven to drugs and drink and, eventually, death, made a masterpiece in the long-overlooked *The Bad and the Beautiful*. Kirk Douglas, never an Oscar-winner in real life, plays a powerful producer who runs roughshod over performers like Lana Turner and writers like Dick Powell in the Hollywood world of agents, hustlers, and hangers-on.

A Star Is Born told a sad story of Hollywood and was a rare case of an original and a remake that were almost equal in quality. The first film, starring Janet Gaynor and Fredric March, and the second, starring Judy Garland and James Mason, were both blockbuster studies of what happens to love when one's star rises while the other's falls. The finish where Norman Maine walks into the ocean to his death and Vicki Lester, in accepting Oscar, introduces herself as "Mrs. Norman Maine" remains one of the most moving moments in movie history. The Hollywood world revolves around Oscar and its impact on the public is enormous.

Until one studies the results of more than fifty years of these ceremonies, one might assume Oscars were won by a Judy Garland or a Cary Grant, a Deborah Kerr, Barbara Stanwyck, Rosalind Russell, Charlie Chaplin, Henry Fonda, James Dean, Paul Newman, Montgomery Clift, or Richard Burton.

It is difficult to believe that Clark Gable's Rhett Butler, Charles Laughton's Captain Bligh, Laurence Olivier's Heathcliff, Marlon Brando's Stanley Kowalski, James Stewart's Mr. Smith, Humphrey Bogart's Rick, Dustin Hoffman's Ratso Rizzo, Katharine Hepburn's Rose, Bette Davis' Margo, and so many more did not win an Oscar.

It is difficult to believe that an Alfred Hitchcock never won for one of his films, that no fantasy ever has won and only one western has won. Or that *Citizen Kane*, *The Grapes of Wrath*, *A Streetcar Named Desire*, *A Place in the Sun*, *Stagecoach*, *Shane*, *High Noon*, *Singin' in the Rain*, *The African Queen*, *The Wizard of Oz*, *Wuthering Heights*, and so many more didn't win an Oscar.

The list is a long one, as has been this book. But if it has served to celebrate the great pictures and performances that didn't win Oscars and if it has made you remember the many that should not be forgotten, it has been worthwhile.

It is the pictures and the performances that count, not the Awards.

BIBLIOGRAPHY

THE AUTHOR used interviews, memory, research, and extensive clip files and read many books in writing this book. The most useful of the reference books were:

50 Golden Years of Oscar by Robert Osborne, designed by Ernest E. Schworck, and published by ESE California, 509 N. Harbor Boulevard, La Habra, California 90631.

Academy Awards Illustrated annuals by Robert Osborne, published by Ernest E. Schworck, ESE. California.

The Film Encyclopedia by Ephraim Katz, published by Thomas Y. Crowell, New York, New York.

The American Movies Reference Book: The Sound Era by Paul Michael, published by Prentice-Hall, Englewood Cliffs, New Jersey.

50 Classic Motion Pictures by David Zinman, published by Crown, New York, New York.

The Great Movies by William Bayer, published by Grosset & Dunlap, New York, New York.

The Great Romantic Films by Lawrence J. Quirk, published by The Citadel Press, Secausus, New Jersey.

The Men Who Made the Movies by Richard Schickel, published by Atheneum, New York, New York.

The Liveliest Art by Arthur Knight, published by Macmillan, New York, New York.

The New York Times Directory of the Film, published by Arno Press/Random House, New York, New York.

Star Stats by Kenneth S. Marx, published by Price/Stern, Sloan, Los Angeles, California.

Abbott and Costello, 192

Abe Lincoln in Illinois, 86, 138, 221, 227

Abel, Walter, 182

Academy Award Nominees and Winners, 22–41; actors and actresses receiving the most nominations and victories, 44–47

Adventures of Robin Hood, The, 141, 173, 178, 179

African Queen, The, 3, 11, 13, 14, 16, 21, 57, 102, 103–104, 141, 145, 146, 151–52, 173, 180, 182, 228; S. P. Eagle, 151; C. S. Forster, 152

Agee, James, 73, 151, 152, 205

Aherne, Brian, 88; *Juarez*, 88, 181

Airport, 107, 120, 122, 181

Albert, Eddie, 76, 180, 182, 186, 194; *Orders to Kill*, 182, 186

Alda, Alan, 98, 196

Aldrich, Robert, 177; *Apache*, 177; *Vera Cruz*, 177; *The Last Sunset*, 177

Alexander, Jane, 7, 107, 129

Algiers, 79, 138, 216

Alice Doesn't Live Here Anymore, 128, 140, 222

All About Eve, 3, 5, 16, 19, 21, 88, 104, 105, 106, 109, 120, 121, 122, 142, 157, 221

All My Sons, 84, 88, 227; Arthur Miller, 227

All Quiet on the Western Front, 82, 142, 178; Louis Wolheim, 82

All That Jazz, 140, 170, 202

All the President's Men, 97, 129, 140, 221, 226, 227

Allen, Woody, 8, 74, 76, 129, 188, 192–93; *Bananas*, 192; *Love and Death*, 193; *Play It Again Sam*, 192; *Sleeper*, 193; *Take the Money and Run*, 192

Altman, Robert, 139, 140, 223; *M*A*S*H*, 140; *Welcome to L. A.*, 223

Ameche, Don, 75–76, 179

American Film Institute, 14, 43, 146

American Graffiti, 3, 140, 222, 224

American in Paris, An, 8, 10, 12, 19, 76, 140, 141, 152, 157, 169, 198, 201

Anatomy of a Murder, 83, 88, 109, 127, 135, 183, 184

Andrews, Dana, 81, 154, 182, 184; *Boomerang*, 81

Andrews, Julie, 70, 108, 119, 199, 202, 203; *Mary Poppins*, 108, 119, 199, 202, 203

Ann-Margret, 181, 197

Anna and the King of Siam, 114, 115, 138

Anna Christie, 84, 110, 133, 140, 214

Annie Hall, 8, 76, 114, 129, 170, 188, 193

Apartment, The, 15, 21, 63, 81, 123, 143, 188, 194

Apocalypse Now, 89, 98, 137, 140, 173, 182; Joseph Conrad's *Heart of Darkness*, 137

Arkin, Alan, 82, 225; *The Russians Are Coming, The Russians Are Coming*, 82; *The Heart is a Lonely Hunter*, 82, 225

Arliss George, 104, 227; *Disraeli*, 227; *The Man Who Played God*, 104

Arnold, Edward G., 163, 164

Around the World in 80 Days, 19, 140, 173, 178, 188; Michael Anderson, 140

Arthur, Jean, 7, 65, 111, 114, 116–17, 163, 164, 174, 181, 193, 194

Astaire, Fred, 7, 8, 10, 76, 109, 119, 168, 169, 171, 198

Astor, Mary, 111, 122, 156, 179, 223; *The Great Lie*, 122

Auntie Mame, 16, 21, 114, 188, 194

Awful Truth, The, 74, 75, 88, 114, 140, 142, 188, 193

Ayres, Lew, 82, 213; *Dr. Kildare*, 82

Bacall, Lauren, 119–120, 219; *Applause*, 120; *The Big Sleep*, 119; *Cactus Flower*, 120; *Dark Passage*, 119

Backus, Jim, 94, 95; *Mr. Magoo*, 94

Bacon, Lloyd, 138; *Action in the North Atlantic*, 138; *Brother Orchid*, 138; *The Oklahoma Kid*, 138

Bad and the Beautiful, The, 122, 145, 227

Bad Day at Black Rock, 83, 136, 141, 173, 177

Bainter, Fay, 122, 205, 215; *The Children's Hour*, 122

Bancroft, Anne, 16, 20, 21, 119, 123, 124, 126, 170, 172; *Fatso*, 126; *Gorilla at Large*, 126; *The Pumpkin Eater*, 126; *Treasure of the Golden Condor*, 126

Bang the Drums Slowly, 99, 146, 181; John Hancock, 181

Bankhead, Tallulah, 53, 106, 107, 212

Barretts of Wimpole Street, The, 211, 214

Barrymore, Ethel, 2, 111, 112, 121; *None But the Lonely Heart*, 121; *The Spiral Staircase*, 121

Barrymore, John, 2, 77, 78, 102, 116, 139, 193, 214; *Twentieth Century*, 193

Barrymore, Lionel, 108, 180, 205, 214, 218, 224

Bartholomew, Freddie, 180, 218; *David Copperfield*, 211, 218

Baryshnikov, Mikhail, 129, 170

Baxter, Anne, 5, 106, 122, 218, 222

Baxter, Warner, 139, 175, 176, 199–200

Beatty, Warren, 7, 80, 97, 98, 123, 129, 171, 175, 197, 206; *All Fall Down*, 98; *Mickey One*, 98

Beau Geste, 88, 134, 145, 173, 178

Beery, Wallace, 19, 98, 181, 207, 214, 218

Begley, Ed, 88; *Patterns*, 88; *12 Angry Men*, 88

Bellamy, Ralph, 88; *Sunrise at Campobello*, 88

Ben-Hur, 19, 20, 143, 178

Bendix, Bill, 182, 186

Bennett, Joan, 78, 193, 214

Benson, Robby, 181; *One on One*, 181

Bergman, Ingrid, 5, 16, 19, 20, 21, 57, 59, 79, 102, 106, 120, 183, 218, 219; *Anastasia*, 106; children, 106; marriages, 106

Berkeley, Busby, 134–35, 138, 142, 168, 169, 198, 199, 200; *Babes in Arms*, 135; *Call Me Mister*, 135; *Footlight Parade*, 135, 199; *For Me and My Gal*, 135; *Girl Crazy*, 135; *Gold Diggers of 1933*, 135, 199; *Gold Diggers of 1935*, 135, 199; *Gold Diggers of 1937*, 134, 199; *Lullaby of Broadway*, 134; *Roman Scandals*, 135; *Rose Marie*, 135; *Strike Up the Band*, 135; *Varsity Show*, 134; *Whoopee*, 135; *Ziegfeld Girl*, 135

Best Years of Our Lives, The, 81, 117, 143, 205, 221

Bickford, Charles, 7, 84, 177, 180, 213, 225; *The Farmer's Daughter*, 84

Bill of Divorcement, 78, 102, 141

Birdman of Alcatraz, 120, 139, 185, 221, 227

Blackboard Jungle, The, 80, 81, 135, 221, 223–24

Blondell, Joan, 181, 208

Blood and Sand, 78, 83, 119, 138, 181; Linda Darnell, 181; Ernest Palmer, 181; Ray Rennahan, 181

Bob & Carol & Ted & Alice, 98, 188, 196–97; Robert Culp, 98; Paul Mazursky, 197

Body and Soul, 57, 89, 90, 135, 180

Boetticher, Budd, 177; *Ride Lonesome*, 177

Bogarde, Dirk, 20

Bogart, Humphrey, 3, 5, 11, 12, 13, 15, 20, 21, 57–59, 60, 63, 89, 101, 103–104, 105, 119, 125, 139, 151, 152, 156, 157, 182, 185, 212, 219, 223, 228; *Desperate Hours*, 185; *San Quentin*, 185

Bogdanovich, Peter, 139, 140, 182, 195, 224

Bolger, Ray, 18, 165, 166, 202

Bond, Ward, 144, 151

Bonnie and Clyde, 11, 14, 98, 127, 128, 135, 171, 183, 186; Robert Benton, 171; Burnett Guffey, 171; David Newman, 171; Robert Penn, 171; Michael Pollard, 171

Borgnine, Ernest, 13, 95, 175

Born Yesterday, 21, 106, 109, 114, 141, 188, 194

Borzage, Frank, 133, 140, 212; *Bad Girl*, 140

Boyer, Charles, 7, 78, 79, 81, 183, 193, 201, 216, 219; *All This and Heaven Too*, 79; *Fanny*, 79, 201

Boys Town, 77, 218, 227

Brando, Marlon, 3, 4, 13, 15, 19, 20, 21, 52, 56–57, 60, 66, 70, 90, 91, 92, 93, 94, 97, 101, 142, 157, 158, 175, 181, 182,

201, 219, 220, 224, 225, 228;
Last Tango in Paris, 220; *The
Men*, 57, 225; *Sayonara*, 219;
The Wild One, 223
Breaking Away, 197
Brennan, Walter, 19, 65, 120,
163, 175, 180
Brent, George, 104, 105, 212, 215
Brice, Fanny, 88, 165
Bridge on the River Kwai, 20, 178
Bridges, Lloyd, 173, 182
Bringing Up Baby, 75, 102, 136,
188, 193
British Film Institute, 14–15, 44
Broadway Melody, 15, 140, 198,
199; Harry Beaumont, 140, 198
Brooks, Mel, 8, 74, 76, 126, 188,
192; *Blazing Saddles*, 192;
High Anxiety, 192; *The
Producers*, 192; *Silent Movie*,
192; *The Twelve Chairs*, 192;
Young Frankenstein, 192
Brooks, Richard, 135, 141, 145,
177, 186, 187; *The Catered
Affair*, 135; *In Cold Blood*, 135,
141, 145, 186; *Crossfire*, 135;
The Last Hunt, 177; *The Profes-
sionals*, 135, 141, 177
Brown, Clarence, 132, 133, 140;
Ah, Wilderness, 133; *Conquest*,
133; *Flesh and the Devil*, 133;
A Free Soul, 133, 140; *The
Human Comedy*, 133, 140;
Idiot's Delight, 133; *Inspiration*,
133; *Intruder in the Dust*, 133;
The Rains Came, 133; *The
White Cliffs of Dover*, 133;
Woman of Affairs, 133; *The
Yearling*, 133
Brynner, Yul, 112, 113, 114, 201
Burstyn, Ellen, 128, 209; *Same
Time Next Year*, 128
Burton, Richard, 7, 12–13, 15, 19,
21, 70, 83, 118, 202, 224, 227;
Camelot, 202
Bus Stop, 120, 221, 225
*Butch Cassidy and the Sundance
Kid*, 11, 12, 14, 15, 21, 95, 97,
140, 171–72, 173; John
Foreman, 171; William
Goldman, 171; Conrad Hall,
171; George Roy Hill, 171;
Katharine Ross, 171
Butterfield 8, 13, 107, 113, 118

Caan, James, 7, 99, 129, 197;
Brian's Song, 99; *Cinderella
Liberty*, 99, 129, 197; *Comes a
Horseman*, 99; *The Gambler*, 99
Cabaret, 14, 124, 140, 169–70,
202; Jay Alleb, 169; Ralph
Burns, 169; Fred Ebb, 169; Cy
Feuer, 169; Bob Fosse, 169;
Joel Gray, 169–70, 202;
Christopher Isherwood, 169,
170; John Kander, 169; Joe
Masteroff, 169; Geoffrey
Unsworth, 169; John Van
Druten, 169; Michael York,
169–70
Cagney, James, 2, 11, 59, 60–61,
67, 84, 119, 139, 185, 194,
199, 202; *City for Conquest*, 84;
Each Dawn I Die, 185; *Kiss

Tomorrow Goodbye, 185; *The
Roaring Twenties*, 185; *White
Heat*, 185
Caine Mutiny, The, 57, 81, 135,
136, 173, 178, 182; Herman
Wouk, 182
Caine Mutiny Court Martial, The,
89
Camille, 3, 16, 21, 78, 110–111,
141, 214, 220
Canutt, Yakima, 152, 153
Capra, Frank, 65, 105, 116, 140,
143, 162, 163, 164, 193, 204,
227; *It's a Wonderful Life*, 143,
204; *Lady for a Day*, 143;
The Name Above the Title,
(autobiography), 143
Captain Blood, 173, 178, 179;
Rafael Sabatini, 179
Captains Courageous, 173, 180;
Rudyard Kipling, 180
Carefree, 168
Carey, Harry, 143, 175
Carey, MacDonald, 182
Carradine, John, 149, 152
Carroll, Diahann, 128, 201;
Claudine, 128
Carroll, Madeleine, 179
Casablanca, 3, 5, 12, 14, 15, 16,
21, 57, 58, 59, 81, 85, 106,
141, 211, 216; Dooley Wilson,
59
Cassavetes, John, 83, 127, 139,
140, 141; *The Dirty Dozen*, 83
Cat Ballou, 177; Elliott Silverstein,
177
Cat on a Hot Tin Roof, 95, 109,
118, 135, 221, 222; Tennessee
Williams, 222
Cavalcade, 15, 142, 211
Champ, The, 19, 132, 207, 211,
218
Champion, 69, 70, 83, 135, 180
Chaplin, Charles, 7, 8, 15, 16, 55,
72, 73, 88, 109, 160, 161, 188,
189, 227; *The Circus*, 73, 160,
188; *The Gold Rush*, 161; *The
Great Dictator*, 73, 145, 160,
188, 189; *Limelight*, 160;
Modern Times, 73, 146, 160,
188, 189; *Monsieur Verdoux*,
73, 160, 188, 189; *The Tramp*,
16, 73
Chatterton, Ruth, 110; *Madame X*,
110; *Sarah and Son*, 110
Chevalier, Maurice, 76, 201
Chinatown, 11, 14, 101, 128,
139, 183, 187
Christie, Julie, 175, 197
Cimarron, 12, 114, 140, 152,
173, 216; Wesley Ruggles, 140
Citizen Kane, 3, 12, 14, 15, 21,
55, 59, 68, 69, 82, 83, 135,
137–38, 146–48, 149, 153,
182, 184, 221, 222–23, 228;
George Coulouris, 147; William
Randolph Hearst, 138, 146,
147, 148; Herman Mankiewicz,
146
City Lights, 7, 14, 15, 72, 73, 160
Clayburgh, Jill, 7, 129; *Pippin*,
129; *The Rothchilds*, 129;
Starting Over, 129; *An
Unmarried Woman*, 129, 197,
211

Cleopatra (1934, 1963), 211
Clift, Montgomery, 3, 5, 7, 13, 15,
20, 21, 57, 90, 91–93, 94, 95,
97, 101, 113, 120, 121, 158,
175, 177, 212, 220, 223, 225,
227; *Freud*, 93; and Libby
Holman, 90; *Monty* by Robert
Laguardia, 92
*Close Encounters of the Third
Kind*, 11, 141, 146, 210; Steven
Spielberg, 141
Cobb, Lee J., 7, 63, 86, 87, 88;
The Brothers Karamazov, 86
Coburn, Charles, 84, 194, 213;
The Devil and Miss Jones, 84;
The Green Years, 84
Cohn, Harry, 109, 119, 143, 173,
204, 227
Colbert, Claudette, 105, 106, 109,
114, 116, 211–12, 220
Colman, Ronald, 179, 193, 203,
212–13, 219
Come Back, Little Sheba, 20, 145,
224; Shirley Booth, 20, 224
Come to the Stables, 121, 122
Coming Home, 3, 13, 57, 89, 99,
100, 107, 219, 220, 221, 225;
Hal Ashby, 220
Conversation, The, 11
Cool Hand Luke, 6, 89, 95, 97;
George Kennedy, 6; Strother
Martin, 89
Cooper, Gary, 19, 54, 65, 117,
163, 173, 174, 175, 178, 181,
182, 194, 227; *Sergeant York*,
68, 163
Cooper, Jackie, 20, 218
Coppola, Francis Ford, 140, 182,
187, 224; *Conversations*, 187
Cotten, Joseph, 3, 81, 82, 137,
147, 211, 222; *Journey into
Fear*, 82; *Portrait of Jennie*, 82,
206; *The Third Man*, 82
Cox, Wally, 57
Crawford, Joan, 90, 105, 106,
108–109, 113, 214, 219;
marriages, 109; *Mildred Pierce*,
109, 141, 211, 219; *Mommie
Dearest*, 109
Cregar, Laird, 83, 181, 186;
Hangover Square, 83; *I Wake
Up Screaming*, 83, 186; *The
Lodger*, 83, 186; *This Gun for
Hire*, 83, 186
Crisp, Donald, 20, 53
Cromwell, John, 105, 138, 179,
212, 227; *The Goddess*, 227; *In
Name Only*, 138; *Made for Each
Other*, 138; *The Prisoner of
Zenda*, 138; *So Ends Our Night*,
138
Crosby, Bing, 76, 192, 199, 201,
224; *Going My Way*, 199; Bob
Hope, 192
Crossfire, 83, 122, 222, 225
Crowd, The, 7, 132, 133, 159,
223; James Murray, 159
Cukor, George, 104, 110, 141,
166, 183, 193, 194, 198, 214;
A Double Life, 141; *Pat and
Mike*, 141; *The Women*, 141
Curtis, Tony, 76, 186, 194,
226–27; *Sweet Smell of Success*,
226, 227
Curtiz, Michael, 141, 178, 179,

180; *Angels with Dirty Faces*,
141; *The Charge of the Light
Brigade*, 141, 178

Dailey, Dan, 76; *When My Baby
Smiles at Me*, 76
Dangerous, 3, 104, 105
Dark at the Top of the Stairs, 81,
126, 224
Dark Victory, 3, 104, 105, 138,
153, 211, 212, 214, 216
Darwell, Jane, 5, 67, 122, 149,
154
Davies, Delmar, 177; *Broken
Arrow*, 177; *Cowboy*, 177; *3:10
to Yuma*, 177
Davies, Marion, 147, 159
Davis, Bette, 3, 5, 16, 19, 20, 21,
54–55, 59, 63, 78, 84, 102,
104–106, 107, 109, 112, 125,
127, 156, 165, 181, 185, 212,
214–15, 216, 219, 224, 228;
All This and Heaven Too, 214;
and Eva Le Gallienne, 104; *The
Old Maid*, 214, 215; *The Private
Lives of Elizabeth and Essex*,
214
Day, Doris, 78, 119, 201;
Calamity Jane, 201; *Pajama
Game*, 201
Days of Heaven, 101, 223; Brooke
Adams, 223; Nestor Almendros,
223; Terence Malick, 223;
Linda Mans, 223; Sam Shepard,
223
Days of Wine and Roses, 84, 127,
221, 225
Dead End, 59, 81, 121, 122, 140,
143, 185, 221, 223; Richard
Day, 223; Leo Gorcey, 223;
Huntz Hall, 223; Billy Halop,
223; Bobby Jordan, 223; Sidney
Kingsley, 223; Marjorie Main,
223
Dean, James, 3, 7, 13, 15, 16, 20,
21, 57, 83, 86, 90, 93–95, 97,
98, 101, 142, 158, 177, 220,
223, 224, 227; and Pier Angeli,
90; biographer David Dalton,
95; and Vic Damone, 90
Death of a Salesman, 61–62, 63,
84, 86, 88, 120, 122, 135, 222,
224; Arthur Miller, 120
Deer Hunter, The, 13, 99, 100,
128, 178, 180, 182
De Havilland, Olivia, 3, 16, 19,
20, 21, 66, 92, 106–107, 178,
179, 212, 216, 217, 225
Deliverance, 180; John Boorman,
180
DeMille, Cecil B., 132, 135, 140,
143; *Cleopatra*, 132; *The
Crusades*, 132; *The King of
Kings*, 132; "Lux Radio
Theatre," 132; *North-West
Mounted Police*, 132; *The
Plainsman*, 132; *Reap the Wild
Wind*, 132, 180; *Samson and
Delilah*, 132; *The Sign of the
Cross*, 132; *The Squaw Man*,
132; *The Ten Commandments*,
132; *Unconquered*, 132; *Union
Pacific*, 132
DeNiro, Robert, 13, 57, 99–100,
101, 181, 182; Stella Adler and

Lee Strasberg, 100; *The Bronx Bull*, 100; *The Last Tycoon*, 99
Derek, John, 92; *Bo Derek*, 92
Dern, Bruce, 89, 100, 219; *Black Sunday*, 89; *The King of Marvin Gardens*, 100; *Smile*, 100
Destry Rides Again, 118, 177; Max Brand, 177; Allen Jenkins, 177; George Marshall, 177; Joe Pasternak, 177
Detective Story, 121, 126, 141, 143, 186; Sidney Kingsley, 186
Devane, William, 98
Devine, Andy, 12, 152
Dial M for Murder, 10, 130
Diary of Anne Frank, 120, 142, 221, 225
Dieterle, William, 135, 136, 140; *Dr. Ehrlich's Magic Bullet*, 136
Dietrich, Marlene, 102, 106, 111, 117–118, 177; and Noel Coward, John Gilbert, Emil Jannings, Erich Maria Remarque, Josef von Sternberg, 117; *The Blue Angel*, 117; *Morocco*, 117; *The Spoilers*, 118
Dinner at Eight, 77, 141, 214
Disney, Walt, 9, 10, 14, 167, 203; *Bambi*, 203; *Cinderella*, 203; *Dumbo*, 203; *Fantasia*, 10, 14, 167; *Pinocchio*, 203; *Sleeping Beauty*, 203; *20,000 Leagues Under the Sea*, 203
Dmytryk, Edward, 136, 182; *Murder My Sweet*, 136; *A Walk on the Wild Side*, 136
Doctor Zhivago, 211
Dog Day Afternoon, 99, 139, 183, 187
Donat, Robert, 12, 56, 65, 68
Donen, Stanley, 140, 169, 198; *On the Town*, 198; *Seven Brides for Seven Brothers*, 198
Donlevy, Brian, 88, 178, 182, 194; *The Glass Key*, 88; *The Great McGinty*, 88, 194; *Two Years Before the Mast*, 88
Double Indemnity, 7, 81, 143, 183
Douglas, Kirk, 7, 69, 70, 155, 177, 180, 186, 203, 227
Douglas, Melvyn, 88, 96, 177–78, 180, 194, 224; *The Best Man*, 88; *Do Not Go Gentle into That Good Night*, 88
Dr. Strangelove, 14, 133, 188, 189, 195–96; Peter Sellers, 196
Dracula, 11, 207, 208; Bela Lugosi, 11, 207
Dressler, Marie, 114, 214; *Min and Bill*, 114
Dreyfuss, Richard, 76, 181, 197
Dunaway, Faye, 127, 128, 171, 187, 227
Dunne, Irene, 7, 74, 111, 114, 115, 193, 216; *Magnificent Obsession*, 216; *Show Boat*, 114
Dunnock, Mildred, 92, 122, 224
Duvall, Robert, 89; *The Great Santini*, 89

Eagle, The, 133; Vilma Banky, 133; Rudolph Valentino, 133
East of Eden, 3, 13, 15, 21, 86, 93, 94, 95, 122, 141, 142, 158, 223; James Basevi, 158; Malcolm Bart, 158; Paul Osborne, 158; Leonard Rosenman, 158; John Steinbeck, 93, 94
Easter Parade, 124, 169
Easy Rider, 14, 101, 222, 224; Peter Fonda, 224
Ebsen, Buddy, 165, 166
Edwards, James, 98
Elmer Gantry, 20, 63, 85, 126, 135, 223, 227; Shirley Jones, 20
Empire Strikes Back, The, 98, 203, 210
Enchanted Cottage, The, 126, 138
Exorcist, The, 11, 128, 140, 203, 209–10; Linda Blair, 209

Fairbanks, Douglas, 79, 134, 179
Fairbanks, Douglas Jr., 117, 178, 179
Falk, Peter, 83; *Murder Inc.*, 83; *Pocketful of Miracles*, 83
Farewell to Arms, A, 88, 211
Farrow, John, 136, 182; *The Big Clock*, 136; *The Old Man and the Sea*, 136; *Two Years Before the Mast*, 136; *Wake Island*, 136, 182
Farrow, Mia, 136, 209, 223
Faye, Alice, 119, 124, 144, 179
Ferrer, Jose, 3, 68, 69–70, 182, 214, 227
Field, Betty, 7, 111, 125, 177, 213; *Tomorrow the World*, 125; *The Southerner*, 125
Field, Sally, 129; "The Flying Nun," 129
Fields, W. C., 8, 71, 73, 74, 161, 162, 165, 188, 190–91, 218; *The Bank Dick*, 162; *Never Give a Sucker an Even Break*, 190; *Poppy*, 190; *You Can't Cheat an Honest Man*, 190
Fitzgerald, Barry, 151, 185, 194
Fitzgerald, Geraldine, 122, 164, 165, 212
Five Easy Pieces, 101, 128, 140, 171, 172, 221, 224; Karen Black, 128, 172; Robert Rafelson, 140
Flaherty, Robert, 142
Fleming, Victor, 140, 166, 180
Fletcher, Louise, 128–29; *Thieves Like Us*, 129
Flying Down to Rio, 119, 168; Dolores Del Rio, 168; Gene Raymond, 168
Flynn, Errol, 52, 54, 55, 78, 79, 90, 105, 139, 178–79, 180; marriages, 78
Fonda, Henry, 3, 5, 15, 20, 57, 65, 66–67, 70, 91, 101, 107, 125, 126, 144, 148, 154, 175, 177, 194, 196, 215, 227; *Young Lincoln*, 227
Fonda, Jane, 16, 19, 20, 21, 107, 128, 177, 219, 220, 225, 226; *Julia*, 226
Fontaine, Joan, 15, 70, 131, 183, 219
Fontanne, Lynn and Alfred Lunt, 107; *The Guardsman*, 107

For Whom the Bell Tolls, 85, 133, 211
Ford, Glenn, 3, 80, 81, 223
Ford, John, 12, 19, 65, 66, 67, 134, 136–37, 140, 143–44, 148, 149, 151, 152, 153, 175–76, 180, 182, 194, 196, 225; *Cheyenne Autumn*, 176; *Four Sons*, 143; *The Iron Horse*, 143; *The Man Who Shot Liberty Valance*, 144, 176; *The Lost Patrol*, 144; *Rio Grande*, 144; *Three Godfathers*, 144
Fort Apache, 12, 144, 176
42nd Street, 14, 199–200; Bebe Daniels, 200; Ruby Keeler, 199–200
Fosse, Robert, 140, 169, 170
Four Daughters, 84, 89, 90, 141; Priscilla Lane, 90
Fraker, William, 177; *Monty Walsh*, 177
Frankenheimer, John, 139, 184, 185; *All Fall Down*, 139; *Grand Prix*, 139; *The Gypsy Moths*, 139; *The Iceman Cometh*, 139
Frankenstein, 11, 207; *Bride of Frankenstein*, 207; Boris Karloff, 11, 207; James Whale, 207
Freed, Arthur, 165, 166, 169
French Connection, The, 140, 183; William Friedkin, 140
Friendly Persuasion, 126, 143, 211
From Here to Eternity, 3, 5, 13, 15, 20, 21, 90, 92, 109, 112, 113, 142, 182, 198, 220, 221; James Jones, 92, 182; Aldo Ray, 92
Front Page, The, 88, 142, 146, 193
Fugitive, The, 12, 144
Funny Girl, 19, 140, 202

Gable, Clark, 3, 4, 12, 15, 20, 21, 52, 53, 54, 55, 56, 60, 63, 65, 68, 76, 93, 101, 105, 112, 116, 120, 121, 165, 166, 177, 179, 182, 211, 219, 220, 228; *Parnell*, 55
Garbo, Greta, 3, 7, 16, 20, 21, 84, 110–11, 117, 133, 138, 165, 194, 214, 219, 220; *Anna Karenina*, 110, 133; and Cecil Beaton, John Gilbert, Mauritz Stiller, 110
Gardner, Ava, 118, 186, 210; *Barefoot Contessa*, 118; *Mogambo*, 118; and Artie Shaw, 118
Garfield, John, 7, 57, 89–90, 91, 92, 93, 99, 101, 179, 180, 184, 206, 219; *Between Two Worlds*, 206; *Dust Be My Destiny*, 90; *Force of Evil*, 90; *Peer Gynt*, 90; and Edith Piaf, 90
Garland, Judy, 7, 10, 16, 18, 20, 21, 78, 93, 107, 111, 123–25, 141, 165, 166, 167, 169, 198, 202, 227; *A Child is Waiting*, 124; marriages, 124
Garson, Greer, 81, 107, 212, 214, 227; *Blossoms in the Dust*, 81,

214; *Mrs. Parkington*, 214; *The Valley of Decision*, 214
Gaslight, 79, 106, 120, 122, 141, 183
Gay Divorcee, The, 10, 76, 119, 168, 198, 200
Gaynor, Janet, 78, 110, 116, 124, 212, 219, 227; *Street Angel*, 110, 212; *Sunrise*, 110, 212
Gazzara, Ben, 83; *The Strange One*, 83
General, The, 7, 14, 15, 73, 160–61, 188, 189; Ephraim Katz, 160–61
Gentlemen's Agreement, 89, 90, 121, 126, 142, 221
Gere, Richard, 99, 101, 187, 223; *American Gigolo*, 101; *Bloodbrothers*, 101; *Yanks*, 101
Giant, 83, 95, 140, 142, 177
Gigi, 19, 141, 198, 201; Leslie Caron, 201; Hermione Gingold, 201; Louis Jourdan, 201
Gleason, Jackie, 96, 181
Gleason, James, 88, 163
Goddard, Paulette, 180; *Reap the Wild Wind*, 180
Godfather, The, 89, 99, 140, 170, 183
Godfather, Part II, The, 15, 99, 140, 183, 187; John Cazale, 99
Going My Way, 76, 142
Golden Boy, 86, 87, 88, 90, 123, 138, 145; Luther Adler, 90
Goldwyn, Sam, 54, 132, 165, 223
Gone With the Wind, 3, 4, 12, 14, 15, 16, 20, 21, 54–56, 65, 68, 85, 105, 107, 137, 153, 164, 166, 198, 211, 212, 216, 220
Goodbye Girl, The, 76, 129, 188, 197
Goodbye, Mr. Chips, 12, 56, 65, 68, 133, 214
Gordon, Ruth, 20, 122, 194–95; *Harold and Maude*, 194; *Inside Daisy Clover*, 122; *Where's Poppa?*, 194
Goulding, Edmund, 138, 140, 212, 214; *The Dawn Patrol*, 138; *Nightmare Alley*, 138
Grable, Betty, 119, 186
Graduate, The, 14, 101, 119, 126, 140, 171, 172, 188; Buck Henry, Lawrence Turman, Calder Willingham, 172
Grahame, Gloria, 122, 139
Grand Hotel, 110, 138, 140, 211, 214
Granger, Stewart, 180; *King Solomon's Mines*, 181
Grant, Cary, 7, 8, 15, 20, 74, 75, 76, 78, 82, 102, 114, 178, 181, 183, 193, 202, 227; *Arsenic and Old Lace*, 193; *Holiday*, 193; *My Favorite Wife*, 193; *People Will Talk*, 193; *Topper*, 193
Grant, Lee, 121; *The Landlord*, 121; *Voyage of the Damned*, 121
Grapes of Wrath, The, 3, 5, 12, 14, 15, 21, 65, 66, 67, 68, 122, 140, 144, 146, 148–49, 151, 221, 223, 228; Nunnally Johnson, 148, 149; Day and Mark Lee Kirk, 149; Russell

Simpson, 149; John Steinbeck, 67, 148; Zeffie Tilbury, 149
Grapewin, Charles, 149, 165
Great Gatsby, The, 83, 100
Great White Hope, The, 98, 107, 129, 146
Great Ziegfeld, The, 75, 111, 140, 198; Robert Leonard, 140
Greatest Performances, The (results of the author's poll of fans and critics), 48–51
Greatest Show on Earth, The, 12, 15, 19, 132, 140, 173, 178
Greenstreet, Sidney, 88, 156
Griffith, D. W., 139, 143; *The Birth of a Nation*, 143
Griffith, Hugh, 20
Guess Who's Coming to Dinner, 102, 103, 114, 135, 188
Gunga Din, 142, 173, 178, 182; Rudyard Kipling, 178
Guns of Navarone, The, 173, 182; J. Lee Thompson, 182
Guy Named Joe, A, 114
Gwenn, Edmund, 20, 63, 74, 205
Gypsy, 114, 119, 120, 202

H. M. Pulman, Esq., 133
Hackman, Gene, 171, 187, 224
Haley, Jack, 10, 18, 124, 166, 202
Hamlet, 3, 6, 12, 68, 126, 140, 152, 211
Hardwicke, Sir Cedric, 180
Hardy, Oliver, 8, 74, 189–90
Harlow, Jean, 166, 181, 214; *Saratoga*, 166
Harris, Julie, 94, 111, 158, 209
Harrison, Rex, 76, 115, 199, 202
Harvey, Laurence, 20, 184
Hathaway, Henry, 135, 177, 178; *Call Northside 777*, 136; *Desert Fox*, 136; *The House on 92nd Street*, 136; *Kiss of Death*, 136
Hawkins, Jack, 20
Hawks, Howard, 61, 92, 116, 136–37, 142, 175, 181, 185, 193, 194, 209; *Ball of Fire*, 136, 194; *The Big Sky*, 175; *The Big Sleep*, 136; *The Crowd Roars*, 136; *The Dawn Patrol*, 136, 181; *Only Angels Have Wings*, 136, 181; *Rio Bravo*, 136, 175, 182; *The Thing*, 209
Hayes, Helen, 19, 107, 120, 165; *The Sin of Madelon Claudet*, 107, 120
Hayward, Leland, 103, 125, 217
Hayward, Susan, 108, 178, 185; as Lillian Roth, 108; marriage to Jess Barker, 108
Hayworth, Rita, 109, 118–19, 138, 181, 213, 219; *Cover Girl*, 119; *Gilda*, 119, 219; *My Gal Sal*, 119; *The Story on Page One*, 119; *You Were Never Lovelier*, 119; *You'll Never Get Rich*, 119; marriage to Aly Khan, 109, 119; marriage to Dick Haymes, 119
Heaven Can Wait, 80, 83, 84, 89, 98, 133, 135, 188, 203, 206, 211; Buck Henry, 98
Hecht, Ben, 61; and Charles MacArthur, 164, 165, 178

Heckart, Eileen, 122; *The Bad Seed*, 122; *Butterflies are Free*, 122
Heflin, Van, 82, 90, 117, 174, 227; *Patterns*, 82, 227
Heiress, The, 16, 21, 90, 92, 106, 107, 143, 211, 212
Henreid, Paul, 3, 57, 58, 59, 81; *Now, Voyager*, 81
Hepburn, Audrey, 13, 20, 108, 114, 184, 194, 199, 227; *Wait Until Dark*, 184
Hepburn, Katharine, 16, 19, 20, 21, 55, 57, 63, 78, 82, 102–104, 107, 114, 151, 152, 193, 202, 214, 219, 228; *Alice Adams*, 211, 213, 214; *The Lake*, 102; *Morning Glory*, 102, 214; *Summertime*, 214; and Robert McKnight, 103; and Dorothy Parker, 102
Here Comes Mr. Jordan, 80, 81, 88, 98, 188, 203, 206; Edward Everett Horton, 80
High and the Mighty, The, 121, 134, 141
High Noon, 3, 12, 14, 65, 142, 146, 173–74, 182, 228; Carl Foreman, 173; Katy Jurado, 174; Otto Kruger, 174
High Sierra, 59, 63, 125, 139, 141, 183, 185
Hill, George Roy, 140
Hiller, Wendy, 20, 213
His Girl Friday, 75, 114, 116, 136, 193
Hitchcock, Alfred, 10, 19, 98, 130–32, 134, 135, 140, 141, 142, 143, 146, 157, 168, 183, 209, 228; *The Birds*, 10, 130, 209; *Foreign Correspondent*, 130, 140, 183; *The Lady Vanishes*, 130; *The Lodger*, 130; *The Man Who Knew Too Much*, 130; *Notorious*, 130, 183; *The Paradine Case*, 130, 183; *Rope*, 130; *Saboteur*, 130, 183; *The Thirty-Nine Steps*, 130; *Under Capricorn*, 130; *The Wrong Man*, 130, 183
Hoffman, Dustin, 13, 15, 20, 21, 57, 100, 101, 172, 177, 218, 227, 228; *Straight Time*, 101
Holbrook, Hal, 98; as Mark Twain, 98; *The Minnesota Strip*, 98
Hold Back the Dawn, 79, 106, 138, 211, 216, 217
Holden, William, 13, 14, 66, 70, 86, 87, 90, 92, 95, 109, 157, 175, 182, 194, 205, 213, 219, 225, 227; *Love Is a Many-Splendored Thing*, 219
Holiday, 102, 141
Holliday, Judy, 20, 21, 106, 109, 114, 194
Holm, Celeste, 89, 121
Holt, Tim, 58, 153, 222
Home of the Brave, 135, 222, 225
Hopkins, Miriam, 109, 111, 225
Houseman, John, 20, 137, 138, 227
How Green Was My Valley, 12, 20, 68, 81, 137, 144, 146, 221
Howard, Leslie, 59, 104, 105, 106, 185, 205, 218–19;

Outward Bound, 205
Hucksters, The, 112
Hud, 88, 95, 96, 97, 141, 177–78; Patricia Neal, 177, 178
Hudson, Rock, 95, 177
Hughes, Howard, 78, 103, 118, 181; *Hell's Angels*, 181
Humoresque, 90, 136, 219; Fannie Hurst, 219
Hunchback of Notre Dame, The, 54, 136, 143, 145, 206; Lon Chaney, 206
Hunter, Kim, 56, 57, 157
Hurricane, The, 85, 144, 180; Jon Hall, 180; Dorothy Lamour, 180
Husbands, 83
Hustler, The, 13, 95, 96, 97, 127, 135, 181
Huston, John, 84, 140, 141–42, 146, 151, 152, 156, 157, 177, 180, 182, 183, 185, 187; *The Asphalt Jungle*, 141, 183, 185; *Beat the Devil* (with Truman Capote), 141, 142, 185; *Fat City*, 141, 146, 180; *The Man Who Would Be King*, 141, 178; *Moby Dick*, 141, 142; *Reflections in a Golden Eye*, 141, 142; *The Roots of Heaven*, 141
Huston, Walter, 84, 152, 223; *The Devil and Daniel Webster*, 84; *Knickerbocker Holiday*, 84

I Am a Fugitive from a Chain Gang, 11, 14, 15, 62, 136, 155–56, 183, 185; Robert Burns, 155; Sheridan Gibney, 155; Helen Vinson, 62
I Never Promised You a Rose Garden, 128, 222, 225; Kathleen Quinlan, 128
I Never Sang for My Father, 88, 146, 222, 224
I Remember Mama, 114, 142
In the Heat of the Night, 15, 97, 140, 171, 183, 186
Informer, The, 3, 12, 14, 52, 140, 144, 146, 149–51, 183, 216, 221; Joseph August, 149; Wallace Ford, 150; Preston Foster, 150; Margot Grahame, 150; Charles Kirk, 149; Una O'Connor, 150; Liam O'Flaherty, 149; Van Nest Polglase, 149; Cliff Reid, 149; Max Steiner, 149, 216
Inherit the Wind, 63, 88, 135, 221
Interiors, 76, 122, 129
Intermezzo, 106, 218–19
Ireland, John, 175, 182
It Happened One Night, 20, 54, 76, 105, 109, 114, 143, 188, 220
Ives, Burl, 86, 224

Jackson, Glenda, 106, 107, 129, 194, 197
Jaffe, Sam, 178, 203, 204
Jagger, Dean, 85, 182; *Bad Day at Black Rock*, 85; *Brigham Young*, 85; *The Eternal Sea*, 85; *Twelve O'Clock High*, 85
Jaws, 11, 89, 173, 181; *Jaws II*, 181

Jewison, Norman, 140, 181; *The Cincinnati Kid*, 98, 181
Jezebel, 3, 104, 105, 122, 141, 143, 214, 215, 216
Johnny Belinda, 12, 82, 84, 107, 108, 121, 136, 211, 213, 216, 221, 225
Johnny Eager, 78, 82, 136
Johnson, Van, 114, 182, 197
Jolson, Al, 7, 14, 199; *The Jazz Singer*, 7, 14, 199; *The Jolson Story*, 199
Jones, James Earl, 98, 107
Jones, Jennifer, 20, 76, 106, 185, 206, 210–11, 219, 227
Judgment at Nuremberg, 13, 20, 63, 90, 93, 118, 124, 135, 221, 225

Kahn, Madeline, 122
Kaufman, George S., 156, 162, 214
Kazan, Elia, 19, 57, 90, 91, 93, 94, 100, 138, 141, 142, 143, 157, 158, 223, 227; Actor's Studio, 92, 93, 95, 98, 99, 142; *America, America*, 142; *A Face in the Crowd*, 142, 227; *Panic in the Streets*, 142; *Viva Zapata*, 142, 145, 181
Keaton, Buster, 7, 8, 15, 73, 160, 161, 188; *The Cameraman*, 73
Keaton, Diane, 8, 76, 114, 129, 170, 187, 193, 219
Kelly, Gene, 7, 8, 10, 76, 119, 169, 171, 198; *Anchors Aweigh*, 76, 169, 198, 201
Kelly, Grace, 109, 124, 131, 173, 201, 224; *Country Girl*, 109, 124, 221, 224; marriage, 109
Kennedy, Arthur, 7, 83–84, 223, 225; *Bright Victory*, 84, 225; *The Glass Menagerie*, 84; *Trial*, 84
Kerr, Deborah, 7, 13, 16, 17, 20, 21, 107, 109, 111–13, 114, 122, 180, 201, 209, 213–14, 219, 220, 227; *The Adventurers*, 112; *Edward My Son*, 112; *Heaven Knows Mr. Allison*, 112; *The Innocents*, 209; *Major Barbara*, 112; marriage, 112
Kerr, John, 112, 219
Key Largo, 119, 121, 141, 185
Kibbee, Guy, 163, 164, 200, 205
Kiley, Richard, 98, 187, 202; *The Little Prince*, 98; *Man of La Mancha*, 98, 202
King and I, The, 112, 113, 201, 202
King, Henry, 135, 179, 180, 182; *The Gunfighter*, 135, 177; *In Old Chicago*, 135, 179–80; *Jesse James*, 135, 177; *Stanley and Livingstone*, 135, 180; *Twelve O'Clock High*, 135, 182; *Wilson*, 135
King Kong, 11, 14, 146, 208
Kings Row, 80, 81, 84, 125, 133, 211, 212, 213; Henry Bellamann, 213
Kitty Foyle, 109, 119, 133, 211, 219
Klute, 21, 107, 140

232

Knight, Arthur (*The Liveliest Art*), 73, 132
Knute Rockne—All-American, 63, 64, 81, 138, 181
Kotto, Yaphet, 98; *Brubaker*, 98; *Report to the Commissioner*, 98
Kramer, Stanley, 135, 142, 173, 182, 196, 214; *The Defiant Ones*, 135; *Home of the Brave*, 135; *On the Beach*, 135; *The Wild One*, 135
Kramer vs. Kramer, 101, 128, 129, 211, 218, 221; Justin Henry, 218
Kubrick, Stanley, 133, 141, 142, 155, 167, 168, 175, 195, 210; *A Clockwork Orange*, 133; *Barry Lyndon*, 133; *The Killing*, 133, 186

Ladd, Alan, 82-83, 117, 174, 177, 186; marriage, 83
Laemmle, Carl, 104, 143
Lahr, Bert, 165, 202
Lake, Veronica, 83, 186
Lamarr, Hedy, 79, 90, 106, 216, 219
Lancaster, Burt, 20, 57, 63, 92, 113, 123, 185, 213, 220, 224, 226, 227
Lanchester, Elsa, 53, 122; *Baby Doll*, 122
Lang, Fritz, 138, 210; *The Blue Gardenia*, 138; *Man Hunt*, 138; *Metropolis*, 210; *The Ministry of Fear*, 138; *Scarlet Street*, 138; *The Woman in the Window*, 138
Lansbury, Angela, 122, 184; *Portrait of Dorian Gray*, 122
Last Picture Show, The, 3, 128, 140, 221, 224
Laughton, Charles, 3, 4, 12, 15, 21, 52-54, 60, 78, 101, 179, 180, 206, 228; *Night of the Hunter*, 184; *Ruggles of Red Gap*, 184
Laura, 81, 85, 135, 141, 183, 184
Laurel, Stan, 7, 8, 74, 189-90
Laurie, Piper, 127, 181; *Francis Goes to the Races*, 127; *Son of Ali Baba*, 127
Lawrence of Arabia, 20, 178
Lean, David, 141; *Summertime*, 141
Leigh, Janet, 131, 132, 157, 184
Leigh, Vivien, 16, 20, 21, 55, 56, 57, 105, 106, 107, 157, 158, 165, 211, 212, 214, 220
Leisen, Mitchell, 138, 217; *Lady in the Dark*, 138
Lemmon, Jack, 15, 19, 20, 21, 63, 67, 97, 194, 196, 225, 227; *Save the Tiger*, 227
Lenny, 100, 101, 128, 140, 222, 227; Lenny Bruce, 227; Valerie Perrine, 128, 227
LeRoy, Mervyn, 66, 136, 140, 155, 165, 179, 184, 185, 196, 212; *Anthony Adverse*, 136, 179; *Thirty Seconds over Tokyo*, 136
Les Miserables, 54, 142, 173, 179
Life of Emile Zola, The, 20, 62, 136, 140, 221

Life with Father, 75, 188
Lifeboat, 107, 130, 141
Light That Failed, The, 125, 134
Lion in Winter, The, 19, 102
Little Caesar, 11, 14, 59, 60, 61, 134, 136, 183, 184
Little Foxes, The, 12, 122, 143, 221, 222, 224; Lillian Hellman, 224
Little Women, 141, 211, 214; Louisa May Alcott, 214
Lives of a Bengal Lancer, 136, 173, 178; Richard Cromwell, 178; Douglass Dumbrille, 178; C. Aubrey Smith, 178
Lloyd, Frank, 52, 53, 140, 142; *The Divine Lady*, 142; *Drag*, 142; *If I Were King*, 142; *Weary River*, 142
Lloyd, Harold, 73, 188; *Feet First*, 188; *Mad Wednesday*, 188; *Movie Crazy*, 188; *Speedy*, 188
Logan, Josh, 65, 120, 196, 213, 225
Lolita, 78, 86, 87; Sue Lyon, 87
Lollobrigida, Gina, 185
Lombard, Carole, 55, 78, 109, 111, 114, 116, 193, 212; *A Perfect Crime*, 116
Lonely Are the Brave, 127, 177; David Miller, 177
Long Voyage Home, The, 12, 85, 144, 151, 173, 176, 178, 180, 182, 221, 222, 225; Ian Hunter, 151; Eugene O'Neill, 151; John Qualen, 151; Joe Sawyer, 151
Looking for Mr. Goodbar, 98, 101, 127, 129, 135, 187
Lorre, Peter, 3, 57, 59, 88, 143, 156, 185, 203, 208; *M*, 88
Lost Horizon, 11, 143, 202, 203-204, 206
Lost Weekend, The, 14, 143, 221, 224
Love Affair, 114, 153, 193, 216
Love with the Proper Stranger, 98, 120
Loy, Myrna, 7, 8, 109, 111, 114, 117, 193
Lubitsch, Ernst, 133, 135, 140, 193, 194; *Broken Lullaby*, 133; *The Love Parade*, 133, 125, 193; *Monte Carlo*, 133, 193; *The Patriot*, 133; *The Smiling Lieutenant*, 133, 193; *To Be or Not to Be*, 133, 135; *Trouble in Paradise*, 193
Lucas, George, 139, 140, 210, 224
Lukas, Paul, 12, 59, 203
Lumet, Sidney, 139, 184; *Long Day's Journey into Night*, 139; *12 Angry Men*, 139
Lupino, Ida, 7, 111, 125, 180; *Devotion*, 125; *The Hard Way*, 125; *In Our Time*, 125; *Moontide*, 125
Lynn, Jeffrey, 90

MacLaine, Shirley, 7, 16, 20, 21, 98, 111, 123, 124, 170; *Being There*, 123; *Irma LaDouce*, 123; *Pajama Game*, 123

MacMurray, Fred, 7, 81, 182, 184, 213; *Captain Eddy*, 81; *Miracle of the Bells*, 81; June Haver, 81
Madame Curie, 81, 136, 214, 221, 227
Magnificent Ambersons, The, 3, 15, 82, 121, 135, 137, 138, 182, 221, 222-23; Stanley Cortez, 222
Malden, Karl, 56, 57, 92, 119, 127, 157, 181
Maltese Falcon, The, 3, 11, 12, 14, 57, 59, 88, 140, 141, 156, 183, 185; Ricardo Cortez, 156; Dashiell Hammett, 156; Hal Wallis, 156
Mamoulian, Rouben, 110, 138, 181, 223; *Applause*, 138; *Becky Sharp*, 138; *City Streets*, 223; *Love Me Tonight*, 138; *Porgy*, 138; *Silk Stockings*, 138
Man for All Seasons, A, 13, 89, 142, 211; Paul Scofield, 13
Manchurian Candidate, The, 122, 139, 183, 184
Manhattan, 76, 128, 193; Mariel Hemingway, 193
Mankiewicz, Joseph, 140, 141, 142, 157, 182, 184; *Five Fingers*, 141, 142, 182; *Julius Caesar*, 142; *A Letter to Three Wives*, 140, 142; *People Will Talk*, 142
Mann, Anthony, 177; *Winchester '73*, 177
March, Fredric, 19, 62, 179, 205, 224, 227; *Death Takes a Holiday*, 205; *Dr. Jekyll and Mr. Hyde*, 19, 206
Marty, 13, 95, 221
Marvin, Lee, 177, 224
Marx Brothers, 7, 8, 74, 161, 162, 188, 191-92; *Animal Crackers*, 191; *The Cocoanuts*, 191; *A Day at the Races*, 191; *Duck Soup*, 191; *Horse Feathers*, 191; *Monkey Business*, 191; *A Night at the Opera*, 161-62, 191
Mason, James, 7, 78, 86, 87, 182, 203, 227; *The Desert Rats*, 86; *Georgy Girl*, 86; *Odd Man Out*, 86
Mason, Marsha, 7, 111, 129, 197; *Chapter Two*, 129; *Promises in the Dark*, 129; Neil Simon, 129
Massey, Raymond, 7, 86, 94, 158, 179, 180, 223, 227
Mature, Victor, 119, 186
May, Elaine, 98, 197; *The Heartbreak Kid*, 197
Mayer, Louis B., 52, 54, 55, 110, 124, 165, 166, 200, 227
McCabe and Mrs. Miller, 98, 175
McCarey, Leo, 140, 142, 193; *The Bells of St. Mary's*, 142; *Good Sam*, 142
McCarthy, Kevin, 92, 209; *Invasion of the Body Snatchers*, 209
McCrea, Joel, 81, 177, 194, 223, 225; *Come and Get It*, 81; *Ride the High Country*, 81; *Sullivan's Travels*, 81; *The Tall Stranger*, 81; *These Three*, 81, 225

McDaniel, Hattie, 56, 107
McGraw, Ali, 219; *Love Story*, 219
McGuire, Dorothy, 57, 111, 126, 219, 224; *Claudia*, 126; *Till the End of Time*, 126; John Swope, 126
McLaglen, Victor, 12, 52, 144, 149, 150, 178, 194
McQueen, Steve, 95, 97-98, 181; *Bullitt*, 98; *The Thomas Crown Affair*, 98; *Wanted, Dead or Alive*, 98
Mean Streets, 99, 140, 223
Meek, Donald, 150, 152
Meet John Doe, 65, 68, 123, 143, 162-63, 193, 221, 227
Meet Me in St. Louis, 124, 141, 165, 202
Menjou, Adolph, 88, 155
Meredith, Burgess, 7, 85, 86, 176, 180, 182; *Day of the Locust*, 86; *Winterset*, 86
Merkel, Una, 177, 200
Merrill, Gary, 5, 106
Middle of the Night, 127
Midnight Cowboy, 13, 15, 21, 101, 221
Milestone, Lewis, 140, 142, 176, 182; *The General Died at Dawn*, 142; *Two Arabian Nights*, 142
Milland, Ray, 178, 180
Minnelli, Liza, 124, 141, 169, 170, 202
Minnelli, Vincente, 124, 140, 169, 198, 227; *Lust for Life*, 141
Miracle on 34th Street, 63, 120, 140, 203, 205; Maureen O'Hara, 205; John Payne, 205; George Seaton, 140, 205
Miracle Worker, The, 21, 126, 135, 141
Misfits, The, 90, 93, 120, 121, 141, 142, 173, 175, 177; Arthur Miller, 177
Mister Roberts, 65, 66, 67, 75, 136, 140, 173, 194
Mitchell, Thomas, 85, 151, 152, 153, 174, 180, 181, 205
Mitchum, Robert, 17, 83, 113, 182, 184, 214; *Cape Fear*, 83; *The Night of the Hunter*, 83, 184
Mix, Tom, 134, 177
Monroe, Marilyn, 20, 93, 111, 120, 121, 127, 177, 185, 194, 220; Joe DiMaggio, 120
Montgomery, Robert, 52, 80, 81, 206; *Night Must Fall*, 81, 184; Elizabeth Montgomery, 81
Moorehead, Agnes, 7, 111, 112, 121, 147, 213, 222; *How the West Was Won*, 112; *Hush, Hush Sweet Charlotte*, 121; *Mrs. Parkington*, 121
The More the Merrier, 81, 116, 142, 188, 194
Morgan, Frank, 88, 165; *The Affairs of Cellini*, 88
Morgan, Helen, 138
Moriarity, Michael, 98, 181
Morley, Robert, 88, 185; *They're Killing the Great Chefs of Europe*, 88
Moulin Rouge, 3, 12, 68, 70, 141, 221, 227

Mourning Becomes Electra, 114, 115, 116

Mr. Deeds Goes to Town, 65, 116, 140, 143, 188, 193

Mr. Smith Goes to Washington, 3, 12, 63–65, 68, 84, 85, 116, 143, 153, 163–64, 188, 193, 221, 227; Alben Barkley, 164; Eugene Pallette, 164

Mrs. Miniver, 81, 107, 122, 143, 211, 212, 214

Muni, Paul, 11, 15, 20, 61–63, 88, 101, 155, 181, 185, 227

Murder on the Orient Express, 106, 120, 139, 183, 184

Murphy, Audie, 177, 182

Mutiny on the Bounty, 3, 4, 12, 15, 20, 21, 52–54, 140, 142, 149, 178; 1962 remake, 52; Charles Nordoff and James Norman Hall, 52

My Darling Clementine, 12, 144, 175, 176

My Fair Lady, 76, 108, 141, 198, 199, 202

My Man Godfrey, 75, 116, 141, 188, 189; Gregory La Cava, 141

My Sister Eileen, 114, 115, 145, 188, 194; Janet Blair, 115

Naish, J. Carroll, 88, 178; *Life with Luigi*, 88; *A Medal for Benny*, 88; *Sahara*, 88

Naked City, The, 145

Nashville, 14, 140, 146, 188, 221, 223

National Velvet, 121, 133, 141, 218

Natwick, Mildred, 122; *Barefoot in the Park*, 122

Negulesco, Jean, 136, 213

Network, 20, 128, 139, 221, 227; Peter Finch, 20, 227

Newman, Paul, 6, 7, 11, 13, 15, 20, 21, 90, 93, 95, 96, 97, 98, 101, 127, 140, 142, 171–72, 177, 178, 213, 220, 224, 227; *The Left Handed Gun*, 95; *Slap Shot*, 181

Nichols, Dudley, 149, 150, 151

Nichols, Mike, 140, 172, 197; *Carnal Knowledge*, 101

Nicholson, Jack, 20, 21, 101, 128, 172, 187, 197, 224; *The Last Detail*, 101, 197; *The Passenger*, 101

Ninotchka, 88, 110, 133, 135, 140, 143, 153, 188, 189, 194

Niven, David, 20, 164, 178, 179, 182, 194, 213

Nolan, Lloyd, 3, 89; *A Hatful of Rain*, 89

Norma Rae, 129, 140, 221

North by Northwest, 10, 75, 130, 182, 183

Novak, Kim, 183, 213, 225

Nun's Story, The, 85, 142, 221, 222, 227

Oberon, Merle, 68, 125, 164, 165, 219, 225

O'Brien, Pat, 3, 63, 64, 181

O'Connell, Arthur, 88, 184, 213

O'Connor, Carroll, 98

Odets, Clifford, 70, 90, 111, 204, 227; *The Big Knife*, 227

Of Human Bondage, 3, 104–105, 126, 138, 214, 216

Of Mice and Men, 86, 125, 140, 142, 153, 173, 176–177; Granville Bates, 177; Roman Bohnen, 176; Lon Chaney Jr., 176; John Steinbeck, 176

Oliver, 20, 146, 198; Carol Reed, 198

Oliver, Edna Mae, 165, 218

Olivier, Laurence, 3, 6, 12, 19, 20, 21, 55, 63, 65, 68–69, 125, 126, 131, 140, 164, 165, 184, 219, 228

On the Waterfront, 20, 21, 56, 70, 86, 142, 198, 221

One-Eyed Jacks, 175

One Flew over the Cuckoo's Nest, 14, 21, 101, 129, 221

O'Neal, Ryan, 219, 223; Tatum O'Neal, 20

Operettas: Deanna Durbin, 200; Nelson Eddy, 200; Kathryn Grayson, 200; Mario Lanza, 200; Jeanette MacDonald, 176, 200; Grace Moore, 200; Lawrence Tibbett, 76

O'Sullivan, Maureen, 136, 180, 218

O'Toole, Peter, 7, 202

Our Town, 125, 126, 133, 203, 205, 223; Thornton Wilder, 205

Ox-Bow Incident, The, 81, 134, 140, 153–55, 173, 177, 182; Francis Ford, 154; Henry Morgan, 154; Lamar Trotti, 153; Walter Van Tilburg Clark, 153

Pacino, Al, 7, 15, 99, 101, 187; *Panic in Needle Park*, 99; *Scarecrow*, 99

Page, Geraldine, 7, 111, 122; *Hondo*, 122; *Summer and Smoke*, 122; *You're a Big Boy Now*, 122

Pakula, Alan J., 139, 140; *Comes a Horseman*, 140; *The Sterile Cuckoo*, 140

Paper Moon, 20, 122, 195

Parker, Eleanor, 126, 186; *Caged*, 126; *Interrupted Melody*, 126; *Pride of the Marines*, 126

Parsons, Estelle, 122, 171, 213

Paths of Glory, 133, 155, 173, 178, 182, 225

Pawnbroker, The, 15, 21, 69, 70, 97, 139, 222, 223; Rod Steiger, 223

Peck, Gregory, 89, 126, 177, 182, 183, 194, 210, 218; *On the Beach*, 210

Peckinpah, Sam, 139, 140, 175; *Junior Bonner*, 140, 175; *Major Dundee*, 140, 175; *Ride the High Country*, 140; *Straw Dogs*, 140

Penn, Arthur, 101, 135, 141, 177; *Alice's Restaurant*, 135, 141; *Little Big Man*, 101, 177

Penny Serenade, 114, 142, 216

Perkins, Anthony, 98, 131, 132, 157; *Desire under the Elms*, 98; *Fear Strikes Out*, 98; *Friendly*

Persuasion, 98; *Lovin' Molly*, 98; *Pretty Poison*, 98

Pete 'n' Tillie, 122, 188, 194

Peters, Jean, 181, 219

Petrified Forest, The, 11, 59, 183, 185

Peyton Place, 83, 118, 135, 202, 211, 223

Philadelphia Story, The, 12, 16, 21, 63, 67, 68, 75, 76, 82, 102, 141, 149, 188, 193; Donald Ogden Stewart, 149

Picnic, 88, 95, 114, 116, 211, 212, 213, 224, 225; William Inge, 213

Pidgeon, Walter, 81, 182, 214, 227

Pillow Talk, 119, 120

Pinky, 112, 121, 142; Jeanne Crain, 112

Place in the Sun, A, 12, 13, 90, 91, 92, 140, 142, 152, 157, 158, 211, 212, 220, 221, 227, 228; Theodore Dreiser's *An American Tragedy*, 92, 158

Poitier, Sidney, 98, 186, 201, 223

Polanski, Roman, 139, 187

Pollack, Sydney, 139, 141, 177

Poor Little Rich Girl, 124

Porgy and Bess, 201; Pearl Bailey, 201; Dorothy Dandridge, 201; Sammy Davis Jr., 201; Brock Peters, 201

Poseidon Adventure, The, 181

Postman Always Rings Twice, The, 89, 90, 118, 183, 184, 219; James M. Cain, 90, 184

Powell, Dick, 76–77, 199, 200, 227

Powell, William, 8, 67, 74, 75, 76, 116, 193, 196

Power, Tyrone, 3, 78, 79, 177, 179, 181, 218; *Nightmare Alley*, 78, 208; Sonja Henie, 78; marriages, 78

Preminger, Otto, 109, 135, 141, 184, 194, 225; *The Cardinal*, 135; *The Man with the Golden Arm*; 135, 225; *The Moon Is Blue*, 135, 194; Max Reinhardt, 135

Preston, Robert, 3, 81, 178, 180, 182, 186, 202, 224; *The Macomber Affair*, 81; *The Music Man*, 81, 202; *The Sundowners*, 81

Price, Vincent, 209; *The Fly*, 209; *The House of Usher*, 209; *House of Wax*, 209; *The Pit and the Pendulum*, 209; *The Raven*, 209

Pride of the Yankees, 122, 133, 181, 227; Lou Gehrig, 181, 227; Babe Ruth, 181

Private Life of Henry VIII, The, 53, 54, 221

Psycho, 10, 98, 130, 131, 132, 141, 157, 168, 183, 209; Robert Block, 132; John Gavin, 132; Joseph Stefano, 132

Public Enemy, 2, 11, 14, 59–60, 61, 134, 183, 185; Mae Clarke, 2, 59–60

Queen Christina, 138, 165

Quiet Man, The, 12, 140, 144, 188, 194

Quinn, Anthony, 19, 154, 181, 182

Rachel, Rachel, 97, 122, 140, 211, 213

Raft, George, 57, 59, 61, 63, 156

Rainer, Luise, 70, 111, 218; *The Good Earth*, 111, 218, 221, 223

Rains, Claude, 7, 57, 58, 59, 80, 83, 84, 163, 164, 179, 213; *Mr. Skeffington*, 84; *Notorious*, 84

Random Harvest, 136, 211, 212–13

Rathbone, Basil, 85, 179, 218; *If I Were King*, 85

Ray, Nick, 95, 138–39, 224; *Bigger than Life*, 138; *In a Lonely Place*, 138; *Johnny Guitar*, 138; *Knock on Any Door*, 138; *The Lusty Men*, 138; *They Live by Night*, 138; and Jean Luc Goddard, 139; and Myron Meisel, 139

Razor's Edge, The, 78, 85, 122, 138, 211, 218

Reagan, Ronald, 80, 81, 181, 212, 213; *The Hasty Heart*, 81; Mrs. Reagan, 84

Rear Window, 10, 130, 131, 141, 183

Rebecca, 10, 12, 67, 68, 130, 131, 140, 146, 149, 151, 183

Rebel Without a Cause, 15, 16, 94–95, 97, 120, 139, 221, 224; Sal Mineo, 94

Red Badge of Courage, The, 141, 178, 182; Stephen Crane, 182

Red River, 12, 90, 92, 136, 145, 173, 175, 182; Noah Beery Jr., 175; Borden Chase, 175; Joanne Dru, 175; Russell Harlan, 175

Redford, Robert, 7, 11, 95, 96, 97, 171–72, 177, 181, 182, 226, 227; *The Candidate*, 97, 227; *Downhill Racer*, 181; *Jeremiah Johnson*, 97, 177; *War Hunt*, 97, 182

Reed, Donna, 20, 205

Remick, Lee, 84, 109, 111, 127, 184, 223, 225, 227; *A Face in the Crowd*, 127; *The Long Hot Summer*, 127

Revere, Anne, 121

Reynolds, Burt, 76, 129, 180

Reynolds, Debbie, 123, 169, 197, 202; *Divorce American Style*, 123, 197; *The Unsinkable Molly Brown*, 123, 202

Ritt, Martin, 140, 141, 177, 223

Ritter, Thelma, 7, 20, 111, 120, 121, 122, 177, 205; *The Mating Season*, 120; *Pickup on South Street*, 120; *With a Song in My Heart*, 120

Robards, Jason, 119, 195, 197, 227; *A Thousand Clowns*, 195

Roberta, 119

Robinson, Bill, 171

Robinson, Edward G., 3, 6, 11, 59, 60, 61, 70, 118, 127, 179, 180, 181, 184, 185, 227; *Two Seconds*, 185

Robson, Mark, 135, 180; *Bright Victory*, 135; *Inn of the Sixth Happiness*, 135
Rocky, 85, 86, 173, 178, 180, 220; Talia Shire, 180, 220
Rogers, Ginger, 109, 116, 119, 168, 169, 198, 200, 214, 219; *The Major and the Minor*, 119; *Tom, Dick and Harry*, 119; *Stage Door*, 214
Roman Holiday, 13, 76, 108, 114, 143, 188, 194
Romance, 110, 133
Romeo and Juliet, 85, 211, 214
Rooney, Mickey, 10, 77, 118, 180, 198-99, 200, 202, 218; *Babes in Arms*, 199, 202; *Strike Up the Band*, 202
Rose Tattoo, The, 20; Anna Magnani, 20
Rosemary's Baby, 122, 139, 209
Ross, Diana, 128; *Lady Sings the Blues*, 128, 202
Rossen, Hal, 136, 140
Rossen, Robert, 90, 135, 140, 180, 181; *All the King's Men*, 135, 140; *The Brave Bulls*, 135; *Johnny O'Clock*, 135; *The Roaring Twenties*, 135; *A Walk in the Sun*, 135
Rowlands, Gena, 7, 111, 127; *Faces*, 127; *Minnie and Moskowitz*, 127; *Opening Night*, 127
Roxie Hart, 88, 134
Russell, Harold, 20
Russell, Rosalind, 3, 7, 8, 16, 21, 111, 114, 115, 116, 119, 193, 194, 202, 213, 225, 227
Ryan, Robert, 83, 175, 180; *Act of Violence*, 83; *They Clash by Night*, 83; *The Woman on the Beach*, 83

Saint, Eva Marie, 92
Sand Pebbles, The, 98, 142
Sanders, George, 5, 88; *Tom Conway*, 88; *The Moon and Sixpence*, 88, marriages, 88
San Francisco, 173
Scarface, 11, 61, 62, 136, 183, 185; Ann Dvorak, 61
Scheider, Roy, 170, 181
Schell, Maximilian, 13, 20
Schenck, Arthur, 166
Schlesinger, Arthur J., 146
Scorsese, Martin, 139, 140, 187, 202, 223; *New York, New York*, 97, 202
Scott, George C., 20, 181, 196
Scott, Martha, 125, 126, 205; *One Foot in Heaven*, 125
Sea Hawk, 84, 141, 178, 179
Sea Wolf, The, 89, 125, 135, 173, 179, 180; Jack London, 135
Search, 90, 92, 141, 145, 221, 225; Ivan Jandl, 225; Jarmila Novotna, 225
Searchers, The, 12, 144, 173, 175, 176, 182; Winton Hock, 176
Seduction of Joe Tynan, The, 98, 128
Segal, George, 89, 194, 214, 224
Selznick, David O., 54, 55, 76,

106, 211, 212, 218; Myron Selznick, 55
Senator Was Indiscreet, The, 75, 188
Separate Tables, 20, 112, 119, 211, 213
Serpico, 99, 146
Seventh Heaven, 110, 133, 140, 211, 212; Charles Farrell, 212
Shadow of a Doubt, 82, 130, 183
Shampoo, 88, 98, 121, 188, 197; Lee Grant, 197
Shane, 12, 14, 82, 83, 117, 142, 173, 174-75, 228; Brandon De Wilde, 174; Loyal Griggs, 174; A. B. Guthrie Jr., 174; Jack Palance, 174; Jack Schaefer, 174; Dimitri Tiomkin, 174
Shanghai Express, 118; Clive Brooks, 118
Shaw, Robert, 89, 181
She Wore a Yellow Ribbon, 12, 144, 176, 182
Shearer, Norma, 55, 88, 107, 108, 109, 110, 214, 219, 224; *The Divorcee*, 108, 110, 214; *A Free Soul*, 108, 214, 224; *Marie Antoinette*, 88, 214; *Their Own Desire*, 108, 214
Sheen, Martin, 98, 182
Sheridan, Ann, 80, 213
Ship of Fools, 135, 211, 214; Simone Signoret, 214; Oskar Werner, 214
Shop Around the Corner, The, 125, 133
Sidney, Sylvia, 122, 223
Simmons, Jean, 126, 135, 197, 201; *The Actress*, 126; *All the Way Home*, 126; *The Happy Ending*, 126, 135
Sinatra, Frank, 5, 7, 20, 92, 118, 184, 198, 201, 225; *Can Can*, 201; *Guys and Dolls*, 201; *High Society*, 201; *The Joker Is Wild*, 201; *On the Town*, 201
Since You Went Away, 138, 211, 212, 216
Singin' in the Rain, 2, 14, 76, 123, 145, 146, 165, 169, 198, 202, 228; Cyd Charisse, 169; Betty Comden and Adolph Green, 169; Jean Hagen, 169; Donald O'Connor, 169
Siodmak, Robert, 136, 141, 186; *The Killers*, 136, 141, 186
Sister Kenny, 3, 85, 114
Skag, 127
Skin of Our Teeth, The, 91
Skippy, 20, 140, 211; Norman Taurog, 140
Sleuth, 6, 141, 142, 184; Michael Caine, 184
Sloane, Everett, 137, 147
Smilin' Through, 211
Snake Pit, The, 3, 12, 16, 106, 107, 221, 225
Snow White and the Seven Dwarfs, 9, 10, 14, 167, 203; Adrienne Castillotti, 167; Marge Champion, 167; Frank Churchill and Larry Morey, 167
Some Came Running, 83, 123
Some Like It Hot, 76, 120, 141, 143, 194

Somebody Up There Likes Me, 95, 142
Sondergaard, Gale, 165, 214
Song of Bernadette, The, 20, 84, 121, 135, 221, 227
Sorry, Wrong Number, 123, 184
Sound of Music, The, 119, 142, 198
Sounder, 128, 140, 221, 223, 225; Cicely Tyson, 128, 223; Paul Winfield, 223
South Pacific, 201; Rossano Brazzi, 201; Mitzi Gaynor, 201; Mary Martin, 201
Spacek, Sissy, 129, 209; *Badlands*, 129; *Coal Miner's Daughter*, 129; *Carrie*, 127, 129, 209
Spellbound, 10, 130, 183
Spiral Staircase, The, 126, 136
Splendor in the Grass, 98, 120, 142
Stagecoach, 3, 12, 14, 85, 144, 146, 152-53, 164, 173, 176, 182, 228; George Babcroft, 152; Ernest Haycox's *Stage to Lourdsburg*, 153; Louise Platt, 152; Elvira Rios, 153; Walter Wanger, 153
Stalag 17, 13, 92, 141, 143, 173, 221
Stallone, Sylvester, 85, 180, 220
Stanwyck, Barbara, 7, 65, 109, 111, 122-23, 163, 184, 194, 217-18, 227; *Ball of Fire*, 123, 163; "Big Valley," 123; *Double Indemnity*, 123, 183, 184; Frank Fay, 123
Stapleton, Maureen, 92, 122; *Lonelyhearts*, 122
Star Is Born, A, 16, 21, 88, 124, 134, 141, 198, 216, 221, 222, 227; Kris Kristofferson, 202
Star Wars, 11, 14, 83, 98, 140, 146, 167, 181, 203, 210, 224
Steiger, Rod, 15, 21, 69, 70, 97
Stella Dallas, 122-23, 132, 217-18; Olive Higgins Prouty, 217
Stevens, George, 116, 140, 152, 158, 174, 177, 178, 194
Stewart, James, 3, 12, 20, 63-65, 67, 68, 76, 82, 101, 102, 125, 131, 144, 163, 164, 165, 177, 183, 184, 193, 204, 227, 228; *The Spirit of St. Louis*, 227
Stewart, Paul, 69, 147
Sting, The, 95, 96, 97, 140, 172, 188
Story of GI Joe, The, 134, 178, 182; Ernie Pyle, 182
Story of Louis Pasteur, The, 61, 62, 136, 140, 221, 227
Strangers, 127
Strangers on a Train, 76, 130, 183; Farley Granger, 183
Strawberry Blonde, The, 119, 139
Streep, Meryl, 128, 182
Streetcar Named Desire, A, 3, 4, 12, 13, 14, 15, 21, 56, 57, 90, 92, 142, 157-58, 220, 221, 228; Charles Feldman, 158; Jessica Tandy, 57
Streisand, Barbra, 19, 124, 202; *Hello Dolly*, 202

Sturges, John, 136, 141, 177, 194; *Gunfight at the OK Corral*, 136; *The Lady Eve*, 194; *The Last Train from Gun Hill*, 136
Sullavan, Margaret, 7, 65, 111, 125, 216, 217; Brooke Hayward *(Haywire)*, 125; *Back Street*, 125, 216; *The Mortal Storm*, 125; *So Ends Our Night*, 125; *The Voice of the Turtle*, 125
Summer Wishes, Winter Dreams, 107, 122
Sun Also Rises, The, 76, 78, 79, 118
Sundowners, The, 13, 16, 17, 21, 83, 107, 112, 113, 142, 211, 214, 219
Sunset Boulevard, 3, 14, 16, 21, 92, 109, 143, 157, 221, 227; Charles Brackett, 157
Sunshine Boys, The, 20; George Burns, 20
Suspicion, 10, 15, 75, 183
Swanson, Gloria, 7, 14, 16, 21, 92, 109-10, 157; *Queen Kelly*, 109; *The Trespasser*, 110; *Sadie Thompson*, 110
Sweet Bird of Youth, 88, 122, 135

Tale of Two Cities, A, 142, 173, 179
Talk of the Town, The, 75, 116, 142, 188, 193
Tamiroff, Akim, 85; *The General Died at Dawn*, 85
Taxi Driver, 99, 140, 183, 187
Taylor, Elizabeth, 12-13, 19, 20, 21, 63, 70, 90, 91, 92, 95, 106, 107, 109, 113, 118, 158, 177, 193, 218, 220, 224; *Raintree County*, 118; *Suddenly Last Summer*, 118; and Eddie Fisher, Nicky Hilton, Mike Todd, John Warner, Michael Wilding, 118
Taylor, Robert, 16, 78, 82, 110, 123, 136, 214, 220; *Three Comrades*, 78; *Waterloo Bridge*, 78
Tea and Sympathy, 112-13, 141, 219; Robert Anderson, 219
Temple, Shirley, 10, 124, 166, 171, 198, 211
Thalberg, Irving, 52, 53, 54, 108, 159, 162; Irving Thalberg Award, 135
Theodora Goes Wild, 88, 114
They Shoot Horses, Don't They?, 16, 21, 107, 139, 141, 222, 225; Michael Sarrazin, 225
Thin Man, The, 75, 117, 135, 188, 189
This Above All, 85, 145
Three Coins in the Fountain, 211
Three Comrades, 125, 225
Tierney, Gene, 184, 218
To Catch a Thief, 75, 130, 183
To Each His Own, 106, 138, 217
To Have and Have Not, 119, 120, 136, 219; *The Breaking Point*, 90
To Kill a Mockingbird, 14, 89, 221, 225

Toland, Gregg, 143, 146, 149, 151, 164
Tom Jones, 20, 188
Tone, Franchot, 52, 91, 109, 178
Top Hat, 10, 76, 119, 168, 202, 216
Torn, Rip, 122, 181
Tortilla Flat, 88, 90
Touch of Class, A, 89, 107, 140, 188, 194, 197; Melvin Frank, 140
Towering Inferno, The, 181
Tracy, Spencer, 19, 20, 21, 63, 88, 101, 103, 114, 134, 141, 177, 179, 180, 185, 193, 218; *The Desk Set*, 193; *Edison the Man*, 227; *Father of the Bride*, 193; *Pat and Mike*, 141, 193; *State of the Union*, 193
Travolta, John, 202, 220; *Grease*, 202; *Moment by Moment*, 220; *Saturday Night Fever*, 202
Treasure of the Sierra Madre, The, 3, 12, 14, 15, 57, 58, 84, 140, 141, 146, 149, 152, 173, 182, 216; Henry Blanke, 152; B. Traver, 152
Tree Grows in Brooklyn, A, 89, 126, 142
Trevor, Claire, 121, 152, 153, 223
Trial, 81, 126
True Grit, 13, 21, 101, 177
Turner, Lana, 78, 109, 118, 127, 184, 219, 223, 227; *By Love Possessed*, 118; Cheryl Crane, 118; marriages, 118
Turning Point, The, 3, 16, 21, 123, 124, 125, 126, 170, 202, 211, 212, 213; Albert Brenner, 170; Leslie Brown, 170; Arthur Laurents, 170; Marvin March, 170; William Reynolds, 170; Herbert Ross, 170; Robert Surtees, 170
Twelve O'Clock High, 173
Twentieth Century, 78, 116, 136
20,000 Years in Sing Sing, 63, 185
Two for the Seesaw, 126
2001: A Space Odyssey, 3, 11, 14, 133, 141, 146, 167–68; Arthur Clarke, 167; Kier Dullea, 167; Gary Lockwood, 167

University of Southern California Performing Arts Council, 14–15, 43, 146

Van Dyke, Woody, 135
Van Fleet, Jo, 93, 94, 122, 158
Vereen, Ben, 170–71
Vertigo, 10, 130, 182, 183
Vidor, King, 7, 19, 132–33, 140, 159–60, 166, 217, 223; *The Actor*, 160; *The Big Parade*, 132; *The Citadel*, 132; *Duel in the Sun*, 132; *Hallelujah!*, 132, 140; *Northwest Passage*, 132, 180; *Our Daily Bread*, 132; *Street Scene*, 132, *War and Peace*, 132
Virginian, The, 175; Owen Wister, 175
Viva Villa, 173, 181; Leo Carrillo, 181; Jack Conway, 181

Voight, Jon, 13, 57, 99, 101, 180, 219, 220, 225
Von Stroheim, Erich, 109, 157

Wagonmaster, The, 175
Walk in the Sun, A, 142, 173, 182; Richard Conte, 182
Walker, Robert, 76, 183, 211
Wallach, Eli, 3, 92, 121, 177
Walsh, Raoul, 138, 139, 175; *In Old Arizona*, 139, 175, 176; *Manpower*, 139; *They Died With Their Boots On*, 139; *What Price Glory?*, 139; *White Heat*, 139
Walters, Charles, 141; *Lili*, 141
Warden, Jack, 88–89
Warner, Jack, 54, 57, 61, 104, 105, 152, 165, 212, 216
Watch on the Rhine, 12, 59, 221, 225
Way We Were, The, 97, 139
Wayne, David, 92
Wayne, John, 12, 13, 20, 21, 92, 101, 134, 139, 144, 151, 152, 153, 175, 176, 177, 180, 194
Weaver, Dennis, 98; "Gunsmoke," 98
Webb, Clifton, 85–86, 184, 194, 218, 219; *Sitting Pretty*, 85, 194
Weissmuller, Johnny, 180; *Tarzan*, 180
Welcome to Hard Times, 175; Burt Kennedy, 175
Weld, Tuesday, 127, 181, 187; *Mothers and Daughters*, 127; *Pretty Poison*, 127
Welles, Orson, 3, 7, 15, 68, 69, 82, 119, 135, 137–38, 142, 146, 147, 148, 153, 180, 218, 222–23; *Chimes at Midnight*, 138; *Journey into Fear*, 137; *The Lady from Shanghai*, 137, 138, 184; *Macbeth*, 138; Mercury Theater, 82, 137, 148; *Othello*, 138; *Touch of Evil*, 137, 138, 182, 184; *The War of the Worlds* (H. G. Wells), 137, 210
Wellman, William, 59, 60, 133, 134, 140, 141, 142, 153, 154, 177, 182, 185; *Battleground*, 134; *Nothing Sacred*, 134; and Buck Jones, 134
West, Mae, 109, 190–91; *My Little Chickadee*, 190; *She Done Him Wrong*, 190
West Side Story, 19, 120, 142, 198, 199, 201; Richard Beymer, 201; George Chakiris, 199, 201; Rita Moreno, 199, 201; Jerome Robbins, 198; Russ Tamblyn, 201–202
What Ever Happened to Baby Jane?, 105, 106, 227
Whitmore, James, 88; *Give 'Em Hell, Harry*, 88
Who's Afraid of Virginia Woolf?, 3, 12–13, 14, 15, 19, 21, 70, 89, 107, 118, 221, 224; Edward Albee, 224
Widmark, Richard, 62–63, 186; *Kiss of Death*, 62–63

Wild Bunch, The, 83, 140, 175; Warren Oates, 175
Wild River, 93, 222, 223
Wilder, Billy, 109, 120, 141, 142–43, 157, 184, 194; *Ball of Fire*, 143; *Sabrina*, 141, 143; with Charles Brackett, 143; with I. A. L. Diamond, 143
Wings, 134, 140, 178, 181, 219; Clara Bow, 219; Adolph Zukor, 219
Winters, Shelley, 92, 120, 158, 227; *A Patch of Blue*, 120
Wise, Robert, 135, 141, 142, 146, 185, 198, 209, 227; *The Day the Earth Stood Still*, 210; *Executive Suite*, 142, 227; *The Haunting*, 209; *I Want to Live*, 141, 142, 185; *The Set-Up*, 142, 180
Witness for the Prosecution, 54, 118, 122, 143, 183, 184
Wizard of Oz, The, 3, 10, 12, 14, 16, 18, 21, 88, 124, 140, 146, 153, 164, 165–67, 198, 202, 228; Harold Arlen, 165; L. Frank Baum, 164, 166; Billie Burke, 165; E. Y. Harburg, 165; Margaret Hamilton, 165; May Robson, 165; Ed Wynn, 165
Woman of Paris, A, 88
Woman of the Year, 103
Woman Under the Influence, A, 83, 127, 140, 141
Women in Love, 107, 129
Wood, Natalie, 16, 94, 119, 120, 176, 197, 201, 202, 205; *Tomorrow Is Forever*, 120; Robert Wagner, 120
Wood, Sam, 133, 181, 182, 194, 205, 213, 219; *Command Decision*, 133, 182; *Good Sam*, 194; *The Stratton Story*, 133
Woodward, Joanne, 95, 97, 107, 213, 225; *The Three Faces of Eve*, 225
Woolley, Monty, 88, 188, 194; *The Man Who Came to Dinner*, 88, 188, 194; *The Pied Piper*, 88; Alexander Woollcott, 194
Wray, Fay, 181, 208
Wright, Teresa, 122
Wuthering Heights, 3, 12, 14, 55, 65, 68–69, 122, 143, 153, 164, 211, 212, 218, 219, 228
Wyler, William, 19, 140, 141, 143, 164, 165, 175, 186, 194, 205, 212, 214; *The Collector*, 141, 143; *Desperate Hours*, 143; *Dodsworth*, 143, 223; *The Letter*, 143, 214; *The Westerner*, 175
Wyman, Jane, 107, 108, 213, 218, 225; *The Yearling*, 218

Yankee Doodle Dandy, 11, 61, 84, 141, 199, 201, 202; George M. Cohan, 11, 199
You Can't Take It with You, 116, 143, 188
Young, Gig, 70, 225
Young, Loretta, 114, 116, 136; *The Farmer's Daughter*, 114, 116
Young, Robert, 75, 133, 180

Zanuck, Darryl, 134, 148
Zinman, David (*50 Classic Motion Pictures*), 146, 148
Zinnemann, Fred, 92, 141, 142, 173, 214, 225; *The Men*, 142; *Oklahoma*, 142